PRISONS, TERRORISM AND EXTREMISM

This volume provides an overview of intervention and management strategies for dealing with terrorist and extremist offenders in prisons.

In reviewing the strategies, interventions and other critical factors when dealing with terrorist and extremist offenders, the focus of this book is not only on current threats and problems but also on key lessons from history. The book assesses the experience of a wide range of different countries and covers an extensive variety of different movements ranging from nationalist groups such as the IRA and ETA, left-wing and right-wing extremists, to religiously motivated movements like Al Qaeda and its affiliates.

Those faced with managing terrorist and extremist prisoners are confronted with a range of options – not all of which are compatible – and there has been enormous uncertainty over what works. This collection provides readers with an up-to-date, informed and accessible account of what is known about terrorists and extremists in prison, what are the key risks and dangers, and what are the critical issues and insights in terms of effective management and reform, as well as the potential implications for wider conflicts.

Written by leading experts in the field, this volume will be of much interest to students of terrorism/counter-terrorism, criminology, security studies and IR in general.

Andrew Silke holds a Chair in Criminology at the University of East London, where he is the Head of Criminology and the Programme Director for Terrorism Studies. He is author/editor of several books on terrorism, including *The Psychology of Counter-Terrorism* (Routledge, 2010), *Research on Terrorism* (Routledge, 2004), and *Terrorists, Victims and Society* (2003).

Political Violence
Series Editors: David Rapoport

This book series contains sober, thoughtful and authoritative academic accounts of terrorism and political violence. Its aim is to produce a useful taxonomy of terror and violence through comparative and historical analysis in both national and international spheres. Each book discusses origins, organisational dynamics and outcomes of particular forms and expressions of political violence.

PRISONS, TERRORISM AND EXTREMISM

Critical issues in management, radicalisation and reform

Edited by Andrew Silke

Routledge
Taylor & Francis Group

LONDON AND NEW YORK

First published 2014
by Routledge
2 Park Square, Milton Park, Abingdon, Oxon, OX14 4RN

and by Routledge
711 Third Avenue, New York, NY 10017

Routledge is an imprint of the Taylor & Francis Group, an informa business

British Library Cataloguing in Publication Data
A catalogue record for this book is available from the British Library

Library of Congress Cataloging in Publication Data
Prisons, terrorism and extremism : critical issues in management, radicalisation and reform / edited by Andrew Silke.
        pages cm. – (Political violence)
        Includes bibliographical references and index.
    1. Political prisoners. 2. Terrorists. 3. Terrorists–Rehabilitation. 4. Prison administration 5. Prisons–Security measures. 6. Terrorism–Prevention.
    I. Silke, Andrew.
    HV8665.P77 2014
    365'.45–dc23   2013024186

ISBN: 978–0–415–81037–1 (hbk)
ISBN: 978–0–415–81038–8 (pbk)
ISBN: 978–0–203–58432–3 (ebk)

Typeset in Baskerville
by Keystroke, Station Road, Codsall, Wolverhampton

Printed and bound in Great Britain by
TJ International Ltd, Padstow, Cornwall

**In fond memory of
Paul Wilkinson
A scholar and a gentleman**

Although many if not most terrorists eventually end up in prison, there has been surprisingly little research on what happens to them while in prison and after they have been released. This volume, edited by a prominent expert in the field, makes an important contribution to fill this gap in our knowledge. Several of the chapters challenge the conventional wisdom that "prisons are universities of terror". Prisons may also provide opportunities for disengagement, deradicalisation and rehabilitation. Wise policies may contribute constructively to facilitate these processes. To achieve this, Professor Silke and his colleagues provide indispensable insights.

Dr. Tore Bjørgo, Professor at the Norwegian Police University College and the Norwegian Institute of International Affairs

Andrew Silke has brought together a truly international group of experts to examine how we understand and manage extremists in our prison systems. The contributors have carefully integrated scientific rigour and effective risk management approaches; they provide much-needed depth and sophistication to thinking about the role of prisons in the management of such prisoners. This book is a must-read for practitioners and policy makers tasked with protecting society from this most formidable of threats.

Professor David Cooke, Glasgow Caledonian University

Radicalization is an issue of such beguiling complexity that it is poorly understood even by those who run our prisons. Andrew Silke has done a great service by bringing together some of the most talented scholars on the radicalisation problem in the world today. This book shows that radicalisation cannot be dealt with through normal techniques of prison management, but only through creative administrative methods informed by the social sciences. The work is destined to become an indispensable guide for the reformers of tomorrow.

Mark S. Hamm, author of The Spectacular Few: Prisoner Radicalization and the Evolving Terrorist Threat

CONTENTS

LIST OF ILLUSTRATIONS

Figures

Tables

ABOUT THE EDITOR

Andrew Silke (BSc Hons, AFBPsS, CSci, CPsych, PhD) is the Head of Criminology and Director for Terrorism Studies at the University of East London. He is internationally recognised as a leading expert on terrorism in general and terrorist psychology in particular. He has a background in forensic psychology and criminology and has worked both in academia and for government. He has written extensively on terrorism and counter-terrorism and is frequently invited to give talks at international conferences and universities throughout the world.

Professor Silke has provided expert advice and testimony in many terrorism-related cases, both in the UK and in the US. He served on the British Psychological Society's working group on the Psychological Risk Assessment of those Convicted or Detained under Terrorist Related Offences. He has worked with a variety of government departments and law enforcement and security agencies. In the United Kingdom these include the Home Office, the Ministry of Justice, the Ministry of Defence, the UK prison service and the London Metropolitan Police, as well as several other UK police forces. Overseas he has worked with the United Nations, the United States Department of Justice, the United States Department of Homeland Security, NATO, the European Defence Agency, the European Commission, and the Federal Bureau of Investigation.

Professor Silke serves by invitation on the United Nations *Roster of Terrorism Experts* and the European Commission's *European Network of Experts on Radicalisation* and formerly on the European Commission's *Expert Group on Violent Radicalisation*. He has provided research advice to both the Royal Society in the UK and the National Academy of Sciences in the US. He has provided invited briefings on terrorism-related issues to Select Committees of the House of Commons and was appointed in 2009 as a Specialist Advisor to the House of Commons Communities and Local Government Committee for its inquiry into the government's programme for preventing violent extremism.

E-mail: andrew_silke@yahoo.co.uk

ABOUT THE CONTRIBUTORS

Jocelyn J. Bélanger is currently a graduate student working under the supervision of Dr. Arie W. Kruglanski at the University of Maryland at College Park. He holds a Bachelor of Science from the Université du Québec à Montréal and a Master's of Science in social psychology from the University of Maryland. He is recipient of the Sciences and Humanities Research Council of Canada Doctoral Fellowship and a member of the Society of Personality and Social Psychology, as well as the Canadian Psychological Association. His research focuses on belief formation, self-regulation, political psychology, and the determinants and implications of goal-structure.

Kurt Braddock received his PhD (2012) in Communication Arts and Sciences from The Pennsylvania State University where he is a research associate at the International Center for the Study of Terrorism and instructs courses related to communication, technology, and terrorism. His research centers on the ways in which various types of persuasive messages affect the radicalization and de-radicalization processes, particularly as they are experienced on the Internet. He has co-edited a book entitled *Terrorism Studies: A Reader* (Routledge, 2011) and his work has appeared in *Terrorism and Political Violence, Communication Quarterly, Journal of Personality*, and other academic publications.

Christopher Dean is a principal psychologist and Head of the Extremism Team at the Interventions Unit in the National Offender Management Service (UK Ministry of Justice). Over the last four years he has worked with a team to develop service-wide guidelines and interventions to help assess and address extremist offending such as the Extremism Risk Guidelines (ERG22+) and Healthy Identity Intervention. His role includes overseeing the effective implementation and delivery of these products and providing consultancy to other groups and agencies within the organisation and government. His previous roles have included delivering, supervising and managing interventions and assessments for sexual and violent offenders at a local and national level.

Gisela Diewald-Kerkmann is a historian of Modern and Contemporary History at the University of Bielefeld, Faculty of History, Philosophy and Theology. Her research interests include the history of National Socialism, history of political violence in the 19th and 20th centuries, and history of terrorism and legal history after 1945. In her habilitation thesis (postdoctoral qualification), which was published in 2009 in the series "Writings from the Federal Archives," she dealt with the theme "Women, Terrorism and Justice. Trials against female members of the RAF and the 2nd-June-Movement." E-mail: *gisela.diewald-Kerkmann@uni-bielefeld.de*

Neil Ferguson (DPhil, University of Ulster, 1998) is a Professor of Political Psychology at Liverpool Hope University. He has been a visiting lecturer to Lock Haven University of Pennsylvania and the University of York, a Research Fellow at University of St Andrews, and previously lectured at the University of Ulster prior to joining Liverpool Hope University in 1996. His research and writings deal with moral development and a number of topics located within political psychology. Dr Ferguson is currently the President of the MOSAIC – Moral and Social Action Interdisciplinary Colloquium.

John Flockton is the Clinical Director and Senior Forensic Psychologist at the High Risk Management Correctional Centre in Goulburn Australia. He has been developing risk assessment approaches with convicted extremist violence offenders with Corrective Services NSW, and continues a consultancy and training role as part of a joint government prisons reform project with corrections, law enforcement and intelligence agencies in Indonesia. He is currently engaged in validation research with the VERA-2, and has been an invited presenter at local and international conferences on emerging Australian extremist violence risk assessment and management practice.

Michele J. Gelfand is a Professor of Psychology and Distinguished University Scholar Teacher at the University of Maryland, College Park and an affiliate of the RH Smith School of Business. She received her PhD in Social/Organizational Psychology from the University of Illinois. Her work explores cultural influences on conflict, negotiation, justice, and revenge; workplace diversity and discrimination; and theory and methods in cross-cultural psychology. She is the co-editor of *The Handbook of Negotiation and Culture* (with Jeanne Brett, Stanford University Press) and *The Psychology of Conflict and Conflict Management in Organizations* (with Carsten De Dreu, Erlbaum) and is the founding co-editor of the *Advances in Culture and Psychology series* and *Frontiers of Culture and Psychology series* (with CY Chiu and Ying-Yi Hong, Oxford University Press).

Liran Goldman works with federal and local law enforcement as a government contractor, analysing domestic issues related to criminal and terrorist activity. She is also working on her PhD in Applied Social Psychology at Claremont Graduate University, studying extreme behaviours and group dynamics – specifically, what motivates an individual to join a terrorist organization or gang. Her education and research have been supported through fellowships from the Department of Homeland Security and The National Consortium for the Study of Terrorism and Responses to Terrorism.

Rohan Gunaratna is Professor of Security Studies at the S. Rajaratnman School of International Studies and Head of the International Centre for Political Violence and Terrorism Research in Singapore. As a part of its mission to build capacity, ICPVTR provided training on insurgent and terrorist rehabilitation in Iraq, Afghanistan, Pakistan, Singapore, Indonesia, Philippines, Sri Lanka, Bangladesh and other countries. He chaired the first International Conference on Terrorist Rehabilitation in Singapore in February 2009. Together with Jolene Jerard and Larry Rubin, he coedited, *Terrorist Rehabilitation and Counter-Radicalisation: New Approaches to Counter-terrorism* (Routlege, 2011) and coauthored *Terrorist Rehabilitation: The U.S. Experience in Iraq* (CRC Press, 2011).

Malkanthi Hettiarachchi (PICT, University of Macquarie, Sydney, Australia) is a Chartered Clinical Psychologist. She has a BA (Hons) Psychology from the University of Peradeniya, Sri Lanka; MSc (Mental Health) from Kings College, University of London; and MSc (Clinical Psychology) from the RMIT University Melbourne. She has worked extensively in community, inpatient and forensic settings (prisons and detention and rehabilitation centres) in Sri Lanka, the UK and Australia. She has experience in designing and implementing rehabilitation programs within secure and community settings; treatment of a range of mental health problems; and psychometric assessment and profiling. She led the specialist team that assessed 9,900 terrorist detainees in Sri Lanka.

Arie W. Kruglanski is a Distinguished University Professor at the University of Maryland and one of the most cited researchers in Social Psychology. His interests have centred on the psychology of judgment and knowledge formation, as well as on the processes of group decision making, goal formation and implementation. He has served as Editor of the *Journal of Personality and Social Psychology: Attitudes and Social Cognition* and the *Personality and Social Psychology Bulletin*. Among other distinctions, he has received the Donald T. Campbell Award for Distinguished Scientific Contribution to Social Psychology, the Humboldt Foundation Life Achievement Award (Forschungpreis), and the NIMH Research Scientist Award Ko5. His publications include over 180 scientific literature articles, chapters, and books on social personality psychology. In 2004 he was appointed as a co-director of a Center of Excellence for Research on the Behavioral and Social Aspects of Terrorism and Counterterrorism, established at the University of Maryland,

College Park. He has also been member of various panels of the National Academy of Science devoted to the social/psychological aspects of terrorism.

John F. Morrison is a Senior Lecturer in Criminology and Criminal Justice at the University of East London (UEL). Prior to joining UEL he was a postdoctoral research fellow at the International Center for the Study of Terrorism (ICST) at Pennsylvania State University. Within this role he was the project manager of ICST's research on modern-day dissident Irish Republican organizations. For his doctoral dissertation, "The Affirmation of Behan?" John analysed the four major splits in the Irish Republican Movement from 1969 until 1997. This research was based on an extensive interview process, as well as the analysis of primary and secondary sources. John holds a PhD in International Relations from the University of St Andrews, an MA in Forensic Psychology from University College, Cork, and a BA in Psychology from University College, Dublin.

Colin Murray is a senior lecturer in law at Newcastle University, having previously been a lecturer there from 2007 to 2012. His current research examines aspects of national security, legal history and public law. His prominent articles include 'In the Shadow of Lord Haw Haw: Guantánamo Bay, Diplomatic Protection and Allegiance' (2011) Public Law 115 and 'Playing for Time: Prisoner Disenfranchisement under the ECHR after *Hirst v United Kingdom*' (2011) 22 King's Law Journal 309. He is also one of the founding members of the academic blog humanrights.ie.

Sulastri Osman is an Associate Research Fellow and the Coordinator of the Radicalisation Studies Programme with the Centre of Excellence for National Security at the S. Rajaratnam School of International Studies, a graduate School of Nanyang Technological University, Singapore. Her research focus is on terrorism and counterterrorism in Indonesia and the wider social and political dynamics surrounding such issues. She is often in Indonesia on fieldwork, which involves conducting interviews with militants convicted on terrorism charges. At present, she is working on various projects aimed at understanding individual motivations for violence and subsequent disengagement from violent activities; the dynamic interface between convicted terrorist inmates and their prison environments; and the role of non-state actors in counterterrorism.

Richard Pickering is the head of Security Group in the National Offender Management Service (NOMS) in the UK and Chair of the NOMS Extremism Board. Prior to this he set up and headed the Extremism Unit within the Prison Service, subsequently NOMS HQ.

Marisa Porges is a research fellow at the Harvard Kennedy School's Belfer Center for Science and International Affairs. She specializes in counterterrorism, with specific emphasis on radicalization and de-radicalization, and detention operations, and with expertise in the Middle East and Afghanistan. For this work, she conducted extensive research in Afghanistan, Saudi Arabia, Yemen, Singapore, and more, interviewing government officials, ex-Taliban and former members of Al Qaeda. Porges was previously a counterterrorism policy adviser at the U.S. Departments of Defense and the Treasury. She has also served as a commissioned naval flight officer, flying for the U.S. Navy. Porges holds an AB in geophysics from Harvard, an MSC from the London School of Economics, and is completing her PhD in war studies at King's College London.

D. Elaine Pressman obtained her PhD in the USA followed by professional appointments in Canada, Asia-Pacific, Europe and the United States. She has over 25 years' experience in research, teaching, diplomacy, and applied behavioural sciences. Her present research interests focus on the development, use and evaluation of risk assessment protocols for violent political extremists, analysis of terrorism financing, professional training and the development of analytic tools to assist in the response to criminal threats. Past affiliations related to this work include the Clingendael Centre for Strategic Studies in The Hague; the Security, Emergency Preparedness and Response Institute, University of Massachusetts, Amherst; and the University of Groningen. She is currently a Senior Fellow in The Norman Paterson School of International Affairs, Carleton University, Ottawa, Senior Fellow with the Terrorism Research and Analysis Project, BSU, FBI Academy and Adjunct Professor (Research) at the Royal Military College of Canada. Her risk assessment work is being used internationally with convicted terrorists.

Kumar Ramakrishna is Associate Professor and Head of the Centre of Excellence for National Security at the S. Rajaratnam School of International Studies, Nanyang Technological University, Singapore. His first book *Emergency Propaganda: The Winning of Malayan Hearts and Minds, 1948–1958* (2002) was described by *The International History Review* as "required reading for historians of Malaya, and for those whose task is to counter insurgents, guerrillas, and terrorists". His most recent book, *Radical Pathways: Understanding Muslim Radicalization in Indonesia* (2009), was identified by *Perspectives on Terrorism* in 2012 as "an important and insightful case study on the pathways to extremism and violent jihad in Indonesia".

Andrew Silke (*see* About the Editor)

Joshua Sinai is a senior manager, national security program, at Infinity Technology, LLC, in McLean, VA, specializing in terrorism and counterterrorism studies. He is also an adjunct Associate Professor/Research at Virginia Tech Center–Arlington. He has also worked as a contractor on behalf of a former company at a U.S. Government counterterrorism center. His articles and book reviews have appeared in academic journals and newspapers. He obtained his PhD in Political Science from Columbia University.

Manuel R. Torres Soriano is Professor of Political Science at Pablo de Olavide University of Sevilla in Spain. He has a PhD in Political Science from the University of Granada. He was a Visiting Fellow at Stanford University, Johns Hopkins University, King's College London, London School of Economics and Harvard University. He is the author of the book, *The Echo of Terror: Ideology and Propaganda in Jihadist Terrorism* (Plaza & Valdes, 2009) (in Spanish). He has received several prizes in recognition of his academic and investigative work, including the National Prize "Defensa" (Ministry of Defense of Spain) for the best investigation for his doctoral thesis. His research topics are terrorism, political communication and cyber-security.

Benedict Wilkinson obtained his PhD at the War Studies Department at King's College London where his research examined the strategies of violent extremism in the Middle East. During his PhD, he also worked as Head of Security and Counter-Terrorism at the Royal United Services Institute, where one of his primary focuses was on domestic extremism and counter-extremism strategy in the UK. He is currently a Lecturer with the Defence Studies Department at King's College London.

Sagit Yehoshua is an applied criminologist, specialising in the psychology and profiling of terrorism. She completed her PhD thesis titled 'The social-psychology profile of terrorist leaders in Israeli prisons' at King's College London University. Her work involves years of studying and teaching the mind-set and conduct of individuals and groups involved in terrorism and political violence. Sagit is a Research Fellow at the Institute of Counter-Terrorism (I.C.T.), Inter-Disciplinary Centre, Herzliya, Israel, and also joined ICSR (International Centre for the Study of De-radicalisation) at King's College London, as an Atkin Research Fellow in 2009.

PART I

Introduction

1

TERRORISTS, EXTREMISTS AND PRISON

An introduction to the critical issues

Andrew Silke

Terrorism is not the same as other types of crime and terrorists are not typical criminals. Inevitably many terrorists and violent extremists end up in prison where they can pose formidable challenges. Such prisoners are unusual and distinctive. As a consequence, their management can pose exceptionally difficult problems in prison and probation settings. Traditionally, however, most countries have had very few prisoners of this type. In the European Union for example, more than half of the member nations currently have no terrorist prisoners at all in their jails and most of the rest have only a handful. But when such prisoners do start to appear in the prison system their impact can be out of all proportion to their numbers.

A range of different types of offenders can potentially fall under the umbrella categories of terrorism and extremism. This can vary from individuals who have been convicted of terrorist offences such as those carried out by the IRA or Al Qaeda; gang members where the gang is partially motivated by racist or extreme ideologies; to members of politically motivated groups such as the Animal Liberation Front, who are prepared to engage in illegal activity which often might not normally be considered as serious as terrorism. The lines between these different types of offender are often blurred, but the common characteristic is that their offending has a political dimension which is not normally seen among criminal offenders. Further, their offending is primarily a group phenomenon, and only rarely do such offenders radicalise and act in isolation. Added to this, prison systems must also be worried about the recruitment or radicalisation of 'ordinary' prisoners into extremist movements, resulting in the 'ordinary' prisoner becoming a much more dangerous individual who could cause serious harm should they be released.

Muddying the waters even further, prison systems sometimes must grapple with ambiguous legal issues when prisoners dubbed as 'enemy combatants' and 'internees' are added to the mix. These categories are often deliberately designed to take prisoners out of traditional criminal justice frameworks and place them somewhere else. Exactly where that somewhere else belongs is messily uncertain. The dividing lines between terrorism, guerrilla warfare and insurgency, for example, have never been clear-cut. For some, inevitably, the terms are completely interchangeable. For others there are important and powerful differences. The common thread running across all three is the use of violence for political purposes, but little else is agreed about, and governments bitterly resist granting 'prisoner of war' status if they can possibly avoid it.

Even using the term 'political prisoner' is shunned. Terrorist prisoners rarely describe themselves as 'terrorists'. Instead they portray themselves as soldiers, freedom fighters, volunteers, partisans, the resistance (at least in their own minds if nowhere else). Normally they bitterly contest any effort to describe them as criminals. Many, though, will refer to themselves as 'political prisoners'.

As a term, political prisoner, still carries its own baggage. A political prisoner may be entirely non-violent. It could, for example, refer to a draught dodger who refuses to serve in the military; a citizen who refuses to pay a particular tax; or a political activist who protests against the government but does not engage in violence. Mahatma Gandhi was imprisoned no less than seven times in his life for non-violent protest. Terrorists who describe themselves as political prisoners try to fall into the same camp, sometimes intentionally but frequently not.

Human rights organisations alert to the problem have moved to segregate the violent from the non-violent, by adding the label 'prisoners of conscience'. For example, Amnesty International define 'prisoners of conscience' as 'men and women detained anywhere for their beliefs, colour, sex, ethnic origin, language or religion, *provided they have not used or advocated violence*' [emphasis added]. In contrast, individuals who have used violence or committed other crimes for political motives are described by Amnesty International as 'political prisoners'. Amnesty International argues that such individuals should receive 'fair and early trials' and not be tortured, but it does not argue that such prisoners should necessarily be released.

This approach to defining a political prisoner is also in keeping with that used by the United Nations. The United Nations developed a definition of what a political prisoner was, in order that such prisoners could be identified and released in a post-conflict amnesty. In describing someone as a political prisoner, the United Nations said the following factors could be considered:

1 The motivation of the offender, that is, whether the offence was committed for a personal or political motive;
2 The circumstances in which the offence was committed; in particular, whether it was committed in the course of or as part of a political uprising or disturbance;
3 The nature of the political objective; whether, for instance, an attempt to overthrow the government or force a change of policy;
4 The legal and factual nature of the offence, including its gravity;
5 The object of the offence, for example, whether it was committed against government personnel or property or directly against private citizens;

6   The relationship between the offence and political objective being pursued, for example, the directness

Under the UN framework most terrorist prisoners could then be reasonably referred to as political prisoners, though, not surprisingly, most governments prefer to avoid this term out of fear that it might transfer some apparent legitimacy to the terrorists and their cause.

Overall, the focus of this book is on individuals who hold extreme political/religious views and who support the use of violence in furtherance of that agenda. The advocation of violence is a crucial element. Individuals who hold radical views but who do not endorse the use of violence are not included here. Neither is this book about 'prisoners of conscience'. The book, though, does encompass the members of terrorist organisations and also the members of groups such as animal rights activists who use violence as part of their campaigns.

'Terrorism' itself is an extremely difficult term to define. Even for those countries that have explicit anti-terrorism laws, many 'terrorist' prisoners have been convicted under other (usually criminal) legislation. Adding to the confusion, terrorism is defined differently in different legal codes and by different countries. To help provide a focus, this volume follows the concise definition provided by Crenshaw (1992) who described terrorism as 'a particular style of political violence, involving attacks on a small number of victims in order to influence a wider audience'. The claims as to what behaviours fit this definition still vary considerably but the focus of this volume is primarily on what can be called 'insurgent' terrorism, which is essentially a strategy of the weak, adopted 'by groups with little numerical, physical or direct political power in order to effect political or social change' (Friedland, 1992).

In practical terms, 'insurgent' terrorists are members of relatively small covert groups engaged in an organised campaign of violence. This violence is often extreme and frequently indiscriminate. The terrorists themselves tend to live isolated and stressful lives and enjoy varying levels of wider support. In the past, groups that fit within this framework have included movements such as the Irish Republican Army, Red Army Faction and the Italian Red Brigades. In the modern era, such groups include Al Qaeda and the jihadi extremists affiliated with it, as well as many others.

Previous research

Our understanding of terrorists and extremists in prison is surprisingly limited. Given the scale of writing and research on terrorism over recent decades – the absolutely overwhelming flood of books and publications in the wake of 9/11 – it is surprising to then see how little has focused on prison issues. This is particularly unexpected because eventually most terrorists will end up in prison. What happens within the prison walls, however, has been largely overlooked for a very long time.

What we do understand about terrorists in prison has sprung mainly from three sources. First are the many autobiographies written by former terrorists who have written extensively on their time in prison (e.g. Baumann, 1975; Schiller, 2009). For them, prison was yet another battleground in the struggle against the state, a contest which was largely hidden from the media and the wider world but which was nonetheless unusually intense given the conditions and the relentless proximity of the two sides. Nelson Mandela summed up well in his own autobiography the typical viewpoint of the prisoner:

> The challenge for every prisoner, particularly every political prisoner, is how to survive prison intact, how to emerge from prison undiminished, how to conserve and even replenish one's beliefs. The first task in accomplishing that is learning exactly what one must do to survive. To that end, one must know the enemy's purpose before adopting a strategy to undermine it. Prison is designed to break one's spirit and destroy one's resolve. To do this, the authorities attempt to exploit every weakness, demolish every initiative, negate all signs of individuality – all with the idea of stamping out that spark that makes each of us human and each of us who we are.
>
> *(Mandela, 1995, p.230)*

The second cluster of understanding emerges particularly from the experience of Irish terrorism. It has been said of Northern Ireland that it is 'the most heavily researched area on earth' (Whyte, 1991). Consequently, a wealth of data exists to describe that protracted and seemingly never-ending conflict. Few regions have experienced terrorism to the extent Northern Ireland has, or for as long as the 'Troubles.' A boon of the intransigence, such as it is, is the wealth of research and knowledge which have emerged. This certainly applied to the prison world which was widely seen as a key arena in the conflict. There now exists a bonanza of books by former terrorists on all sides – almost all of whom spent considerable time in prisons (e.g. O'Doherty, 1993; Collins, 1997; O'Rawe, 2005; Sands, 1993; Adair, 2009). There are even books by former prison staff describing their experiences (e.g. McKee, 2009). Added to this are academic studies dealing both with current and former prisoners (e.g. Lyons and Harbinson, 1986; Crawford, 1999; McEvoy, 2001; Bates-Gaston, 2003; Burgess, Ferguson & Hollywood, 2007; O'Donnell, 2011; Dwyer, 2013), and a bewildering array of more general works all of which usually give considerable prominence to the prison story in the Irish conflict and some of which focus nearly exclusively on what happened in the prisons (e.g. Ryder, 2000; Beresford, 1987; Clarke, 1987).

The final cluster is also the youngest, though it will probably soon eclipse the others. It is disconcerting to note that most of the literature on terrorism has been published since 9/11. The avalanche of paper on the topic in the aftermath of the collapse of the twin towers absolutely dwarfs what went before. Of course, most of this work has focused on the peculiar threats posed by Al Qaeda and its kin, but caught in the backwash of this flood has been a steadily growing body of work looking at militant jihadis in prisons and detention facilities around the world (e.g. Boucek, 2008; Ashour, 2010; Neumann, 2010; Hamm, 2013).

Radicalisation – and even more so, de-radicalisation – are the buzzwords in these accounts, and it is not a coincidence that radicalisation, too, is in truth a post-9/11 child. No one talked of the IRA being radicalised, or Shining Path, or ETA or the Red Army Faction – though they all certainly were by our modern understanding. After 9/11 it became awkward to talk about people 'becoming' terrorists, 'joining' terrorist groups, or being 'recruited'. Those terms were too banal, too ordinary. Ordinary terms might imply ordinary processes, and worse, ordinary solutions. They had to make way for something more exotic, more extreme. 'Radicalisation' fitted the bill nicely.

Radicalisation carried with it, though, the promising prospect of *de-radicalisation* – the exotic flip-side of the new terminology. If people could be radicalised into terrorism, perhaps they could also be de-radicalised? (Which sounded so much more sophisticated than saying if they joined a terrorist group, maybe they could eventually leave it.) Regardless, in the years which followed, one nation after another has introduced de-radicalisation programmes to deal with terrorist prisoners, and this troubled endeavour has gradually spawned a literature casting a usually cold eye on the effectiveness and impact of such work (e.g. Barret and Bokhari, 2009; Horgan, 2009; Horgan and Braddock, 2010; Silke, 2010, 2011).

Radicalisation, de-radicalisation and disengagement

The current volume is the result of a deliberate effort to pull together an up-to-date and expertly informed assessment of what we know about terrorists, extremists and prison. This is a highly emotive area dogged by widely held myths, profound political controversy, and interspersed with genuine tales of shocking abuse, negligence and mismanagement. In such an environment, making calm, rational assessments and conclusions can be a hazardous task. The task is not helped by the fact that the evidence base on which to make sensible judgements has in the past been astonishingly sparse. Given both the ongoing critical relevance of the subject and the growth of fresh research and information in a number of areas, it seemed an apt time to try to pull together some of the most important lessons and insights of the past fifty years. As a result, this volume tries to take a holistic and wide-ranging approach to the problems and issues raised by terrorist and extremist offenders in prison settings. Critical issues around management strategies, radicalisation and de-radicalisation, reform, and risk assessment, as well as post-release experiences, are all explored in detail. The role that prisoners play in the conflicts beyond the jail walls is also examined, with case studies illustrating how prisoners can play a critical role in bringing about a peace process or alternatively in sustaining or even escalating campaigns of violence.

The initial section of the book is concerned with setting a historical context to the volume and with tackling critical concepts such as radicalisation. The history of prison and terrorism is poorly understood as, with many things in the field today, it tends to be overshadowed by 9/11 and its aftermath. The result is that important early works such as Von Tangen Page's ground-breaking *Prisons, Peace and Terrorism* (1998) are largely overlooked today. Colin Murray in Chapter 2 tries to address such shortcomings, at least in a UK context, and outlines the development of prison policy towards terrorist and extremist prisoners throughout the twentieth century, and how these systems adapted, under the Prevent Strategy, to the risks posed by terrorist inmates in the last decade. He particularly explores the often-heard argument that locking terrorists away in prisons simply produces universities of terror, and leads to a high risk of radicalisation spreading among other prisoners. The evidence, he argues, challenges simplistic assumptions that terrorist 'kingpins' are free to radicalise other inmates and that the prison authorities are powerless to prevent such activity as a result of human rights concerns.

In Chapter 3, Joshua Sinai, outlines how and when prison radicalisation occurs. Drawing particularly on cases from the U.S. prison system, he sketches some of the critical themes and patterns. Importantly, Sinai looks not only at cases which led to individuals becoming directly involved in terrorism, but also looks at other outcomes such as involvement in extremism (but not terrorism) and a range in between. The chapter tries to assess what it means to be radicalised in a prison setting, and what the genuine scale of the problem is.

Liran Goldman takes these themes a further step on. Again drawing particularly on the U.S. experience, she highlights what it is that makes prisoners such an appealing population for extremists to target and why prison environments can be such suitable environments for radicalisation. Like Sinai, Goldman is interested in the processes involved in prison radicalisation. She explores these and draws particular attention to the nexus between prison gangs and terrorist organisations and the role of religion. The chapter concludes by examining the release of radicalised prisoners, noting some key weaknesses in the U.S. prison system in particular, and providing suggestions on how to effectively counter prison radicalisation.

Countering radicalisation is also the focus for the next chapter by Kurt Braddock. He explores the concept of de-radicalisation and describes how it has been approached in a number of different prison systems. In particular, Braddock looks closely at two of the most important modern de-radicalisation programmes – the Yemeni and Saudi initiatives – and focuses on the reliance on persuasive communication as a cornerstone for de-radicalisation. The chapter considers some of the psychological implications of such an approach, and in particular draws out issues around psychological reactance and emotional arousal, both of which may seriously undermine attempts to de-radicalise. As a result of this analysis, Braddock provides some recommendations for improving future de-radicalisation initiatives.

The initial phase of the book closes with a chapter by John Morrison, who provides an alternative perspective on the radicalisation/de-radicalisation debate. Morrison's chapter deals primarily with the Northern Ireland case, which is by far the richest one we currently have in terms of evidence and source material. It is widely recognised that the paramilitary prisoners played a key role in the development and eventual acceptance of the Good Friday Peace Agreement in

Northern Ireland. Indeed, on a number of occasions senior UK government ministers travelled to HMP The Maze to hold critical face-to-face meetings with paramilitary prisoners. In exploring how the prison experience impacted on individuals and organisations, this chapter concludes that while prison did not lead to the de-radicalisation of prisoners, it did lead to an increased willingness to consider and support non-violent solutions to the conflict. It is a finding which has important implications for thinking about whether prison should be concerned primarily with de-radicalisation or with disengagement when it comes to these types of prisoners.

Critical issues in management, risk assessment and reform

Having introduced many of the major concerns in this area the book now moves to consider applied issues in how such prisoners are managed and assessed in different settings. This section opens with a chapter by Chris Dean, who charts how the UK developed a ground-breaking psychologically informed intervention to address extremist offending. As Dean argues, our understanding about what works with terrorist offenders is still in its infancy. In the past decade, however, the UK's National Offender Management Service (NOMS) came under increasing pressure to try to develop interventions which could be used with the growing number of extremist prisoners within the system. The chapter describes the key principles, content and goals which underlie the new programme. In particular, the chapter draws attention to the importance of the programme's focus on exploring and addressing identity issues with prisoners and how this can be crucial to both understanding and preventing extremist offending.

Risk assessment of terrorist prisoners has emerged as a particularly critical issue in the field. How can one tell if a prisoner is still dangerous or not? What are valid measures to assess risk and what type of evidence is worth examining? Chapter 8, written by yours truly, tries to bring together recent developments in this area. There is generally good recognition that standard risk assessment tools do not work well with terrorists and extremists. However, recent years have seen the emergence of new tools and the chapter assesses these new measures as well as drawing on the author's experience of conducting risk assessments of terrorist prisoners in a variety of settings.

One of the new risk assessment measures mentioned in Chapter 8 is VERA-2 (Violent Extremist Risk Assessment). The following chapter is written by the developers of this tool, Elaine Pressman and John Flockton, who outline the background to VERA-2 and how it was developed specifically for use with ideologically motivated violent offenders. The chapter discusses the use of VERA-2 in different countries and the authors argue that it has been found to contribute empirically supported and offence-related information to assist risk management decisions. It is employed as one component of a multi-modal risk assessment process with information obtained from law enforcement, intelligence and judicial sources and is used in addition to other accepted standardised assessment tools.

The next chapter by Sagit Yehoshua looks at prisoner management and risk assessment in a very different context: security prisoners in Israeli jails. Drawing on detailed interviews with terrorist prisoners in Israel, Yehoshua suggests that it is a mistake to view prison purely as a 'university of terror'. As with the findings described earlier by John Morrison in Northern Ireland, Yehoshua concludes that different factors can actually lead to prisoners becoming less violent and extreme – even in a context where there are no de-radicalisation programmes and no peace process on the outside world. Certain factors, such as the length of time spent in prison, the support the prisoner receives from their social environment and their fellow inmates, as well as gaining education while in prison and taking part in leadership roles, can lead to positive and pragmatic changes in how prisoners understand and approach the wider political conflict.

Key case studies

It is difficult to underestimate the importance of context when considering terrorists and extremists in prison settings. A wide range of very different groups and individuals are classed as 'terrorist' and there can be profound differences in the conflicts and societies which have spawned them. Assuming that all such prisoners are going to be the same is perhaps the quickest route to making serious errors in their management and attempted reform. That terrorists come in difference guises has already been touched upon in the volume, but this next section consciously builds on this by focusing on important case studies involving different forms of terrorism and different time periods.

The section opens with a chapter by Richard Pickering, who examines how the National Offender Management System (NOMS) in England and Wales has reacted to terrorist prisoners over the past ten years. Terrorist prisoners have been a periodic feature in English jails stretching back well over a century, but there is wide recognition that the growth in Al Qaeda-related prisoners since 9/11 presented what were seen as unique challenges to the system. Pickering explores how NOMS tried to react to this new problem and the chapter explores key issues around security and operational management, staffing, reducing reoffending, public protection and managing intelligence.

Marisa Porges then examines what is probably the most important case study with regard to Al Qaeda-related/inspired prisoners. Saudi Arabia has been at the cutting edge in terms of attempting to rehabilitate extremist prisoners in the past decade, though there has been tremendous controversy surrounding the success or failure of the Saudi efforts. Porges provides a detailed account of what it is that the Saudis have been attempting to do through a range of prison-based and post-release programs. The chapter describes the key elements of the government's strategy, exploring both religious and non-religious dimensions to the work. Importantly, Marisa argues that the Saudi strategy in this area has not been a static one, but has grown and changed over time to address the country's specific geo-political and security requirements, and the needs of its extremist prisoner population. The chapter provides a thorough evaluation of the success and failures of the programme and explores what are the real lessons the Saudi strategy provides for other countries.

Switching focus away from Muslim extremists, Arie Kruglanski and his fellow authors assess the case of the Liberation Tigers of Tamil Eelam (LTTE) in Sri Lanka. Sri Lanka has been the location for one of the most violent and long-running conflicts of the past thirty years. In 2009 major fighting ended with the comprehensive military defeat of the LTTE but the country is still dealing with the legacy of the conflict. This chapter is based on recent research on detained members of the LTTE in various Sri Lankan centres where up to 12,000 prisoners were held following the group's defeat. The chapter provides a fascinating case study of de-radicalisation efforts in a context of a particularly bitter conflict, but one where fighting beyond the prison walls has ended.

Kumar Ramakrishna in the following chapter returns to the issue of Islamist extremists, this time in the context of the experience of Singapore. As a richly multicultural society – yet one which is both wealthy and stable – the Singapore experience provides a fascinating counterpoint to the other case studies dealing with jihadi extremism which usually stem from the Middle East. Overall, the number of extremists Singapore found itself dealing with was quite small, but the country took the threat very seriously and invested enormous resources and effort to try to tackle the problem. Ramakrishna describes and analyses the 'Three Rings' of Singapore's terrorist rehabilitation and broader counter-ideological programme. The Inner Ring seeks to rehabilitate Singaporean radical Islamist terrorist detainees, the Outer Ring then extends the counter-ideological effort to the detainees' families, while, finally, the Outermost Ring seeks to create cognitive firewalls against violent extremist ideology amongst the wider Singaporean Muslim community. Ramakrishna argues that the Singaporean experience shows that a fully developed, multi-faceted, resource-intensive counter-ideological program is needed to deal with the problem of violent extremists in prison. Importantly, he also highlights the need for involving multiple stakeholders and for work to extend beyond prison walls.

Indonesia's experience with terrorist prisoners presents yet a further contrast and this is the focus of the next chapter by Sulastri Osman. Indonesia has been experiencing violence from several different sub-state groups in recent decades. The most notorious of these groups is Jemaah Islamiyah, which has drawn attention because of its connections with groups like Al Qaeda and its involvement in attacks such as the Bali bombings in 2002. Drawing on recent research in the region – including interviews with several extremists – Sulastri assesses the nature and extent of radicalisation in Indonesian prisons and also examines the role and impact of de-radicalisation initiatives which have been run by civil society organisations.

The following chapter by Gisela Diewald-Kerkmann looks back in history to the remarkable case of the Red Army Faction prisoners in West Germany in the 1970s. The Baader Meinhof group, a.k.a. The Red Army Faction, was one of the most notorious terrorist groups of the 1960s and 1970s. It was also a group which posed enormous challenges for the prison system as the number of prisoners belonging to the organisation grew (including most of its original leadership cadre). Yet despite the high-profile nature of the group and the very significant role that imprisonment played, remarkably little attention has been paid to this case in recent analyses of the problems around terrorists and prison. Gisela's account of what happened in this case provides an overview of the group in prison and what role the prison experience played (for better and worse).

The final case study is provided by Manuel R. Torres Soriano who examines the Spanish experience in this area. Soriano reviews Spain's prison policy as an anti-terrorist instrument, exposing its strengths and weaknesses, and the key lessons that can be incorporated for other countries with a similar context. Drawing both from a comprehensive review of the literature as well as in-depth interviews with prison officials, policy makers and members of the Spanish Police, Soriano concludes that prison policy can be a very important instrument in the fight against terrorism. The Spanish experience highlights that disengagement is very difficult to achieve in the presence of strong terrorist organisations willing to use extreme violence to neutralise government programmes. Soriano judges that the Spanish practice of trying to avoid the concentration of prisoners in the same jail ultimately proved a useful tool for weakening the control of the organisation over its members.

Post-release experiences

The final section of the book tries to consider what happens to terrorist and extremist offenders after they are released. Our understanding on this issue is even murkier than our understanding of the prison experience. Everyone asks the obvious – and important – question of 'do they return to violence' (the evidence seems to be that remarkably few do) but show extraordinary little interest beyond that.

Ben Wilkinson starts the discussion by considering how probation services have worked with former terrorist prisoners in England and Wales. In particular, the past ten years have seen the release of well over 200 prisoners who had been convicted of involvement in some form of terrorist activity related to Al Qaeda or an affiliated cause. The release of these prisoners has posed a major challenge for the probation service, amid feverish media fears that the released prisoners pose a high risk for re-engaging in terrorism and extremism. Drawing on interviews with probation staff, this chapter provides a balanced assessment of how released prisoners are managed and assessed, and describes how the release and probation process has worked with regard to these types of prisoners. The key challenges and difficulties faced by those involved in the process are identified and assessed. Wilkinson highlights there is an enormous need for an increasing focus and investment in rehabilitative programmes at this stage rather than offender management.

Neil Ferguson then completes the book and returns us to the Troubles in Northern Ireland. As he points out, it is estimated that somewhere between 20,000 and 32,000 men and women were incarcerated for politically motivated offences during the course of the conflict. Political prisoners and the nature of imprisonment in Northern Ireland made a huge impact on the intensity of the conflict, the wider politics of the region and ultimately the peace process. Drawing on research with former political prisoners, Ferguson explores the impact of imprisonment on the individual prisoners and also on the wider Northern Irish peace project. He highlights the role of former prisoners working at the interface between Protestant and Catholic communities to reduce communal tensions. The chapter also illustrates how the experiences gleaned in Northern Irish prisons offer some important lessons to those managing political prisoners in other geographical locations.

Concluding thoughts

Our knowledge of managing and intervening with violent extremists in prison settings is very limited. On many issues we currently have almost no published research, and much of what does exist is of poor quality. This deficiency unquestionably represents one of the most serious obstacles to developing effective strategies for promoting and facilitating disengagement from terrorism.

In reviewing the strategies, interventions and other critical issues for dealing with terrorist and extremist offenders, the focus of this book is not only on current threats and problems but also on drawing critical lessons from important historical cases. To do this effectively the book consciously considered the experience of a wide range of different countries in dealing with terrorists in prison, and focused on a variety of different movements ranging from nationalist groups such as the IRA, ETA and the LTTE, to ideologically motivated groups such as the Red Army Faction, to religiously motivated groups like Al Qaeda and its affiliates.

In pulling together the chapters, a key advantage of the collection has been the depth and range of experience of the contributors. Among the writers are practitioners, policy makers and leading researchers, with enormous experience of dealing with terrorists and extremists in prison settings. Most chapters are based on direct experience of working with terrorist prisoners and several are written by authors who have interviewed scores of such prisoners (current and former) as part of their work.

Ultimately, the book highlights the range of different – and sometimes contradictory – approaches that have been taken to try to manage and intervene with terrorist prisoners. Robust evaluations of these different strategies have by and large not been carried out and claims of success or failure must all be treated with caution. This volume, however, tries to add to the available knowledge and does focus attention on what can be regarded as the most reliable evidence to date. Emerging from this pool of knowledge, one thing that is very clear is that there is no magic formula for handling such prisoners.

Ultimately, those faced with managing terrorist and extremist prisoners are faced with a range of options – not all of which are compatible – and where there can be enormous uncertainty over what will work and what will not. This collection aims to bring much needed clarity and insight to this issue and to provide readers with an up-to-date, informed and accessible account of what is known about terrorists and extremists in prison, what are the key risks and dangers, and what are the critical issues and insights in terms of effective management, reform and the potential implications for wider conflicts. It is left to the reader to judge if it succeeds in that task or not.

References

Adair, J. (2009). *Mad Dog*. London: John Blake Publishing.

Ashour, O. (2010). *The De-Radicalization of Jihadists: Transforming Armed Islamist Movements*. London: Routledge.

Barret, R. and Bokhari, L. (2009). 'De-radicalization and rehabilitation programmes targeting religious terrorists and extremists in the Muslim world: An overview.' In Tore Bjørgo and John Horgan (Eds.) *Leaving Terrorism Behind*, pp.170–280. New York: Routledge.

Bates-Gaston, J. (2003). 'Terrorism and imprisonment in Northern Ireland: A psychological perspective.' In A. Silke (Ed.). *Terrorists, Victims and Society: Psychological Perspectives on Terrorism and Its Consequences*, pp.233–255. Chichester: Wiley.

Baumann, B. (1975). *Wie Alles Anfing*. Munich: Trikont Verlag.

Beresford, D. (1987). *Ten Men Dead: Story of the 1981 Hunger Strike*. London: Grafton.

Boucek, C. (2008). *Saudi Arabia's 'Soft' Counterterrorism Strategy: Prevention, Rehabilitation, and Aftercare*. Carnegie Papers, Middle East series 97. Washington, DC: Carnegie Endowment for International Peace.

Burgess, M., Ferguson, N., & Hollywood, I. (2007). 'Rebels' perspectives of the legacy of past violence and of the current peace in post-agreement Northern Ireland: An interpretative phenomenological analysis.' *Political Psychology*, 28, 69–88.

Clarke, L. (1987). *Broadening the Battlefield: H-blocks and the Rise of Sinn Fein*. Dublin: Gill and MacMillan.

Collins, E. (with McGovern, M.) (1997). *Killing Rage*. London: Granta Books.

Crawford, C. (1999). *Defenders or Criminals: Loyalist Prisoners and Criminalisation*. Belfast: Blackstaff Press.

Crenshaw, M. (1992). 'How terrorists think: What psychology can contribute to understanding terrorism.' In L. Howard (Ed.), *Terrorism: Roots, Impact, Responses*, pp.71–80. London: Praeger.

Dwyer, C. (2013). '"They might as well be walking around the inside of a biscuit tin": Barriers to employment and reintegration for "politically motivated" former prisoners in Northern Ireland.' *European Journal of Probation*, 5/1, pp. 3–24.

Friedland, N. (1992). 'Becoming a terrorist: social and individual antecedents.' In L. Howard (Ed.), *Terrorism: Roots, Impact, Responses*, pp.81–93. London: Praeger.

Hamm, M. (2013). *The Spectacular Few: Prison Radicalization and the Evolving Terrorist Threat*. New York: New York University Press.

Horgan, J. (2009). *Walking Away from Terrorism: Accounts of Disengagement from Radical and Extremist Movements*. Oxon, UK: Routledge.

Horgan, J. and Braddock, K. (2010). 'Rehabilitating the terrorists? Challenges in assessing the effectiveness of de-radicalization programmes.' *Terrorism and Political Violence*, 22/2, pp.267–291.

Lyons, H.A. & Harbinson, H.J. (1986). 'A comparison of political and non-political murderers in Northern Ireland, 1974–84.' *Medicine, Science and the Law*, 26, 193–198.

Mandela, N. (1995). *Long Walk to Freedom*. Boston: Back Bay Books.

McEvoy, K. (2001). *Paramilitary Imprisonment in Northern Ireland: Resistance, Management and Release*. Oxford: OUP.

McKee, W. (2009). *Governor.* Dublin: Gill & Macmillan.

Neumann, P. (2010). *Prison and Terrorism: Radicalisation and De-radicalisation in 15 Countries.* London: ICSR.

O'Doherty, S. (1993). *The Volunteer: A Former IRA Man's True Story.* London: Harper Collins.

O'Donnell, R. (2011). *Special Category: The IRA in English Prisons, Vol. 1 1968–1978.* Dublin: Irish Academic Press.

O'Rawe, R. (2005). *Blanketmen.* Dublin: New Island.

Ryder, C. (2000). *Inside the Maze.* York: Methuen Publishing.

Sands, B. (1993). *Writings from Prison.* Cork: Mercier Press.

Schiller, M. (2009). *Remembering the Armed Struggle: Life in Baader-Meinhof.* London: Zidane Press.

Silke, A. (2010). 'Terrorists and extremists in prison: psychological issues in management and reform.' In Andrew Silke (Ed.) *The Psychology of Counter-Terrorism.* London: Routledge.

Silke, A. (2011). 'Disengagement or deradicalization: A look at prison programs for jailed terrorists.' *CTC Sentinel*, 4/1, pp.18–21.

Von Tangen Page, M. (1998). *Prisons, Peace and Terrorism: Penal Policy in the Reduction of Political Violence in Northern Ireland, Italy and the Spanish Basque Country, 1968–97.* New York: Palgrave Macmillan.

Whyte, J. (1991). *Interpreting Northern Ireland.* Oxford: Oxford University Press.

2

"TO PUNISH, DETER AND INCAPACITATE"

Incarceration and radicalisation in UK prisons after 9/11

Colin Murray[1]

Out of sight, out of mind?

Lord Bingham once explained that the objectives behind sentencing in serious cases of terrorism differed from those applicable to ordinary criminal trials. Terrorism cases were of such 'abnormal' seriousness (*R v Turner*, 1975) that 'the object of the court will be to punish, deter and incapacitate; rehabilitation is likely to play a minor (if any) part' (*R v Martin*, 1999, p.480). He was speaking in the context of a Provisional IRA member's appeal against the sentence imposed for plotting a series of coordinated attacks on electricity substations around London. Despite the grave 'political, economic and social threat presented by this conspiracy', Lord Bingham led the Court of Appeal in reducing the appellant's sentence from 35 years to 28 years. Since Al Qaeda's attacks of 11 September 2001 ('9/11'), Lord Bingham's conception of the criminal justice system's role in terrorism cases has attracted considerable attention, with the Australian courts enthusiastically repeating that the criminal law exists in this context to 'punish, deter and incapacitate' (*R v Roche*, 2005). That Lord Bingham spoke in the course of a decision reducing an excessive sentence is forgotten.

In the UK, the Blair government's most prominent response to the 9/11 attacks was to introduce executive measures designed to circumvent the criminal law's strictures. In October 2001 the Anti-Terrorism, Crime and Security Act was enacted, permitting detention without trial of foreign nationals who the Home Secretary 'reasonably suspects' of involvement in international terrorism. The low standard of proof necessary for such detention, by comparison to the standard required for criminal prosecution, coupled with the admissibility of evidence which cannot be used to support a prosecution, meant that detention without trial could serve as a means of side-stepping the strictures of the criminal law. The courts, however, subjected the executive measures introduced by UK governments since

2001 to intense scrutiny, including ruling that detention without trial was incompatible with human rights under the European Convention (ECHR) and restricting the use of the replacement Control Orders regime to the point when, in 2011, the Coalition Government abandoned it in favour of Terrorism Prevention and Investigation Measures.

Alongside these cases, however, the courts assiduously delivered decisions which facilitated criminal law responses to terrorism. The courts have not called into question, or radically reinterpreted, the 'precursor' offences such as acts preparatory to terrorism or undertaking training for terrorist purposes enacted under the Terrorism Act 2006 with the aim of criminalising even early-stage terrorist activity. In *R v Da Costa* (2009), for example, the courts rejected claims by the defendants that the offence of receiving 'training in skills' for terrorist purposes could not encompass activities as loosely related to a terrorist purpose as fitness training. Similarly, in *R v A* (2010), the Court of Appeal accepted that whilst the 'acts preparatory' offence was particularly broad, 'Parliamentary intention was to embrace preparatory acts which are not so proximate to the acts of terrorism as to amount to attempts in law'. For writers such as Conor Gearty, such flexibility is inherent in the nature of criminal law, with 'the substance of the crimes themselves and the procedural framework for their detection and punishment being in a perpetual state of flux' (2008, p.189).

The domestic judiciary's receptiveness towards counter-terrorism adaptions to the criminal justice system indicates the continuing attractiveness of Lord Bingham's mantra. Nonetheless, in the era of suicide terrorism, academics including Bruce Ackerman (2006), questioned criminal law's deterrent effect upon individuals intending to commit such attacks. The courts have responded to such concerns in cases like *Barot*, reaffirming the faith of many judges in the criminal law's capacity to undermine terrorism:

> Many [terrorists] are unlikely to be deterred by the length of the sentence that they risk, however long this may be. Indeed, some are prepared to kill themselves in order to more readily kill others. It is, however, important that those who might be tempted to accept the role of camp followers of the more fanatic, are aware that, if they yield to that temptation, they place themselves at risk of very severe punishment.
>
> *(R v Barot, 2007, p.45)*

The effect of such judicial decisions has been to partially refocus the UK's counter-terrorism policy from executive measures to the criminal law (Walker, 2011). For security analysts based at institutions such as the Royal United Services Institute and the Quilliam Foundation, this approach carries long-term risks.[2] These security analysts argue that the UK's reliance upon criminal law responses could generate a 'second wave' of terrorist attacks, emanating from individuals released after serving relatively short terms of imprisonment for terrorism-related offences and from individuals radicalised whilst imprisoned for offences which were not terrorism-related (e.g. Clarke and Soria, 2010). The former concern, resultant from the application of precursor offences, such as the training and acts preparatory offences considered above, to peripheral individuals involved in nascent plots (whose behaviour would not have attracted criminal sanction outside the terrorist context), is to a certain extent negated by the small numbers of such individuals. On 31 December 2010, only 123 individuals were imprisoned in Great Britain on the basis of terrorism/extremism offences (Anderson, 2012). Moreover, convicted terrorists who are subsequently released from prison will likely remain the subject of extensive surveillance by the security services. Few individuals planning future terrorist attacks would risk contact with such figures. This contribution focuses instead upon the latter claim that convicted terrorist prisoners are involved in widespread efforts to radicalise their fellow inmates. It first evaluates claims regarding radicalisation amongst the prison population, before turning to consider the detention regime in place for those convicted of terrorism related offences in UK prisons. As we shall see, the criminal justice system's near-absolute focus in terrorism cases on punishment, deterrence and incapacitation does not stop at the prison gates. Such prisoners are subjected to a prison regime intended to maintain these goals, one which the courts have sustained in the face of challenge.

The threat of radicalisation within prison populations

Prisons are frequently portrayed as potential 'incubators for terrorism' (Pantucci, 2009), although such claims are often heavily caveated, as demonstrated by Anthony Whealy's discussion of prison radicalisation in Australia:

> [T]here is anecdotal evidence emerging from Australian prison conditions to suggest that Islamist radicalisation is occurring among prisoners within the gaol population. Once again, it is impossible to know how accurate reports of this kind are.
>
> *(Whealy, 2010, p.35)*

Seeking to combat this dearth of evidence, prominent figures in two influential think-tanks, Michael Clarke from the security-focused RUSI and James Brandon from the extremism-focused Quilliam Foundation, conducted research which they interpreted as establishing that prison radicalisation posed a serious threat to UK security. Writing in 2009, Clarke and his co-author Valentina Soria first developed their prisoner radicalisation thesis, drawing a direct connection between the imprisonment of convicted terrorists and the risk of radicalisation:

> Prisons around the world are universities of terror and there is no reason to believe that the UK's will not be the same. The ninety-odd convictions, of which the security services can be proud, will have their own longer-term consequences for which the government must be prepared.
>
> *(Clarke and Soria, 2009, p.52)*

A year later Clarke and Soria returned to the issue of radicalisation in a second article, noting the additional impetus that the number of individuals convicted of terrorism offences had swelled from 90 to 230. Whilst they admit that much of the evidence they draw upon is 'necessarily circumstantial', they conclude that 'jihadist radicalisation' was a particular problem 'in the eight high-security institutions where most terrorist prisoners are kept' (Clarke and Soria, 2010, p.29). These conclusions are supported by Brandon's (2009) contemporary research, which argues that Islamist extremists linked to Al Qaeda are actively recruiting in UK prisons. Brandon draws extensively upon convicted terrorists' accounts of their time in prison to substantiate this claim, but whilst many of these accounts detail contact between these individuals and other Muslim prisoners, and even attempts by convicted terrorists to adopt leadership roles amongst Muslim prisoners, few of these published accounts suggest overt radicalisation. Whilst Brandon can evidence figures such as Rachid Ramda, who would ultimately be extradited to France and convicted of involvement in the 1995 attacks on the Paris metro, leading Friday Prayers, he can only conjecture that he used this position of influence to radicalise his fellow inmates. Even where convicted terrorists do claim to have recruited their fellow prisoners, such claims must be regarded in light of their imperative to inflate the importance of jihadist movements.

Despite the shortcomings in such research, its impact upon UK counter-terrorism policy has been profound. The UK's Counter-Terrorism Strategy (CONTEST) proceeds on the basis of the premise that prisons are institutions in which individuals will likely become radicalised:

> Evidence and intelligence suggest that the ideology of violent extremism gains influence through individuals and groups who actively promote it: the messenger is as important as the message. Radicalisers exploit open spaces in communities and institutions, including . . . prisons.
>
> *(HM Government, 2011a)*

This assertion of the importance of prisons in the UK's counter-radicalisation strategy requires us to consider whether this indeed constitutes a novel problem, and the adequacy of the prison authorities' reaction to the issue.

Penology and political violence in the twentieth century

UK governments have grappled with the particular problems of detaining individuals suspected or convicted of involvement in political violence through much of the twentieth century. In responding to Irish irredentism, lessons regarding the detention of those involved in political violence, or merely suspected of such involvement, have been repeatedly learned, forgotten and relearned by the UK authorities.

In the wake of the Easter Rising in 1916, the UK authorities used the war-time Defence of the Realm Regulations to detain 3,500 individuals suspected of involvement in Irish Republicanism (Townshend, 1998). These individuals could thereafter be held indefinitely without trial, and around 2,000 detainees were transferred to internment camps, including former POW camps at Reading and at Frongoch in North Wales. Many had no involvement in the Rising whatsoever, but in the camps such individuals, embittered by their mistaken detention, came under the influence of those who had participated. Frongoch became for Irish Republicanism 'a veritable political university and military academy' (O'Mahoney, 1987, p.58), with the internees using their detention 'to lay the foundations of the reorganization of the national movement' (Townshend, 1998, pp.81–82). One of David Lloyd George's first acts as prime minister in December 1916 was to approve the release of remaining detainees, with the Chief Secretary for Ireland expressing to the House of Commons his hope that this action would produce 'good results' for the situation in Ireland. The damage, however, had been done. From Frongoch's huts would spring much of the IRA's leadership in the War of Independence, fought between 1919 and 1921.

With the partition of Ireland in 1922 seemingly 'solving' the Irish Question, the UK authorities forgot the lessons of Frongoch for radicalisation, or at least came to question their significance. In the middle years of the twentieth century IRA prisoners like Seán Mac Stíofáin, convicted for his part in a raid on an Officer Training Corps armoury in 1953, could regularly associate with their fellow prisoners. Mac Stíofáin, who would go on to become the first Chief of Staff of the Provisional IRA, later wrote of how, in Wormwood Scrubs, he and other republican inmates were schooled in asymmetric warfare by imprisoned members of the Greek-Cypriot EOKA (Mac Stíofáin, 1975, p.79). When, at the end of the 1960s, the 'Troubles' once again erupted in Northern Ireland, the authorities repeated the mistakes of Frongoch. Amid claims that the normal criminal justice process could not cope with rising levels of political violence, the Stormont-based Northern Ireland Government commenced internment in August 1971. Hennessey (1997, p.194) described the basis of internment as 'an arbitrary trawl through Catholic areas detaining all young men, rather than an intelligence led effort'. Members of the IRA were swept up alongside innocent individuals apt to be radicalised by such a deprivation of their right to liberty, and held together at internment facilities like the camp at the former RAF Long Kesh base, south of Belfast (the site of the future Maze Prison). Since internees had not been convicted of criminal offences, they were not subject to the same restrictions of prison work or uniform as convicted criminals, and were able to freely associate within such camps. Once again, such camps became an 'important sector' in the Republican struggle (Mac Stíofáin, 1975, p.73).

As the number of internees increased into September 1971, the UK Government wrung its hands and committed additional army units in support of the beleaguered RUC, with the Home Secretary assuring Westminster that whilst internment was 'a hideous measure' he did 'not regard it as hideous as a campaign of murder and terrorism' (*Hansard*, 22 September 1971, cc2-157). By the time the UK government prorogued the devolved Stormont arrangements in March 1972, almost 1,000 people had been interned, almost all of them Catholic (Donohue, 2001, p.62). Facing a further upsurge in violence, however, the government sought to abandon this ineffective policy. A report prepared by Lord Diplock, a senior judge, proposed that the criminal justice system, rather than military-led internment, should take the lead in combating political violence. The courts, in Lord Diplock's opinion, had 'in general held the respect and trust of all except the extremists of both factions' (Diplock, 1972, p.13). Judge-only trial processes could be used to tackle the dangers of jury intimidation or jury sympathy for the aims of those involved in political violence that the Stormont government had cited when it introduced internment. By attempting to draw legitimacy from the modified criminal justice system, and the increasing number of convictions of terrorist suspects, the government once again had to confront the issue of how to deal with offenders convicted of involvement in political violence within the prison system.

From 1972 onwards, in response to a prison hunger strike, prisoners in Northern Ireland convicted of terrorism-related offences had been subject to 'Special Category Status', entitling them to similar treatment to internees. Many such prisoners were moved to the same compounds as internees. Lord Gardiner attempted to highlight to parliament the dangers of policy in terms of the radicalisation of prisoners:

> The housing of male special category prisoners in compounds means that they are not closely controlled as they would be in a normal cellular prison, discipline within compounds is in practice exercised by compound leaders, and they are more likely to emerge with an increased commitment to terrorism than as reformed citizens.
>
> *(Gardiner, 1975)*[3]

By the mid-1970s internment had been phased out of use, even if the power would not be removed from the statute book until 1998 (Colville, 1990; Donohue, 2001). Judges may have continued to describe 'bomb outrages' and 'acts of political terrorism' as 'wholly abnormal', (e.g. see *R v Turner*) but they did so in order to justify extended sentences for individuals convicted of such activities, not to question the criminal justice system's capacity to deal with such offenders. Through these policy changes the UK government sought to change public opinion, both nationally and internationally, toward its counter-terrorism policy. As Clive Walker (1984) notes, this new criminalisation strategy held distinct attractions for the government, coaxing public opinion into adopting 'a perception of the terrorists which corresponds to that of the state – in other words, the terrorists are viewed simply as criminals, so their treatment as such is acceptable. Unsurprisingly, the government came to regard Special Category Status as dissonant with its efforts to portray terrorists as criminals.

Special Category Status was abolished in 1976 and a succession of riots, blanket protests, dirty protests and ultimately hunger strikes ensued. The details of the protests and their impact on the UK's penal policy in the context of the 'Troubles' has been thoroughly documented elsewhere, with prisoners belonging to both loyalist and republican groups ultimately gaining extensive concessions regarding their status (Campbell, McKeown and O'Hagan, 1994). Often physically separated from the remainder of the prison population in Northern Ireland, in some cases following the end of the 1980–81 hunger strikes, prisoners of different factions were even housed in entirely separate accommodation. This can hardly be seen as a success for counter-radicalisation, however, as such segregation was a key demand by paramilitary prisoners (Colville, 1992). Indeed, such separation provided them with a barrier against informants, thereby facilitating disruptions of prison routine and even escape attempts. After the mass breakout from HMP Maze in 1983, the then Chief Inspector of Prisons noted that 'the segregation of Provisional IRA prisoners . . . made it easier for them to plan and execute the escape' (Hennessey, 1984). The UK government thereafter sought to adopt what one Northern Ireland Secretary called a 'clear stand' against the separation of different paramilitary factions. De facto separation of groups of prisoners committed to each other's destruction would, however, continue throughout the 'Troubles', with nominally 'shared' facilities like canteens divided by staggered dining times.

Such general separation of paramilitary prisoners from the remainder of the prison population was not attempted in Scottish, Welsh and English prisons during the 'Troubles'. Successive governments perceived the potential for such prisoners recruiting their fellow inmates to be slight, due to the particular character of the conflict in Northern Ireland. For the most part, as one former republican prisoner told *An Phoblacht*, Sinn Fein's newspaper, in 1988, '[t]he Irish political prisoners usually get on fairly well with the other prisoners in the jail, but there is always that gap between them'. Nonetheless, due to escape risks, such prisoners did influence the development of restrictive High Security Units (HSUs) in UK prisons, with the Unit at HMP Belmarsh in particular being designed to house paramilitary prisoners. Although some paramilitary prisoners were occasionally segregated from the remainder of the prison body ('removal from association' under the Prison Rules), this power was often employed as a standard disciplinary policy or to protect such individuals from their fellow inmates following high-profile terrorist attacks.

Political violence and UK prisons after 9/11

By the late 1990s, accompanied by the efforts to bring the 'Troubles' in Northern Ireland to an end through the Good Friday Agreement, the Prison Service was acutely aware of the particular difficulties in handling prisoners convicted of involvement in political violence (McEvoy, 1998). Nonetheless, the experience of dealing with large bodies of prisoners involved in the ethno-nationalist conflict in Northern Ireland did not always translate directly into the context of managing offenders linked to, or inspired by, Al Qaeda in the aftermath of the 9/11 attacks.

Whilst a number of prisoners had been convicted of involvement in international political violence from the 1980s onwards (*R v Basra*, 1989; *R v Al-Banna*, 1984), including attempts to perpetrate mass casualty attacks (*R v Hindawi*, 1988), special arrangements were not put in place for these prisoners over and above the standard regimes in high security prisons. For the most part, the UK prison authorities did not attempt to segregate such prisoners and radicalisation was not regarded as a particularly serious threat. Nezar Hindawi's case is instructive. In 1986, Hindawi was convicted of attempting to destroy an El Al Boeing 747 carrying 375 people using a bomb planted in his then fiancée's baggage, without her knowledge (*R (Hindawi) v Secretary of State for Justice*, 2011). He was sentenced to 45 years imprisonment, 'not a day too long' in the words of Lord Lane CJ. His willingness to carry out such a mass casualty attack and his 'extreme views about the enemies of Palestinians', in many ways made Hindawi the prototypical Islamic-extremist inmate. The first decade of his imprisonment was spent in an HSU, permitting Hindawi limited interaction with his fellow prisoners. Hindawi's links with the Syrian Intelligence Service indicated to the authorities that he might, with outside assistance, seek to escape. By 1997, however, such concerns had receded and the authorities reclassified Hindawi as a Category A prisoner. By 1999 he was reclassified once again as a Category B prisoner, and by 2006 as a Category C prisoner. Despite the seriousness of Hindawi's offences, by process of regular review of the threat to society and escape risk which he posed, the prison authorities were able to progressively downgrade the restrictiveness of his prison conditions.

Hindawi's imprisonment would in many ways act as a blueprint for the prison regimes imposed upon Islamist extremists incarcerated from 2001 onwards. Cells in HSUs, developed to house prisoners like Hindawi and paramilitary prisoners linked to the 'Troubles', are now routinely used to house terrorist prisoners on remand and post-conviction. In the *Ahmed Ali* case, involving appeals lodged by prisoners convicted of involvement in the 'Airline Bomb Plot' of August 2006, Thomas LJ detailed how the appellants had been held for extended period in the HSU at Belmarsh, 'often described as prison within a prison', which imposed 'intrusive and strict security procedures' (*R v Ahmed Ali & Others*, 2011). These procedures, developed to securely detain individuals where the likelihood of an escape attempt was high, also allow prison authorities to hamper any efforts by individuals convicted of involvement in terrorism to radicalise members of the general prison population. Whilst preparing a 2012 report evaluating the threat of radicalisation amongst the UK prison population, members of the UK Parliament's Home Affairs Select Committee interviewed one of HMP Belmarsh's Muslim chaplains. The committee noted that, despite Belmarsh holding a particularly high percentage of Muslim prisoners (20 per cent, compared with 12 per cent across all UK prisons), the Imam was not particularly concerned with the threat of radicalisation posed by the presence of high-profile individuals such as Abu Hamza, as he 'was more likely to influence the High Security Unit prisoners than other prisoners, owing to the detention regime' (Home Affairs Select Committee, 2012, p.39).

Furthermore, prison Imams, and other prison staff, are expected to complete Security Intelligence Reports (SIRs) should any issue arise which could affect 'the security of the establishment or public protection' (Home Affairs Select Committee, 2012, p.39). SIRs are the cornerstone of what the UK Counter-Terrorism Strategy refers to as 'enhanced arrangements for collecting intelligence relating to prisoners suspected, or convicted of terrorist related activities or extremism' (HM Government, 2011a). Such arrangements continue to apply even if prison authorities no longer deem it necessary, for security reasons, to hold particular inmates in HSUs. Michael Spurr, the Chief Executive Officer of the National Offender Management Service (NOMS), explained to the Committee the steps which would be taken if such monitoring indicated that a prisoner was attempting to radicalise other inmates:

> [I]f we had evidence of individual risk or attempts to radicalise or create disorder in the establishment, we would respond to that and we could manage individuals in tighter security, for example, in periods of segregation or in close supervision centres, which have particularly high levels of security.
>
> *(Home Affairs Select Committee, 2012)*

Nonetheless, SIRs are not solely focused on counter-terrorism detainees and, as the most recent inspection report from Belmarsh makes clear, few of the 8,400 SIRs completed in 2010 concerned radicalisation (HM Chief Inspector of Prisons, 2011a, p.71).

The 'War on Terror' has not, therefore, seen a radical reorganisation of how UK prisons manage offenders convicted of involvement in political violence. Many such inmates continue to be held initially in HSUs, although at times in the last decade, particularly after significant counter-terrorism operations, the limited HSU provision in UK prisons has been at 'full stretch' (HM Chief Inspector of Prisons, 2006, p.5). Many terrorist prisoners will therefore ultimately be transferred, following risk assessments, out of an HSU and find themselves in a position to mingle with the remainder of the prison population, as demonstrated by the accounts which Brandon (2009) draws upon in his research. At this point, however, monitoring regimes continue to assess whether these individuals pose a threat to the management of the prison, specifically with regard to efforts to radicalise their fellow inmates. Furthermore, in recent years an increased effort has been placed on challenging the ideology of such individuals by the prison authorities (Home Affairs Select Committee, 2012). These efforts, whether in prison or upon release,[4] ordinarily involve focused interactions intended to fundamentally alter the individuals' ideals (de-radicalisation) or at the very least to persuade them to end associations with violent groups (disengagement).

Legal challenges to the detention conditions of terrorist prisoners

As with many aspects of contemporary penal policy, the concept of 'risk management' seems, on a preliminary assessment, to be the primary influence upon detention conditions of prisoners convicted of terrorism or terrorism-related offences (Maurutto and Hannah-Moffat, 2006). The Prison Act 1952 permits the authorities to hold inmates in any prison, and also allows government to make regulations for the management of prisons. Such regulations, now contained within the Prison Rules 1999, allow prison governors to segregate an inmate from other prisoners, in the interests of good order, to discipline the prisoner or to protect the prisoner.

This power gives prison governors the ability to remove prisoners from association where they perceive a risk of radicalisation, but it is not without its limits. The Strasbourg-based European Court of Human Rights recognises that prisoners do not lose their ECHR rights simply because of imprisonment (see *Dickson v UK*, 2008). For example, Article 3 of the ECHR prevents any treatment of prisoners which would amount to inhuman or degrading treatment. Neumann (2010) has argued that this rule prevents countries from attempting the 'permanent isolation of terrorist prisoners', and indeed, ECHR jurisprudence has long recognised that a combination of complete sensory and social isolation would indeed contravene Article 3. The principle that prisoners should not be completely isolated is embedded within the UK's Prison Rules, with the specific rule on classification of prisoners, for example, making clear that '[n]othing in this rule shall require a prisoner to be deprived unduly of the society of other persons'.

Notwithstanding this limitation, the ECHR institutions have given considerable leeway to member states concerning inmates who pose serious security risks. When members of the Red Army Faction imprisoned in Germany in the 1970s sought to challenge their segregation from other prisoners, the Strasbourg institutions recognised that restrictions short of such total isolation may not reach the threshold of inhuman or degrading treatment, depending upon factors such as 'the particular conditions, the stringency of the measure, its duration, the objective pursued and its effects on the person concerned' (*Ensslin, Baader and Raspe v Germany*, 1978, p.109). Where high-profile terrorist inmates are at issue, ECHR states can often successfully argue that isolation is necessary. In the case of Ramirez Sanchez (*Ramirez Sanchez v France*, 2007) the claimant, better known as Carlos the Jackal, failed to persuade the European Court that eight years of solitary confinement breached his Article 3 right. Beyond these Article 3 concerns, imprisonment may necessarily curtail many of an individual's other rights, including the right under Article 8 to private and family life, but such restrictions will ordinarily be acceptable if prison authorities can supply adequate justifications for their actions. Given the leeway contained within these rights, applicable in domestic cases since the enactment of the Human Rights Act 1998, the prison authorities enjoy considerable powers to counter radicalisation, short of total isolation. Uses of these powers which have been challenged in the courts include both the separation of groups of terrorist prisoners from the main prison population and the segregation of individual terrorist prisoners.

The *Bary* case involved several claimants held at HMP Long Lartin pending deportation or extradition on the basis of suspected involvement in terrorism (*R (Bary and Others) v The Secretary of State for Justice*, 2010). From 2005 onwards such individuals were held in a specific 'Detainee Unit' at Long Lartin, separated from the remainder of the prison population. Contact with other members of the prison population was extremely limited after December 2008, when the governor issued a notice that the detainees would be restricted to the Detainee Unit in all activities other than healthcare appointments. The governor claimed that this process recognised the status of the detainees as distinct from convicted prisoners, but admitted in correspondence with HM Inspectorate of Prisons that he also considered the isolation of the unit from the remainder of the prison to be a means of 'maintaining the safety of some high profile inhabitants of the unit and to managing issues of radicalisation of prisoners' (*R (Bary and Others) v The Secretary of State for Justice*, 2010, p.22). One of the detainees then held at Long Lartin was Abu Qatada, described by Aikens LJ as 'an iconic figure in the jihadist movement', and the governor explained at the time that his policy was in part intended to rebut widespread media allegations that Qatada was actively radicalising Muslim inmates within the general prison population. This focus on 'media handling' was not repeated in response to the legal challenge to the separation of the Detainee Unit prisoners from the rest of the prison body, but it indicates the pervasive impact upon prison policy of the media's fixation upon the idea that terrorist ringleaders had embarked upon radicalising their fellow inmates. The Divisional Court recognised that concerns regarding media coverage could not justify the separation of detainees:

> [A]t the outset [the governor] was clearly concerned with the possibility of allegations in the press and other media that either the detainees were having a 'cosy' time or that they could dictate the terms of their detention regime. It is now accepted that this could not be a valid reason for changing the regime.

Despite this evidence that the separation of detainees held at Long Lartin constituted an exercise in media management, the court accepted that other justifications could exist, and that the important issues under Articles 3 and 8 were, 'the risk [the detainees] present to other prisoners, not in this case so much by way of direct violence but by way of propagandising' and 'whether the risks which they present justify and/or are proportionate to the conditions and regime in place' (*R (Bary and Others) v The Secretary of State for Justice*, 2010, p.43). In spite of 'the unsatisfactory way in which the rationalisation for the decision ha[d] evolved since December 2008' and the lack of intelligence suggesting a specific radicalisation threat, the Court accepted that it was reasonable to respond to the general threat of radicalisation posed by Abu Qatada, who was able to 'exercise a malign influence on other Muslims, including prisoners, and in particular, on impressionable young men, many of whom might be susceptible to his brand of extremism'. This reasoning may well be taken to justify the isolation of Qatada himself, but the Court went further, recognising that 'if the other detainees continued to use the main prison and [Qatada] was, in fact, determined to attempt to radicalise others in the main prison . . . he could try to persuade other detainees to assist him' (*R (Bary and Others) v The Secretary of State for Justice*, 2010, p.80). This construction of a hypothetical worst-case scenario demonstrates the Court's eagerness to find a justification for the degree of isolation practiced in the Detainee Unit. Despite the Court's best efforts, as Nick Hardwick, HM Chief Inspector of Prisons would note in June 2011, the rationale for the on-going separation of detainees 'appeared obscure as sentenced terrorists faced no such restriction in the main prison and not all detainees posed the same level of risk' (HM Chief Inspector of Prisons, 2011b, p.5).

The group separation practiced in the *Bary* case remains an exception in current UK practice (although one still reflected in the management of loyalist and republican prisoners in Northern Ireland (see HM Chief Inspector of Prisons, 2009), with prison authorities being more likely to segregate specific prisoners on the basis of attempting to radicalise their fellow inmates, than to separate out a body of inmates. Hussain Osman, for example, convicted of involvement in the failed 21 July 2005 attacks on the London transport network, complained on the now defunct website muslimprisoners.com that he had been segregated for four weeks for attempted radicalisation (Gardham, 2012). In *King, Bourgass and Hussain* (*R (King, Bourgass and Hussain) v Secretary of State for Justice*, 2012), the latter claimants were both prisoners convicted of serious terrorism-related offences. Kamel Bourgass, the lead conspirator in the 2003 'Ricin Plot', was segregated on several occasions during his imprisonment in HMP Whitemoor to preserve prison order and discipline, on the basis that he was 'responsible for an escalation of violence in the Prison "for faith related reasons" and that his influence over other prisoners was a threat to good order and security'. Whilst Maurice Kay LJ accepted that this segregation, for up to six months at a time, 'probably did engage Article 8 at some stage', he concluded that it was justified on the basis set forth by Lord Bingham in another segregation case (not related to radicalisation), *R (Munjaz) v Mersey Care NHS Trust* (2005), as 'it is used as the only means of protecting others from violence or intimidation and for the shortest period necessary to that end'. In reaching this decision, the Court of Appeal emphasised the risk posed by the prisoner but, in contrast to *Bary*, considerable attention was also given to the safeguards in place over the segregation of individuals:

> One only has to recall the circumstances that gave rise to the segregation decisions in relation to Bourgass . . . to appreciate the necessity for urgency. Moreover, the initial decisions, which cannot last more than 72 hours, are subject to early and regular periodic review thereafter, at which point the prisoner can make representations to the [Segregation Review Board].

Despite the Review Board in Bourgass's case relying on information obtained from an undisclosed source as sufficient to justify maintaining his segregation, raising concerns regarding the fairness of the hearing under Article 6 ECHR, Kay LJ was willing to follow the High Court in giving considerable leeway to prison authorities in dealing with the 'realities of the situation' of managing terrorist prisoners.

Murphy and Whitty (2007) assert that 'UK prison governance has become enveloped by the discourses of risk and rights', a view strongly supported by these cases. In terms of risk assessment, however, these judgements also fit squarely within

Murphy and Whitty's identification of 'a longstanding appellate court reluctance to become involved in adjudicating on expert opinion in relation to risk assessments of prisoners' (p.803). *Bary* and *King, Bourgass and Hussain*, however, are not simply prison management cases. They mark the intersection between prison governance and counter-terrorism, likewise an area in which 'questions of risk are often central' (Poole, 2008, p.259), and indicate that at this intersection the courts are particularly reliant on the executive's risk assessments. These cases, furthermore, bear out Tom Poole's (2008) warning, that recourse to human rights arguments would not necessarily inhibit security-focused government policies in many cases. All of the qualified rights, like the right to private and family life relied upon in these cases, are contingent upon official risk assessments, which form the basis of judicial decisions as to whether the particular interference with these rights is proportionate. In *Bary* and *King, Bourgass and Hussain*, the respect shown by the courts towards the prison authorities' 'expert' risk assessments, meant that these executive opinions were able to 'infiltrat[e] judicial decisions' supposedly made on the basis of human rights concerns. The challenge for the courts, unconvincingly addressed in these cases, remains in assessing whether such a risk assessment rests less upon expertise than upon the 'gut feeling' of an official.

Together, these cases provide little guidance on when the judiciary would intervene and rule that the segregation of inmates on the basis of their alleged efforts to radicalise other prisoners breached their human rights. The back-stop provided by Strasbourg jurisprudence, which confirms that complete isolation of an inmate would contravene the ECHR, remains in place, but where terrorism is at issue, a broad range of responses short of complete isolation have not been ruled out. Together, *Bary* and *King, Bourgass and Hussain* emphasise the willingness of the UK's courts to facilitate the operations of the prison authorities in countering radicalisation. The prison authorities' limited reliance upon the most far-reaching disciplinary powers in their arsenal would appear, therefore, to result less from the 'external' judicial protection of human rights norms than from that key 'internal' constraint upon prison management, the professional judgement of prison personnel.

Conclusion

In recent decades, the courts have consistently asserted that the use of political violence 'to destabilise the community or exert pressure [on the authorities] must be met with severe deterrent sentences' (e.g. *R v Cruickshank and O'Donnell*, 1995). In other words, the courts have made a close connection between punitive sentences and the protection of the community. The aim of 'incapacitating' such individuals through such sentences would be undermined, however, if the prison authorities did not enjoy adequate tools to prevent them from radicalising their fellow inmates. This contribution has sought to explain the methods employed by the prison authorities to prevent such radicalisation and to consider the approach of the courts to challenges to these methods under human rights legislation. As cases such as *Bary* and *King, Bourgass and Hussain* show, human rights legislation has not impeded the application of highly restrictive detention regimes to prisoners considered to pose a serious risk of radicalising other inmates.

The threat of prison radicalisation has often been presented as a caricatured process whereby imprisoned terrorist masterminds whisper in the ears of their fellow inmates whilst the prison authorities watch on, helpless in the face of human rights restrictions. The debate over prison radicalisation, however, seems to be shifting. There is no discernible pressure from prison authorities for new powers over inmates to constrain radicalisation, and instead their attention has focused on the effective use of their existing powers. First, the NOMS's counter-radicalisation efforts are no longer focused almost exclusively on 'grooming' by prisoners convicted of, or on remand for, terrorism or terrorism-related offences. Instead, the NOMS has extended oversight regimes beyond such offenders, focusing instead on identifying 'at risk' inmates on the basis of 'intelligence and the engagement . . .with individual offenders' (Home Affairs Select Committee, 2012, p.52). This development is necessary in light of the recognition, in the government's Prevent Strategy, that:

> [S]ome people who have been convicted for non-terrorism-related offences but who have previously been associated with extremist or terrorist networks have engaged in radicalising and recruitment activity while in prison.
>
> *(HM Government, 2011b)*

Nonetheless, at a time when prison inspection reports cite improved relations between Muslim inmates and staff in prisons like Belmarsh (see HM Chief Inspector of Prisons, 2011a), the danger remains that an overzealous application of the Prevent Strategy will only serve to reinforce a perception amongst Muslim prisoners that they are under perpetual suspicion of constituting a terrorist threat. Such a focus would be particularly misplaced in the context of increasing far-right militancy.

Moreover, the authorities have begun to focus attention on the support of offenders after they leave prison. In the prison radicalisation debate, considerable academic and media attention has focused upon individuals like Richard Reid, Muktar Ibrahim and Jermaine Grant, all supposedly radicalised whilst in Feltham Young Offenders Institute (Nawaz, 2012). Many such prisoners, however, convert or manifest faith as part of the 'temporary and opportunistic alliances' forged to create a support network during incarceration (Home Affairs Select Committee, 2012, p.90). In such circumstances, as Home Office Minister Crispin Blunt recognises, '[c]onversion to Islam does not equal radicalisation' (Blunt, 2012). Instead, many offenders are in fact particularly susceptible to radicalisation immediately after their release from prison, when there is 'a tendency for a family to reject the offender' (Home Affairs Select Committee, 2012, p.65). As Neumann's (2010, p.27) report indicates, much of Richard Reid's radicalisation took place immediately after his release, 'when he became involved with a group of extremists at Brixton Mosque'.

The efforts by Brandon and Clarke and Soria to highlight the threat of prison radicalisation by convicted terrorists resonates with policy makers, who are often all too eager to identify internal threats capable of justifying the continuation of extensive counter-terrorism powers (Hamm, 2009). But their warning of direct radicalisation by inmates convicted of terrorism or terrorism-related offences risks perpetuating a caricature of radicalisation which obscures the complexity of this issue. Nonetheless, after more than a decade in which such voices have held sway over penal policy, enhanced monitoring of vulnerable inmates and mentoring upon release finally suggest that this aspect of the UK's Prevent Strategy is undergoing a necessary evolution.

Notes

1   My thanks to Kevin J. Brown (Newcastle University), Fiona de Londras (Durham University) and Aoife O'Donoghue (Durham University) for their advice and comments upon earlier drafts of this article. Any errors remain my own.
2   Considerable academic literature suggests the issue of counter-terrorism policy should be conducted through extraordinary measures or embedded within the criminal justice system. For more on this see Gross and Ní Aoláin (2006).
3   Lord Gardiner was drawing upon the work of an official committee he had chaired, the report of which had been largely side-lined by the then government; see Lord Gardiner (1975).
4   For an evaluation of one mentoring programme operating in the West Midlands from 2009 onwards, see Spalek and Davies (2012).

References

Ackerman, B. (2006). *Before the Next Attack: Preserving Civil Liberties in an Age of Terrorism*. New Haven: YUP.
Anderson, D. (2012). *Report on the Operation in 2011 of the Terrorism Act 2000*. London: The Stationery Office.
Blunt, C. (2012). 'Letter to the Editor.' *The Times* (12 January 2012).
Brandon, J. (2009). *Unlocking Al-Qaeda. Islamist Extremism in British Prisons*. London: Quilliam.
Campbell, B., McKeown, L. and O'Hagan, F. (1994). *Nor Meekly Serve My Time: The H Block Struggle 1976–1981*. Belfast: Beyond the Pale.
Clarke, M. and Soria, V. (2009). 'Terrorism in the UK: Confirming its modus operandi.' *RUSI Journal*, 154/3, pp.44–53.
Clarke, M. and Soria, V. (2010). 'Terrorism: The new wave.' *RUSI Journal*, 155/4, pp.24–29.
Dickson v UK (2008) 46 EHRR 41, 68.
Donohue, L. (2001). *Counter-Terrorism Law and Emergency Powers in the United Kingdom, 1922–2000*. Dublin: Irish Academic Press.
Ensslin, Baader and Raspe v Germany (1978) 14 DR 64, 109.
Gardham, D. (2012). 'Muslim prisoners issue rallying call from behind bars.' *The Telegraph* (19 February 2012).
Gearty, C. (2008). 'The superpatriotic fervour of the moment.' *Oxford Journal of Legal Studies*, 28(1), pp.183–200.
Gross, O. and Ní Aoláin, F. (2006). *Law in Times of Crisis: Emergency Powers in Theory and Practice*. Cambridge: Cambridge University Press.

Hamm, M. (2009). 'Prison Islam in the Age of Sacred Terror.' *British Journal of Criminology*, 49(5), pp.667–685.

Hansard HC Deb vol 823 cc2-157 (22 September 1971).

Hennessey, J. (1984). *A Report of an Inquiry by HM Chief Inspector of Prisons into the Security Arrangements at HM Prison Maze.* London: The Stationery Office.

Hennessey, T. (1997). *A History of Northern Ireland: 1920–1996.* London: Macmillan.

HM Chief Inspector of Prisons (2006). *Report on an Unannounced Full Follow-up Inspection of HMP Belmarsh, 3–7 October 2005.* London: The Stationery Office.

HM Chief Inspector of Prisons (2009). *Report on an Unannounced Full Follow-up Inspection of HMP Maghaberry, 19–23 January 2009.* London: The Stationery Office.

HM Chief Inspector of Prisons (2011a). *Report on a Full Unannounced Inspection of HMP Belmarsh, 6–15 April 2011.* London: The Stationery Office.

HM Chief Inspector of Prisons (2011b). *Report on an Unannounced Follow-up Inspection of the Detainee Unit at HMP Long Lartin, 4–6 April 2011.* London: The Stationery Office.

HM Government (2011a). *CONTEST: The United Kingdom's Strategy for Countering Terrorism.* London: The Stationery Office.

HM Government (2011b). *Prevent Strategy.* London: The Stationery Office.

Home Affairs Select Committee (2012). *Roots of Violent Radicalisation.* London: The Stationery Office.

Lord Colville (1990). *Review of the Northern Ireland (Emergency Provisions) Acts 1978 and 1987.* London: The Stationery Office.

Lord Colville (1992). *The Operational Policy in Belfast Prison for the Management of Paramilitary Prisoners from Opposing Factions.* London: The Stationery Office.

Lord Diplock (1972). *Report of the Commission to Consider Legal Procedures to Deal with Terrorist Activities in Northern Ireland.* London: The Stationery Office.

Lord Gardiner (1975). *Report of a Committee to Consider, in the Context of Civil Liberties and Human Rights, Measures to Deal with Terrorism in Northern Ireland.* London: The Stationery Office.

Mac Stíofáin, S. (1975). *Memoirs of a Revolutionary.* Edinburgh: Cremonesi.

Maurutto, P. and Hannah-Moffat, K. (2006). 'Assembling risk and the restructuring of penal control.' *British Journal of Criminology*, 46, pp.438–454.

McEvoy, K. (1998). 'Prisoners, the Agreement and the political character of the Northern Ireland Conflict.' *Fordham International Law Journal*, 22/4, pp.1539–1576.

Murphy, T. and Whitty, N. (2007). 'Risk and human rights in UK Prison Governance.' *British Journal of Criminology*, 47/5, pp.798–816.

Nawaz, M. (2012). 'I was told: "No one messes with the Muslims in here"'. *The Times* (11 January 2012).

Neumann, P. (2010). *Prison and Terrorism: Radicalisation and De-radicalisation in 15 Countries.* London: ICSR.

O'Mahony, S. (1987). *Frongoch: University of Revolution.* Dublin: FDR Teoranta.

Pantucci, R. (2009). 'UK prisons: incubators for terrorism?' *The Guardian* (4 February 2009).

Poole, T. (2008). 'Courts and conditions of uncertainty in "times of crisis"'. *Public Law*, pp.234–259.

R v A (2010) EWCA Crim 1958.

R v Ahmed Ali & Others (2011) EWCA Crim 1260; [2011] 2 Cr. App. Rep. 22.

R v Al-Banna (1984) 6 Cr. App. R. (S) 426.

R v Barot (2007) EWCA Crim 1119, [45].

R (Bary and Others) v The Secretary of State for Justice (2010) EWHC 587 (Admin).

R v Basra (1989) 11 Cr. App. R. (S) 527.

R v Cruickshank and O'Donnell (1995) 16 Cr. App. R. (S) 728, 730 (Lord Taylor CJ).

R v Da Costa (2009) EWCA Crim 482.

R v Hindawi (1988) 10 Cr. App. Rep. (S) 104.

R (Hindawi) v Secretary of State for Justice (2011) EWHC 830 (QB), [5] (Thomas LJ).

R (King, Bourgass and Hussain) v Secretary of State for Justice (2012) EWCA Civ 376.

R v Martin (1999) 1 Cr. App. Rep. (S) 477, 480.

R (Munjaz) v Mersey Care NHS Trust (2005) UKHL 58; (2006) 2 AC 148.

R v Roche (2005) 188 FLR 336, 358 (McKechnie J).

R v Turner (1975) 61 Cr.App.R. 67, 90 (Lawton LJ).

Ramirez Sanchez v France (2007) 45 EHRR 49.

Spalek, B. and Davies, L. (2012). 'Mentoring in relation to violent extremism: A study of role, purpose, and outcomes.' *Studies in Conflict & Terrorism*, 35/5, pp.354–368.

Townshend, C. (1998). *Ireland: The 20th Century*. London: Arnold.

Walker, C. (1984). 'Irish republican prisoners: Political detainees, prisoners of war or common criminals?' *The Irish Jurist*, 19, pp.189–225.

Walker, C. (2011). *Terrorism and the Law*. Oxford: OUP.

Whealy, A. (2010). *Terrorism and the Right to a Fair Trial: Can the Law Stop Terrorism? A Comparative Analysis*. Available at: http://www.professionalstandardscouncil.gov.au/lawlink/Supreme_Court/ll_sc.nsf/vwFiles/whealy0410.pdf/$file/whealy0410.pdf, accessed 10 July 2012.

PART II

Radicalisation, de-radicalisation and disengagement

3

DEVELOPING A MODEL OF PRISON RADICALISATION

Joshua Sinai

Introduction

As criminal offenders, many terrorist leaders, associates and supporters have served time in prison throughout history. Further, many prisoners who begin their sentences as "non-extremists" are at risk of radicalising while behind bars. This can happen because they possibly possess personal vulnerabilities that make them susceptible to extremism – such as strong disaffection with their predicament as inmates and a violent disposition to begin with – and can combine with enabling factors such as living in close proximity to offenders who hold extremist ideologies (of one sort or another), as well as unresolved conflicts around the world that might affect their co-religionists. As a result, prisons have become known as "incubators" of violent extremism, and large numbers of susceptible inmates throughout the world have become radicalised into violent extremism while incarcerated in prisons, with some of them following their release ending up committing terrorist acts in "civilian" society.

This chapter's objective is to present a model of some of the critical patterns involved in the radicalisation of prison inmates. The model draws particularly on cases from the American prison system. The United States has one of the world's largest inmate populations, and like other countries its prisons have long served as permissive environments for the spread of extremist ideologies of all political and religious varieties, with a minority of these prisoners ending up engaging in terrorist activities. Though grounded in American examples, the phases and indicators identified in the model are expected to have relevance for prison systems in other countries.

Defining prison-based radicalisation

Within the context of the American penal system, prisoner radicalisation is defined as the process by which prisoners during the course of their incarceration adopt extremist views, especially beliefs that violent measures must be employed to achieve the political components of militantly religious and political objectives (U.S. Department of Justice, 2004). Within the parameters of the prison system, such extremism includes strong intolerance of specific racial or social groups regarded as adversaries, religious exclusivity, and unreasonable or extreme requests for accommodation based on their religious beliefs (Gryboski, 2012).

The magnitude of the threat

While extremist views, whether White Supremacist or Black Nationalist (and especially its Islamist component embodied by the Nation of Islam) have always been prevalent among America's prisoner population, including gang members who have developed their own forms of extremist beliefs, few of them had engaged in large-scale terrorist activities in the U.S. or overseas. It was only after the 9/11 attacks that Muslim extremism, in particular, became a growing concern to Western prison officials.

Demonstrating the severity of this threat, a number of court cases since 9/11 have involved Americans such as Jose Padilla, Kevin James, Michael Finton, and James Cromitie, who converted to Islam while incarcerated in American prisons, and upon their release from custody attempted to carry out terrorist operations in America. In the case of Padilla, he had travelled overseas to an Al Qaeda camp in Pakistan where he underwent training in terrorist warfare in preparation for an attack in America. In other cases, such as Farah Mohamed Beledi, a 27-year-old Somali American gang member from Minneapolis, Muslim-born prisoners became radicalised in prison, and then further radicalised upon their release, with Beledi ending up in Somalia fighting on behalf of al Shabaab, an Al Qaeda affiliate.

It is important to point out that only a very small percentage of converts to Islam in American prisons have become violent extremists upon their release, or, in a few cases, even while in custody. According to one estimate, between 1968 and 2009 there were 46 cases in which incarceration in an American prison contributed to radicalisation into violent extremism, leading eventually to an actual terrorist attack or thwarted plot against Western targets (Hamm, 2011).

For Caucasian prisoners, conversion while in prison into white supremacist extremism also represented a major national security threat, with numerous examples of such radicalised prisoners joining these gangs' "civilian" groups upon their release and then carrying out violent acts on their behalf. In 2010, there were an estimated 27,000 white supremacist gangs with 788,000 members nationwide, with 50,000 incarcerated in the prison system, with most of them members of such prison gangs (Keteyian, 2010).

Other than such newspaper accounts, official statistics are not available on the ideological or religious orientation of inmates in the U.S. prison system, limiting the ability to precisely assess the potential for political and religious extremism by Islamic or white supremacist inmates upon their release. As long as such figures are considered "rough" and imprecise, it is possible to extrapolate from the general makeup of the prison population to estimate the size of the populations, inside prison and those that are annually released, in order to assess the size of the radicalised prison population that represents a potential terrorist threat. First, according to one estimate, in 2011, 1.6 million people were incarcerated in U.S. prisons, with 95 percent of them due eventually to be released (Useem, 2011). Each year, U.S. prisons release an estimated 730,000 inmates (Useem, 2011).

Among the minority of the overall population who seek religion while impris- oned in U.S. municipal, state and federal correctional institutions, some 80 percent turn to the Muslim faith, numbering between 30,000 to 40,000 annually, with some 350,000 American prisoners converting to Islam between 2001 and 2011 (Useem, 2011). Many of these Muslim prisoners were Sunni or Nation of Islam followers, and were not considered as a risk to turn to terrorist violence (although they had a high criminal recidivism rate), so only a minority of the 350,000 converts to Islam might be considered to be of the extremist Salafi jihadi variety with a potential affinity for Al Qaeda and its affiliates.

Second, it is important to note that included in the general population of prisoners (according to a September 30, 2010 official figure) were more than 251 individuals with a history of or nexus to international terrorism (IT) and 111 indi- viduals with a history of or nexus to domestic terrorism (DT) (Federal Bureau of Prisons, 2013). Although precise numbers are unavailable, it can be assumed that many if not most of the prisoners were convicted for Al Qaeda-related offenses.

This discussion focuses on radicalisation within the prison system managed by the U.S. Bureau of Prisons. It does not focus on the situation of Muslim prisoners who are incarcerated in the Guantanamo Bay detention camp, which is managed by the United States military and located within the Guantanamo Bay Naval Base, Cuba. That facility was established in 2002 by the Bush Administration to hold detainees captured from the wars in Afghanistan and Iraq, with those detainees already radicalised into violent extremism. Since 2002, nearly 800 Muslim detainees have been incarcerated at Guantanamo, with a majority released since then to their countries of origin. As of September 2012, an estimated 170 detainees remained incarcerated at Guantanamo.

A model of critical patterns leading to radicalisation into violent extremism and terrorism in the U.S. prison system

In order to assess the significance of the terrorist threats presented by radicalised U.S. prisoners, it is necessary to analyse the general processes of radicalisation that characterise their progression into violent extremism. In general, radicalisation into violent extremism and terrorism involves a complex interaction of multiple processes, both in prison and outside (e.g. Borum, 2011; Silke, 2011). Significantly, within the U.S. prison context, most of those who undergo the radicalisation process begin their incarceration with no particularly strong religious or ideological affiliation.

The radicalisation processes they experience include the following factors, which are broken down into seven phases of progressively escalating risk behaviours and activities. This model draws in particular from the work of Goldman (2010) and Silber and Bhatt (2007) and the general layout of the model is described in Table 3.1.

Phase 1: Personal factors

Unlike individuals in the outside "civilian" world who typically lead "ordinary" lives, prisoners who are susceptible and vulnerable to becoming extremists generally do not come from middle-class or professional backgrounds and typically have a previous criminal history. Moreover, their arrest and incarceration often serve as a shock. Living in a prison environment is difficult, with prisoners forced to face the consequences of their crimes, adapt to a new, lonely, and harsh lifestyle and, when possible, prepare to rehabilitate themselves for future release. Such personal pressures also serve to make them feel alienated and disassociated from the rest of society. Most incarcerated prisoners, as a result, experience negative personal factors of one sort or another that might be associated with those who radicalise into violent extremism, although very few of them will actually become terrorists. Nevertheless, the literature on radicalisation among prisoners highlights the following negative personal factors as contributing factors – especially when combined with the indicators in the successive phases.

Contributing personal factors are a history of violent behaviour, anti-social attitudes, and a combination of personal crisis and low self-esteem. A tiny proportion of such individuals may suffer from mental health disorders – though it is important to note that most terrorists do not suffer from such disorders. However, many will express a sense of victimisation (i.e., that their predicament was caused by others) and feelings of compromised identity and alienation. They also seek a means to wipe away their previous criminal deeds. At this point, as spiritual seekers they will seek a religious meaning to interpret and resolve their spiritual discontent (Hamm, 2008), including their need to "start anew" by wiping away their criminal past, and will seek to adopt an empowering religion, while their political grievances will lead them to seek an empowering ideology.

Finally, although this factor may come earlier in the phase, with severe over-crowding, hostility and violence common within prisons, it is often a struggle for prisoners merely to survive unscathed through their daily routines, ranging from a need not only to overcome loneliness, but to secure protection against daily violent threats by other prisoners, especially those that seek supremacy and advantages over them.

In such cases, prisoners will either revert back to their previous gangs who maintain a presence in their prisons or join new ones that promise safety and security. As many gangs have themselves become radicalised into espousing religio-ideological

TABLE 3.1 Phased model of prison radicalisation

Phase 1: Pre-Radicalisation Personal Factors	Phase 2: Situational/ Contextual Factors and Enablers	Phase 3: Self-Identification	Phase 4: Indoctrination	Phase 5: Militancy	Phase 6: Post-Prison Release Terrorism	Phase 7: Post-Attack Re-incarceration
(I-1) History of violent behaviour	(II-1) Presence of extremist social networks religious-based gangs, that provide physical and social support and protection	(III-1) Begin to explore extremist ideologies/religions	(IV-1) Intensification of extremist beliefs	(V-1) Adopt Extremist ideology calling for violence against adversaries	(VI-1) Join extremist "gateway" organisation	(VII-1) If not killed in terrorist attack and apprehended, resume previous six phases
(I-2) Anti-social attitudes	(II-2) Presence of extremist ideologies	(III-2) Begin to gravitate away from old identities	(IV-2) Follower/ discipleship under extremist "indoctrinators"	(V-2) Self-Designate themselves as "warriors" for the cause	(VI-2) Join terrorist cell	
(I-3) Personal crisis, low self-esteem	(II-3) Presence of charismatic inmate leader(s)	(III-3) Begin to associate with like-minded extremists		(V-3) Accept duty to participate in violent activities	(VI-3) Plan to conduct terrorist attack	
(I-4) Mental health disorders	(II-4) Presence of extremist prison chaplains					
(I-5) Sense of victimisation	(II-5) Outreach programs by external extremist organisations that distribute extremist materials					

TABLE 3.1 Continued

Phase 1: Pre-Radicalisation Personal Factors	Phase 2: Situational/ Contextual Factors and Enablers	Phase 3: Self-Identification	Phase 4: Indoctrination	Phase 5: Militancy	Phase 6: Post-Prison Release Terrorism	Phase 7: Post-Attack Re-incarceration
(I-6) Feelings of compromised identity and alienation	(II-6) Presence of terrorist "kingpins"					
(I-7) Low Self esteem and need to belong to empowering religion/ideology	(II-7) "Virtual" presence by terrorist organisations					
(I-8) Seek to wipe away previous criminal deeds						
(I-9) Spiritual seeking						
(I-10) Need an external entity to blame for their personal problems						
(I-11) Political grievances						
(I-12) Need for physical protection						

extremism, a growing trend is for prisoners to join such gangs to fulfil their need for such overall protection and a sense of personal empowerment.

Phase 2: Situational/contextual factors and enablers

Radicalisation does not occur in a vacuum, but is facilitated by myriad situational factors that serve as enablers in driving the susceptible and vulnerable prisoners to the next phases in the radicalisation process. These include the presence of extremist social networks that provide the physical protection and social support that such prisoners are seeking. Such social networks might include religious- or ideology-based gangs or cellmates. Cellblocks serve as areas that are difficult to reach even by prison officials, so small cells can operate with relative ease in asserting their influence over the prisoners in those areas (Goldman, 2010).

The religio-ideological gang model, in particular, has a strong influence on the radicalisation process because it provides prisoners with an organisational structure and an outlet in which they can conduct their daily lives (Hamm, 2008). In exchange for protection from other prisoners who threaten them, gangs such as Jam'iyyat Ui-Islam Is-Saheed, or JIS, demand that prisoners follow their violent message, including following it upon their release from prison (Hamm, 2008). It must be pointed out that even for prison gangs that exhibit such extremist components, criminal enterprises such as drug trafficking, and not their extremist beliefs, largely drive their activities within the prison environment.

Another important enabler is the presence of extremist religions and ideologies in empowering prisoners who feel powerless and are seeking a higher meaning to their lives. These extremist beliefs also serve to justify these prisoners' already violent tendencies (Mueller, 2006). An example of such extremist religio-ideologies is what is termed "prison Islam" or "Prislam," consisting of "gang-like cliques" that use cut-and-paste versions of the Qur'an to give a religious layer and justification to their violent and criminal activities (Hamm, 2008). This form of "Jailhouse Islam" is unique to prison because it incorporates into the religion the values of gang loyalty and violence.

"Prislam" is especially appealing and attractive to prisoners for several reasons. First, for those with the predispositional personal factors associated with Phase I, those who revert or convert to this type of empowering Islam (Indicator II-2) will now be protected by their fellow inmate adherents (Indicator II-1). Second, such an empowering religio-ideology promises a new and unique community that is part of a large and growing inmate community where prisoners feel equal, they will be rehabilitated and become a new person with their past crimes wiped away, with the added benefit of being part of a larger subculture of fellow "true believers" outside the prison environment and around the world.

Although these prisoners are provided with a community, also important is the presence of charismatic inmate leadership. As described by Max Weber, charismatic leadership entails "a certain quality of an individual personality by virtue of which he is set apart from ordinary men and treated as endowed with supernatural, superhuman, or at least specifically exceptional powers or qualities" (Weber 1968, p.241). Inmate leadership that possesses such attributes, in fact, is considered one of the most important proselytising factors in prisoner radicalisation (Hamm, 2008). A particular concern in this regard involves the presence of extremist prison chaplains. In addition to radicalising prisoners through their sermons and counselling, they can also distribute extremist pamphlets and books to the prisoners.

Another important enabler is the outreach activities by representatives of extremist gateway organisations, such as social clubs or political movements that conduct activities and distribute extremist literature to prisoners. Gateway organisations play a role in what is considered a "slippery slope" in facilitating the pathway of some of their adherents into violent extremism, even if they themselves remain "non-violent." Because of the importance of establishing rapport with prison inmates, some of these "representatives" will be former inmates or "missionary" volunteers. The literature distributed by such organisations and their outreach "volunteers" at prisons promote extremist beliefs such as, in the case of white supremacists, promoting ethnic and racial hatred, encouraging the overthrow of the government and terming prison officials as agents of "illegal" government authority. In such a way, they serve to promote a violent and racially charged prison atmosphere which they hope will radicalise prisoners towards their violent beliefs.

Another enabler is the presence of terrorist "kingpins" who are locked up in the prison system and who conduct their own form of "outreach" to other inmates, indoctrinating them to regard "fallen" terrorists as martyrs and heroes to be emulated. As "die-hard" veteran extremists, these imprisoned terrorists already constitute not only first-order prison extremists, but they are now fully capable of radicalising other inmates on their own and guiding them to supportive infrastructures upon their release. Examples of such incarcerated terrorist "kingpins" include Ramzi Yousef and Sheikh Omar Abdel-Rahman, both of whom were convicted for their involvement in the first bombing of the World Trade Center in 1993. These are among an estimated two dozen Al Qaeda terrorists who were incarcerated in U.S. prisons, including others implicated in the 1993 World Trade Center bombing, the 1998 East African embassy bombings, the 1999 millennial plot to bomb the Los Angeles International Airport, the 2000 bombing of the USS Cole, and others.

A final enabler is the "virtual" presence of terrorist organisations, such as Al Qaeda and its affiliates, whether on the Internet or via their extremist publications, which serves to inspire the incarcerated prisoners.

Phase 3: Self-identification

In this phase, such individuals who are searching for spiritual and ideological guidance begin to "self-identify" with other extremist individuals, religio-ideologies, or movements whose messages and narratives resonate with their own personal experiences, disaffections and grievances. As explained by Silber and Bhatt (2007, p.6), in this phase "individuals, influenced by both internal and external factors, begin to explore extremist ideologies/religions, gradually gravitating away from their old identities and associate themselves with like-minded individuals and adopt their ideology as their own." In this way, this phase serves as the catalyst that sets off the rest of the phases in the radicalisation process.

Some of the specific indicators associated with this phase are likely to include the beginnings of an exploration of extremist ideologies and religions available in their prison environment, gravitating away from their former identities, and associating with other like-minded extremists.

This process might be repeated over time for those prisoners who are in the process of "experimenting" with various extremist religions and ideologies that proliferate within the confines of a prison.

Phase 4: Indoctrination

Following the consolidation of the "self-identification" phase, the process of actual indoctrination into the extremist religions and ideologies begins. It is here that the individual's extremist beliefs are progressively being intensified by the agents of indoctrination, whether gang leaders, terrorist "kingpins", extremist chaplains, volunteer "missionaries," or other agents of extremism.

Phase 5: Militancy

In this phase, the individual's extremist religion and ideology are now fully adopted. The adherents now fully accept their individual duty to participate in militant activities and self-designate themselves as "holy warriors" for their cause.

Phase 6: Post-prison-release terrorism

Upon their release from prison, while many former convicts return to society intent on rehabilitating themselves and integrating into society, some return with an "axe to grind" as they seek opportunities to carry out acts of retribution against their perceived enemies. According to Kurzman (2011), 12 Muslim Americans who had been radicalised in U.S. prisons conducted terrorist offenses between 9/11 and 2011. Radicals of this nature engage in at least three types of post-incarceration retribution activities.

In the first, their radicalisation process will intensify upon their release, but still without a turn to terrorist activities. As an example of such a pathway, Jose Padilla, known as the "dirty bomb" plotter, who converted to Islam while incarcerated in a Florida jail. While in jail, a fellow inmate directed him to a mosque in Ft Lauderdale, Florida for when he was released in the late 1990s. At the mosque, Padilla met Adham Amin Hassoun, who had set up a local office of Benevolence International, a charity that reportedly was used as a front for Al Qaeda. Hassoun allegedly financed a trip to Egypt for Padilla, from where he eventually made his way to Al Qaeda's training camps in Afghanistan.

In a similar vein, Farah Mohamed Beledi, a 27-year-old Somali American from Minneapolis, was a gang member who had been convicted of a number of crimes, including assault with a deadly weapon. After being released from prison after serving two years, he began attending the Abu Bakar As-Saddique Islamic Centre in Minneapolis, where he reportedly became further radicalised, and was soon on his way to fight on behalf of al Shabaab in Somalia (King, 2011).

In a later example, in September 2009 Michael Finton, who had been radicalised in an Illinois state prison, plotted to assassinate U.S. Congressman Aaron Schock and destroy the federal courthouse and office building in Springfield, Illinois.

In the second type of post-incarceration retribution, those who have progressed along the radicalisation pathway as "fully fledged" incarcerated militants may already have begun planning for a terrorist attack during their incarceration, whether as a "lone wolves" or as members of a terrorist cell. An example of a cell that had been radicalised in prison,involves Kevin James, a former Nation of Islam adherent. In 2005, James formed a jihadi group called Jami'iy yat Ul-Isla Is Saheeh (JIS) while serving time at California's Folsom Prison. He recruited other prisoners while they were incarcerated, and after their release the group carried out a series of armed robberies in Los Angeles, in order to finance their terrorist operations against local government and Jewish targets.

In a third type, such operational planning might begin following their release from prison, again, whether as "lone wolves" or as part of a cell. An example of such a case was seen in June 2011 when James Cromitie, who had been radicalised in a New York prison, was scheduled to be sentenced for his leading role in a conspiracy to attack troop transports at an Air National Guard base in Newburgh, New York, as well as attacking a synagogue and Jewish community centre in New York City.

For terrorist groups, especially foreign ones, gaining some new recruits with a background in prison gangs is desirable because, as U.S. citizens, this provides them greater operational flexibility *within* the United States compared to foreign-born potential recruits. Moreover, prison gang members also have experience in illegal or violent activity and feel disenfranchised from the U.S. government or society. Such recruits are not without their disadvantages, however. Indeed, former inmates can be detrimental to the terrorist groups because they are already "known" to law enforcement authorities, which may limit their operational flexibility, especially if they attempt to fly to foreign countries of concern that might be tracked by government counterterrorism agencies.

Phase 7: Post-attack re-incarceration

In this final phase, among those former prisoners that are not killed in the course of their terrorist attacks and are subsequently apprehended by law enforcement authorities, once they are re-incarcerated, then the previous six phases will likely repeat themselves. Notable examples of former prisoners who were subsequently arrested and incarcerated for attempting to carry out terrorist attacks include Jose Padilla, Kevin James, Michael Finton, and James Cromitie.

Potentially, this seven-phase radicalisation cycle can keep repeating itself with a continuous pool of newly incarcerated inmates filling the ranks of those who complete their prison sentences and are released into society.

Conclusions

In testing this model against cases of incarcerated inmates who embark on the pathway from initiation radicalisation into potential terrorism, several factors need to be considered.

First, while Phase I's "pre-radicalisation personal factors" are significant in preparing the ground for potential radicalisation, many of these factors characterise a majority of the inmate population, with very few of them in relative terms likely to turn to terrorist activities upon their release.

Second, Phase II's "situational/contextual factors and enablers" are therefore crucial in providing potentially susceptible and vulnerable inmates with the means to advance on the radicalisation pathway into violent extremism. These factors and enablers, their activities and publications, need to be carefully monitored and tracked by prison officials. Decreasing their proselytising capability, in fact, is likely to positively affect the next phases along the radicalisation pathway of self-identification, indoctrination, and militancy.

Third, another important factor to consider is whether certain prison environments are more susceptible to radicalisation than others. For example, maximum security prisons house larger numbers of violent offenders; are severely more overcrowded; are underfunded for rehabilitation work; and their wings, cellblocks and prison yards are typically already more politically charged and polarised (Hamm, 2011).

Finally, it is important to consider the indicators involved in Phase VI's "post-prison-release terrorism" because its alternative outcomes can result in such former inmates either turning to peaceful, non-violent activity or violent extremist activities.

In assessing the likelihood of an incarcerated inmate's radicalisation into violent extremism, no single phase or indicator can be considered as causal, since a combination of indicators is necessary for an individual to embark on the trajectory from initial radicalisation into terrorism. Although this model is sequential, inmates, just like a society's general population, do not necessarily follow a linear progression into extremism and terrorism and some phases and factors may overlap. For the self-identification, indoctrination, and militancy phases, social ties with other prisoners may be key in influencing the susceptible inmates to become an extremist and "go operational" in Phase VI's "post-prison-release terrorism." For other inmates, post-release foreign travel to an extremist region or involvement in an extremist "gateway" organisation may be the crucial factors in their turn to terrorism. For others, upon their release a significant "trigger" event, such as an international controversy, may be the critical variable in their decision to embark on violence. The radicalisation process can also occur quickly or slowly, publicly or privately, whether the former inmate joins a terrorist group or becomes a "lone wolf." Finally, the radicalisation process will invariably vary from one inmate to another, depending on specific conditions and circumstances, whether individually or in combination.

References

Borum, R. (2011). "Understanding terrorist psychology." In Andrew Silke (Ed.). *The Psychology of Counter-Terrorism*, pp.19–33. London: Routledge.

Federal Bureau of Prisons (2013). *State of the Bureau 2010*. U.S. Department of Justice.

Gryboski, M. (2012). "Prison chaplains believe religious extremism common in jail, but not a threat," *Christian Post*, March 22, 2012, http://www.christianpost.com/news/prison-chaplains-believe-religious-extremism-common-in-jail-but-not-a-threat-71936/

Goldman, B. (2010). "Radicalization in American prisons," *Publications in Contemporary Affairs*, http://www.theepicproject.org/?page_id=285.

Hamm, M. (2008). "Prisoner radicalization: Assessing the threat in U.S. correctional institutions," *NIJ Journal*, 261. http://www.nij.gov/journals/261/prisoner-radicalization.htm.

Hamm, M. (2011). *Locking Up Terrorists: Three Models for Controlling Prisoner Radicalization.* www.indstate.edu/ccj/crinst/Locking%20Up%20Terrorists.docx

Keteyian, A. (2010). "The violent world of white supremacist gangs," *CBSNews.com*, September 5, 2010.

King, P. (2011). Statement of Chairman King June 15, 2011. *Compilation of Hearings on Islamist Radicalization – Volume I, Hearings Before The Committee on Homeland Security, House of Representatives, One Hundred Twelfth Congress, First Session, March 10, June 15, and July 27, 2011, Serial No. 112–9.* http://www.gpo.gov/fdsys/pkg/CHRG-112hhrg72541/pdf/CHRG-112hhrg72541.pdf Statement

Kurzman, C. (2011). *Muslim-American Terrorism Since 9/11: An Accounting.* Chapel Hill, NC: Triangle Center on Terrorism and Homeland Security. http://tcths.sanford.duke.edu/about/documents/Kurzman_Muslim-American_Terrorism_Since_911_An_Accounting.pdf

Mueller, R. (2006). *Remarks for Delivery by FBI Director Robert Mueller at City Club. Cleveland, Ohio, June 27.* (Transcript)

Silber, M. and Bhatt, A. (2007). *Radicalization in the West: The Home-grown Threat.* New York: New York City Police Department.

Silke, A. (2011). "Terrorists and extremists in prison: Psychological issues in management and reform." In Andrew Silke (Ed.). *The Psychology of Counter-Terrorism*, pp.123–134. London: Routledge.

Useem, B. (2011). *Testimony Of Professor Bert Useem, Purdue University, Committee on Homeland Security, U.S. House of Representatives Hearing On The Threat of Muslim-American Radicalization in U.S. Prisons, June 15, 2011.* http://homeland.house.gov/sites/homeland.house.gov/files/Testimony%20Useem.pdf

U.S. Department of Justice (2004). *A Review of the Federal Bureau of Prisons' Selection of Muslim Religious Service Providers.* Washington, DC: Office of Inspector General.

Weber, M. (1968). *Economy and Society.* University of California Press.

4

FROM CRIMINALS TO TERRORISTS

The US experience of prison radicalisation

Liran Goldman

Since 2001, Al Qaeda has become a global entity – a 'network of networks' – with each franchise acting locally and largely independent of each other. This has led to terrorist attacks becoming inspired by Al Qaeda ideologies more so than actually being orchestrated by Al Qaeda. Thus, an unintended consequence of Al Qaeda's decentralisation has been the organisation's transition to a 'movement' fuelled by ideology. This flexibility enables the ideology to take root anywhere, resulting in increased concerns about home-grown terrorism (Carpenter, Levitt, Simon, & Zarate, 2010; Cilluffo, Cardash, & Whitehead, 2007; Downing, 2009).

A setting that may be an especially fertile breeding ground for radicalisation and recruitment to terrorist organisations is prison. While there is no doubt that radicalisation is occurring in prisons throughout the world, evidence of radicalisation in Western countries has been surfacing in recent years (Brandon, 2009; Cilluffo et al., 2006; Neumann, 2010). Because the United States has the highest incarceration rate in the world, prisoners in the United States may be at a high risk of being radicalised by terrorist organisations (Anti-Defamation League, 2002; Cilluffo et al., 2006, 2007). Of course, radicalising prisoners is not a new phenomenon, a new approach for Islamic extremists, or unique to Western countries (Brandon, 2009; Cilluffo et al., 2006, 2007; Neumann, 2010).

While radicalisation appears to be the exception among prisoners rather than the rule, it is unclear how large or small the threat may actually be (Cilluffo et al., 2006). The limited evidence of cases of prison radicalisation in the United States suggests that the probability of prisoners conducting mass-scale terrorist attacks is quite small (Austin, 2009; Cilluffo et al., 2006). But according to testimony at a House Committee Hearing on Islamic radicalisation in the United States, Michael Downing (2011), Chief of the Counterterrorism and Special Operations Bureau at Los Angeles Police Department, noted that 'radicalisation of even a small population of these individuals holds high consequence for people in the United States and around the world.' So while magnitude may not be quantifiable, the threat does exist. And if the issue of domestic radicalisation – especially in prisons – is not addressed, then the United States risks being unprepared, potentially facing a much larger problem.

Owing to a dearth of empirical research on prison radicalisation, very little is known about how the process is incited and sustained, especially in the United States. Hence, the following chapter will address what is known about prison radicalisation, but will also go further by explaining the processes involved from a social scientific perspective. Although the current focus is on radicalisation by Islamists, the processes explored in this chapter are applicable to any extremist group trying to radicalise and recruit prisoners. Finally, countermeasures that may be effective in counteracting or preventing prison radicalisation will also be explored.

The allure of prison radicalisation

Individual, social, and environmental factors all have the potential to influence radicalisation and the willingness to join a terrorist organisation. As such, it is necessary to understand two important and related issues related to prison radicalisation. First, what makes prisoners an appealing population for extremists to target? And second, why are prison environments especially favourable for radicalisation?

Criminals versus terrorists

Terrorists are uniquely different from criminals. Traditional criminals are generally unable to continue their illicit activities while incarcerated. Extremist criminals, however, are quite the opposite. Some may even welcome imprisonment because of the opportunity to continue spreading propaganda by authoring publications, teaching their ideological beliefs, and recruiting other inmates (Anti-Defamation League, 2002; Brandon, 2009; Neumann, 2010). As Frank Cilluffo (2006), Director of the Homeland Security Policy Institute at George Washington University, testified to the U.S. Senate 'prisons have always been an incubator for radical ideas, in part because there is a captive audience.' For example, while in prison, Hitler wrote *Mein Kampf*, Stalin recruited inmates to participate in the Bolshevik Revolution, Sayyid Qutb (known for his ties to the Muslim Brotherhood) wrote *Milestones*, a manifesto well known for its radical Islamist tone, and Abu Musab al Zarqawi rose from petty criminal to feared leader of Al Qaeda in Iraq.

More worrisome, however, is that the conversion of prisoners to extremism creates a new breed of terrorist. For starters, psychologists have confirmed that terrorists are psychologically normal. Violent criminals, on the other hand, tend to suffer from mental disorders and can be unstable (Alderdice, 2007; Post, 2007; Silke, 2008) – which can yield a potentially explosive (no pun intended) situation. Also, when politically or religiously motivated extremists interact with 'ordinary' criminals, they create opportunities for terrorists' ideological fervour to be combined with traditional offenders' criminal tendencies (Neumann, 2010). Conventional terrorists are committed to jihad and have acted outside socially accepted norms, often through criminal behaviour. But criminals who have been recruited to participate in terrorist efforts become jihadists who know how to access and handle weapons (Useem, 2011). Therefore, while it has been suggested that the dynamics of terrorism changed when Al Qaeda '1.0' – a hierarchical terrorist organisation with authoritarian control – evolved into Al Qaeda '2.0' – an organisation that functions as a decentralised autonomous network (Post, 2007) – if home-grown radicalisation inspired by Islamist ideology continues to increase, especially in prisons, we may be on the verge of Al Qaeda 3.0.

Prisoners: the perfect audience

In the extremist's eyes, prisoners are a great target population for recruitment and radicalisation because of certain characteristics found among many inmates. Prisoners with racist tendencies, who harbour anti-government sentiments, or are simply angry about their incarceration, make especially good targets for recruitment. These individuals are likely to be more receptive to sentiments that glorify anti-social and anti-state violence (Anti-Defamation League, 2002; Brandon, 2009; Hamm, 2008). Further, prisons may be environments especially conducive to radicalisation as terrorist recruits tend to be young, unemployed, alienated, express the need for self-importance, and harbour feelings centring around the need to belong to a group – all characteristics that are common among prisoners (Cilluffo et al., 2006).

An added benefit for extremists is that the prison setting breeds a vulnerable population ripe for recruitment. Prisoners are especially susceptible to radicalisation efforts because they have often been abandoned by their family or friends and are thus separated from their typical social networks (Anti-Defamation League, 2002; Cilluffo et al., 2007; Neumann, 2010). In other words, prisoners by nature are alienated and socially isolated, which makes them at a higher risk of being radicalised because they are captive audiences. Extremists of all kinds, in part, prey on that alienation (Cilluffo et al., 2007). This alienation often drives prisoners to seek protection, seek meaning, and establish an identity (Cilluffo et al., 2007; Hamm, 2008; Neumann, 2010), which results in prisons becoming unique environments where individuals are especially likely to explore new beliefs and associations.

These behaviours and conditions are typical in the prison environment and play a role in prison radicalisation as they increase inmates' susceptibility to extremist and militant interpretations of Islam (Neumann, 2010). Such circumstances produce individuals who may be easier to radicalise and recruit than those individuals in the general population. According to Dr. Fathali Moghaddam (2004), professor of psychology and director of the conflict resolution program at Georgetown University, isolation is an important precondition for the evolution of terrorist organisations because isolation heightens group conformity and cohesion.

Taking a step back and applying this precondition at the individual level, social psychologists have found that individuals who possess a strong need to belong as well as a strong need to achieve a stable identity will often turn to a group to fill these needs, with the group's identity becoming incredibly important to an individual's self-concept over time (Post, 1985; Tajfel & Turner, 1979; Turner, Hogg, Oakes, Reicher, & Wetherell, 1987). In fact, evidence suggests that when becoming radicalised, it is common for individuals to experience long periods of intense social interaction with a small group, which relieves feelings of isolation (Silke, 2008). Individuals who feel isolated are also more likely to experience an exaggerated perception that their in-group is more homogeneous than it really is. In other words, the perceived differences between the in-group (e.g., Muslims) and the out-group (e.g., Westerners) are exaggerated (Oakes, Haslam, & Turner, 1994). This can intensify the isolation and feelings of alienation that prisoners feel, providing them not only with even more motivation to seek out other similar group members (e.g., Muslims) but also to accept the opinions and beliefs of other group members. This sets the stage for the radical thinking that promotes terrorism.

Processes involved in radicalisation

Understanding radicalisation can be difficult, largely because every terrorist group maintains its own specific ideology, objectives, communities from which support is obtained, and its own form of violence (Carpenter et al., 2010; Richardson, 2006). Further complicating matters, the rise in home-grown terrorists, consisting primarily of individuals inspired by Al Qaeda, makes it difficult to identify exactly how individuals turn to terrorism. So whether extremist inmates are working independently or in conjunction with a larger terrorist network, different attitudes and approaches for radicalisation and recruitment may be utilised in the prison setting (Neumann, 2010).

At the same time, though, the radicalisation process experienced by prisoners is very similar to the radicalisation process experienced outside prison. In both settings, social identity plays a key role in radicalisation. As an explanation of why inmates turn to terrorism, social science research has found that individuals who perceive their future to be bleak and uncertain are more likely to attempt to belong to a group because the group provides a script for how people should behave and what to think, thereby reducing uncertainty (Hogg, 2006, 2007, 2012). Additionally, the more uncertain one is, the higher the chances that the individual will seek a group higher in entitativity – i.e., a group that appears cohesive, clearly structured, and distinct from other entities (Hogg, 2006, 2012; Hogg, Meehan, & Farquharson, 2010; Hogg, Sherman, Dierselhuis, Maitner, & Moffitt, 2007). This can make 'extreme groups' (e.g., cults, terrorists, gangs) more appealing and attractive as they provide individuals with a more rigidly defined, highly prescriptive social identity (Hogg, 2012; Hogg et al., 2007). Accordingly, joining a terrorist organisation is largely a group phenomenon (Silke, 2008). This is supported by numerous cases where the most common methods to radicalise and recruit prisoners were through gangs or religion in prisons.

Gangs and terrorists

Terrorists' interests in criminal enterprises have been growing, which creates the potential for a nexus between prison gangs and terrorist organisations (Anti-Defamation League, 2002; Cilluffo et al., 2006; Hamm, 2008) – but this relationship between gangs, prisons, and terrorism is not new. Jeff Fort, for example, was a gang leader incarcerated in Chicago in 1965 who founded the group El Rukn, an Islamic splinter group of the street gang The Almighty Black P. Stone Nation. Through El Rukn, Fort arranged a $2.5 million deal in 1985 with the Libyan government to attack U.S. police stations, government facilities, military bases, and passenger airplanes (Cilluffo et al., 2006). Fort, however, became religious and converted to Islam while in prison but founded El Rukn only after he was released (Schatzberg & Kelly, 1997). Considering some more recent cases of domestic radicalisation – e.g., dirty-bomber Jose Padilla, conspirator on the Mumbai attacks David Headley, the Little Rock recruiting centre shooter Carlos Bledsoe, and Colleen La Rose also known as Jihad Jane, etc. – only a few served time in prison before showing support for jihad (Padilla and Headley) and, of these, only Padilla had ties to gangs. Thus, it is possible that prison gangs' contribution to extremism may be a more recent phenomenon. What is known about prison gangs, though, suggests these groups may be incredibly effective avenues for promoting radicalisation.

Outside prison, when asked why they join gangs, many gang members say something along the lines of, 'it was simply the thing to do' (Del Carmen et al., 2009, p. 65). This reasoning contrasts directly with outside observers' beliefs that individuals are actively recruited into gangs rather than people deciding to join of their own accord (Bliss-Holtz, 2011; Del Carmen et al., 2009). The same can be said of domestic radicalisation, as many Americans have decided to wage jihad without direct pressure from others. Closer inspection of the processes involved in becoming a gang member suggests two primary reasons for joining: social networks and protection (Decker & Van Winkle, 1996; Peterson, Taylor, & Esbensen, 2004; Taylor, 2009; Thornberry, Krohn, Lizotte, Smith, & Tobin, 2003). These factors are incredibly similar to the reasons cited as influencing the decision to join prison gangs. Whether prison gangs are working in conjunction with a terrorist organisation or extremist groups create their own gangs, these groups are well positioned to take advantage of the alienation, isolation, and vulnerability of prisoners. In fact, radicalisation closely follows a prison gang model: the most vulnerable – usually consisting of individuals who are alienated because they are no longer in contact with their friends or family – are targeted by charismatic leaders (Hamm, 2008, 2009). These individuals are more likely to join gangs or extreme groups because they gain a sense of belonging or receive necessary protection (Cilluffo et al., 2007; Neumann, 2010). Only later do these individuals actually adopt extremist views and ideologies (Stern, 2010).

Most street gangs, though, are not ideologically motivated; divisions tend to be based on racial, ethnic, or geographic distinctions. But while many prison gangs do acknowledge being motivated by an ideology, part of the method of compelling individuals to join prison gangs does include the appeal of some sort of 'unifier' which is generally derived from racial or ethnic identities such as white, black, or Hispanic (Anti-Defamation League, 2002). In fact, while prisoners can be 'converted' and radicalised by terrorist inmates, in Western countries it is much more likely that prisoners will be radicalised through Muslim gangs. According to a report on prison radicalisation published by the International Centre for the Study of Radicalisation and Political Violence (ICSR), 'like traditional prison gangs, Muslim prison gangs are based on religious (sometimes also ethnic) affiliation and provide members with a strong sense of identity and in-group loyalty. Moreover, they allow members to articulate their grievances and protect them against other gangs or groups of prisoners' (Neumann, 2010, p. 28). Further, according to Chief Downing's (2011) testimony to the House Committee on Homeland Security, not only are the most dangerous inmates gang members – they are violent, territorial, operate continuously while in prison – but many gang members are uniting and crossing over to the 'Muslim' side.

Individuals who join prison gangs primarily for protection often cut ties with the gang once they are released (Anti-Defamation League, 2002). Similarly, inmates who have been radicalised may not continue on the same path once they are released as their social circumstances may change. This may be especially true for prisoners who have joined a radical group such as a prison gang for protection. A potential explanation for this lies in research that has found that individuals are more likely to participate in collective behaviour when they feel they will get something out of it (Tropp & Brown, 2004). In other words, those who join prison gangs for protection are less likely to benefit from their gang membership upon release (i.e., they no longer need the same kind of protection), so they separate themselves from the group. Once freed from prison, these individuals typically do not need the same protection they required in prison (Neumann, 2010).

Some individuals, however, do remain ideologically committed after release (Anti-Defamation League, 2002). It is possible that the individuals who are most likely to maintain ties with a gang are those who joined to gain a sense of belonging. When individuals become incarcerated, the quickest way to establish their identity is through affiliation with a gang. Among those who first become involved in gangs outside prison, identity as a gang member becomes a permanent part of that individual's social awareness. After joining a gang, the group's views become central to the individual's life, shaping his or her identity and personality (Decker & Van Winkle, 1996; Del Carmen et al., 2009; Moore, 1978; Stretesky & Pogrebin, 2007). These same processes are likely to occur in individuals who join prison gangs.

Religion and terrorists

As is the case with the relationships between gangs, terrorism, and prisons, the relationships between religion, terrorism and prisons are not novel concepts. For example, James Ellison founded the extremist group Christian Group Covenant,

Sword and Arm of the Lord (CSA) in 1978. Ellison connected with Robert G. Millar while incarcerated, who was leader of the radical 'Christian Identity' movement. After Ellison was released, he established a compound with CSA followers, which was eventually raided by authorities who found homemade landmines, U.S. Army anti-tank rockets, and cyanide that was intended to poison a city's water (Cilluffo et al., 2006). More recently, Kevin Lamar James founded Jami'iy yat Ul-Islam Is Saheeh (Assembly of Authentic Islam) while in New Folsom State Prison in California in 1997. One of James' 'disciples' who had been released from prison recruited other members from a local mosque. The group advocated jihad against the U.S. government and supporters of Israel and was plotting to attack numerous government and Jewish targets in the state (Brandon, 2009; Cilluffo et al., 2006; Useem & Clayton, 2009). Finally, Daveed Gartenstein-Ross, a Jew who converted to Islam, has come forward with his experience working for Al Haramain Islamic Foundation from 1998 to 1999. According to Gartenstein-Ross (2006, 2007), Al Haramain distributed radical literature – a Wahhabi-Salafi version known as the Noble Qur'an – to prisoners who were curious about Islam. The literature that was dispersed was filled with contempt for non-Muslims and openly advocated global jihad. Al Haramain also collected personal information on inmates who requested Islamic literature including these inmates' names, prisoner numbers, release dates, and address outside of prison. This information was input into a database (which, at the time of Gartenstein-Ross's account, had upwards of 15,000 individuals), and although Al Haramain appears not to have abused this information, it could easily have been used to follow-up with prisoners and potentially to allow for terrorist recruitment.

These examples highlight the very real possibility that religion has and can be used in prison settings to radicalise inmates. Regardless of religious or ethnic background, new convicts tend to feel insecure, uncertain, and afraid when they enter prison. As an attempt to alleviate the anxiety associated with these feelings, and to obtain a sense of identity, many inmates turn to religion (Hamm, 2008, 2009).

Typically, conversion does not equal radicalisation. Conversion can be a step towards radicalisation, but not all converts are radicalised terrorists (Cilluffo et al., 2006; Federal Bureau of Investigation, 2006). Further, discovering religion or converting can aid in the rehabilitation of prisoners by increasing these prisoners' self-discipline as well as helping them improve their interactions with other inmates and prison staff (Hamm, 2008). Participation in a religion can be positive by providing inmates with discipline, direction, and a sense of purpose they previously lacked (Cilluffo, 2006; Collins, 2006).

Taking advantage of these circumstances, imprisoned extremists may offer food, friendship, and spiritual support to new prisoners (Brandon, 2009). It is important to note, though, that the concern is not about prisoners who convert to Islam. Rather, the concern is violent extremists who use Islam in prisons to spread hateful ideology and justify violent acts (Collins, 2006; van Duyn, 2006). Additionally, it must be considered that religious radicalisation is not unique to Islam (Cilluffo,

2006). According to Los Angeles County Sheriff Lee Baca (2011), since 9/11, domestic non-Muslims have been responsible for almost 80 terror plots within the U.S., while domestic and International Muslims have been behind just over 40 terror plots. As such, it is important to have a general understanding of how any religion – not just Islam – is used to entice prisoners to join terrorist efforts.

Radicalisation in prisons is more likely to begin through personal relationships than through preaching (Brandon, 2009). However, because 'ordinary Muslim prisoners' and 'new converts' typically have limited knowledge of Islam or are poorly educated, these inmates' understanding of Islam is dependent upon what they are exposed to in prison (Brandon, 2009; Cilluffo et al., 2006). Additionally, while many inmates in U.S. prisons are likely to have been exposed to mainstream Christianity, most inmates are unlikely to have had much exposure to or experience with Islam prior to incarceration which may actually make radicalising Western prisoners easier because they can be easily persuaded to adopt Islamist ideologies that will help them to turn away from crime, drugs, and alcohol and provide them with a 'new start' (Brandon, 2009; Cilluffo et al., 2006; van Duyn, 2006).

Ideology can be spread to prisoners through a number of means. As illustrated in Gartenstein-Ross's account of Al Haramain, some extremist groups publish periodicals targeted towards prisoners, which can serve as prisoners' connection to the outside world. Other extremists simply visit inmates. With this method, religion often plays a role as inmates are allowed access to religious services and personnel. Extremist organisations that are adept at hiding their true motives from prison authorities may use members to provide religious services to inmates (Anti-Defamation League, 2002). Plus, contract, volunteer, and staff personnel who enter the prison system with the intent to recruit or radicalise can be extremely influential and persuasive as they are viewed by inmates as holding a position of authority (Brandon, 2009; van Duyn, 2006). This can be done by setting an example for other Muslim prisoners to follow, such as not cracking under pressure or ostensibly living a pious and humble life in prison. In this approach, 'leaders' display confidence, serenity, and certainty, which can be highly attractive to insecure prisoners. Once authority has been established, leaders begin spreading their ideology, often through small prayer circles (Brandon, 2009).

While prisoners have a right to worship, in the United States there is a shortage of suitably qualified religious authorities and academically credentialed experts to review the religious materials entering prison systems or even the provided sermons. Consequently, there are no standard procedures for determining whether the material prisoners are exposed to is appropriate (Cilluffo et al., 2006). As a result, under-qualified and radical chaplains have been allowed to enter prisons. While chaplains are required to have a Master of Divinity degree issued by an accredited institution, a relatively small number of chaplains are available. As a result, many prisons use contracted religious service providers and volunteers who are *not* required to have formal religious training. Due to a lack of personnel, those providing religious services are often not properly vetted, nor are the services consistently supervised or monitored (Cilluffo et al., 2006). In fact, Cilluffo (2006) noted in a U.S. Senate hearing on prison radicalisation, 'prisoners often take on this role themselves. Their converts may in large part have had no prior exposure to Islam and have no means to put the radical message into context. The only version some may ever learn is a cut-and-paste version of the Qur'an that incorporates violent prison gang culture, known as jailhouse Islam or Prislam.'

Keeping this in mind, the prisons that provide the best environments for radicalising inmates are those that are overcrowded and have a shortage of chaplains to provide religious guidance (Hamm, 2008). Of course, while it is always important to remember that very few converts turn to radical beliefs and later participate in terrorist action, it is equally important to point out that this can and does happen (Hamm, 2009).

Release from prison

The term 'prison radicalisation' usually refers to individuals being radicalised in prison, not that terrorist plots are being formulated in prison. In most cases, inmates who adopt radical Islamist ideologies while incarcerated commit terrorist acts only after they are released – if they engage in terrorism at all. Many of those who adopt extreme Islamist ideologies in prison often disregard these beliefs upon release (Brandon, 2009; Cilluffo et al., 2006; Hamm, 2008). Although it is only in rare instances that prisoners move from radicalisation to actual recruitment and participation in terrorist activities, the phenomenon does, in fact, occur.

While it is certainly possible to radicalise prisoners, a few examples of incarcerated individuals who eventually participated in terrorism suggests that prison may only set a foundation; what happens after prison may be equally important. Richard Reid, the 'shoe bomber' and Muktar Ibrahim, the leader of the July 21, 2005 London bomb plot, are two well-known terrorists who appear to have been radicalised in European and American prisons. These two individuals' paths towards radicalisation followed similar trajectories: both were in prison in the mid-1990s, during which time Reid converted to Islam and Ibrahim adopted extreme Islamist ideologies. However, both of these individuals were not 'terrorists' the moment they were released. They were further radicalised at mosques they began attending after they were released (Brandon, 2009; Neumann, 2010). This suggests that while it is possible to be completely radicalised in prison, prison may also act as a point of entry or precondition for further radicalisation after release from prison.

The adoption of radical Islamic beliefs may often begin in prison, but those beliefs can also deepen after release (Dunleavy, 2011; Neumann, 2010). Current prisoners are certainly vulnerable to radicalisation, but so are recently released inmates. They often leave prison with very little financial, emotional, or family support. Knowing this, radical groups may attempt to fill this void by providing social and financial support to released prisoners (Cilluffo, 2006; Cilluffo et al., 2006, 2007). As Cilluffo (2006) testified in a congressional hearing on prison radicalisation, 'by providing for prisoners in their time of greatest need, radical organizations can build upon the loyalty developed during the individual's time in prison.' Cilluffo further points out that this is a tactic often used by gangs and white supremacist groups. Thus, targeting prisoners after they are released can be just as effective – if not more so – than targeting those who are currently incarcerated.

Weaknesses and counter-measures

The process of radicalisation within prisons is not fully understood as most of our knowledge comes from a limited number of cases. As a consequence, it is difficult to develop effective intervention techniques (Cilluffo et al., 2006; Saathoff, 2006). However, greater awareness of where weaknesses lie in our prison systems and greater vigilance can help mitigate the potential for prisoners to be radicalised into terrorists (Anti-Defamation League, 2002). While the need for protection and loss of identity are conditions that create a ripe breeding ground for terrorist recruitment, some root causes can be identified that lead to such issues. Poorly run and overcrowded prisons increases the threat of radicalisation as the safety of inmates cannot be ensured, thereby increasing the chances prisoners will turn to gangs for protection. Also, overcrowded prisons often have a lack of personnel available to appropriately monitor inmates (Hamm, 2008; Neumann, 2010). Moreover, the limited number of legitimate Muslim religious service providers, inability to track prisoners after their release, and lack of social support provided to prisoners to help them reintegrate into society (which leaves them vulnerable to recruitment by radical groups that do provide social support) all increase the risk of radicalisation (Cilluffo et al., 2006).

Much can be done to address these issues. State and local correctional institutions clearly need more resources for both manpower and training (Anti-Defamation League, 2002). Specifically, informative and educational materials on prisoner radicalisation to raise awareness would be beneficial. Many other steps can be taken (Cilluffo, 2006; Neumann, 2010; Saathoff, 2006; van Duyn, 2006):

- Establishing protocols for vetting prison contractors and volunteers, especially those who provide religious services
- Improving monitoring of prisoners and their activities
- Developing the ability to identify inmates associated with radical groups
- Developing the ability to track inmates after they are released
- Developing the ability to track those who provide religious services in prisons
- Improving information sharing not just among law enforcement officials, but also prison personnel

Further, while some prisons may already have policies following some of the above suggestions, local and state facilities would benefit from establishing standard protocols. For example, it is not unheard of that prisons within the same state have different approaches to providing access to religious services and material for inmates (Cilluffo, 2006). Such inconsistencies, though, leave the door open for extremists to take advantage of loopholes and other vulnerabilities.

Overall, prison systems are challenged with both detecting and preventing radicalisation. To some degree, it is important to maintain a level of political correctness and acknowledge when implementing new policies that conversion does not equal radicalisation, nor are Muslims the only group guilty of radicalising prisoners (Neumann, 2010). But it is equally necessary to be aware that the United States has the highest incarceration rate in the world with more than 2.3 million prisoners and Islam happens to be the fastest growing religion in prison (Thompson, 2011). Consequently, to adequately and appropriately address issues of prison radicalisation, such facts must be considered when creating and implementing policies aimed at preventing or detecting prison radicalisation.

Conclusion

Some sceptics argue against placing too much time, effort, energy, or resources on the issue of prison radicalisation in the United States, claiming that the evidence suggests radicalisation in U.S. prisons is extremely low (e.g., Useem & Clayton, 2009). However, even a low level of radicalisation is still a cause for concern, especially in the context of such a large prison population. Realistically, only a few people are needed to coordinate and carry out a terrorist plot that can harm hundreds or thousands of people. And, because home-grown radicalisation in the United States is increasing (Carpenter et al., 2010; Downing, 2011), this suggests it would not be unrealistic to see an upsurge in prison radicalisation as well. The mere knowledge that prisoners have been radicalised is evidence alone that prison radicalisation can and does happen. Therefore, it is imperative to understand why and how radicalisation occurs in prisons.

References

Alderdice, J. (2007). 'The individual, the group and the psychology of terrorism.' *International Review of Psychiatry*, 19, 3, pp. 201–209.

Anti-Defamation League (2002). *Dangerous Convictions: An Introduction to Extremist Activities in Prisons*. Washington, DC: ADL, at http://www.adl.org/learn/Ext_Terr/dangerous_convictions.pdf (Accessed March 27, 2012).

Austin, J. (2009). 'Prisons and fear of terrorism.' *Criminology & Public Policy*, 8, 641–646.

Baca, L. D. (2011). *Statement to the House Committee on Homeland Security on Islamic Radicalization in the U.S. March 10, 2011*. Retrieved March 27, 2011 from http://www.c-spanvideo.org/program/298377-2

Brandon, J. (2009). 'The danger of prison radicalization in the West.' *CTC Sentinel*, 2, 1–4.

Bliss-Holtz, J. (2011). 'Broken schools + broken homes + broken neighborhoods = street gangs?' *Issues in Comprehensive Pediatric Nursing*, 34, 1–3.

Carpenter, J. S., Levitt, M., Simon, S., & Zarate, J. (2010). *Fighting the Ideological Battle: The Missing Link in U.S. Strategy to Counter Violent Extremism*. Washington, DC: The Washington Institute for Near East Policy.

Cilluffo, F. (2006). *Statement to the Committee on Homeland Security and Governmental Affairs on Prison Radicalization: Are Terrorist Cells Forming in U.S. Cell Blocks?* Hearing September 19, 2006. Transcript available via http://www.access.gpo.gov/congress/senate

Cilluffo, F. J., Cardash, S. L., & Whitehead, A. J. (2007). 'Radicalization: Behind bars and beyond borders.' *Brown Journal of World Affairs*, 13, 113–122.

Cilluffo, F., Saathoff, G., Lane, J., Cardash, S., Magarik, J., Whitehead, A., Raynor, J., Bogis, A., & Lohr, G. (2006). 'Out of the shadows: Getting ahead of prisoner radicalization.' *A Special Report by the Homeland Security Policy Institute at The George Washington University and the Critical Incident Analysis Group at The University of Virginia*, Washington, DC: The George Washington University, 8, at http://www.heathsystem.virginia.edu/internet/ciag/publications/out_of_the_shadows.pdf (Accessed March 27, 2012).

Collins, S. M. (2006). *Statement to the Committee on Homeland Security and Governmental Affairs on Prison Radicalization: Are Terrorist Cells Forming in U.S. Cell Blocks?* Hearing September 19, 2006. Transcript available via http://www.access.gpo.gov/congress/senate

Decker, S. H. & Van Winkle, B. (1996). *Life in the Gang: Family, Friends, and Violence*, New York: Cambridge University Press.

Del Carmen, A., Rodriguez, J. J., Dobbs, R., Smith, R., Butler, R. R., & Sarver, R. (2009). 'In their own words: A study of gang members through their own perspective.' *Journal of Gang Research*, 16, 57–76.

Downing, M. P. (2009). 'Policing terrorism in the United States: The Los Angeles Police Department's convergence strategy.' *The Police Chief*, 26, 1–9.

Downing, M. P. (2011). *Statement to the House Committee on Homeland Security on Islamic Radicalization in the U.S.* June 15, 2011. Retrieved March 27, 2011 from http://www.c-spanvideo.org/program/300053-1

Dunleavy, P. (2011). *The Fertile Soil of Jihad: Terrorism's Prison Connection*. Washington, DC: Potomac Books.

Federal Bureau of Investigation, Counterterrorism Division (2006). *The Radicalization Process: From Conversion to Jihad*. Washington, DC: Government Printing Office, May 2006.

Gartenstein-Ross, D. (2006). *Statement to the Committee on Homeland Security and Governmental Affairs on Prison Radicalization: Are Terrorist Cells Forming in U.S. Cell Blocks?* Hearing September 19, 2006. Transcript available via http://www.access.gpo.gov/congress/senate

Gartenstein-Ross, D. (2007). *My Year Inside Radical Islam: A Memoir*. New York: The Penguin Group.

Hamm, M. S. (2008). 'Prisoner radicalization: Assessing the threat in U.S. correctional institutions.' *National Institute of Justice Journal*, available at http://www.ojp.usdoj.gov/nij/journals/261/prisoner-radicalization.htm#note8

Hamm, M. S. (2009). 'Prison Islam in the age of sacred terror.' *British Journal of Criminology*, 49, 667–685.

Hogg, M. A. (2006). 'Social identity theory.' *Contemporary Social Psychological Theories* (pp. 111–136). Stanford University Press.

Hogg, M. A. (2007). 'Uncertainty-identity theory.' In M. P. Zanna (Ed.), *Advances in Experimental Social Psychology* (Vol. 39, pp. 69–126). San Diego, CA: Academic Press.

Hogg, M. A. (2012). 'Uncertainty-identity theory.' In P. A. M. Van Lange, A. W. Kruglanski, & E. T. Higgins (Eds.), *Handbook of Theories of Social Psychology* (pp. 62–80). Thousand Oaks, CA: Sage.

Hogg, M. A., Meehan, C., & Farquharson, J. (2010). 'The solace of radicalism: Self-uncertainty and group identification in the face of threat.' *Journal of Experimental Social Psychology*, 46, 1061–1066.

Hogg, M. A., Sherman, D. K., Dierselhuis, J., Maitner, A. T., & Moffitt, G. (2007). 'Uncertainty, entitativity, and group identification.' *Journal of Experimental Social Psychology*, 43, 135–142.

Moghaddam, F. (2004). 'Cultural preconditions for potential terrorist groups: Terrorism and societal change.' *Understanding Terrorism: Psychosocial Roots, Consequences, and Interventions* (pp. 103–117). Washington, DC: American Psychological Association.

Moore, J. (1978). *Homeboys: Gangs, Drugs, and Prison in the Barrios of Los Angeles.* Philadelphia, PA: Temple University Press.

Neumann, P. R. (2010). *Prisons and Terrorism: Radicalisation and De-radicalisation in 15 Countries.* London: International Centre for the Study of Radicalisation and Political Violence (ICSR).

Oakes, P. J., Haslam, S. A., & Turner, J. C. (1994). *Stereotyping and Social Reality.* Oxford: Blackwell.

Peterson, D., Taylor, T. J., & Esbensen, F. (2004). 'Gang membership and violent victimization.' *Justice Quarterly,* 21, 794–815.

Post, J. (1985). 'Hostilite, conformite, fraternite: The group dynamics terrorist behaviour.' *International Journal of group Psychotherapy,* 36, 211–224.

Post, J. M. (2007). *The Mind of the Terrorist: The Psychology of Terrorism from the IRA to al-Qaeda.* New York: Palgrave Macmillan.

Richardson, L. (2006). 'The roots of terrorism: An overview.' In L. Richardson (Ed.) *The Roots of Terrorism* (pp. 1–13). New York: Routledge.

Saathoff, G. (2006). *Statement to the Committee on Homeland Security and Governmental Affairs on Prison Radicalization: Are Terrorist Cells Forming in U.S. Cell Blocks?* Hearing September 19, 2006. Transcript available via http://www.access.gpo.gov/congress/senate

Schatzberg, R. & Kelly, R. J. (1997). *African American Organized Crime: A Social History.* New Brunswick, NJ: Rutgers University Press.

Silke, A. (2008). 'Holy warriors: Exploring the psychological processes of jihadi radicalization.' *European Journal of Criminology,* 5, 99–123.

Stern, J. (2010). 'Mind over martyr: How to deradicalize Islamist extremists.' *Foreign Affairs,* 89, 95–108.

Stretesky, P. B. & Pogrebin, M. R. (2007). 'Gang related gun violence: Socialization, identity, and self.' *Journal of Contemporary Ethnography,* 36, 85–114.

Tajfel, H. & Turner, J. C. (1979). 'An integrative theory of intergroup conflict.' In W. G. Austin & S. Worchel (Eds.), *The Social Psychology of Intergroup Relations.* Monterey, CA: Brooks-Cole.

Taylor, S. S. (2009). 'How street gangs recruit and socialize members.' *Journal of Gang Research,* 17, 1–27.

Thompson, B. (2011). *Statement to the House Committee on Homeland Security on Islamic Radicalization in the U.S. June 15, 2011.* Retrieved March 27, 2011 from http://www.c-spanvideo.org/program/300053-1

Thornberry, T. P., Krohn, M. D., Lizotte, A. J., Smith, C. A., & Tobin, K. (2003). *Gangs and Delinquency in Developmental Perspective,* New York: Cambridge University Press.

Tropp, L. R. & Brown, A. C. (2004). 'What benefits the group can also benefit the individual: Group-enhancing and individual-enhancing motives for collective action.' *Group Processes & Intergroup Relations,* 7/3, 267–282.

Turner, J. C., Hogg, M. A., Oakes, P. J., Reicher, S. D., & Wetherell, M. S. (1987). *Rediscovering the Social Group: A Self-Categorization Theory.* Oxford: Blackwell.

Useem, B. (2011). *Statement to the House Committee on Homeland Security on Islamic Radicalization in the U.S. June 15, 2011.* Retrieved March 27, 2011 from http://www.c-spanvideo.org/program/300053-1

Useem, B. & Clayton, O. (2009). 'Radicalization of U.S. prisoners.' *Criminology & Public Policy,* 8, 561–592.

van Duyn, D. (2006). *Statement to the Committee on Homeland Security and Governmental Affairs on Prison Radicalization: Are Terrorist Cells Forming in U.S. Cell Blocks?* Hearing September 19, 2006. Transcript available via http://www.access.gpo.gov/congress/senate

5

THE TALKING CURE?

Communication and
psychological impact in prison
de-radicalisation programmes

Kurt Braddock

Introduction

In the ten years following the September 11th attacks, it has become clear that although military force and the disruption of terrorist activity are key components of combating terrorism, they are not sufficient to fully mitigate the threat of violent extremism. It is not enough to simply remove active terrorists from operation. It is also vital to stem the flow of new and recidivist offenders from engaging in terrorism. To do so, the beliefs and attitudes that drive violent behaviour must be addressed; otherwise, there is a risk for violent extremists to return to the battlefield again and again.

One concept that has received increased attention from terrorism researchers as a potential method for countering violent extremism has been referred to as "de-radicalisation". Although the literature offers a wide range of specific definitions for de-radicalisation, it generally refers to a psychological process through which an individual abandons his extremist ideology and is theoretically rendered a decreased threat for re-engaging in terrorism. The effectiveness of de-radicalisation is a topic of much debate, but it is apparent that many governments believe in its merit as a tool for combating violent extremism within their countries' borders. Government-regulated initiatives intended to stem violent extremism through de-radicalisation have emerged around the world, with various types of programmes materialising in Northern Ireland, Colombia, Indonesia, the Philippines, Malaysia, Singapore, Norway, Sweden, Germany, Egypt, Jordan, Algeria, Tajikistan, Saudi Arabia, Yemen, and others. Although the programmes vary in their respective approaches to promoting psychological rehabilitation of former terrorists, they all feature a common component: the inclusion of communicative activities with those they mean to prevent from re-offending. Theological debate, dialogue, and psychological counselling have all been used as tools for promoting de-radicalisation.

These communicative actions have psychological implications for the subject being targeted. None of these implications have been satisfactorily studied in relation to de-radicalisation, and as a result, are poorly understood in this context.

The purpose of this chapter is to explore de-radicalisation and present how it has been approached, understood, and implemented. First, the concept of de-radicalisation will be explained. Next, to illustrate some ways de-radicalisation has been approached, the programmes based in Yemen and Saudi Arabia will be described and claims of the programmes respective successes will be presented. Finally, this chapter will present some potential implications of the various communicative approaches applied in the Yemeni and Saudi programmes with a particular emphasis on how communication may affect the programmes' impact.

Radicalisation and de-radicalisation

To understand how de-radicalisation has been conceptualised and approached, it is first necessary to review how researchers and government officials have come to understand individual motivations for engaging in terrorism. In the past, several scholars have tried to explain terrorism using individual psychological models (Taylor, 1988; Taylor and Quayle, 1994), economic and rational choice models (Elster, 1986; Gupta, 2008; Sandler, Arce and Enders, 2008), and what have become known as "root causes" (Bjørgo, 2005). Although many of these explanatory models and perspectives have contributed to our understanding of terrorist motivation, they have also been criticised as incomplete or incorrect. Individual psychological models that emphasised psychopathy or major mental illness as a risk factor for engaging in terrorism have been effectively dismissed (Horgan, 2008; Merari, 1990; Silke, 1998; McCauley, 2002). Similarly, explanations for violent extremism in terms of frustration, narcissism, or unresolved childhood conflicts have also been criticised as limited in scope or lacking empirical support (Horgan, 2003; McAllister and Schmid, 2011; Borum, 2004). The association between economic factors and terrorism remains ambiguous; and root causes perspectives, while insightful regarding conditions that serve as structural risk factors for terrorism in the long run, are general in nature and emphasise social problems that yield a number of negative outcomes of which terrorism is only one (Bjørgo, 2005). Despite years of concerted effort on the part of some terrorism researchers, the pursuit for causal explanations for terrorism based on static traits, conditions, or root causes has yielded little headway.

As a result, many contemporary terrorism researchers have abandoned attempts to identify a terrorist personality or profile founded on static features. Instead, researchers have sought explanations for violent extremism by adopting perspectives that emphasise a "more dynamic, comprehensive account of the social and psychological processes leading to terrorism" (Moghaddam, 2005, p.161). It is this shift in focus from static traits to dynamic processes that gave rise to a perspective that explains terrorism in terms of a process of gradual belief and attitude change toward an extremist ideology. Although there have been multiple definitions for it within the academic and intelligence sectors, the social and psychological process by which an individual adopts an extremist ideology has often been referred to as *radicalisation*. Explications that fully illustrate the complexity of radicalisation have been featured elsewhere, and thus will not be attempted here (see Braddock, 2012; Sedgwick, 2010). But it is vital to recognise that the assumption that violent extremism results from specific social factors and a process-based assimilation of a radical ideology influences the ways in which the problem of violent extremism is approached. The logic behind de-radicalisation is that if an individual can adopt radical beliefs and attitudes that make him a risk for engaging in terrorism, he can also abandon those beliefs and attitudes and become less of a threat for engaging in terrorism.

However, the question remains: What exactly is de-radicalisation and how does it occur? Government initiatives intended to promote de-radicalisation often fall short of defining the process and as a result, there exists no standardised conceptualisation for it. Despite this, some academics have attempted to formally delineate the term. Horgan (2009) provides the most comprehensive treatment of the concept (as well as related issues), arguing that de-radicalisation is "the social and psychological process whereby an individual's commitment to, and involvement in, violent radicalisation is reduced to the extent that they are no longer at risk of involvement and engagement in violent activity." He goes on to say that de-radicalisation can also refer to a specific initiative that is geared towards achieving a reduction of risk for re-engagement in terrorism through addressing the specific and relevant disengagement issues. However, one should be warned that despite the connotations surrounding the term, de-radicalisation should not be considered a psychological return to some pre-radicalised state. Once an individual has sought out and engaged in terrorism, it is altogether unlikely that that individual can be "turned" or "de-programmed" (Horgan, 2009). Rather, de-radicalisation can be considered a process by which an individual's threat for re-engaging in terrorism is minimised.

Yemen: the Religious Dialogue Committee

The Yemeni Religious Dialogue Committee was created in the wake of three high-profile terror attacks. One of those attacks was the September 11th operation by Al Qaeda in 2001. In response to the 9/11 attacks, the Bush administration made clear that not only would terror groups be targeted for military force, but also that those countries that host terror groups would likewise be targeted. Following this doctrine, the United States military began strikes against Afghan targets on October 7, 2001 to rout Al Qaeda and its host governing body, the Taliban. For his part, Yemen's President Saleh voiced support for the American-led "Global War on Terror" and appeared to be prepared to support the United States in this endeavour (Lumpkin, 2006).

However, two other attacks in and around Yemen in the early 2000s illustrated that dealing with violent extremists in Yemen would present a unique challenge to

Saleh and his advisers. A year before the September 11th attacks, Al Qaeda conducted a suicide attack against the USS *Cole* while it was refuelling in the Harbour of Aden, killing 17 American sailors. Abd al-Rahim al-Nashiri, Al Qaeda Persian Gulf Operations Chief and Yemeni national, was found to be the commander of the USS *Cole* operation (Lumpkin, 2006). Following the attack on the USS *Cole*, President Saleh ordered a security crackdown on domestic terrorists operating within Yemen's borders. Yemeni forces arrested hundreds of suspected militants in 2001 and 2002, but Al Qaeda proved resilient (Johnsen, 2004).

The second attack in Yemeni territory occurred on October 6, 2002. A small boat packed with explosives rammed a French oil tanker called the MV *Limburg*. The attack killed a Bulgarian crewman and caused significant damage to the oil tanker. As with the attack on the *Cole*, Al Qaeda claimed responsibility and al-Nashiri was again implicated as the operational commander (Lumpkin, 2006).

Although the attack on the USS *Cole* in October of 2000 and the September 11th attacks in 2001 prompted President Saleh to act against Al Qaeda in Yemen, the *Limburg* attack was significant in that it (a) illustrated that Yemeni nationals were operating on behalf of Al Qaeda within Yemen, (b) showed the Yemeni government that Al Qaeda was still capable of functioning despite the security crackdown, and (c) represented Al Qaeda's first successful attack on an oil target (Lumpkin, 2006). In spite of his attempts to punish militants in Yemen, President Saleh was widely perceived as incapable of stamping out terrorism through security crackdowns alone. This doubtlessly led to the widespread view within Yemen that the American government would take counter-terrorist measures in Yemen into its own hands to protect its interests unless Saleh produced a viable solution to violent extremism (Horgan and Braddock, 2010). It was around this time that the Yemeni government determined that an alternative method to dealing with terrorism was needed if Al Qaeda was to be defeated there (Johnsen, 2004).

The alternative method that was developed came in the form of the Yemeni Committee for Dialogue, which was developed shortly after the bombing of the *Limburg*. Once known as the "re-education programme," the foundations of the prison-based initiative rely on three fundamental pillars of Islamic belief: the Qur'an, the sunna (Islamic traditions that are thought to date back to the Prophet Mohammed), and hadiths (the sayings that were attributed to the Prophet Mohammed) (Horgan and Braddock, 2009). Five religious scholars were chosen to form what would become Yemen's Religious Dialogue Committee (RDC). Hamoud al-Hitar, a widely respected Yemeni judge was appointed by Saleh as the head of the RDC.

The RDC was founded on the idea that because attacking civilians for a political cause has "faulty intellectual foundations" (Johnsen, 2004), the ideologies that promote terrorism can be argued against. Successful arguments ought to weaken or reverse beliefs and attitudes that support terrorist activity (al-Hitar, n.d.). To achieve this, the RDC primarily used open debate with militants that had been captured. Specifically, al-Hitar claimed that because many militants had memorised several parts of the Qur'an as justifications for their actions, the RDC sought to challenge the militants' beliefs based on their understanding of the verses and hadiths within the Qur'an itself (Johnsen, 2008). The RDC openly invited the captured militants to use the Qur'an to justify attacks on civilians, and when they struggled with this, the RDC used passages within the Qur'an that renounce the use of violence against civilians and promotes respect for other religions (Brandon, 2005). These debates occurred in small group settings – with no more than five to seven militants gathered at any one time. After several weeks of debate, if the prisoners renounced the use of violence and their membership with the terrorist groups of which they were a part, they were released and offered training to facilitate the procurement of legal employment.

In the time immediately following its inception and implementation, the RDC was perceived as an inventive and effective approach to fighting terrorism within Yemen. Senior Yemeni officials voiced their support for the programme, and curious governments invited al-Hitar to travel to their countries to share the secrets of ideological dialogue and its effectiveness (Willems, 2008). However, later years saw the RDC's practices and claims of effectiveness called into question (Schanzer, 2003).

Of particular concern were the circumstances under which prisoners qualified for release from custody. In essence, participation in dialogue through the RDC qualified suspected militants for release and vocational training. However, many questioned whether terrorists could be reformed on the basis of talking alone. Abdullah al-Faqih, professor of political science at Yemen's Sana'a University, conceded that it is very difficult to alter radical beliefs through dialogue or to determine the extent to which belief change has occurred (Willems, 2008). These worries reflected the chief question surrounding the release strategies of the RDC: How can we know that suspected militants who denounce violence do so because they have changed their beliefs and not simply to escape custody?

Doubts about the effectiveness of the RDC to de-radicalise prisoners were accentuated by questions about stated rates of recidivism. The RDC operated with the backing of a Yemeni government that had a strong interest in curbing terrorism within its borders, which gave rise to scepticism about the truthfulness of stated recidivism rates. Al-Hitar claimed that between 2002 and 2005, 364 suspected militants had undergone treatment and had been released, and described their progression as "encouraging" and "positive" (Brandon, 2005). In one interview, al-Hitar went so far as to claim that "those influenced by Al Qaeda were persuaded [to renounce violence and their group membership] at a 98% rate" (Oudah, 2008). Although the number of militants released by the RDC is verifiable, the number that returned to their violent activities is not. Furthermore, the locations in which released prisoners returned to the battlefield has proven to be another complicating factor in ascertaining accurate recidivism rates for the RDC. Al-Hitar has not clarified whether he constitutes former participants fighting in Iraq, Afghanistan, or the Israeli-Palestinian conflict as "failures" of the programme (Boucek, Beg and Horgan, 2009). As a result, it is possible that rates of successful belief change claimed by al-Hitar are inflated to the extent that the RDC considers some areas defensible environments for terrorism.

Currently, the status of the RDC is uncertain. Al-Hitar left his post as head of the RDC after being appointed the Minister of Islamic Affairs in Yemen. As a result of al-Hitar's leaving, the dialogue programme ceased operation in 2008 (Oudah, 2008). Although al-Hitar expressed interest in reviving the programme in the future, the political climate and continued violence in Yemen since the programme's ending suggests that doing so would be a difficult endeavour. Despite initial promise as a soft approach to dealing with terrorism, the RDC seems to have been abandoned due to a lack of transparency, suspicious reports of recidivism rates, and continued scepticism on the part of Yemen's allies.

Saudi Arabia: the Advisory Committee Counselling Programme

In May of 2003, 34 people were killed in a series of attacks against Western housing targets around Riyadh (BBC News, 2003). A source connected to the Emergency Response and Research Institute claimed that the coordinated nature suggested Al Qaeda's involvement (Emergency Response and Research Institute, 2003). These suspicions were verified when arrests related to the attacks included members of Al Qaeda (PBS Online News, 2003). Fifteen Saudi citizens were found to have taken part in the attacks. Despite a history of strong counter-terrorism operations, the Riyadh attacks illustrated that Al Qaeda could not only penetrate Saudi Arabia's borders, but also recruit its citizens to participate in attacks within the country.

Following the Riyadh compound attacks, the Saudi government developed a new series of "soft" measures intended to de-legitimise interpretations of the Qur'an that the kingdom determined to be incorrect and/or violent (Boucek, 2007). One of these measures to combating terrorism was a special initiative developed to rehabilitate extremists using a combination of open dialogue and psychological counselling and evaluation. The Saudi initiative, which was called the Advisory Committee Counselling Programme, is housed under the Saudi Ministry of the Interior, which is responsible for domestic security, civil defence, and counter-terrorist activity. Prince Mohammed bin Nayef, who is the third-highest ranking official in the Saudi Ministry of the Interior, serves as the head of Saudi Arabia's rehabilitation efforts (Boucek, 2008).

The chief goals of the Counselling Programme are to facilitate the abandonment of radical ideologies among those that have expressed beliefs and attitudes that promote the use of terrorism and to reintegrate these individuals into Saudi society. The primary targets of the programme are those who have expressed beliefs consistent with radical ideologies, but do not yet have "blood on their hands". Although individuals who have engaged in active terrorist activity are eligible for the programme, they do not qualify for early release (Boucek, 2007; Neumann, 2010).

The Saudi Counselling Programme is comprised of four subcommittees: the Religious Subcommittee, the Psychological and Social Subcommittee, the Security Subcommittee, and the Media Subcommittee (Boucek, 2008; Murphy, 2008). Each of these subcommittees is charged with a separate aspect of the overall counselling and rehabilitation process.

Comparable to the Yemeni RDC, the Saudi Religious Subcommittee is composed of religious clerics, religious experts, and university scholars and is responsible for discussing participants' experiences and interpretations of the Qur'an and Islamic duty. In these discussions, members of the Religious Subcommittee challenge participants on their violent interpretations of Islam, with the goal of persuading them to adopt a more moderate ideology (Barret and Bokhari, 2009). This aspect of the Saudi programme is based on the assumption that individuals will obey those they perceive to be legitimate authorities on an issue.

The Psychological and Social Subcommittee is comprised of mental health professionals, including psychologists and psychiatrists, to evaluate participants for psychological problems and determine the extent to which participants are adhering to the de-radicalisation programme. This subcommittee is also responsible for taking care of participants' families in their absence and organising logistic reintegration into Saudi society after completing the programme. This includes the provision of cars, money, and vocational prospects to those that complete the programme (Verma, 2008).

Although participants in the Saudi programme are eligible for release from prison (with the exception of those that actively engaged in terrorism), they are not released on their own recognisance. The Security Subcommittee monitors participants during and after their release from custody to ensure they do not become a violent threat to the kingdom (Boucek, 2008). In coordination with the Psychological and Social Subcommittee, the Security Subcommittee recommends which participants are safe to release. In addition, after they are released, participants are informed that the Security Subcommittee will monitor them in both overt and covert ways (Boucek, 2008). In sum, the Security Subcommittee maintains close watch over participants both during and after their treatment. With tight restrictions on what participants may do and with whom they may associate, the Security Subcommittee offers a contingency plan in the event that some participants return to violence.

The Media Subcommittee serves as the information branch of the Saudi programme. Primarily geared towards outreach, the Media Subcommittee performs research on the best ways to reach Saudis at risk for violent radicalisation with carefully executed media campaigns. To this end, the Media Subcommittee develops persuasive material to be used both within the Saudi Counselling Programme and as pre-emptive warnings to those who have not yet become radicalised (Horgan and Braddock, 2010).

Although the Saudi programme is comprised of these four subcommittees, the Religious Subcommittee is primarily responsible for the counselling aspects. When members of the Religious Subcommittee first meet with potential participants of the programme, they are told that they may choose one of two options: They may either take part in a rehabilitation process and renounce their loyalty to the terrorist movement of which they are a part, or they can face prosecution for terrorist-related offenses and be sent to a Saudi prison (Henry, 2007). If the individual chooses to undergo rehabilitation, Saudi officials ask participants what they did and why they did it, and allow participants to respond freely and without interruption. After this, members of the Advisory Committee respond by showing how participants' interpretations of Islam are incorrect, and offer a more moderate interpretation of the Qur'an upon which the remainder of the rehabilitation programme is based (Boucek, 2007).

From here, participants are enrolled in one of two counselling programmes. In the first, participants engage in short counselling sessions that last no more than a few hours. Although many participants verbally recant their dedication to an extremist ideology after one session, they are usually compelled to attend several sessions after they admit to abandoning their beliefs (Boucek, 2007). The other programme more closely resembles an official counselling initiative, and is analogous to a six-week workshop in which officials from the various subcommittees work with up to twenty participants at once (Horowitz, 2008). During the course of this six-week programme, participants are instructed about loyalty, terrorism, and Saudi-approved interpretations and rules of jihad. Participants may also partake in classes related to psychological health and self-esteem improvement. Once this six-week course is completed and participants pass a psychological evaluation, they move on to the aftercare portion of the programme.

The aftercare component of the Saudi de-radicalisation initiative is actually comprised of various smaller programmes, each designed to satisfy a specific psychological or economic need of the participants (Horowitz, 2008; Verma, 2008). After the Saudi Advisory Committee determines that a participant is eligible for the aftercare programme, that participant is taken to a rehabilitation facility (the Care Rehabilitation Centre) where he lives in an environment that is very different from that of a Saudi prison. Detainees are able to go outside, socialise with other inmates, and engage in physical activity on the facility's property, among other freedoms not afforded to traditional prisoners. Counselling sessions that had begun during the initial six-week initiative continue while the participant spends time at the Care Rehabilitation Centre.

Individuals who undergo rehabilitation at the Care Rehabilitation Centre are treated differently based on the circumstances surrounding their incarceration. Detainees who were involved with terrorist-related activity domestically or in Iraq spend time speaking with counsellors. Those who return from the U.S. detention facility in Guantanamo Bay undergo psychological counselling and tailored instruction intended to facilitate their reintegration into Saudi society (Allam, 2007).

In addition to the psychological counselling and social support by the initial six-week programme and the Care Rehabilitation Centre, detainees are also given assistance in getting a job, a means to travel, money, and a place of residence. The families of detainees are also used as a means by which to support their recovery. Using positive reinforcement, the Ministry of the Interior provides social support programmes to facilitate families' trips to visit the detainees. However, the Ministry of the Interior also holds families of programme participants financially and socially responsible if the participant reverts to the behaviours that led to his incarceration.

Saudi officials have claimed that participants in the programme are successfully rehabilitated between 80% and 90% of the time (Boucek, 2008). In 2007, Prince bin Nayef said that of 3,000 participants in the programme, fewer than 35 had returned to terrorism, yielding a success rate of over 97% (Boucek, 2008). These claims of success have caused the Saudi programme to be closely monitored, particularly to detect recidivism among participants (see Chapter 12 in this volume for more on the Saudi case).

Psychological implications of communicative aspects of de-radicalisation

Although the Yemeni and Saudi initiatives use different approaches to de-radicalisation, each of these (and other) programmes feature communicative tenets. At their core, the communicative components of the de-radicalisation initiatives are deliberately constructed as persuasive. The Yemeni religious debates are designed to persuade using Qur'anic arguments. The Saudi programme uses a six-week instructional programme and extensive psychological counselling, both of which are based on communication, to persuade its participants. Each of these communicative practices has its own respective psychological effects, both expected and unexpected. Although the communicative aspects of de-radicalisation programmes can lead to the reduced risk of terrorism by mitigating the influence of a violent ideology on an individual, there are also unintended consequences to communicative interventions that may run counter to that objective.

This section will detail two psychological effects that may result from the communicative strategies of many de-radicalisation initiatives. First, because many de-radicalisation initiatives feature communication strategies that do not mask their persuasive intent, it is possible that participants may psychologically revolt against beliefs and attitudes the initiative means to instil. Thus, the Theory of Psychological Reactance, which relates to a message recipient's rebellion against overt persuasive attempts, will be discussed. Second, many of the communicative practices of de-radicalisation initiatives are sure to arouse various types of emotion in those who undergo them, which can be persuasive in both expected and unexpected ways. Accordingly, effects of guilt and anger, two kinds of "discrete emotions" resulting from communication in the programmes, will also be explored.

Psychological reactance

Psychological Reactance Theory (PRT) is based on the premise that individuals must fulfil basic needs for survival and that "given some minimal level of valid knowledge about oneself and the environment, freedom to choose among different behavioural possibilities will generally help one to survive and thrive" (Brehm, 1966, p.2). PRT is generally considered a theory of social influence that is geared towards explaining human behaviour when free behaviour is constrained (Burgoon, Alvaro, Grandpre and Voulodakis, 2002). Reactance is considered a motivational psychological state geared towards re-establishing the freedom to perform behaviours that have been restricted (or threatened with restriction).

According to PRT, forms of persuasive communication represent a possible threat to behavioural freedom (Brehm, 1966; Brehm and Brehm, 1981). Humans' need for autonomy in determining their own beliefs, attitudes, and behaviours is based on the assumption that people have a strong preference to perceive themselves as in control of their own fates. As such, when an individual's freedom is threatened with proscription, that individual will feel psychological pressure to re-establish the threatened freedom (Heilman and Toffler, 1976). One way that an individual can restore the lost freedom is through participating in the proscribed behaviour or embracing the forbidden beliefs or attitudes (Brehm, 1966). Research investigating the restoration of lost freedoms has demonstrated that certain persuasive messages result in effects opposite to those that are intended (Worchel and Brehm, 1970). Simply stated, persuasive messages can cause the target of the messages to perform the very acts or adopt the very beliefs that are being discouraged.

Given the persuasive nature of many de-radicalisation initiatives' communicative practices, this effect can have implications for the effectiveness of such initiatives. Recall that the Yemeni and Saudi programmes both involve some form of discussion in which participants' beliefs are overtly challenged and state-sanctioned beliefs, attitudes, and behaviours are openly encouraged. Evidence supporting PRT suggests that these practices may result in participants psychologically rejecting the beliefs and attitudes being promoted and reinforcing those beliefs and attitudes that led to their incarceration (Burgoon et al., 2002). For those individuals who fail to abandon their radical beliefs, psychological reactance may be one explanation.

Practically speaking, PRT can inform the development of future de-radicalisation initiatives. Although the argument-based discussions of current programmes are often treated as indispensable, the methods by which the persuasive messages embedded in those discussions are delivered can be refined so as to minimise the likelihood of arousing psychological reactance. For example, as part of the Saudi Counselling Programme, the Religious Subcommittee openly challenges participants on their interpretations of Islam and attempts to persuade them to adopt a government-approved version of the religion. PRT predicts that some participants may attempt to restore their decisional freedom by defying the Religious Subcommittee's messages and strengthening their resolve to violent religious extremism. To avoid this, the Saudi initiative (as well as others) can mask their persuasive intent in these discussions. Rather than overtly challenging participants' beliefs during discussions, more subtle forms of persuasion may prove effective.

For instance, narrative persuasion, which consists of covertly embedding persuasive messages in stories with plots, characters, settings, and scenes, has been shown to influence message recipients' beliefs, attitudes, intentions, and behaviour (Braddock, 2012). Some narratives include characters that adopt (or avoid) a promoted (or dissuaded) set of beliefs or behaviours as a means to persuade the message recipient. Other narratives are geared towards arousing specific emotions (see below) that may motivate the adoption of promoted beliefs or behaviours. Regardless of the mechanisms by which they are persuasive, all narrative persuasive messages share one commonality: the persuasive intention of the narrative is not overt. By reading, viewing or hearing carefully produced narratives rather than being explicitly challenged on their beliefs, participants may be more inclined to accept persuasive messages.

Of course, initiative participants may suspect that narratives (like all other communication they would encounter as part of their de-radicalisation) are intended to persuade them. However, in the case of narratives, the persuasion would not be overt or forceful. This is critical in avoiding psychological reactance. No matter how arguments are constructed in the context of de-radicalisation programmes – whether embedded in a narrative or presented in some other way – they may be less susceptible to rejection if the persuasive intent is disguised. By masking the persuasive intent of the messages, officials may be less likely to arouse the perception of a threat to participants' decisional freedom. Thus, there would be a reduced possibility that participants would experience subsequent psychological reactance that would cause the reinforcement of their radical beliefs and attitudes.

Discrete emotional arousal: guilt and anger

Various theories of emotion have the same four principles at their core. First, emotions have intrinsic adaptive purposes. Second, emotions arise from stimuli that are personally relevant. Third, each emotion has a unique objective represented by an action tendency meant to guide cognitive and physical activity. Fourth, emotions organise and motivate behaviour (Nabi, 2002; Lazarus, 1991). Based on the action readiness and physiological changes resulting from the experience of an emotion, perceptions, cognitions, and behaviours are organised in line with that emotion's action tendency (Nabi, 2002). These effects render the experience of emotion persuasive.

Noted psychologist Richard Lazarus (1991) identified seven emotions as having distinctive action tendencies. These emotions are fear, guilt, disgust, anger, sadness, envy, and happiness. Participants in de-radicalisation initiatives are likely to experience some of these emotions in response to the communicative components of their rehabilitation. Functional theories of emotion suggest that the experience of these emotions may have implications for the extent to which de-radicalisation may occur.

Although it is to be expected that participants will experience a wide range of emotions during their incarceration, some emotions are more likely to (a) be aroused in response to attempts to alter participants' viewpoints, and (b) influence the efficacy of their attempted de-radicalisation. Of the emotions identified by Lazarus, it seems most plausible that participants may feel guilt and anger during their communicative interactions with programme officials.

Guilt results from an individual's perception that he has violated an internalised moral or ethical code (Ausubel, 1955; Izard, 1977) and has a strong action-motivation tendency to repair past damages or to recompense for not correcting injustices (Tangney, Miller, Flicker and Barlow, 1996). In the context of de-radicalisation, it may prove difficult to elicit guilt from participants given that their internalised moral codes may justify the use of violence against civilians, and thus, they will feel no remorse for thoughts and actions that support those moral codes. So, to provoke feelings of guilt, the Yemeni and Saudi programmes emphasise participants' violation of "true Islam." The purpose of this is to provide participants with a new internalised moral code with respect to their religion. By redefining the nature of what it means to think and behave like a good Muslim, the Saudi and Yemeni programmes create the opportunity for participants to reflect upon their past attitudes and behaviours and think about how they violated their new notion of Islam. If successful, the guilt felt by participants will render them more prone to adopting beliefs, attitudes, and behaviours that reduce their risk for re-engaging in terrorism.

Successful elicitation of guilt, however, may be difficult among committed radicals. The extent to which they are psychologically adherent to their violent ideologies may dictate how guilt may affect their de-radicalisation. Further, communication research has shown that guilt often co-occurs with other emotions that hinder the de-radicalisation process. One of the most common emotions with which guilt is associated is anger.

Anger is generally elicited in response to the interference of achieving one's goals or demeaning offenses against oneself or one's loved ones. It is related to a desire to strike out at, attack, or gain retribution against the source of the anger (Tangney et al., 1996; Averill, 1982). Research has demonstrated that intentionally induced anger is positively related with attitude change (Nabi, 2002). However, communication that is designed to provoke guilt or fear has been shown to unintentionally induce anger at times. When this occurs, anger has been shown to negatively correlate with attitude change (Dillard and Peck, 2000; Pinto and Priest, 1991). Presumably, unintentionally induced anger is likely directed at the source of the message in response to what audience members perceive as attempts to deceitfully influence their emotions (Pinto and Priest, 1991; Coulter and Pinto, 1995).

In the context of de-radicalisation, it is possible that participants who perceive an attempt to manipulate their emotions (by attempting to induce feelings of guilt, sadness, fear, or shame) may feel anger towards programme personnel. If this occurs, attempts at de-radicalisation can be undermined due to a mistrust of and aggression towards programme personnel. Therefore, the unintentional provocation of anger represents a threat to the de-radicalisation programmes' effectiveness.

To avoid this potential effect, emotional appeals should be used with caution. In the previous section, it was said that preventing psychological reactance required creative and covert options to presenting messages intended to de-radicalise. The use of emotional appeals as components of a de-radicalisation programme should be approached with the same level of subtlety to ensure effectiveness. Carefully developed narratives, visual material, and debate points may successfully evoke guilt (or other motivating emotions) more effectively than obvious attempts to manipulate participants' emotions. Although the evocation of emotions that make de-radicalisation more difficult will be inevitable, architects of successful initiatives will attempt to minimise the extent to which emotional appeals are conspicuous.

Concluding remarks

The Yemeni Religious Dialogue Committee and the Saudi Counselling Programme are only two examples of initiatives geared toward de-radicalisation. Although they represent only a small sample of the various types of programmes that have emerged the world over, they include an integral aspect of how de-radicalisation has come to be approached: persuasive communication. Fundamentally, de-radicalisation initiatives engage in a particular type of persuasion intended to alleviate the threat of terrorism and promote beliefs and attitudes that are non-violent. Various programmes have experienced different degrees of success in practising their persuasive communication, but some of the ways in which de-radicalisation is attempted may bring about effects opposite to those that are intended. Current and future programmes should seek to understand these communicative effects and consider them when developing best practices for reducing the risk of an individual's re-engagement in violent extremism.

References

Al-Hitar, H. (n.d.). *Dialogue and its Effects on Countering Terrorism: The Yemeni Experience*, pp.1–18.

Allam, H. (2007). 'To stanch the spread of radical Islam, Saudi Arabia woos detainees.' *McClatchy newspapers*, May 25, 2007, http://www.mcclatchydc.com/159/story/16043.html.

Ausubel, D. (1955). 'Relationships between shame and guilt in the socializing process.' *Psychological Review*, 62, 378–390.

Averill, J. (1982). *Anger and Aggression: An Essay on Emotion*. New York: Springer-Verlag.

Barret, R. and Bokhari, L. (2009). 'De-radicalization and rehabilitation programmes targeting religious terrorists and extremists in the Muslim world: an overview.' In Tore Bjørgo and John Horgan (eds.) *Leaving Terrorism Behind*, pp.170–280. New York: Routledge.

BBC News (2003). 'Saudi Bombing Deaths Rise,' May 13, 2003, http://news.bbc.co.uk/2/hi/middle_east/3022473.stm.

Bjørgo, T. (2005). *Root Causes of Terrorism: Myths, Reality, and Ways Forward*. Oxon, UK: Routledge.

Borum, R. (2004). *Psychology of Terrorism*. Tampa: University of South Florida, http://works.bepress.com/randy_borum/1/.

Boucek, C. (2007). 'Extremist reeducation and rehabilitation in Saudi Arabia.' *Terrorism Monitor*, 5/16, http://www.jamestown.org/single/?no_cache=1&tx_ttnews[tt_news]=4321.

Boucek, C. (2008). *Saudi Arabia's 'Soft' Counterterrorism Strategy: Prevention, Rehabilitation, and Aftercare*. Carnegie Papers, Middle East series 97. Washington, DC: Carnegie Endowment for International Peace.

Boucek, C., Beg, S. and Horgan, J. (2009). 'Opening up the jihadi debate: Yemen's Committee for Dialogue.' In Tore Bjørgo and John Horgan (eds.) *Leaving Terrorism Behind*, pp.181–192. New York: Routledge.

Braddock, K. (2012). 'Fighting words: the persuasive effect of online extremist narratives on the radicalization process.' Ph.D. Dissertation, The Pennsylvania State University.

Brandon, J. (2005). 'Koranic duels ease terror.' *Christian Science Monitor*, February 4, 2005, http://www.csmonitor.com/2005/0204/p01s04-wome.html.

Brehm, J. (1966). *A Theory of Psychological Reactance*. New York: Academic Press.

Brehm, S. and Brehm, J. (1981). *Psychological Reactance: A Theory of Freedom and Control*. New York: Academic Press.

Burgoon, M., Alvaro, E., Grandpre, J. and Voulodakis, M. (2002). 'Revisiting the Theory of Psychological Reactance: communicating threats to attitudinal freedom.' In James Price Dillard and Michael Pfau (eds.) *The Persuasion Handbook: Developments in Theory and Practice*, pp.213–232. Thousand Oaks, CA: Sage.

Coulter, R. and Pinto, M. (1995). 'Guilt appeals in advertising: what are their effects?' *Journal of Applied Psychology*, 80/6, 697–705.

Dillard, J. and Peck, E. (2000). 'Affect and persuasion: emotional responses to public service announcements.' *Communication Research*, 27/4, 461–495.

Elster, J. (1986). 'Introduction.' In Jon Elster (ed.) *Rational Choice*, pp.1–33. Oxford, UK: Basil Blackwell.

Emergency Response and Research Institute (2003). 'Terrorist Attack on western residences in Riyadh, Saudi Arabia.' *EmergencyNews*, May 12, http://www.emergency.com/2003/saudi_bmbs_051203.htm.

Gupta, D. (2008). *Understanding Terrorism and Political Violence*. London: Routledge.

Heilman, M. and Toffer, B. (1976). 'Reacting to reactance: an interpersonal interpretation of the need for freedom.' *Journal of Experimental Social Psychology*, 12, 519–529.

Henry, T. (2007). 'Get out of jihad free.' *Atlantic Monthly*, June 2007, http://www.theatlantic.com/doc/200706/saudi-jihad.

Horgan, J. (2003). 'The search for the terrorist personality.' In Andrew Silke (ed.) *Terrorists, Victims, and Society: Psychological Perspectives on Terrorism and its Consequences*, pp.3–28. Chichester, UK: John Wiley & Sons.

Horgan, J. (2008). 'From profiles to pathways and roots to routes: perspectives on psychology on radicalization into terrorism.' *The ANNALS of the American Academy of Political and Social Science*, 618, 80–94.

Horgan, J. (2009). *Walking Away from Terrorism: Accounts of Disengagement from Radical and Extremist Movements*. Oxon, UK: Routledge.

Horgan, J. and Braddock, K. (2009). 'Assessing the effectiveness of current de-radicalization initiatives and identifying implications for the development of U.S.-based initiatives in multiple settings.' Final Report to Human Factors Division, Science and Technology Directorate, U.S. Department of Homeland Security.

Horgan, J. and Braddock, K. (2010). 'Rehabilitating the terrorists? Challenges in assessing the effectiveness of de-radicalization programs.' *Terrorism and Political Violence*, 22, 267–291.

Horowitz, A. (2008). 'What's the best way to stop terrorism? (a) Political intervention, (b) torture, (c) pampering: The Saudi government believes it's found the answer.' *The Sunday Telegraph*, July 13, 2008, p.8.

Izard, C. (1977). *Human Emotions*. New York: Plenum.

Johnsen, G. (2004). 'Terrorists in rehab.' *Worldview Magazine*, 17/3, http://www.worldview magazine.com/issues/article.cfm?id=139&issue=34.

Johnsen, G. (2008). 'In Yemen, a benevolent alternative to Osama bin Laden.' *New American Media*, January 20, 2008, http://news.ncmonline.com/news/view_article.html?article_id=be013890b8c48cf458e54f95b8708629.

Lazarus, R. (1991). *Emotion and Adaptation.* New York: Oxford University Press.

Lumpkin, J. (2006). *USS Cole Bombing.* Available at: http://globalsecurity.org/security/profiles/uss_cole_bombing.htm.

McAllister, B. and Schmid, A. (2011). 'Theories of terrorism.' In Alex Schmid (ed.), *The Routledge Handbook of Terrorism Research*, pp.201–293. New York: Routledge.

McCauley, C. (2002). 'Psychological issues in understanding terrorism and the response to terrorism.' In Chris Stout (ed.), *The Psychology of Terrorism: Theoretical Understandings and Perspectives*, pp.3–30. Westport, CT: Praeger.

Merari, A. (1990). 'The Readiness to kill and die: suicidal terrorism in the Middle East.' In Walter Reich (ed.), *Origins of Terrorism: Psychologies, Ideologies, Theologies, States of Mind*, pp.192–207. Washington, DC: Woodrow Wilson Center Press.

Moghaddam, F. (2005). 'The staircase to terrorism: a psychological exploration.' *American Psychologist*, 60, 161–169.

Murphy, C. (2008). 'Saudis use cash and counseling to fight terrorism.' *Christian Science Monitor*, August 21, 2008, http://www.csmonitor.com/World/Middle-East/2008/0821/p01s01-wome.html.

Nabi, R. (2002). 'Discrete emotions and persuasion,' In James Dillard and Michael Pfau (eds.), *The Persuasion Handbook: Developments in Theory and Practice*, pp.289–308. Thousand Oaks, CA: Sage.

Neumann, P. (2010). *Prisons and Terrorism: Radicalism and De-Radicalisation in 15 Countries.* London: The International Centre for the Study of Radicalisation and Political Violence.

Oudah, A. (2008). 'Judge Hamoud al-Hitar, Minister of Islamic Affairs, talks about using dialogue to confront extremists.' *Yemen Observer*, June 4, 2008, http://www.yobserver.com/reports/10014374.html.

PBS Online News (2003). 'Saudi Arabia arrests at least five linked to Riyadh bombings,' *PBS Online News Hour*, May 28, 2003, http://www.pbs.org/newshour/updates/riyadh_05-28-03.html.

Pinto, M. and Priest, S. (1991). 'Guilt appeals in advertising: an exploratory study.' *Psychological Reports*, 69, 375–385.

Sandler, T., Arce, D. and Enders, W. (2008). *Transnational Terrorism.* Copenhagen: Copenhagen Consensus Center.

Schanzer, J. (2003). 'Yemen's al-Qaeda amnesty.' *Frontpage Magazine*, November 28, Available at: http://archive.frontpagemag.com/readArticle.aspx?ARTID=15244.

Sedgwick, M. (2010). 'The concept of radicalization as a source of confusion.' *Terrorism and Political Violence*, 22, 479–494.

Silke, A. (1998). 'Cheshire-Cat logic: the recurring theme of terrorist abnormality in psychology research.' *Psychology, Crime, and Law*, 4, 51–69.

Tangney, J., Miller, R., Flicker, L. and Barlow, D. (1996). 'Are shame, guilt, and embarrassment distinct emotions?' *Journal of Personality and Social Psychology*, 70/6, 1256–1269.

Taylor, M. (1988). *The Terrorist.* London: Brassey's.

Taylor, M. and Quayle, E. (1994). *Terrorist Lives.* London: Brassey's.

Verma, S. (2008). 'Terrorists 'cured' with cash, cars, and counseling: controversial Saudi rehab program aims to reform jihadists returning from U.S. prisons.' *The Globe and Mail*, September 11, http://www.theglobeandmail.com/news/world/article708655.ece.

Willems, P. (2004). 'Judge Hamoud al-Hitar praised: the Dialogue Committee is known internationally.' *Yemen Times*, December 16–19, http://yementimes.com/article.shtml?i=799&p=community&a=2.

Worchel, S. and Brehm, J. (1970). 'Effect of threats to attitudinal freedom as a function of agreement.' *Journal of Personality and Social Psychology*, 14, 18–22.

6

A TIME TO THINK, A TIME TO TALK

Irish Republican prisoners in the Northern Irish peace process

John F. Morrison

Introduction

The mid 1970s and early 1980s in Northern Ireland are rightly remembered as being among the most violent years of the Troubles. Perhaps paradoxically, this chapter will argue that this period should also be considered as the beginning of the Republican Movement's gradual advance towards the acceptance of peaceful politics. At the dawn of the Troubles, in the early 1970s, the Irish Republican Movement, most notably the newly established Provisional IRA, was experiencing an influx of new young recruits. Many of this young membership, as well as those who joined in the late 1960s, would go on to play a significant role in shaping the course of Irish Republicanism. It was under their leadership that the Provisional IRA took part in a sustained and brutal terrorist campaign during the Troubles. However, it is also under this leadership that the majority of the Irish Republican Movement eventually accepted the necessity for peaceful politics in the place of armed force. This politicisation was only made possible by an extended process of internal debate at both leadership and rank and file levels. One of the most prominent forums for this strategic debate was within the Republican prison populations.

The purpose of this chapter is to look at the role prison – as a forum – played in the gradual acceptance of peaceful politics by the majority of those within the Irish Republican Movement. It will assess the central role which the debates within the prisons played in the gradual dismantling of the traditional abstentionist policy,[1] and the eventual cessation of sustained paramilitary violence. The main concentration within the chapter is on the lead-up to the 1986 split within Provisional Republicanism. This saw the formation of dissident groupings Republican Sinn Fein (RSF) and the Continuity IRA (CIRA). This is a split which ostensibly took place after the dropping of the abstentionist policy to Dail Eireann. It is the process in the lead-up to this split which laid the foundations for the ultimate, gradual, politicisation of the majority of the Republican Movement. By understanding this process one can begin to understand how the Provisional Irish Republican Movement ultimately ended their prolonged terrorist campaign.

Gradual politicisation

One of the key elements of the successful politicisation was how the leadership gradually brought this about while retaining the armed strategy throughout. This 'armalite and ballot box' strategy succeeded in appeasing a number of potential detractors and resultantly weakened the position of the dissidents. The gradualism allowed the leadership to ease their membership into the organisational transition from a terrorist movement into the democratically political organisation they are today. The retention of the core membership throughout was vital to the success of the politicisation process, and therefore the constant engagement with and appreciation of the expectations of the base was essential to the successful implementation of change. A key element of this base was, and for many still is, the prison population.

This chapter is predominantly based on the analysis of the perceptions of leading and rank and file members of Irish Republicanism, both those who spent time within prison and those who did not. This includes the views of individuals who stayed with Sinn Fein and the Provisional IRA as well as those who left to form or join a dissident grouping. Similarly it also analyses the perspectives of some members who left organised Irish Republicanism completely. By utilising these viewpoints one can see how they wish for this role to be portrayed, and the importance they place on the prisons in the overall history of Irish Republicanism. This should not be considered as anything near a comprehensive commentary on the politicisation of Irish Republicanism, or on penology during the Troubles. Its aim is merely to introduce the reader to the centrality of the prisons in the process which eventually led to peaceful politics. Neither should it be regarded in any way as a justification for the ongoing terrorist activity of the Provisional IRA during this period. The work presented in this chapter originated from my doctoral dissertation which analysed splits in Irish Republicanism between 1969 and 1997 (Morrison, 2010). The quotations utilised, unless otherwise stated, derive from interviews carried out by the author during this doctoral research. These interviews took place between 2007 and 2010.

Throughout the 1970s a large proportion of Provisional Republicans were either imprisoned or interned. The paramilitary prison populations ranged from national and local leadership figures down to ordinary rank and file members, to those with no organisational affiliation at all and the wrongfully imprisoned. Within the prisons the Republican inmates organised as they would on the outside in an organisational command structure. At this time, especially from the mid-1970s onwards, leadership figures within the prisons such as Gerry Adams were openly questioning the direction the movement was taking, and the long-term strategies of the national leadership. This can be seen as the origins of the process which led to his ultimate takeover of the national leadership with his mainly northern affiliates. The external context of a weakening Republican Movement meant that the Republican community was more receptive to critical questioning of the long-term strategy. Within this context prisoners were being asked to think not just militarily but also politically. They were advised to educate themselves on other revolutionary struggles, as well as the Irish one, and see how this could be applied to the situation in Northern Ireland. There was encouragement to look beyond a purely armed campaign and to develop their political thinking. Critical to this, and in stark contrast to the Goulding leadership of the 1960s,[2] was that the prison leadership was not calling for a complete move away from the armed struggle but that a continued armed campaign would be complemented by a strengthened political strategy. This important differentiation allowed this discussion to be more inclusive and did not isolate as many as the political discussions of the 1960s. Joe Doherty, a Provisional IRA prisoner at the time recalls the role which Adams played within the prison, and the discussions which he led:

> I remember Gerry Adams in the jail. We were all sitting there and he says 'you know the armed struggle is only a means to the end, not the end. Youse (sic) are politicians.' And people said 'we're not really, we're army'. 'No you have to develop your consciousness in here . . . Politics is important and the armed struggle is only a means to an end, and not the end.' So everything I think we see now with Sinn Fein today, I think Adams and them people actually foreseen that. They probably knew that the armed struggle was outmoded, but you couldn't do it because you would have been overthrown, the army would have turned against them.

These discussions led to the gradual acceptance of the utility of the introduction of a political element to the Republican struggle among the prison population. The prisons provided the time and the space for the Republicans to actively discuss, argue and think about how this could add to or detract from the armed struggle. It provided the perfect platform for those in favour of a more political struggle to introduce to and convince others of the necessity of this political element while simultaneously questioning the present tactics of the movement. Mitchell McLaughlin a leading Sinn Fein figure outlines this viewpoint:

> So I think out of the perhaps initial very violent background, and then people through internment and imprisonment, actually having the time. Because when you were in prison you were removed from that day-to-day almost kind of survival, or conflict. They began to reflect on these arguments, began to examine whether the current kind of structures of republicanism was fit for purpose.

An inevitable consequence of these discussions about the importance of a political element was the debate surrounding electoral politics. As in the lead up to the 1969/70 split which saw the formation of the Provisional IRA, there was an innate scepticism about Republican participation in electoral politics and the potential consequences of members taking their seat upon election. However, within the confines of the prison environment the pros and cons of Republican involvement were able to be discussed. There were those within the prisons who were strong advocates of electoral involvement and they utilised their time inside to discuss and open others up to the possibility. The debate was one which continued both within the prisons and externally within the Republican community through the 1970s, 80s and 90s and even into the twenty-first century. The gradual and continuous process of the discussions went on to shape the strategic path taken by the movement.

These discussions over the long-term strategy taking place within the prisons had an obvious influence on those who were present and taking part in the process. However, they also had an external influence on the wider Republican community. Within Republican circles throughout the 1970s and 1980s the Republican prison population was held in high regard. Their opinions and actions were listened to and appreciated. While many externally would not have been privy to the breadth of the internal discussions taking place, there was a strategic utilisation by the prisoners of the Republican publications to outline their critical analysis of the 'Republican struggle.' The most prominent example of this is the series of articles believed to be penned by Gerry Adams but published under the pen name 'Brownie' which appeared in the northern Republican newspaper *Republican News* between August 1975 and February 1977. While detailing his experiences of prison life the articles also provided a vehicle for 'Brownie' to be critical of national leadership while also putting forward the recommendation of placing a stronger emphasis on the political element of the struggle. These articles proved significantly influential within the Republican population as they introduced the wider community to the debates and discussions which were taking place within the prisons at the time. 'Brownie' was one of the methods utilised to gradually introduce this debate into the wider Republican population (e.g. Brownie, 1975).

Those who stayed with the Provisionals after the 1986 split look to these political debates within the prisons as a positive and necessary step in the process of modern-day Irish Republicanism. However, those who exited to form the Continuity IRA and Republican Sinn Fein regard this in a negative manner. They deem it as the start of the downfall of the 'true' Irish Republicanism. The influence of these debates, both within and outside the prisons, are seen by them as moving the focus away from the armed campaign and towards a corrupt and illegitimate political process. An obvious divide was forming between the northern and the southern leadership and within the prison the northern influence is blamed for the ultimate acceptance of Dail Eireann. The blame is laid at their door for not fully understanding the significance of dropping the abstentionist policy to the Dail. In their eyes this was an 'illegitimate' prospect, one that could not be supported in the eyes of those who eventually moved away from the Provisionals in 1986.

> I have a suspicion that that [the discussion to drop abstentionism to the Dail] originated probably in Long Kesh camp in the 1970s and again it is people

looking for a shortcut to an all-Ireland Republic and I have a suspicion that it was . . . Well inevitably it was in Long Kesh, it was mostly Northern people. I do feel that unfortunately within the north there is this kind of foolish attitude towards the twenty-six county state.[3]

The obvious influence of these prison debates came with the impact the prisoners had after their release. Many of the leaders of the discussions within the prisons acquired prominent positions within the national and local leadership of the IRA and Sinn Fein. There were great expectations that leaders such as Gerry Adams who, while introducing the political element to the campaign, would also lead the Provisionals in a sustained armed resistance against the British presence in Northern Ireland.

I think in Adams people had a great expectation of him. I think in many ways Adams was trying to influence the debate out there with the Brownie columns and influence Seamus Twomey, who was Chief of Staff of the IRA.[4]

Within their leadership roles they extended the discussions which had taken place and introduced the issues to the wider population. They did this through internal local discussions but also through public speeches and addresses.

I remember at Bodenstown, maybe about 1978 or thereabouts, or in some keynote interview or speech, it might not have been Bodenstown, saying that there could be no military victory for any side, that the problem in the north was a political problem and it needed a political solution. That caused all sorts of controversy in a certain generation of Republican leaders, and for me it was just so obvious.[5]

Even though this process did eventually result in a split within the movement it was a minimal division of the organisation. The actions and preparation taken by the Adams/[Martin] McGuinness leadership throughout the process significantly contributed to minimising the effect of the split. The gradual introduction of a critical voice to the debate on Republican strategy was one of the most significant factors at play. The similarities between the intentions the Goulding leadership and the achievements of the Adams/McGuinness leadership are unmistakable. Goulding wished to fully politicise the movement and bring it away from the armed campaign, but failed. However, it was the Adams/McGuinness leadership who gradually achieved this with the Provisionals. The critical difference between the two situations is that the Goulding leadership attempted to change too much too soon. In contrast, the Provisional leadership of the late 70s and early 80s gradually introduced the idea of a strengthened political arm to the movement while stating that they wished to maintain the armed struggle. This showed a connection between the dissenting voices and the membership and wider Republican population. However, in order to successfully make these changes the young leadership first had to get themselves into positions of power within the movement, without gaining too many internal enemies in the process. Similar to the politicisation process, prison provided a forum both to question the current leadership, and to put forward the argument for the necessity for change in the national leadership. Again this was a gradual process, one which many of those who later joined the Continuity IRA and/or Republican Sinn Fein in '86 once again trace back to the mid-1970s, and particularly the ceasefire of 1974/75.

1974/75 ceasefires

The cessation referred to was initiated in December 1974 after a meeting between leading Republicans and Protestant clergymen[6] in Feakle, Co. Clare. In the aftermath of the Feakle talks, discussions continued between the Provisionals and intermediaries about the possibility of a December ceasefire. The Provisionals announced a ten-day cessation on December 20th 1974. This was extended to last until January 17th, while the Provisionals negotiated with Northern Ireland Office (NIO) officials. However, the Republicans brought it to an end as their demands had not been met. The end of the ceasefire was marked by continued bombings and attacks in both England and Northern Ireland. The following month, on February 9th, the Provisionals announced an indefinite ceasefire and again entered into negotiations with the British. Key to their demands was the construction of a plan for British withdrawal from Northern Ireland. These talks and ceasefire eventually came to a close with no development on the Provisionals' demands (Bew and Gillespie, 1999; Bowyer Bell, 1989). The ceasefire officially ended in November 1975. However, during the period of the ceasefire there was growing unrest within the Provisional movement about the handling of the talks by the leadership. A number of members broke the ceasefire, oftentimes claiming their actions under names other than the Provisional IRA. This discontent was evident not only within the communities but also among the Republican prisoners and internees. The talks were led on the Republican side by Ruairi O'Bradaigh and Daithi O'Conail who are characterised by many as principal members of the old southern leadership of the time, both of whom would ultimately lead members in the newly formed Republican Sinn Fein and Continuity IRA in 1986. These negotiations have been much maligned by the Provisionals as having a detrimental effect on the movement. However, O'Bradaigh defends his and the leadership's position of entering into and continuing with the negotiations:

> The invitation was from the British government to 'discuss structures of British disengagement from Ireland.' Now how could one refuse that? Except that they were being deceitful, but how could one refuse that?

His position is that the Republican negotiators were led to believe that there was a possibility of achieving British withdrawal from Northern Ireland. However, there was a failure to agree on the proposed timeline, and that the British would not publicly announce their intention for withdrawal. The ceasefire and the protracted negotiations have been criticised both during and in the years after their existence. In both instances criticisms have principally, but not exclusively, come from the newly emerging northern leadership of the time. The accusation is that the lengthy nature of the combined cessation and talks, which resulted in no real benefits for Republicanism, led to a sense of disillusionment among the membership and supporters. There was a growing belief that the Provisional leadership of the time had effectively run its course. They no longer knew how to move the Republican movement forward and it was therefore time for a new leadership to take over.

> I think it [1975 ceasefire] had a big effect. If you like the then, and I stress then, young leadership would have seen that period as a time where the old days, it was totally out-manoeuvred by the British in terms of how they were dealing with them, what was on offer and the reality of it. After that had run its phase, it was time to move on.[7]

The viewpoint expressed is that the leadership of the time were politically naïve and consequently unable to pragmatically deal with the British. They had brought the movement as far as they possibly could, and therefore it was time for a change, both in personnel and policy.

> In terms of the ceasefire, this is without being overly critical, I think the leadership was military as opposed to political. That doesn't mean you can't be military and political or that you can't have military thoughts when you are political, but really I think it was politically naive. I mean the Brits were saying things like they were going to leave, but they weren't. They were saying that there was an economic argument that it was inevitable to leave. But all of that was frankly a bit of bullshit to try and prolong the ceasefire and make it harder for them to go back to armed struggle, to all of those things.[8]

Throughout the negotiations there were critical voices coming out especially from the prisons about the way the national leadership was handling the situation and questioning the benefits which the talks and ceasefire had for the Republican cause. The criticisms were chiefly coming from leading northern Republicans, such as Gerry Adams and Ivor Bell. These individuals had a significant influence on the prison population, as well as on Republicans external to the prison.

> People who were in jail, like Adams and Ivor Bell and other people who were querying what was going on and their influence would have been felt amongst the prison population, some of whom were coming out of jail and also in late August 1975 Adams started to write for *Republican News* . . . So there was a big lot disillusioned about what was going on in '75. And also it had been felt that the IRA had lost its way.[9]

The longer the negotiations went on without any significant benefits for the Republican cause the more demoralising it became for the membership. The newly emerging leadership used this demoralisation as an opportunity to begin their gradual takeover of the movement both politically and militarily.

> To be quite critical, I think that there wasn't a particularly strong view of British objectives at the time, and the ceasefire then created tensions. I suppose then at that point you have a new . . . the other side of the ceasefire in late 1975/76 you begin to see a new leadership emerge, a leadership that has brought the movement right along to where we are today.[10]

The members of this new leadership, which gradually came into position in the late 1970s and early 1980s, look upon this as an essential transition which was carried out for the good of Republicanism. While not arguing with the point that it was these negotiations which laid the foundations necessary for the new leadership to take over, a number of interviewees during my research were still critical of the move to acquire power. They specify that individuals within this newly emerging leadership were using the situation for their own personal and selfish benefits. It was not necessarily the case that they were opposed to the actions of the O'Bradaigh leadership at the time. However, they saw this as an opportunity to utilise the disillusionment within Republicanism not only to acquire positions of power but to also isolate certain leadership members.

> I think it was probably called for the best reasons, but I think it was used by certain individuals within the Provisional Movement to enhance their status.[11]

Those Republicans who exited in 1986 believe that the criticism of the 1975 leadership was mainly utilised in the years subsequent to the events as opposed to at the time. Some of these emerging leaders were already in positions of power at the time of the ceasefire and negotiations, yet failed to speak out against them at the time. However, in later years they utilised the situation to critically assess the old leadership. They wished to frame this as a failed leadership, one which had significantly damaged the Republican cause. They believe that there was not necessarily a purely negative sentiment among the rank and file at the time. Many saw the benefits of the extended ceasefire as it allowed for those on the run to return home and for the PIRA to re-organise where necessary.

> There seemed to be developments only in terms of entering into truces, we didn't see these truces in the way Adams and [Martin] McGuinness would later, you also have to bear in mind McGuinness was seen by us as a key leader and he wasn't making his opposition to the truce known then in the way that he would later.[12]

The poor handling of the 1975 ceasefire and negotiations became a prominent aspect in the subsequent years of the negative portrayal of the 'old southern' leadership by their new northern counterparts. It was utilised to illustrate how they were out of touch and were unable to move Republicanism forward. However, it most notably provided the catalyst for a more focused discussion to take place about the utility of a more dominant political strategy to work alongside the armed campaign.

Beyond '86

As the years and decades after show, the leadership only introduced significant changes when they believed that they had the support of the majority of members. As with the lead up to 1986, a key element of this support was that of the prison population. In 1994 major inroads were made in a burgeoning peace process. In February of that year Gerry Adams was granted a forty-eight hour visa to the United States by President Bill Clinton, a gesture which showed America's expectation that Adams would be able to deliver a move for the Republican Movement away from armed struggle. Similarly, the Irish government removed the broadcasting ban on Sinn Fein members. These actions can be regarded as a show of faith in the possibility of the Sinn Fein leadership bringing about a cessation of violence. From early to mid-1994 the possibility of such a ceasefire was being discussed at leadership levels within the Provisional Movement. The topic was first broached in discussions about the possibility for a short exploratory cessation. While talks had collapsed between Republicans and the British, they continued between Republicans and the SDLP and the Irish government, and therefore shifted from targeting British withdrawal to the establishment of a pan-nationalist front. These talks developed a blueprint for future Republican strategies and actions. However, what the Republican leadership was telling their membership was different to what they were telling the other negotiators. While negotiations were often times fraught, eventually on August 31st 1994 the Army Council of the Provisional IRA announced a four-month ceasefire, which was later extended. This announcement was in the acceptance of a fourteen-point proposal issued by Irish Taoiseach Albert Reynolds. This cessation was greeted with celebrations across the whole island of Ireland as well as in Great Britain.

In order to ensure organisational support for the cessation the leadership had been preparing all levels of membership and support for a significant period prior to the actual declaration. This was highlighted both in the external Republican community and within the Republican prison communities. The leadership met with their communities to discuss the potential for a cessation and to gauge the levels of support or resistance within these communities to the proposals, and the entire politicisation process. They were also preparing members for what they could realistically expect from the process and how this would benefit the entire process seeking to achieve their ultimate and immediate goals.

That's what was good about coming up to the ceasefire. I think Adams and the people went out into all the Sinn Fein Cumanns. And in the prison [Martin] McGuinness and Gerry Kelly was almost in there every other week, the British allowed them to come in. Everybody went into the canteen, McGuinness was there asking questions and taking questions preparing everybody for 'you know the reality is we're going to enter negotiations, we might not get a united Ireland. Be realistic, look at the bigger picture.'[13]

It was this persistent preparation and engagement with all levels of membership which allowed the leadership to gauge the sentiment within the movement and as a result they were aware when the timing for change, in this case a cessation of IRA violence, was right. This preparation prior to each change, not just the 1994 ceasefire, allowed them to gauge the levels of support and the potential for splits within the movement. Therefore, they were able to pursue their desired course at the most opportune time when their leadership was not being challenged and also when the opposition to the proposed change was at its weakest point. The more control the leadership had over the context in which the changes were implemented, the more potential they had for success. However, the leadership does not always have control of the external context in which the change is being made. Therefore, the most opportune time for change is when external events have as minimal impact on the internal changes as possible.

Clearly you didn't bring all people with you. But one of the accomplishments of the leadership of both Oglaigh na hEireann and Sinn Fein is that they brought by far the majority of their members with them into the process, through the process and out the other side of the process. I don't think it was humanly possible to avoid some of the disaffections.[14]

Conclusion

From the origins of Irish Republicanism right up to today the role and authority of the Republican prisoners has been both influential and respected by the external membership. They have at times played a significant role in altering the course of the 'struggle' while also shifting the external perception of the movement. The most cited and analysed example of this is clearly that of Bobby Sands and his fellow hunger strikers in 1981. However, this issue has been covered by a number of authors, and does not require any further analysis (e.g. O'Rawe, 2005; Beresford, 1987). What the present chapter has aimed to do is to show that even beyond the high-profile hunger strikes that the role of the Republican prisoners played a significant role in the evolution and politicisation of the movement. It has aimed to give readers an understanding of how Irish Republicans, both mainstream and dissident, perceive the role which the prisons and prisoners played. The time spent incarcerated provided the inmates with an opportunity to assess the future of the Republican Movement, and their position within it. It allowed them the opportunity, either intentionally or unintentionally, to influence the future of the movement and for them to, at times, manoeuvre their way to the top. In essence it provided them with a time to think, a time to talk.

Notes

1 This refers to the traditional Irish Republican policy whereby any Sinn Fein member elected to Dail Eireann, Stormont or Westminster would abstain from taking their seats on strategic and policy grounds as by their very nature these three houses were seen to promote the partition of Ireland.
2 Cathal Goulding was Chief of Staff of the IRA at the time of the 1969/70 split which saw the birth of the Provisional IRA. In the lead up to the split, Goulding and his supporters proposed to fully politicise the Republican Movement by dropping the traditional abstentionist policies to Dail Eireann, Stormont and Westminster and completely moving away from the utilisation of force to achieve their aims.
3 Sean O'Bradaigh.
4 Anthony McIntyre.
5 Gerry Adams.
6 Members of this group were in contact with the Northern Ireland Office (NIO).
7 Pat Doherty.
8 Gerry Kelly.
9 Danny Morrison.
10 Tom Hartley.
11 Anonymous current member of the 32 County Sovereignty Movement and former member of the Provisional IRA.
12 Anthony McIntyre.
13 Joe Doherty.
14 Mitchell McLaughlin.

References

Beresford, D. (1987). *Ten Men Dead: Story of the 1981 Hunger Strike*. London: Grafton.
Bew, P. and Gillespie, G. (1999). *Northern Ireland: A Chronology of the Troubles, 1968–99* (revised 2nd edition). Dublin: Gill & Macmillan Ltd.
Bowyer Bell, J. (1989). *The Secret Army: The IRA* (revised 3rd edition). Dublin: Poolbeg.
Brownie (October 18 1975). 'Active abstentionism.' *The Republican News*. p.6.
Morrison, J.F. (2010). *The Affirmation of Behan? An Understanding of the Politicisation Process of the Provisional Irish Republican Movement Through an Organisational Analysis of Splits from 1969 to 1997*. Phd dissertation submitted to the School of International Relations, University of St. Andrews, Scotland.
O'Rawe, R. (2005). *Blanketmen*. Dublin: New Island.

PART III

Critical issues in management, risk assessment and reform

7

THE HEALTHY IDENTITY INTERVENTION

The UK's development of a psychologically informed intervention to address extremist offending

Christopher Dean

> I kept thinking: this isn't who I am, it's not who I want to be. I could no longer agree with what they thought and what they did.
>
> *(Van de Valk & Wagenaar, 2010 p.57)*

Introduction

How we intervene to prevent people from committing terrorist or extremist acts continues to be an enduring and significant issue. Whilst the primary focus on 'intervention' in the consciousness of governments, media, academia and the public is often on military, police or government activity, far less focus has been on the role of specific programmes to 'rehabilitate' extremist offenders or to prevent those who may be vulnerable to such offending. This is often referred to as 'soft intervention' or part of the 'battle for hearts and minds'. It is argued that understanding and addressing the ideas, motives and emotions that mobilise such activity is equally important as other forms of intervention to address this issue. However, our knowledge and understanding about how we can effectively work with individuals to divert them from supporting or committing such acts is still in its relative infancy. Programmes of this nature are small in number, operating in a just a handful of jurisdictions, inevitably embedded in the cultures and societies in which they are developed and delivered, and limited information is typically known about the structure, rationale or approaches underlying them.

This chapter outlines a psychologically informed intervention that has been developed centrally by the National Offender Management Service (NOMS) part of Her Majesty's Ministry of Justice. It describes its development, its broad approaches and goals, its methods, content and principles of delivery. Interventions based on psychological and sociological principles and evidence have received less coverage in the literature and some of the key concepts and principles are highlighted to broaden awareness and understanding. Our experiences to date suggest that those individuals who've turned their backs on being involved in extremist activity and offending appear to have done so because it no longer fulfils their expectations, priorities or values in life. Perhaps most importantly, involvement no longer seems to reflect the type of person they want to be and therefore it becomes something they no longer want to identify with. The role of identity is considered central in understanding why many individuals become involved in extremist activity but also why they may choose to leave such involvement behind. Exploring and working with identity issues explicitly underlies the focus and approach of this intervention. This chapter also seeks to highlight the emerging significance of working with identity issues through interventions in this field to bring about meaningful change.

Context

In 2008 a small team comprising psychologists, a probation officer and a Muslim chaplain were brought together at Interventions Unit within NOMS. Interventions Unit is a group which over a couple of decades has developed proven expertise and international recognition for developing robust intervention programmes to address offending behaviour across the whole spectrum of offending (from sexual offending to offending resulting from substance misuse). The key remit of this group was to develop appropriate ways of trying to prevent extremist offending through the delivery of specific interventions. Whilst delivering this work with convicted extremist offenders would be the key focus for this work, preventing such offending being committed by other offenders who may be on a pathway to engaging in such activity would also be an issue.

It became quickly apparent to us that there were no off-the-shelf interventions that we could simply adopt into our service or simply refine for this purpose. Internationally, interventions to address this type of offending – especially at an individual level – are in their early stages of development. There was no simple model, theory or rationale on which to base interventions to address what is a very complex issue. Whilst interventions being developed in other countries can inform interventions in the UK, contextual differences need to be considered carefully (e.g. El Said, 2012). Given this, we adopted some key principles early on to steer our work based on early learning and experience:

1   In some other jurisdictions (e.g. Singapore, Saudi Arabia) there was an emphasis on taking a holistic approach in addressing this issue through addressing psychological, social and religious issues when appropriate to do so. This seemed sensible and flexible and contributed to the multi-disciplinary composition of our team.
2   We needed to ensure that any interventions were culturally and organisationally sensitive and we needed to be cautious about assuming that approaches taken in other jurisdictions (or services) would easily translate.

3   We believed that building on the principles underlying effective intervention with other offenders would provide a good foundation, but we would need to test whether these applied to this group and be prepared to accommodate differences that emerged.

4   We needed to keep an open mind and not be driven by assumptions or knowledge about other offenders when there may be specific differences with this group (e.g. taking care not to pathologise such offending).

When we embarked on this work we engaged in an extensive process of reviewing the literature (not just in the field of extremism but from other fields and drawing on our expertise in addressing other forms of offending behaviour). We also engaged with international partners about ongoing work in this area and emerging learning. We engaged over a significant period of time in one-to-one interviews and/or casework with extremist offenders whose affiliation was with various groups or causes (e.g. the far-right, Al Qaeda and Animal Liberation). Over time this work has informed the compilation of both manualised interventions and assessment. These include the Healthy Identity Intervention (as described here), the Al Furqhan course (which specifically focuses on challenging justifications for violence based on Islamic scripture) and The Extremism Risk Guidelines (ERG22+) (see HM Government, 2011 a, b). All of these were then piloted in a number of prisons and community regions in England. These were evaluated, revised and refined for delivery across the service. To date, nearly a third of convicted extremist offenders have engaged in one or more of these interventions and many more have had ERG assessments completed on them. The experience of those delivering these interventions continues to feed into the ongoing evolution of this work. We recognise this work is still in its relative infancy and are acutely aware of cultural differences which may limit the generalisability of learning and approaches across jurisdictions. More detail about our learning and experiences from delivering these interventions and casework is outlined in other articles and papers (see Lloyd & Dean, 2012; Lloyd, 2012; Dean, 2012; HM Government, 2012 a, b).

It is important to emphasise that these interventions are just part of a much wider strategy – which includes many other approaches, processes and policies – that collectively assist in addressing this form of offending. Our experience suggests that broader contextual circumstances (e.g. healthy relationships, feeling safe, opportunities to walk away from groups or causes) are equally if not more important than specific targeted interventions in this endeavour.

The development of the intervention

What works

The Healthy Identity Intervention has been designed and developed based on a range of different sources, theories, models and data. These include the evidence-base for effective interventions with other offender groups (the 'What Works' literature); the small literature on effective intervention with extremist offenders; direct casework with extremist offenders; the Extremism Risk Guidelines (and its associated evidence base); cross-agency governmental reports and data; the desistance literature (including why individuals disengage from extremist offending); the broader literature on extremist offending; and numerous research and theoretical models from the psychological and sociological literature.

It is based on established approaches to address offending behaviour as well as those which are more innovative and seem to have particular value with this group of offenders. There is now an expansive literature – much of which is based on empirical research – which has helped to develop our understanding of what makes interventions effective in addressing many forms of offending behaviour i.e. the 'What Works' literature. This focuses on how intervention content, context, delivery and management can all impact on effectiveness. This evidence is increasingly being used by governments to commission interventions on the basis of effectiveness and value for money. The value of this evidence in informing interventions to address extremist offending has also been recognised in the literature (Mullen, 2010). It is not in the scope of this chapter to outline in detail the various principles and features associated with effective correctional intervention but these can be found elsewhere (Andrews & Bonta, 2006; Andrews & Dowden, 2005; Dowden & Andrews, 2004; Lipsey & Cullen, 2007).

A key principle from this literature is that effective interventions are usually those which target the factors or circumstances that directly contribute to offending occurring (often labelled as criminogenic factors). This may seem common sense, but history suggests this is not a principle that has been routinely employed. In developing our interventions we wanted to be confident we knew what factors were important to target (i.e. those that contribute to extremist offending) to ensure effectiveness. Over time we identified a number of factors that did seem significant within and across individual cases which provided targets for intervention. However, not all these factors and circumstances necessarily applied to each individual and therefore developing an appropriate assessment framework was essential.

It is unusual for any group of offenders to be the same and extremist offenders appear to be no different. Similarly, the motivations, circumstances and reasons for why individuals commit the same types of offence are often varied and complex. In the early days of this work there was an assumption that most of these offences would be committed to bring about political or social change or to fight for a moral cause. However, over time this was recognised as clearly not the case. Some offenders appear to become engaged in such activity because of more conventional criminal motives (e.g. to make money, for the excitement or simply for the gratification of committing violence) and for others to fulfil more intrinsic or existential needs and desires, e.g. the need for status, belonging or meaning. A consequence of not using rigorous assessment is that assumptions are made about motivations and therefore any subsequent plans to provide appropriate intervention or manage risk become spurious. For some extremist offenders more conventional intervention programmes seem appropriate (e.g. to address violence generally or anti-social attitudes), for others minimal or no targeted programmes may be required, whereas some may require the type and level of intervention outlined here.

The importance of assessment

The Extremism Risk Guidelines (ERG22+) were developed to help assess each individual, and the personal and contextual circumstances which contributed to their offending and/or are likely to contribute to such offending in the future. A detailed account of the development and content of these guidelines is outlined elsewhere but an overview is helpful in understanding the intervention approaches adopted (Lloyd & Dean, 2012). These guidelines adopt a case formulation approach, a method of analysing the specific individual and contextual circumstances in an individual's life that appear to have a functional link to their offending. It is particularly appropriate for idiosyncratic offending where we can be less certain about its causes or functions. This method is well established in forensic and clinical settings where it is commonly used in the assessment of problematic clinical behaviours and presentations (Hart & Logan, 2011). Using this approach to assess extremist offenders is recommended in the literature (Roberts & Horgan, 2008; Dernevik et al., 2009; Gudjonsson, 2009). Structured Professional Judgement is employed in which the assessor uses their discretion to consider how certain factors may impact on risk issues and how these risks (or personal needs) may need to be addressed through interventions or risk management strategies. A framework is provided to help make these judgements systematic, considered and transparent. Assessors consider three dimensions: (1) engagement, (2) intent and (3) capability.

Engagement refers to the circumstances or factors which may motivate an individual to engage with an extremist group, cause or ideology and also to offend. This dimension captures the emotional aspect of both involvement and offending. Intent refers to the circumstances or factors which may enable the individual to be willing or prepared to offend on behalf of the group, cause or ideology. This allows us to examine the reasons why individuals may or may not be prepared to offend rather than simply being engaged with the group or cause. Finally, capability refers to the circumstances which may enable someone to actually commit a particular offence of concern. Collectively these dimensions help build a picture of an individual, including circumstances which may prevent or protect them from engaging in such offending.

Twenty-two factors have been identified which seem to contribute to extremist offending and these typically map on to the three dimensions of engagement, intent and capability. Assessors are asked to consider these to ensure they do not neglect specific circumstances which may contribute significantly to offending. This assessment is dynamic in that it can measure the impact of changes in people's lives on their level of engagement, intent or capability (including the impact of intervention on these areas). The intervention incorporates these guidelines in a number of ways. 1) Interventions have been designed around addressing these specific factors. 2) The assessment is completed on participants to identify the specific factors and circumstances which need to be targeted by the intervention. 3) An Intervention Plan is completed to identify how intervention can target areas of concern. 4) The intervention is flexible so that sessions are completed on those areas which are most relevant for each participant.

Integrated approaches

The intervention incorporates three broad approaches drawn from current models of offender rehabilitation. The first is the Risk-Need-Responsivity Model which underlies many offending behaviour programmes (Andrews & Bonta, 2006; Bonta & Andrews, 2007). This model is based on three key principles related to risk, need and responsivity that have been associated with effective intervention (Hanson et al., 2009). In essence these principles state that the intensity and duration of the intervention needs to match the risk and need level of the offender and that intervention should target those who are most risky and needy. Intervention should target areas of risk which directly contribute to an individual's offending which are changeable (e.g. criminogenic needs). Intervention needs to be responsive to individual circumstances, including how the intervention is actually delivered, e.g. motivational, intellectual, demographic differences. Intervention should draw on a general personality and cognitive social learning perspective of human behaviour to enable change. In accordance with this model, the interventions try to address those factors and circumstances that are believed to cause individuals to commit extremist offences. The assumption here is that by changing or removing these factors through intervention, individuals will be less likely to offend.

The second approach focuses on facilitating those circumstances which are believed to make people desist. The assumption here is that if we know what circumstances make people choose not to offend, we can try to facilitate these processes through intervention to prevent offending. This approach is consistent with the 'desistance' literature that has evolved over recent years (Lebel et al., 2008; Maruna, 2001, 2004; Maruna & Roy, 2007; Sampson & Laub, 1993, 1995). The focus here is on understanding why individuals come to points in their lives when they decide that they no longer want to offend or be part of lifestyles which contribute to such offending. What are the circumstances and reasons why people 'move on' and how do they sustain this commitment without turning back to offending? Such circumstances include disillusionment about their current position in life or the presence of other priorities or relationships which encourage them to become an 'ex' offender (Maruna, 2001). There is also a small but growing litera-ture around why extremist offenders may choose to desist. This has particularly focused on why such individuals choose to disengage from an extremist group, cause or ideology and through this process come to desist (Bjorgo, 2009; Horgan, 2009; Jacobsen; 2010). Many of the circumstances which appear to contribute to these processes overlap with those in the wider desistance literature supporting this approach.

The third approach draws on the Good Lives Model of offender rehabilitation (Day et al., 2010; Ward & Stewart, 2003; Ward et al., 2007). This approach has been used for explaining why offending occurs, as well as for understanding why offenders may desist. A key concept in this model is the idea that offending is not an 'abnormal' process. Offenders seek to satisfy the same needs or goods as non-offenders but it is how they go about achieving these which can often lead to problematic, harmful and destructive behaviours. Therefore the aim of intervention is to empower, equip and support offenders in satisfying these needs without having to harm others or offend in the process. This is particularly significant to extremist offenders because many of the processes which seem to contribute to engagement and offending do not appear 'abnormal' but rather are processes which many people may experience at times in their lives, e.g. becoming over-identified, accepting values and beliefs without question, wanting to be politically active. Similarly, there are a number of needs or goods which extremist offenders appear to engage with an extremist group, cause or ideology to satisfy, which are also shared by non-offenders, e.g. the need for excitement, status/significance and belonging. Whereas other people may seek these needs through opportunities in contexts that do not lead to harm (e.g. vocations, clubs, hobby groups) this is not the case for extremist offenders. Other aspects of this approach which make it particularly relevant includes its 'holistic' focus and its appreciation for the role that personal identity, values and agency can play in rehabilitation.

All of these approaches have well-documented strengths and weaknesses (Serrin & Lloyd, 2011). They have all been incorporated to try and ensure the interventions are effective, to utilise all of their strengths and to offset their weaknesses. All have specific resonance for intervening with extremist offenders. It is important for interventions to recognise and address factors and circumstances which contribute to offending and desistance (Porporino, 2010). In addition, interventions also need to try and facilitate intrapersonal circumstances which may moderate the transition between offending and desistance, e.g. a sense of hope and agency, changes to identity and changes to personal beliefs and expectations (Porporino, 2010; Serrin & Lloyd, 2011).

In summary, these approaches are integrated in the intervention which seeks to:

1 Address factors and circumstances which make people engage with an extremist group, cause or ideology.
2 Address factors and circumstances which make people prepared and willing to offend on behalf of an extremist group, cause or ideology.
3 Facilitate circumstances which promote disengagement.
4 Facilitate circumstances which promote desistance.

Identity as a unifying construct

The construct of identity is central to the intervention. Many of the factors associated with why people seem to commit these offences are related directly or indirectly to identity issues. Some people engage with a group or cause because they lack a sense of personal purpose, meaning or worth; some because they have a desire to see themselves as superior or special; whereas others may come to 'over-identify' with the group, cause or ideology or develop 'us and them' thinking because of whose side they choose to identify with. Identity issues seem to underlie those factors typically associated with why people engage and are motivated to offend, as well as those which typically enable people to offend. It can also help to explain the emotional drive behind such actions given the role identity appears to play in people's own sense of purpose, security and worth (Vignoles et al., 2006). Similarly, various models and theories which seek to explain the processes through which individuals come to commit extremist offences (radicalisation models) are grounded in or include consideration of identity issues (Arena & Arrigo, 2004; Liht & Savage, 2008; Schwartz et al., 2009). Even at the level of government policy, 'identity issues' or 'threats to identity' have been recognised as central to why people commit extremist offences (HM Government, Home Office, 2011). In addition, the desistance literature focuses on how changes to identity (or personal narratives or stories) and the development of alternative identities may be crucial to why people desist (Maruna, 2001). Addressing identity issues is also consistent with other approaches to rehabilitation outlined previously.

Identity connects the internal worlds of people with the social worlds they live in. In this sense a focus on identity can ensure intervention remains holistic. It focuses on how changes to the person, their relationships, employment and social lives etc. may all be important in bringing about change. Changes in these wider aspects of people's lives – for example, changing life priorities, conflicts in personal beliefs, values or commitments and changing relationships with family members or peers (Bjorgo, 2009; Jacobsen, 2010; Sampson and Laub, 1993) – have also been associated with desistance generally and disengagement more specifically. Changes to personal lives often impact on our social worlds and vice versa. Focusing on identity can try to ensure interventions focus on individuals in their social context, which is particularly relevant to extremist offending. It helps facilitators and participants to understand why developing certain relationships in their lives can have an impact on who they are as people and why this may be important to prevent them from offending.

The notion of identity is also beneficial to effective intervention in other ways. There are existing theories, models, research and knowledge about identity issues which can be drawn on to develop intervention approaches (Kroger, 2007). Whilst this is a broad area and fragmented between disciplines and areas of practice, addressing identity issues has been the focus of interventions to address other social or psychological problems, especially in adolescence (Kroger, 2007). This focus can also make the work inherently motivational and engaging. Identity is literally at the heart of who and what we are. It motivates existential needs and drives (e.g. for purpose, belonging, security) which influence our daily actions (Vignoles et al., 2006). Intervention can therefore focus on what really matters to individuals rather than just tinker with more peripheral issues in their lives. It prevents offenders from being seen by others (and seeing themselves) as just a 'bag of risks', which has been a criticism of interventions more widely (Ward et al., 2007). It ensures that intervention recognises desistance and disengagement as processes that involve changes in how someone perceives and approaches various aspects of their life, rather than just a narrow focus on one or two risk factors (Serrin & Lloyd, 2011). Finally, this focus supports a sense of 'hope' and new beginnings which feature so strongly in why certain individuals believe they have been able to move away from offending (Maruna, 2004).

Purpose and outcomes

As with all offending behaviour interventions, the ultimate purpose is to prevent individuals from committing future offences. The intervention tries to achieve this through 1) ending or reducing an individual's engagement with a specific extremist group, cause or ideology that promotes offending (especially those aspects that contribute to harm) and 2) reducing an individual's readiness to offend on behalf of an extremist group, cause or ideology. The notion of *engagement* is particularly helpful for understanding this type of offending (Horgan, 2005) and *disengagement* for understanding why individuals may no longer offend (Jacobsen, 2010; Horgan, 2009). Our experience suggests that considering the process of *identification* is as important in understanding offending and how best to intervene. When people begin to define themselves by their engagement with a group, cause or ideology this appears to carry an additional significance. It has been argued that extremists rarely engage with a group or cause because of an ideology but this 'hardens' as identification increases and acts as 'the cement' of the shared extremist identity (Van de Valk & Wagenaar, 2010).

To engage does not always mean to identify. Our experiences suggest that some individuals may associate themselves with a group, cause or even ideology but not choose to identify – or define themselves – with it, for example, where engagement provides opportunities for criminal activity or where people become associated simply because of friendship but remain ignorant to the motives and ideas of a group or cause. The nature of someone's engagement (or identification) seems to have implications for which interventions are likely to be appropriate and effective and this is incorporated into our interventions. Similarly, equally helpful concepts from our observations are the processes of *de-identification* – where people choose to change or end their identification or affinity with a group, cause or ideology – and *dis-identification* where people come to define themselves in opposition to a group, cause or ideology which they once identified themselves with (Ashforth, 2001).

These concepts enrich some of our understanding of what we are trying to achieve through intervention. Trying to encourage someone to reconsider an identity that may fulfil such strong needs in them is an incredibly difficult task. One of the most salient realisations from this work is recognising that when people are heavily identified, it is unlikely they will give this up unless opportunities are present to develop or strengthen new aspects to their identity that can also meet these needs and enable them to 'get on' in the communities and environments they find themselves in. Prisons may provide limited opportunities to develop more positive identities (and giving up an extremist identity can carry significant challenges) (Liebling & Straub, 2012) but our experience suggests such steps are still possible. There is a fine balance between enabling extremist offenders to find and create opportunities to give them incentive and hope in dis-identifying with extremist groups etc., whilst also restricting opportunities to maintain security and control.

As McCauley and Segal (1989) point out, extremist offenders are typically either becoming engaged, remaining engaged or in the process of dis-engaging. Recognising the procedural and dynamic nature of this relationship is helpful and is consistent with broader understandings of desistance (Serrin & Lloyd, 2011). Disengagement, like desistance, is not necessarily a linear or sequential process; in many ways this may be 'a process that involves reversal of decisions, indecision, compromise and lapses' (Burnett 2004, p.169). We have found that disengagement often seems to involve individuals taking small steps at different points in their sentence and sometimes reverting back to old commitments and behaviours even when progress is gradually being made. The extent to which someone may need to disengage may also reflect the extent to which they were engaged in the first place. If engagement was or is only peripheral, intensive interventions may not always be necessary or appropriate. This similarly applies to desired outcomes whereby individual progress needs to be measured against their current level of identification or engagement: e.g. for those who are heavily identified, the process of simply engaging in these interventions and coming to question their continued identification may represent considerable progress, but this may not be the case for those who have already arrived at this stage. We recognise that interventions can have different roles for different individuals. For some, intervention can bring about significant change and steps to disengage, for others it can consolidate and reinforce decisions and opinions already made, and for others it can provide a space for all parties to understand their offending and current position more clearly. In all these cases those delivering need to be considerate and responsive to the circumstances of each individual participant.

Goals

The central aims of the intervention – to promote disengagement and reduce an individual's willingness to offend on behalf of an extremist group, cause or ideology (i.e. desistance) – have been translated into five specific intervention goals (outlined below). These goals have emerged from our understanding of why people engage and offend as well as our understanding of why people disengage and desist. The modules and sessions of the interventions work towards meeting one or more of these goals. Clearly, all these goals may not be relevant or appropriate for each participant. Issues such as whether the interventions are being used on those convicted or not for extremist offences, the individual's role and nature of engagement and their current level of disengagement are important to consider.

1 Fulfilling needs legitimately – This goal is about helping individuals meet their personal needs and desires without having to be involved with an extremist group, cause or ideology. Many individuals seem to become engaged and are motivated to offend because these actions enable them to fulfil strong personal needs or desires such as personal status or significance, belonging or meaning, excitement or adventure. Ways in which interventions facilitate this goal include helping individuals identify opportunities to develop alternative commitments to meet their needs, by questioning how adequately their involvement really meets their needs and exploring any dissatisfaction or disillusionment with their involvement.

2 Reducing offence-supportive attitudes, beliefs and thinking – This goal is about challenging and addressing attitudes or beliefs that enable individuals to support or commit direct harm against other groups of people. Many offenders seem to have been able to commit these types of offence when they have adopted attitudes and beliefs which justify such offending and demonise and dehumanise other groups of people. Ways in which interventions facilitate this goal include exposing inconsistencies or inaccuracies in these beliefs, reducing identification with a group or cause (which can begin to weaken the bonds of ideology) and by making it more difficult for them to see other groups in simplistic ways through diluting 'us and them' stereotypes and recognising the complexity of other people's values and commitments and commonalities between groups (i.e. raising integrative complexity; Liht & Savage, 2008; Suedfeld & Tetlock, 1977).

3 Increasing emotional tolerance and acceptance – This goal is about helping participants to express, tolerate and cope with powerful emotions in alternative ways to denigrating or harming others. Many offenders seem to have become engaged and offend because they are motivated by strong and sometimes overwhelming emotions (e.g. threat, humiliation, powerlessness) often triggered by perceptions of how events impact on those things they strongly identify with and care about. Ways in which interventions can facilitate this goal include making individuals more aware of how their emotions are associated with their values and beliefs, helping them to tolerate emotions more effectively and 'let go' of these, and making changes in their life to make circumstances which impact on the things they identify with feel less personal.

4 Increasing personal agency – This goal is about empowering participants to take more responsibility for who they are, how they live their lives and the personal commitments they make. Many offenders seem to offend because they go through a process of unquestioningly adopting a shared identity which supports extremist offending and can sideline the influence of their personal identity or agency over their behaviour. Ways in which interventions facilitate this goal include educating individuals about how and why people can adopt the values and beliefs of others without question, reconnecting them with their personal identity rather than just being defined by the extremist group, cause or ideology and supporting them in taking steps to form new commitments to reflect who they want to be in order to meet their needs (including helping them to manage intimidation and pressure from others to prevent them from disengaging).

5 Expressing values and pursuing goals legitimately – This goal is about encouraging participants to use alternative ways to realise their goals or express their commitments without needing to offend or harm others. Many individuals seem to commit these offences because they were not able to express their values through legal means or because they felt personally entitled and justified to offend because their cause is greater than the rule of law. Ways in which interventions facilitate this goal include challenging individuals about their sense of entitlement to offend for a specific cause (or on behalf of a group of people), exploring whether such behaviour is counter-productive to their cause and through examining the consequences of such behaviour on other people.

The Healthy Identity Intervention(s)

The Healthy Identity Intervention seeks to address both the reasons why people are motivated to engage and offend and also those attitudes, beliefs and perceptions that enable them to offend. At their simplest level, they provide an opportunity for participants to take stock and reflect on who they are, who they want to be and how they want to live their lives in the future. They encourage participants to reflect on and re-examine the commitments they have made in their lives, especially those associated with their engagement or identification with an extremist group, cause or ideology. They invite participants to consider whether these continue to reflect the type of person they want to be and enable them to 'get on' in life in as they wish to. They challenge them to explore any doubts or disillusionment they may have about their involvement in order to facilitate disengagement. They help participants understand both the reasons for their engagement and/or offending and to develop strategies which may prevent these circumstances from resulting in future offending. They help them to explore how they can achieve what they got from their engagement and/or offending but in alternative ways and through different commitments, e.g. relationships, interests, employment and values. They challenge participants' sense of entitlement to offend for personal (political) reasons and help them find alternative ways of expressing their values without having to offend. They also challenge their attitudes, beliefs and perceptions of other 'out groups', which can make harming others more difficult in the future. Ultimately, the interventions encourage participants to 'move on' in their lives, to embrace new commitments and feel empowered to walk away.

Method of delivery

The intervention is delivered on a one-to-one basis (or two facilitators to one participant). Some participants have openly verbalised their relief about this method of delivery. The individual format has a number of obvious benefits over a group format, the most important of which is helping participants to get in touch with their own personal values and beliefs rather than being overly influenced by those of their associates.

The relationship between the facilitator/s and the participant is viewed as crucial to facilitating change and disengagement. Facilitators acknowledge that identity issues are not unique to offenders and this common ground can help address issues of stigmatisation. Differences and commonalities between facilitators and participants (especially along identity lines such as religion or race) can also be explored to challenge beliefs where such differences have been used to justify violence previously.

The intervention is intended to be experienced as a collaborative process in which participants engage because they see this as being in their own interests, rather than just as an act of compliance or a means to an end. Interventions are flexible in that facilitators can decide which sessions they want to complete for each individual. The sessions selected are those which are assessed as being most relevant and responsive to target the risks, needs and circumstances of each participant. The interventions target the areas that matter most for each individual and the goals will be different for each participant. Facilitators are given a significant degree of discretion over how they use sessions to help participants progress. Helping participants work towards achieving the overall goals of the interventions is seen as more important than following sessions in a prescriptive manner.

Interventions which use a variety of methods have been found to be more effective (Pearson et al., 2002) and the Healthy Identity Intervention also uses a range of different methods. Some methods try to challenge and change ways of thinking as well as encouraging individuals to behave in different ways to those which have or could contribute to offending. Interventions which seek to change patterns of thinking and behaviours associated with offending (cognitive-behavioural approaches) have been found to be more effective than other approaches (e.g. Landenberger & Lipsey, 2005; Wilson et al., 2005). Most of the methods used here are also used in other offending behaviour interventions, e.g. pro-social modelling, cognitive restructuring, or using motivational approaches. These are widely cited in the 'What Works' literature as being effective in bringing about changes in offending behaviour (Andrews & Bonta, 2006). Some, however, are more specific and distinct but also play a central role, e.g. identity development work, psycho-social education and opportunity creation. The Healthy Identity Intervention therefore uses a balance of tried and tested approaches alongside more innovative ones. Given the emphasis of these interventions on facilitating a process (i.e. disengagement), they do not focus as much on equipping individuals with new skills as other offending behaviour programmes typically do. Where such skills are deemed necessary to reduce risk, other interventions may be necessary.

Content

The Healthy Identity Intervention is divided into two separate interventions, Healthy Identity Intervention: Foundation (HIIF) and Healthy Identity Intervention: Plus (HIIP). Whilst the two interventions are delivered in their own right, they are best considered as two components of one intervention given their overlap in aims, goals, approaches and outcomes. They have been defined as separate interventions for a number of reasons, primarily to target the amount of intensity of intervention appropriately. Sessions can be used flexibly across the two interventions if required.

The interventions are intended to help direct further intervention work, opportunities or actions which may help participants to progress, e.g. helping participants appreciate why strengthening certain relationships, gaining further knowledge, insight or skills or focusing on different priorities in their life could be in their interests. They are not intended to be delivered in a vacuum from the social worlds in which they live. They actively encourage and support participants in engaging with their social worlds in different and fresh ways to more effectively enable them to 'move on'. They are not ideologically based or intended to re-educate participants in a particular set of beliefs. They do, however, allow for exploration and challenge of beliefs, ideas and attitudes, particularly those which directly contribute to offending behaviour. Addressing and challenging inaccurate, unhelpful or distorted beliefs and attitudes is just one aspect of the interventions.

The HIIF is typically used as a low-intensity intervention for those individuals who have engaged opportunistically or superficially (and do not particularly identify) with an extremist group, cause or ideology. The HIIF can also prepare individuals to engage effectively in more intensive intervention work (i.e. the HIIP). It can be used to identify further intervention work and opportunities to progress and to develop plans for their future. Sessions are informally divided into three modules, (1) engagement and insight, (2) mindfulness and (3) moving on.

> Engagement and insight sessions focus on the participants' needs and values, helps them explore what is important in their lives, what motivates them and how they can work towards these goals without having to offend in the future. They encourage participants to recognise discrepancies between their offending (and or engagement with an extremist group, cause or ideology) and their needs, values and beliefs. This can motivate participants to reconsider their past and/or current engagement with an extremist group etc. Sessions encourage participants to develop different strategies, opportunities and means through which they can work towards these goals which may lead them away from future offending.

Mindfulness sessions help participants to manage and tolerate specific thoughts or feelings which may impair their daily lives, their ability to engage fully in intervention work and/or their ability to relate to staff. These sessions encourage participants to use strategies which can help them to manage challenging feelings, including feelings of injustice, threat and grievance.

Moving on sessions help participants consider how they can move forward with their lives in a way that fits with their values, beliefs and needs. They also look at concrete ways in which they can make progress including skills they can develop, opportunities they can make and take, relationships they can form or strengthen and any additional intervention work they may need.

The HIIP is a medium- to high-intensity intervention for individuals who clearly identify (or have identified) with an extremist group, cause or ideology. It focuses directly on encouraging participants to disengage from an extremist group, cause or ideology and increasing their inhibitions about harming others on behalf of this group. It provides a space through which opportunities can be identified and developed outside sessions to allow participants to build new commitments (or re-strengthen old commitments) to help move them away from commitments associated with offending, e.g. taking steps to re-build family relationships. Sessions are divided into seven modules.

Foundation sessions allow the participant–facilitator relationship to develop and familiarise the participant with the nature and style of the intervention. Participants begin to explore how they have come to be the person they are today (their identity), why they became or have become interested and engaged with an extremist group, cause or ideology and, when relevant, to explore the reasons why they offended.

Personal identity sessions allow participants space to explore and re-examine specific commitments they have made in their lives (or are in the process of making) and how beneficial these really are in helping them get on with their lives. They allow participants to think about the best ways of making commitments which will allow them to get what they want from life without having to offend.

Group involvement sessions encourage participants to explore the nature of their relationship to the group (or shared identity). In particular, participants are encouraged to consider their dissatisfaction with being engaged and/or the costs this may have on their lives. It challenges commitments that have caused problems in their lives as well as those which support offending and also encourages participants to develop fresh commitments which may support disengagement.

Self-image sessions help participants explore how they can make changes in their life to maintain a desired self-image/identity without needing to be engaged with an extremist group, cause or ideology or needing to offend.

Group conflict sessions help participants to understand and develop strategies for dealing with feelings such as threat which are associated with taking sides and ultimately engaging in conflict. They challenge 'us and them' thinking and thinking which demonises and dehumanises other groups of people and try to reduce such perceptions and thinking.

Seeking change sessions challenge participants to reconsider and question the legitimacy of offending to achieve and express their own ideological or political goals and values. They help participants explore how they can achieve these goals or express these values through legitimate activity.

Concluding sessions encourage participants to reflect on the learning and progress they have made, consolidate the strategies they will take to move forward with their lives and support their sense of 'moving on'.

Delivery

In line with principles of effective intervention, standards have been established about who is qualified to complete this work, the training required, and ongoing support and supervision needed, etc. The interventions are delivered by psychologists or experienced probation staff. They are typically familiar and experienced in delivering intervention work, confident and competent with having discretion over how sessions are run, but are also able to follow a loose structure. The staff are also therapeutically orientated, psychologically-minded and openly reflective about their practice. All facilitators attend a structured training course. Support and supervision is provided when required to try and ensure the interventions are delivered as intended and staff are supported (i.e. to preserve intervention integrity). Manuals have been produced to provide some structure and guidance to how the interventions are delivered (e.g. style of delivery, how to handle specific issues that may surface, how to approach participants, etc).

Conclusions

The Healthy Identity Intervention(s) provide a systematic, evidence-based framework through which psychological and social issues associated with extremist offending can be addressed. To date, the impact of this work has been largely positive although inevitably this has varied depending on those delivering the work, where it has been delivered and the circumstances of each participant. As with other programmes to address offending behaviour, knowledge can only evolve gradually to answer which interventions work effectively with whom, when, where and why.

Whilst this intervention is focused on broadly psychological and social issues, it has also been found to support, contextualise and reinforce intervention work specifically focused on addressing those who use Islamic scripture to justify offending for their cause. Many themes and issues considered in both interventions overlap such as religious identity, group conflict, us and them thinking, demonisation and dehumanisation of others, etc. The relationship between religiously informed interventions and those which are psychologically informed is an interesting one worthy of continued analysis.

The association of identity issues with extremist offending and with disengagement and desistance and effective intervention approaches provides a central concept around which interventions can address those psycho-social issues which can contribute to such offending. This knowledge and understanding may in time also have value in informing operational policies and organisational activities that help to support individual disengagement or may help with broader initiatives to counter-terrorism.

References

Andrews, D. A. & Bonta, J. (2006). *The Psychology of Criminal Conduct* (4th edition). Newark, NJ: LexisNexis.

Andrews, D. A., & Dowden, C. (2005). 'Managing correctional treatment for reduced recidivism: A meta-analytic review of program integrity.' *Legal and Criminological Psychology*, 10, 173–187.

Arena, M. P., & Arrigo, B. A. (2004). 'Identity and the terrorist threat: An interpretative and explanatory model.' *International Criminal Justice Review*, 14, 124–163.

Ashforth, B. E. (2001). *Role Transitions in Organisational life: An Identity-Based Perspective.* Hillsdale, NJ: Lawrence Erlbaum.

Bjorgo, T. (2009). 'Processes of disengagement from violent groups and the extreme right.' In J. Horgan & T. Bjorgo (Eds.) *Leaving Terrorism Behind: Individual and Collective Disengagement.* Oxon: Routledge.

Bonta, J. and Andrews, D. (2007). *Risk-Need-Responsivity Model for Offender Assessment and Rehabilitation* (User Report 2007-06). Ottawa, ON: Public Safety Canada.

Burnett, R. (2004) 'To re-offend or not to re-offend? The ambivalence of convicted property offenders,' In S. Maruna & R. Immarigeon (Eds) *After Crime and Punishment: Pathways to Offender Reintegration.* Cullompton: Willan Publishing.

Day, A., Casey, S,. Ward, T., Howells, K. & Vess, J. (2010). *Transitions to Better Lives: Offender Readiness and Rehabilitation.* Cullompton: Willan Publishing.

Dean, C. (2012). 'Intervening effectively with terrorist offenders,' *Prison Service Journal*, 203, 31–37.

Dernevik, M., Beck, A., Grann, M., Hogue, T. & McGuire, J. (2009). 'The use of psychiatric and psychological evidence in the assessment of terrorist offenders.' *Journal of Forensic Psychology and Psychiatry*, 20(4), 508–515.

Dowden, C., & Andrews, D. A. (2004). 'The importance of staff practices in delivering effective correctional treatment: A meta-analysis of core correctional practices.' *International Journal of Offender Therapy and Comparative Criminology*, 48, 203–214.

El Said, H. (2012). *De-radicalising Islamists: Programmes and their Impact in Muslim Majority States.* International Centre for the Studyof Radicalisation (ICSR). London: Kings College.

Gudjonsson, H. (2009). 'The assessment of terrorist offenders: A commentary on the Dernevik et al article and suggestions for future directions.' *Journal of Forensic Psychology and Psychiatry*, 20(4), 516–519.

Hanson, K. R., Bourgon, G., Helmus, L., & Hodgson, S. (2009). 'The principles of effective correctional treatment apply to sexual offenders: A meta-analysis.' *Criminal Justice & Behaviour*, 36(9), 865–891.

Hart, S. & Logan, C. (2011). 'Formulation of violence risk using evidence-based assessments: the structured professional judgment approach.' In P. Sturmey and M. McMurran (Eds.). *Forensic Case Formulation.* Chichester, UK: Wiley-Blackwell.

HM Government, Home Office (2011). *Prevent Strategy.* London: Home Office Publications.

HM Government – National Offender Management Service (2011a). *Extremism Risk Guidelines: ERG 22+ Structured Professional Guidelines for Assessing Risk of Extremist Offending.* London: Ministry of Justice Publications.

HM Government – National Offender Management Service (2011b). *Healthy Identity Intervention: Delivery & Facilitator Manuals.* London: Ministry of Justice Publications.

HM Government – National Offender Management Service (2012a). *Extremism Intervention Pilot: An Evaluation.* London: Ministry of Justice Publications.

HM Government – National Offender Management Service (2012b). *Extremism: A Digest of Learning.* London: Ministry of Justice Publications.

Horgan, J. (2005). *The Psychology of Terrorism.* Oxon: Routledge.

Horgan, J. (2009). *Walking Away from Terrorism.* Oxon: Routledge.

Jacobsen, M. (2010). Terrorist Drop-outs: learning from those who have left. *Policy Focus,* 101. Washington Institute for Near East Policy.

Kroger, J. (2007). *Identity Development: Adolescence through Adulthood.* Thousand Oaks, CA: Sage.

Landenberger, N. A. & Lipsey, M. W. (2005). 'The positive effects of cognitive-behavioral programs for offenders: A meta-analysis of factors associated with effective treatment.' *Journal of Experimental Criminology,* 1, 451–476.

Lebel, T.P., Burnett, R., Maruna, S., & Bushaway, S. (2008). 'The "Chicken & Egg" of subjective and social factors in desistance from crime.' *European Journal of Criminology,* 5(2), 131–159.

Liebling, A. & Straub, C. (2012). 'Identity challenges and the risks of radicalisation in high security custody.' *Prison Service Journal,* 203, 15–23.

Liht, J. & Savage, J. (2008). 'Identifying young Muslims susceptible to violent radicalisation: Psychological theory and recommendations.' In Mary Sharpe (Ed.), *Suicide Bombers: The Psychological, Religious and Other Imperatives. NATO Science for Peace and Security Series: E: Human and Societal Dynamics,* pp.5–25. Amsterdam, Netherlands: IOS Press.

Lipsey, M. W. & Cullen, F. T. (2007). 'The effectiveness of correctional rehabilitation: A review of systematic reviews.' *Annual Review of Law and Social Science,* 3, 271–296.

Lloyd, M. (2012). 'Learning from casework & the literature.' *Prison Service Journal,* 203, 23–31.

Lloyd, M. & Dean, C. (2012). 'The development of structured guidelines for assessing risk in extremist offenders.' Submitted for publication.

Maruna, S. (2001) *Making Good: How Ex-Convicts Reform and Rebuild Their Lives.* Washington: American Psychological Association.

Maruna, S. (2004). 'Desistance from crime and explanatory style: A new direction in the psychology of reform.' *Journal of Contemporary Criminal Justice,* 20, 184–200.

Maruna, S., & Roy, K. (2007). 'Amputation or reconstruction? Notes on the concept of "knifing off" and desistance from crime.' *Journal of Contemporary Criminal Justice,* 23(1), 104–124.

McCauley, C. R. and Segal, M. (1989). '*Terrorist Individuals and Terrorist Groups: The Normal Psychology of Extreme Behaviour.*' In J. Groebel and J. H. Goldstein (Eds) *Terrorism,* p.45. Seville: Publicaciones de la Universidad de Sevilla.

Mullen, S. (2010). 'Rehabilitation of Islamist terrorists: Lessons from criminology.' *Dynamics of Asymmetric Conflict,* 3(3), 162–193.

Pearson, F. S., Lipton, D. S., Cleland, C. M., & Yee, D. S. (2002). 'The effects of behavioural/cognitive-behavioral programs on recidivism.' *Crime and Delinquency,* 48(3), 476–496.

Porporino, F. (2010). 'Bringing *sense* and sensitivity to corrections: From programmes to "fix" offenders to services to support desistance.' In J. Brayford, F. Cowe & J. Deering (Eds.). *What Else Works? Creative Work With Offenders,* p.61–85. Collumpton: Willan Publishing.

Roberts, K. & Horgan, J. (2008). 'Risk Assessment and the Terrorist.' *Perspectives on Terrorism,* 2(6), 3–9.

Sampson, R. & Laub, J. (1993). *Crime in the Making: Pathways and Turning Points Through Life.* Cambridge, MA: Harvard University Press.

Sampson, R. J. & Laub, J. H. (1995). 'Understanding variability in lives through time: Contributions of life-course criminology.' *Studies on Crime and Crime Prevention,* 4, 143–158.

Schwartz, S. J., Dunkel, C. S. & Waterman, A. S. (2009). 'Terrorism: An identity theory perspective.' *Studies in Conflict & Terrorism*, 32, 537–559.

Serrin, R. C. &, Lloyd, C. D. (2011). 'Examining the process of offender change: The transition to crime desistance.' *Psychology, Crime and Law*, 15(4), 347–364.

Suedfeld, P. & Tetlock, P. (1977). 'Integrative complexity of international communications in international crises.' *The Journal of Conflict Resolution*, 21(1) 169–184.

Van de Valk, I. & Wagenaar, W. (2010). 'The extreme right: Entry and exit.' *Racism and Extremism Monitor*. Anne Frank House.

Vignoles, V., Regalia, C., Manzi, C., Golledge, J. and Scabini, E. (2006). 'Beyond self-esteem: Influence of multiple motives on identity construction.' *Journal of Personality and Social Psychology*, 90, 2, pp.308–333.

Ward, T., Mann, R. E. & Gannon, T. A. (2007). ,Good lives model of offender rehabilitation: Clinical implications.' *Aggression and Violent Behavior*, 12(1), 87–107.

Ward, T. & Stewart, C. (2003) 'Criminogenic needs and human needs: A theoretical model.' *Psychology, Crime and Law*, 9, 125–43.

Wilson, D. B., Bouffard, L. A., & MacKenzie, D. L. (2005). 'A quantitative review of structured, group-oriented, cognitive-behavioral programs for offenders.' *Journal of Criminal Justice and Behavior*, 32, 172–204.

8

RISK ASSESSMENT OF TERRORIST AND EXTREMIST PRISONERS

Andrew Silke

Our understanding of the risk assessment of terrorist and extremist prisoners is in its infancy, yet this is clearly a critical issue. History provides us with many examples of prisoners who have emerged from jail more hard-line and more dangerous than when they entered. The most wanted terrorist on the planet at the time of writing, Ayman al-Zawahiri, the current leader of Al Qaeda, is a former extremist prisoner. He was arrested and imprisoned in Egypt in the early 1980s because he had links with the assassins of the Egyptian President Anwar Al Sadat. While incarcerated he was brutally tortured. Zawahiri was already a radical before he entered prison, but when he emerged he had become even more committed to the cause and considerably more dangerous and powerful. His prison experience served only to harden his zeal; he became a leader among his fellow prisoners and emerged as a prominent spokesman for the cause. Upon release he assumed the overall leadership of Egyptian Islamic Jihad, committing that movement to a campaign of extreme violence, and ultimately merging the organisation with Al Qaeda in the 1990s. Prison did not reform Ayman al-Zawahiri, it did not rehabilitate him and it certainly failed to de-radicalise him. It only succeeded in making him more dangerous.

In considering risk assessment of terrorists and extremists in prison settings there are a range of essential issues to consider. To start with, not all terrorist and extremist prisoners are the same. Terrorists are surprisingly heterogeneous and they defy simple categorisation into one type or profile. This applies as much to entire terrorist movements as it does to individuals, and there are a potentially bewildering array of terrorist groups to deal with (e.g. Ganor, 2008; Marsden and Schmid, 2011). Big categories such as Religious, Revolutionary, Anarchist and Nationalist/ Separatist can be further split and divided into ultimately potentially hundreds if not thousands of sub-categories. Naturally there is considerable variation between these different types of movements on important factors, not least around the movement's structure and membership, but also crucially around the level and nature of the violence the groups are prepared to encourage and engage in. As a result, each movement needs to be considered in its own political, social and aspirational context – the individual members who are the focus of the risk assessment are not divorced from this.

Even if one is comfortable with the particular type of movement being dealt with, there then follows the formidable challenge of the specific context of the individual. At its most basic level, any effort to deal with the risk assessment of terrorists needs to be robust enough to confront the tricky question of how would one potentially have assessed Osama Bin Laden, but also, similarly, how it would have played out with Nelson Mandela, and what would have been the result at different points in both men's lives? It is a mistake to assume that the individual's motivation will overlap 100 per cent with the stated rationale of the movement they are associated with. The motivation of young men and women to join the US military, for example, is rarely because they are immersed in the intricacies of US foreign policy and are 100 per cent in agreement with the government's aims and plans. Other factors – more immediately personal factors – tend to play a much more important role in explaining why they join. Similarly, for terrorists, joining a movement is often more about small-scale personal and social issues rather than the all-encompassing result of fully embracing a political or religious ideology.

Bearing this potential disconnect between *knowing the movement* and *knowing the individual,* a further important issue is to recognise that there are different types of roles around terrorist activity and this too results in very different types of terrorist prisoners.

Figure 8.1 outlines the broad categories of who is of concern when we think of terrorism and extremism within prison contexts. Four broad groupings exist, and as the figure illustrates, we should not expect that the factors which apply clearly to one group will also apply equally strongly to the others. There will certainly be

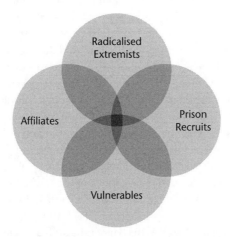

FIGURE 8.1 The different populations of concern for terrorist risk assessment in prison

overlap in places, but there will also be differences, and this means that effective risk assessment processes will need to be nuanced.

In considering the different groupings, the first and most obvious are those prisoners who entered prison already holding extremist views and who had engaged in extremist actions in the outside world. We can refer to these as the 'True Believers'. Even here, however, there is significant variety between the different types of activity the prisoners may have been involved with. Some will have carried out – or have planned to carry out – extremely serious acts of violence. Others will have engaged in different types of activity which, while not directly violent themselves, were unmistakably intended to help or encourage others to commit violence. Thus the group will include killers, bombers, would-be suicide terrorists, and so forth, as well as ideologues, recruiters, fund-raisers and on-line propagandists. A few with longer careers may have engaged in a whole gamut of activity ranging from the relatively mild to the incredibly dangerous. Individuals who were very violent in their teens and twenties, in later decades may pose no serious risk of direct violence themselves, but could perhaps have moved into important iconic, ideologue and leadership roles. Thus the focus of the risk assessment inevitably will vary not only across different individuals but also across the lifespan of the same individual.

The second group of concern are prisoners who have been convicted of involvement in extremism or terrorism, but where there are good reasons to suggest that they were not actually radicalised when they did so. It is often assumed that radicalisation is an absolute necessity before you can have terrorist behaviour, but this is not the case. Such prisoners may have been unaware of the seriousness of what they were involved in, or possibly they were coerced into playing a role. They may for example have been friends or family members of 'True Believers', but overall they will generally tend to have been individuals at the periphery of plots and activism. Nevertheless, within the prison system they tend to be treated as full-blown 'terrorists'.

Within the prison world, a third important group are 'ordinary decent' prisoners who have been radicalised *within* prison, possibly as a result of contact with extremist prisoners. These converts to the cause are distinctive because their prior behaviour outside had no political involvement whatsoever, and thus risk assessment processes with some of these prisoners may be unaware that extremism is even an issue. The spread of radicalisation among such individuals has been a recurring obsession with prison authorities, for understandable reasons, and high profile cases such as the Spaniard José Emilio Suárez Trashorras, the British 'shoe bomber' Richard Reid, and the American José Padilla, convicted of trying to assemble a radiological bomb, stand as a clear warning about the potential danger posed to the outside world by these types of prisoners (Silke, 2011a). That said, the scale of such recruitment has rarely matched the often fevered expectations of the outside world (a point made with telling precision by Mark Hamm through the title of his book on the subject: *The Spectacular Few*).

The final group can be classed as the 'vulnerables'. These again will be 'ordinary decent' prisoners who, while at the moment may not have radicalised, may nevertheless still be assessed as vulnerable to joining the 'Spectacular Few' in the right circumstances. Assessment here may resolve around issues of whom to allow such prisoners to affiliate and co-habit with as well as considering potential programmes to inoculate resistance to radicalisation.

Thus any system for risk assessment and management needs to recognise that it will potentially have to deal with very different groups of extremists and potential extremists. Some of the differences between these prisoners will be very subtle, and others much more obvious. As a consequence, some issues which are absolutely critical for one type of prisoner may be far less important for others.

An example from my own experience can illustrate this. My very first visit to a prison was in the early 1990s to Cork prison in Ireland. This was a medium-sized facility intended for medium- and low-risk offenders. In one prisoner's cell, however, the walls were covered with Irish Republican paraphernalia and slogans supporting the IRA. Within Ireland, IRA and other militant Republican prisoners are all normally held in the country's high-security prison at Portlaoise, where the Irish military provide additional security. Why, I asked staff, was this prisoner in Cork? Shouldn't he be at Portlaoise? 'Ah', they responded. 'He's not the real thing. He's a wannabe.'

It was clear that the staff did not regard this prisoner as a serious threat. His explicit sympathy for the terrorist group and his collection of group-related paraphernalia – which in other contexts would act as major warning signs of radicalisation – were essentially dismissed here as trivial. The staff understood that it was highly unlikely that the IRA would be interested in recruiting him – the default position of the IRA in the 1990s was to view 'ordinary prisoners' as scumbags, and they never showed interest in radicalising or recruiting them. While the prisoner may have liked to have been linked with the IRA, this would not have been reciprocated by the movement. Overall, the staff's understanding both of the prisoner's background and the nature of the terrorist group, meant that they had no serious worries that this prisoner should be treated as a terrorist or extremist. If the staff, however, had been less familiar with the terrorist group or had lacked experience of dealing with 'real' terrorists and extremists, then the reaction would almost certainly have been both very different and unnecessary.

Recidivism in terrorist cases

Terrorist prisoners have very low reconviction rates. Bakker (2006) found that of 242 jihadi terrorists in Europe, 58 had a previous criminal record (24 per cent). In only 6 cases, however, was this prior record for terrorism-related offences (2.5 per cent). Sageman (2004) found a similar picture, albeit with a slightly smaller sample of jihadi terrorists (172 individuals), where again roughly one-quarter had a prior criminal record, though these were all for ordinary crime rather than politically motivated crime.

Overall, probably less than five per cent of all released terrorist prisoners will be re-convicted for involvement in terrorist-related activity. For some groups the figure is potentially even lower. In England and Wales from 11 September 2001 to 31 March 2008, there were 196 convictions for terrorist-related offences, most of which were connected to Al Qaeda-related extremism. Many of these individuals received relatively short prison sentences and by early 2009, nearly 100 had already been released back into society. These prisoners were released before the UK had introduced programmes in prison aimed at de-radicalising terrorist prisoners, but to date none have been re-arrested or convicted for subsequent involvement in terrorist activity. There is no evidence that any have attempted to engage in terrorist activity overseas. One has been convicted for another crime – tax fraud – though this was recognised as being purely for personal gain and not to benefit a cause.

In Northern Ireland, as part of the Good Friday Peace Agreement in 1998, 453 paramilitary prisoners were released. By 2011, just 23 of these prisoners had been recalled to custody (5 per cent). Of these 23, just 10 were recalled for alleged involvement in further terrorist offending (2.2 per cent) with the remainder being recalled for purely criminal activity.

If this is what can occur in the absence of a de-radicalisation programme, we should not be too surprised then when countries who do run such programmes are able to announce re-offending rates which also appear remarkably low. For example, the Saudis for a number of years claimed a 100 per cent success rate with their programmes though that allegedly perfect result has not borne up to closer scrutiny. The official position has moved to a more realistic alleged reoffending rate of just under 3 per cent – though as Marissa Porges highlights in this volume, some estimates give a higher re-offending level. Other chapters in this volume rightly raise doubts about how accurate these and other spectacularly successful claims are, but there is still a general acceptance that the overall reconviction rate for all released terrorist prisoners is low.

The experience of imprisonment normally changes terrorist prisoners. There are many individual case studies cases to support this (e.g. O'Doherty, 1993), but stronger evidence also comes from more systematic research such as Crawford (1999) who interviewed 70 former paramilitary prisoners in Northern Ireland (as well as a small number of non-paramilitary prisoners). He found that all of the prisoners reported that imprisonment increased their level of political awareness (e.g. 'we hadn't a clue about republicanism'). What is particularly interesting is that Crawford also found that this increasing political awareness led most prisoners (70 per cent) to eventually believe that a political settlement to the conflict was the only logical solution (rather than continued violence).

Ferguson has found a similar picture with Republican prisoners. Most of the prisoners remained highly sympathetic to the cause but either no longer believed that violence was the most effective way to achieve the movement's aims and/or were no longer willing to break the law themselves on behalf of the movement. As one Muslim prisoner I interviewed in a UK jail put it, 'the cause is a moral cause', while adding that he no longer believed that violence was the best way to achieve it.

What are the appropriate issues to focus on?

Several writers have attempted to identify issues which are worth focusing on in terms of assessing risk in cases of terrorism (e.g. Rehabilitation Services Group, 2011; Cole, Alison, Cole and Alison, 2012; Kebbell and Porter, 2012; Monahan, 2012; Pressman and Flockton, 2012a). For those who have produced more detailed models, the number of specific variables typically ranges anywhere between 17 and 31, but Figure 8.2 provides an overview of the general clusters around which most variables usually form.

Ideology

Ideology plays a significant role in facilitating political violence though it is probably a mistake to view it as the most important factor. Recruits to terrorist movements often have a simplistic understanding of the ideology the movement's leadership endorses. Indeed, for some, a deeper ideological understanding only comes after time spent in prison with other members which allows them time for detailed debate and discussion. In assessing risk, key issues to consider are whether the individual's behaviour or attitudes endorse a movement's ideological values. To properly do this, the assessor needs to have an understanding of the ideological framework of the particular movement.

FIGURE 8.2 Key factors for terrorist risk assessment

Capability

Individuals may have attitudinal sympathy to a movement's ideology but lack the capability to act on these. For example, the Cork prisoner mentioned earlier was of concern because of his attitudes but not because of his capability (as the movement was highly unlikely to want to recruit him or be associated with him). The more experience and training an individual has, the higher the level of capability.

Political and social environment

Terrorism does not occur in a vacuum. Terrorist campaigns are strongly influenced by the wider political and social contexts in which they occur. This environment can either support and encourage violence, or inhibit and undermine it. Of particular importance here is the constituent community the terrorists are most associated with. It is important to consider the perceptions the individual prisoners hold of this community environment. As Crenshaw (1988) highlights, 'the actions of terrorists are based on a subjective interpretation of the world rather than objective reality. Perceptions of the political and social environment are filtered through beliefs and attitudes that reflect experiences and memories.'

Affiliations

Terrorism and violent extremism are generally group phenomenon. Research on radicalisation highlights that social factors are probably the single most important element in the radicalisation process (e.g. Silke, 2003, 2008). Camaraderie, social support and a sense of belonging can all be powerful incentives for becoming and staying involved with a group. Any risk assessment needs to consider the affiliations of individual prisoners. Who do they prefer to spend time with? Other terrorism-related offenders? A crucial issue to consider is the degree of choice the prisoner can exercise here. For example, a prisoner who is held on a wing with a large proportion of terrorist prisoners is likely to have considerable contact with them even if he or she would prefer otherwise. In some cases, a prisoner may have explicitly requested to join (or be separated from) other terrorist prisoners, which in itself will reveal much about their general political and social outlook.

Emotional factors

A range of emotional motivational factors have been highlighted as important in understanding involvement in terrorism. These primarily cluster around issues of grievance, perceived injustice, anger and revenge. Most terrorists believe at the time of their offending that their actions are morally justified, and various psychological processes (such as deindividuation, mortality salience, moral disengagement and risky shift) appear to play an important role in facilitating active involvement in terrorism (e.g. Bandura, 1990; Silke, 2003, 2008; Pyszczynski et al., 2006).

Behaviour in custody

Behaviour in custody is an important factor for every prisoner in terms of risk assessment. Terrorist and extremist prisoners who engage in violence against staff and other prisoners, participate in political protests (e.g. hunger strikes) or actively attempt to compromise the operation or security of the prison (e.g. escape attempts) are clearly showing strong commitment to the cause and a willingness to engage in serious violence on behalf of it. In contrast, prisoners with a good behavioural record have shown an ability to comply with the regime and this may indicate a genuine desire for reform. For example, how jihadi prisoners relate to prison imams may provide considerable insight into their general outlook and attitude. Other important issues to consider are whether the prisoner has shown a willingness to complete prison programmes which have been designed specifically for extremist prisoners (e.g. the Healthy Identities programme used in the UK, and described in Chapter 7 in this volume). If they have engaged with such programmes, the outcome of such involvement is obviously a significant issue to consider.

Disengagement factors

One problem with many models of risk assessment is that they tend to focus more on factors linked with individuals becoming terrorists (radicalisation) and often largely ignore factors associated with individuals leaving terrorism (disengagement). Given that we are generally dealing with individuals who have been imprisoned because of terrorist activity, the fundamental question is arguably not about whether the factors associated with becoming involved are present – in most prison-based cases they historically inevitably will be – but rather are the factors associated with disengagement currently present?

Disengagement from terrorism and extremism is usually brought about by a complex set of processes (e.g. Bjørgo and Horgan, 2009; Horgan, 2009; Reinares, 2011; Silke, 2011b). These elements can interact, and picking out the primary cause in the case of any one person can be very difficult. In considering whether disengagement has occurred or is occurring for a particular individual some factors worth considering include:

- Aging. In general, individuals are less likely to remain actively involved in terrorism the older they get.
- Experiencing a turning-point event (this may include incarceration, serious injury, death of a friend, divorce). Usually this is a profoundly aversive experience related to their involvement in extremism.
- The development of delayed deterrence. An increase in the fear of physical harm, future incarceration, or both. Recognising that continued involvement will inevitability have serious costs while at the same time questioning their ability to cope with these costs. There is an overall increase in the anxiety connected with a terrorist life.

- Expressing disillusionment with the movement. Is the individual showing increased dissatisfaction with the movement's policies, leadership and activities? Does he or she disagree with the overall strategy and objectives (e.g. willingness to negotiate) or with specific operational tactics (e.g. the targeting of civilian areas).
- Other negative emotions as a result of continuing involvement in terrorism. This can relate to interpersonal disputes and clashes with other group members. A growing sense that the individual no longer 'fits in' or has been betrayed or disregarded by other members and supporters.
- Perceiving that the wider political and social environment has changed and that political violence is no longer necessary, or, no longer supported by their constituents, leading to a reappraisal for the need or justification for continued terrorism.
- Contemplation time away from one's offending environment, allowing the individual to evaluate past decisions and re-assess life goals, provoking a re-evaluation of their involvement in terrorism.
- Expressing changed priorities. An increased focus on wanting a 'normal' life. Expressing a desire for investing in a marriage and a career, and showing more respect and concern for children, especially their own children.

Sources of information

Having reviewed the issues which are likely to be of most use when considering risk assessment in the context of a terrorist prisoner, the next critical step is to identify what sources of information can provide the necessary insight to inform this assessment. Overall, the main sources of data used for risk assessments for other types of prisoners will broadly also apply to terrorist and extremist prisoners:

1   Interview(s) with the individual being assessed
2   Specialised testing
3   Third-party information (e.g. court reports, prison documentation, police reports, etc.)

Prisoner interviews

Interviews with the prisoner are the most important source of information. Interviews alone, however, should not be relied upon to reach the assessment as prisoners will frequently try to minimise the seriousness of their actions (including denying their guilt of some or all of their convictions), present their behaviour and attitudes in the best possible light, and in some cases blatantly lie. With those caveats in mind, a detailed interview nonetheless provides the best prospect to properly explore most if not all of the issues identified in the preceding section as being of importance. As a consequence it is not surprising that many terrorist groups ban their members from participating in such interview processes, or if they do participate, to do so with minimal interaction and monosyllabic answers. IRA prisoners in Northern Ireland, for example, as a matter of routine refused to be involved in such processes, while more recently in England and Wales, roughly one-third of jihadi prisoners have also refused to take part in the interviews connected to the ERG22+ assessment (more on this below).

While a prisoner's refusal to be interviewed can be – and usually sensibly is – interpreted as evidence of continued extremism, this is not always the situation. In one case in my experience, a prisoner had refused to participate in risk assessment interviews. When he eventually agreed to be interviewed, he did so with considerable hostility, suspicion and monosyllabic responses. The assumption made by many was naturally that this indicated he was still a radicalised extremist. Time revealed a more complex issue. The prisoner's initial refusal and first interviews occurred after he had been moved to a prison much further away from his family home, making what had been frequent family visits now very difficult and consequently rare. This led to the prisoner growing increasingly depressed and convinced that the prison authorities were out to get him. He became convinced that the risk assessment interviews were yet another way to try to make life difficult for him. His refusal and reluctance to engage with the process was not the result of continued radicalisation but was rather about much more personal factors. When he was eventually transferred to a prison closer to his family his attitude transformed and he engaged positively and highly productively with both the risk assessment process and anti-extremism programmes.

Specialised testing

Generally, research on the risk assessment of offenders has found that third-generation clinical-actuarial risk assessment measures are consistently the most reliable; however, no such tools have yet been properly validated for terrorist prisoners. Some early writers argued that tests which were developed for and regularly used on other forensic populations, such as HCR20 and PCL-R, could be usefully used to help risk assessments with terrorist prisoners (Roberts and Horgan, 2008). Certainly, such tools have been used in at least a few terrorist cases. However, a growing consensus has built up since then that the disadvantages of using these tests outweigh the advantages. Overall, these tests are poorly designed for terrorist and extremist prisoners and in general their use should be avoided (e.g. Dernevik et al., 2009; Monahan, 2012; Pressman and Flockton, 2012b). Even the authors of the tests have themselves expressed serious reservations about their use with terrorist prisoners (e.g. Hart, 2010) and overall it seems preferable to look elsewhere for appropriate tests.

As alternatives, there are currently at least two measures which have been specifically designed for use with terrorist prisoners and which are currently in use in prison settings. These are the Extremism Risk Guidance 22+ (ERG22+) which is used in England and Wales, and the Violent Extremist Risk Assessment (VERA-2) which is in use in Australia. It is likely that other models will emerge in the coming years.

Extremism Risk Guidance 22+ (ERG22+) is an assessment tool developed by the NOMS Operational Intervention Services Group and was launched in 2011 (Rehabilitation Services Group, 2011). The ERG assesses offenders on 22 factors which are theoretically related to extremist offending (the '+' in the title is a reflection that the model will consider other factors beyond the 22 if they are shown to be relevant to a particular case). ERG is a theoretical model, and as yet, does not have an evidence base demonstrating clear links to future offending. As the authors of the test highlight:

> The ERG factors are essentially working hypotheses to account for how an individual became engaged and to capture the features of their mind-set, their intentions and their capability for terrorism. None of these factors has a demonstrated link with future offending, so are as yet unproven. As such the ERG cannot predict risk with any certainty, but directs attention to aspects of the individual associated with their offending where intervention may be targeted or proportionate risk management approaches deployed.

ERG22+ does not provide a specific risk assessment score for an offender (in the same manner that a system such as OASys does), partly because the evidence base is much weaker and the influence of the 22 factors on risk outcomes is not yet known. The 22 factors currently all carry equal weighting in the assessment, but this is likely to change as the number of longitudinal follow-ups on prisoners assessed through the measure increases.

VERA-2 is in many respects a similar model to the ERG22+, which is not surprising as both models are derived from a review of essentially the same literature relating to terrorism. A detailed account of VERA-2 is provided in Chapter 9 in this volume, so it makes sense to be succinct in considering it here. In brief, VERA-2 is built around assessing individuals on 31 factors. There is, not surprisingly, considerable overlap with many of the factors identified in ERG22+, though the VERA-2 factors include six protective factors (Pressman and Flockton, 2012a). In contrast to ERG22+, VERA-2 does supply an overall risk assessment score for the individual terrorist. Like the UK test, VERA-2 currently gives equal weighting to the different factors in arriving at this score and this state of affairs is likely to change as follow-up data become available.

Overall it is not possible to say at the moment which of these two tests is more reliable, but it would be surprising if they produced startlingly different conclusions on the same individual given both tests have considerable similarities in origin and structure. A small-scale study by Beardsley and Beech (2013) found that the VERA-2 factors appeared to be relevant and supported its use for risk assessment, but we must wait for more robust evaluations of both models. What is clear is that both are almost certainly more useful for assessing terrorist risk assessment than any pre-existing tests which were not explicitly designed for terrorist prisoners.

Third-party information

Third-party information includes court reports, prison reports and other prison documentation, police reports, assessments by prison and probation staff, etc. This is usually the most readily available information for the risk assessment process.[1] This material plays a major role in informing the overall assessment and is also critical for guiding interviews with prisoners. In cases where the prisoner refuses to be interviewed, the risk assessment will essentially depend solely on this material.

While this material is more usually reliable, it should still be considered through a critical lens. For example, in my own risk assessments I am always very keen, where possible, to have the opinions of prison staff who have worked with the prisoner. The close proximity means that such staff can often have very remarkable and useful insights and I traditionally place weight on their views. I adopted a somewhat more critical view after reading one particular staff assessment in support of the release of a prisoner. The statement was unremarkable in the points made and indeed was very similar to many other statements I had previously seen for other prisoners. To quote from the assessment:

> [The prisoner] has shown himself to be an orderly, disciplined prisoner, not only in his own person, but also with reference to his fellow prisoners, among whom he has preserved good discipline. He is amenable, unassuming, and modest. He has never made exceptional demands, conducts himself in a uniformly quiet and reasonable manner, and has put up with the deprivations and restrictions of imprisonment very well. He has . . . exercised a helpful authority over other prisoners. . . . He is invariably polite and has never insulted the prison officials.
>
> During his . . . detention while awaiting trial and while under sentence, he has undoubtedly become more mature and calm. When he returns to freedom, he will do so without entertaining revengeful purposes against those in official positions . . . He will not agitate against the government, nor will he wage war against other nationalist parties. He is completely convinced that a state cannot exist without internal order and firm government. In view of the above facts, I venture to say that his behaviour while under detention merits the grant of an early release.

The problem here, unfortunately, was that the prisoner in question was Adolf Hitler.

That this assessment (supporting his release just nine months into a five-year sentence) had been so shockingly wrong, and had so badly misread the man and what he was capable of, gave me serious pause for thought. Ultimately, all evidence, whether it comes from the prisoner or other sources, needs to be considered in a critical framework.

Conclusions

Our understanding of the risk assessment of terrorists and extremists may be in its infancy, but there is no denying that we have still witnessed enormous progress in the last ten years alone. It is very likely we will make even further progress over the next decade. The field has moved from a position where such prisoners were very poorly understood in terms of risk assessment frameworks, and where the default position was to assume that such work was either almost impossible, or else that such prisoners would always be high risk, no matter what.

The legacy of both of these misguided perspectives is still with us and there is no question that risk assessment of these types of prisoners faces unique and serious challenges. That said, sensible risk assessment is possible in these cases. The development of theoretically informed measures to do this certainly represents a significant step forward, as is the growing recognition and acceptance of the different issues which need to be considered for these prisoners.

Risk assessment of terrorist prisoners is a work in progress. Though the picture is improving, it is still important to bear in mind the current limitations in our knowledge and competence in working with such prisoners. There remain serious gaps in the evidence base and it is likely to be some time before the current theoretical models can be properly validated by solid research evidence. In the long term, a great deal of further work is needed to identify the most reliable factors for understanding the motivations and vulnerabilities associated with prisoners becoming involved in or disengaging from terrorism. For now, the only certainty is that this will remain a complex but vitally important issue.

Note

1   However, in some cases the available material can be surprisingly limited in some respects. For example, this can happen when prisoners have not actually been convicted or where much of the alleged evidence against them has not been disclosed (such as with the deeply unsatisfactory Control Order regime used in various incarnations in the UK in the 2000s).

References

Bakker, E. (2006). *Jihadi terrorists in Europe, their characteristics and the circumstances in which they joined the jihad: an exploratory study*. The Hague: Clingendael Institute.

Bandura, A. (1990). 'Mechanisms of moral disengagement.' In W. Reich (Ed.), *Origins of Terrorism: Psychologies, Ideologies, Theologies, States of Mind* (pp.161–191). Cambridge: Cambridge University Press.

Beardsley, N. and Beech, B. (2013). 'Applying the violent extremist risk assessment (VERA) to a sample of terrorist case studies.' *Journal of Aggression, Conflict and Peace Research*, 5/1, pp.4–15.

Bjørgo, T. and Horgan, J. (2009). *Leaving Terrorism Behind*. New York: Routledge.

Crawford, C. (1999). *Defenders or Criminals: Loyalist Prisoners and Criminalisation*. Belfast: Blackstaff Press.

Cole, J., Alison, E., Cole, B. and Alison, L. (2012). *Guidance for Identifying People Vulnerable to Recruitment into Violent Extremism*. University of Liverpool. Available at: http://www.nhserewash.com/safeguarding/IVP_Guidance_Draft_v0.3_web_version.pdf

Crenshaw, M. (1988). 'The subjective reality of the terrorist.' In R. O. Slater and M. Stohl (Eds.), *Current Perspectives on International Terrorism* (pp.12–46). London: Macmillan.

Dernevik, M., Beck, A., Grann, M., Hogue, T. and McGuire, J. (2009). 'The use of psychiatric and psychological evidence in the assessment of terrorist offenders.' *Journal of Forensic Psychiatry & Psychology*, 20/4, pp.508–515.

Ganor, B. (2008). 'Terrorist organization typologies and the probability of a boomerang effect.' *Studies in Conflict & Terrorism*, 31/4, 269–283.

Hamm, M. (2013). *The Spectacular Few: Prison Radicalization and the Evolving Terrorist Threat.* New York University Press: New York.

Hart, S. (2010). 'Risk for terrorism: a multi-level, multi-disciplinary approach to threat assessment.' Paper presented at the *American Psychology-Law Society Annual Conference*, March 18–20, Vancouver.

Horgan, J. (2009). *Walking Away from Terrorism: Accounts of Disengagement from Radical and Extremist Movements.* Oxon, UK: Routledge.

Kebbell, M. and Porter, L. (2012). 'An intelligence assessment framework for identifying individuals at risk of committing acts of violent extremism against the West.' *Security Journal*, 25/3, pp.212–228.

Marsden, S. and Schmid, A. (2011). 'Typologies of terrorism and political violence.' In A. Schmid (Ed.), *The Routledge Handbook of Terrorism Research* (pp.158–200). London: Routledge.

Monahan, J. (2012). 'The individual risk assessment of terrorism.' *Psychology, Public Policy, and Law.* 18/2, pp.167–205.

O'Doherty, S. (1993). *The Volunteer: A Former IRA Man's True Story.* London: Harper Collins.

Pressman, D. E. and Flockton, J. (2012a). 'Calibrating risk for violent political extremists and terrorists: the VERA 2 structured assessment.' *The British Journal of Forensic Practice*, 14/4, pp.237–251.

Pressman, D. E. and Flockton, J. S. (2012b). 'Applied risk assessment for violent political extremists and terrorists using the VERA 2.' Paper presented to the *British Psychological Society: Division of Forensic Psychology Annual Conference* Terrorism Symposium, Cardiff, Wales, 28 June 2012.

Pyszczynski, T., Abdollahi, A., Solomon, S., Greenberg, J., Cohen, F. and Weise, D. (2006). 'Mortality salience, martyrdom, and military might: the great Satan versus the axis of evil.' *Personality and Social Psychology Bulletin*, 32/4, 525–537.

Rehabilitation Services Group (2011). *Extremism Risk Guidance 22+: Summary and Overview.* National Offender Management Service.

Reinares, F. (2011). 'Exit from terrorism: a qualitative empirical study on disengagement and deradicalization among members of ETA.' *Terrorism and Political Violence*, 23/5, pp.78–803.

Roberts, K. and Horgan, J. (2008). 'Risk assessment and the terrorist', *Perspectives on Terrorism*, 2/6, pp.–9.

Sageman, M. (2004). *Understanding Terrorist Networks.* Philadelphia: University of Pennsylvania Press.

Silke, A. (2003). 'Becoming a terrorist.' In A. Silke (Ed.), *Terrorists, Victims and Society: Psychological Perspectives on Terrorism and Its Consequences* (pp.2–53). Chichester: Wiley.

Silke, A. (2008). 'Holy warriors: exploring the psychological processes of jihadi radicalisation.' *European Journal of Criminology*, 5/1, pp.9–123.

Silke, A. (2011a). 'Terrorists and extremists in prison: psychological Issues in management and reform.' In Andrew Silke (Ed.), *The Psychology of Counter-Terrorism* (pp.12–134). London: Routledge.

Silke, A. (2011b). 'Disengagement or deradicalization: a look at prison programs for jailed terrorists.' *CTC Sentinel*, 4/1, pp.18–21.

9

VIOLENT EXTREMIST RISK ASSESSMENT

Issues and applications of the VERA-2 in a high-security correctional setting

D. Elaine Pressman and John Flockton

Introduction

The risk assessment of individuals who are convicted of terrorist and violent extremist offences is of increasing importance to corrections officials worldwide. These risk assessments impact sentencing, correctional classification, placements, program interventions and release determinations. It is essential that the risk assessment protocol for terrorists and violent extremists not be the same as those known as 'psychiatric risk assessments' as these are more appropriate for use with individuals more commonly found to have clinical or personality disorders, psychopathy, impulsivity and other known criminogenic risk indicators.

Terrorists and other perpetrators of ideological violence are 'normal' individuals who have conscious control of their actions. They are committed to an ideology that enables them to justify or excuse even the most catastrophic events on the basis that their acts are undertaken to serve the greater good. Currently used standardised risk assessment tools for general violence have not been validated on ideologically motivated violent offenders and these offenders are known to differ significantly in motivation, background and other characteristics from non-ideological violent offenders. As a result, the predictive validity of these tools, when used with violent extremists, is compromised.

The Violent Extremism Risk Assessment protocol (Version 2), abbreviated as the VERA-2 (Pressman & Flockton, 2010, 2012a) was developed to address the need for an offence-specific, utilitarian and relevant risk assessment tool. It is being used in high-security prison settings in several countries with convicted terrorists. Additional applications for the tool are being explored.

The VERA-2 is an analytic-predictive risk assessment approach that is specific to offenders of violent acts carried out in furtherance of ideological objectives and is consequently differentiated from 'psychiatric-predictive' tools. The structured professional judgement methodology, which is used in the VERA-2, is a recognised and reputable approach. Offence-specific risk indicators were included following consultation with experts with both operational knowledge and empirical experience with terrorists. The low base rate of terrorists, problems with population compliance and the relatively long sentences received by this group of offenders have created limitations for actuarial and statistical data for the indicators. As a result, the indicators employed in the VERA-2 were validated by experts in terrorism who scrutinised them for their significance in identifying risk of future violence. In addition, they were supported by 'lessons learned' analyses of violent extremists by terrorism researchers and judged to have face validity by correctional and security experts with experience of working with terrorists.

There are specific aspects of the violent extremist population that enhance the ability to make an assessment of risk. The rational and conscious decision-making capability of these offenders, their known intentions, and the nature of their ideological goals are examples of elements that support risk analysis and assessment. If one has free will, is committed to specific ideological goals and also has the intention and capacity to act with unlawful violence in furtherance of these goals, then supportive data is an assist but is not a necessity for the formulation of a reasoned judgment of future risk. The VERA-2 approach, which uses a systematic, structured and analytical protocol, applies credible risk indicators that are measurable according to defined criteria. This transparent and replicable approach is defensible as 'best practice' available at this time. Training in the VERA-2 is required by users to support the reliability of the ratings as well as ensuring users have a comprehensive understanding of the benefits and caveats of the approach.

Terrorists, violent extremists and violent offenders

Since 2003, there has been growing agreement as to the distinctive features of acts of unlawful violent extremism. The United States Federal Bureau of Investigation (FBI) and the United States Department of Defence (DOD) now define such acts in terms of identifiable elements. A terrorist incident is 'a violent act or an act dangerous to human life, in violation of the criminal laws of the United States, or of any state, to intimidate or coerce a government, the civilian population or any segment thereof, in furtherance of political or social objectives' (FBI, 2001). This definition includes both actions that have the intention to cause harm to persons or property and those acts that cause actual harm or loss of life in furtherance of ideological objectives. The United States Department of Defence defines terrorism as the calculated use of unlawful violence or threat of unlawful violence, to inculcate fear and to coerce, or to intimidate governments or societies in the pursuit of goals that are generally political, religious, or ideological (Department of Defence, 2010). These definitions are a refinement of the five characteristics of terrorism suggested some decades ago by Schmid & Jongman (1988). The United Kingdom Terrorism Act of 2000 (c.11) defines terrorism as an act of violence for political, religious or ideological purpose or objective or cause (United Kingdom, 2000). Such definitions are consistent with other Western anti-terrorism acts.

Terrorists and violent extremists differ in significant ways from non-ideological common violent offenders, but not from each other in terms of the pertinent risk indicators. Terrorists and violent extremists both use calculated unlawful violence to further political, religious or ideological goals. They intend the violence to harm specific persons or property, to coerce and intimidate governments or other officials and to alter public opinion. Terrorist attacks have the specific property of having the intention to cause fear and terror in civilian populations or decision makers. Not all acts of violent extremism have this psychological intention as an objective. Violent environmentalists, for example, may target property and intend to cause significant damage but they do not necessarily plan to kill others or cause fear in the public domain. Violent anti-abortionists have assassinated abortion doctors and cause significant damage to clinics but generally have not demonstrated an interest in indiscriminate civilian killing, or maximum diffuse destruction. Terrorist acts are referred to as violent extremism by governments and constitute a subset of ideologically motivated violence. Terrorists are violent extremists. The risk factors that relate to violent extremists for this reason also apply to terrorists.

The differences between non-ideologically motivated violent offenders and violent extremists are many and they are significant. The former are known to engage in acts generally due to motivations such as personal gain, addictions, criminogenic needs, and impulse control problems (Marzuk, 1996; Silke, 2003). In contrast, violent extremists are motivated by ideologies, beliefs, and social, religious and political causes. The groups differ in their interest in publicity. Violent extremists advertise their attacks and they communicate their goals whereas ordinary violent criminals try to avoid detection and attention (LaFree & Dugan, 2004). Ordinary violent criminals regularly exhibit personality disorders, psychopathy, uncontrollable aggression, behaviour problems, and/or other mental or clinical disorders. These features are not generally present in terrorists (Sageman, 2004; Nesser, 2004; Post, 2005; Precht, 2007; Silber & Bhatt, 2007; Pressman, 2009; Mullins, 2011), whose dominant feature is their 'normality' (Crenshaw, 1981, 1995, 2000). Both terrorism experts and knowledgeable psychiatrists assert that terrorists are not mentally ill or psychologically disordered (Horgan, 2003; Post, 2005, 2007). Despite this, Silke (2003) pointed out that a 'steady stream of psychologists and psychiatrists' since the early 1970s have continued to push the erroneous idea that terrorists suffer from mental illness, damaged psyches and deviant personalities. To counter such incorrect assertions, Post, a terrorist expert and psychiatrist, emphasised that terrorists and violent extremists are not only to be considered psychologically 'normal' in the sense of not being clinically psychotic, but they are also not depressed, severely emotionally disturbed, nor are they crazed fanatics (Post, 2005). Furthermore, he notes that terrorist groups and organisations regularly screen out emotionally unstable individuals because they represent a security risk (Post, 2005, 2007). An increasing amount of empirical research supports this position as the most credible interpretation (Silke, 2003; Horgan, 2003, 2005, 2008, 2012; Kruglanski & Fishman, 2006; Merari, 2005, 2010).

This is not to argue that there are never mentally unbalanced or pathological individuals in terrorist organisations or among those who act as lone-wolf terrorists. The point to be made is that such individuals are 'the exception rather than the rule' (Silke, 2003). Furthermore, 'these exceptions' would not be included in the 'rationally normal' violent extremist population of relevance to the VERA-2 identified population.

Terrorists do not typically have histories that include early patterns of violence, dismal poverty, poor childrearing, educational failure, other socio-economic related deprivation or a record of past crime (Bakker, 2006; Silber & Bhatt, 2007). This finding was underscored by the results of a recent review of Australian offenders classified as terrorists. It was found that they did not have prior criminal records and none of the offenders were 'legally exculpated' on the grounds of suffering from mental health issues (Mullins, 2011). Overall, it was concluded that there was nothing remarkable about the backgrounds of the Australian terrorists that distinguished them from the rest of the population in terms of traditional investigative profiling or that differentiated them from other studies previously undertaken in Europe and elsewhere (Mullins, 2011). In terms of education and skills, terrorists are more educated, more employable and more skilled than common violent criminals (Merari, 2010). They were not notably different from the general population in terms of education, occupation, or income (Kreuger & Maleckova, 2002; Kreuger, 2007; Mullins, 2011). They are sociable rather than isolated and they had a high number of friends rather than being incapable of positive inter-personal relationships (Taher, 2011). The aforementioned distinctive characteristics of violent extremists were considered in the development of the VERA-2 risk indicators. Consequently, these risk indicators differ fundamentally from the risk indicators used for non-ideologically motivated violent offenders.

The development of the VERA-2

The VERA (Violent Extremist Risk Assessment) protocol was developed in 2009 as an offence-specific assessment tool for violent extremists and terrorists with pertinent risk indicators for this limited population (Pressman, 2009). The VERA was revised in 2010 as the VERA-2 (Pressman & Flockton, 2010) following constructive feedback from its early use with terrorists in a high-security prison. Additional consultation and comments received from experts in law enforcement, forensic psychology, violent extremism and terrorism supported the revisions.

The need for a dedicated tool was highlighted by results obtained from an analysis of the risk indicators used to predict recidivism in general violent offenders. These risk items were demonstrated to have limited relevance to terrorists (Pressman, 2009). Less than one-third of the items on the HCR-20 (Webster et al., 1997, 2001), a well-known and accepted risk assessment tool for general violence, were found to be applicable to violent extremists and terrorists (Pressman, 2009). Furthermore, a recent study, undertaken in a high-security correctional facility, compared risk assessment results for a group of convicted terrorists and a comparable matched group of non-ideological violent offenders on four standardised risk assessment tools. Significant differences between the groups were found for all four of the standardised risk assessment tools used (Pressman & Flockton, 2012b). This supports the dubious legitimacy of even those standardised risk assessment tools, developed for general violence, when applied to violent extremists. It also further jeopardises any previously assumed validity of the results for the recidivism of this population. The two groups were compared on four well-known risk assessment tools for general violence. These risk assessment tools included the Historical-Clinical-Risk-Management-20 or the HCR-20 (Webster et al., 1997), the Level of Service Inventory or the LSI-R (Andrews & Bonta, 2000), the Psychopathy Checklist: Screening Version or the PCL:SV (Hart, Cox & Hare, 2003), and the Violence Risk Scale-Screening Version or the VRS-R (Wong & Gordon, 2000).

Skeem and Monahan (2011) reviewed all risk assessment methodologies that could be considered for use with terrorists, including the unmodified clinical risk assessment, modified clinical risk assessment, structured professional judgement, modified actuarial risk assessment, and unmodified actuarial risk assessment. It was concluded that the structured professional judgement approach was the 'preferable' method. The four categories of risk indicators (ideology, grievances, affiliations and moral emotions) thought to offer 'most promise' for a risk assessment approach for terrorists (Monahan, 2012) are also reflected in the VERA-2 risk indicators.

The VERA-2 risk assessment was developed to be a generic approach for the range of violent extremists. This eliminates potential bias that would tarnish an approach used with only one ideology considered particularly heinous by assessors. The VERA-2 can be used equally with the spectrum of 'unlawful violent extremists'. This includes violent right-wing extremists, violent left-wing extremists, violent animal rights extremists, violent environmentalists, violent anarchists, violent anti-abortionists, violent Al Qaeda inspired extremists, violent political rejectionists such as 'Sovereign Citizens', and all other violent offenders motivated by social, religious or political ideologies. All are assessed with the same protocol and risk indicators.

The final risk decision is not based alone on VERA-2 interviews. All available information, reports and intelligence from multiple sources is used to determine the ratings for each indicator and the final risk judgement. A detailed picture of the ideological nature, motivators, background, training, capacities, world view and other relevant aspects is constructed for each offender using the VERA-2 risk indicators within the provided framework. This snapshot represents the unique constituent elements of risk at a given time for a specific individual in a given situational context.

The final risk decision is not determined in an additive manner but is a professional judgement. This judgement is made subsequent to a consideration of the available information restructured and integrated into the VERA-2 risk indicators and then rated. As with all risk assessments, the quality of the assessment is dependent on the nature of the information upon which it is based. Many experts have agreed that risk assessments have a greater chance of being accurate if decisions are made using a transparent and systematic protocol with a rating system

(Monahan, 1981, 2012; Monahan & Steadman, 1994; Webster et al., 1997, 2001; Bonta, Law & Hanson, 1998; Dolan & Doyle, 2000; Douglas et al., 2002; Hanson, 2005; Ogloff, 2009; Hart & Logan, 2011). The VERA-2 uses such a systematic and structured approach.

At all times at which risk assessments are undertaken, it is important to establish if ideological motivation has played a role in the violent acts of offenders. In correctional settings, offenders may well be convicted of 'ordinary' violent offences such as murder or manslaughter despite being motivated by extremism and the furtherance of their ideological viewpoint. The only person convicted of involvement in the worst terrorist attack in Canadian history, the Air India Flight 182 bombing on June 3, 1985 in which 329 were killed, was sentenced for manslaughter and a perjury, and not a terrorism offence. Nidal Hasan, the United States Army psychiatrist who was arrested after horrific shootings that killed 13 and injured 32 at Fort Hood, Texas on November 5, 2009, is indicted on counts of pre-meditated murder and attempted murder despite the likely involvement of ideological motivation. Ordinary criminal offences, such as murder, arson or manslaughter, may be considered more pragmatic for prosecutions even when there is evidence of ideological motivation for the violent act. An offence-specific tool for extremist violence should be added to the battery of protocols and assessments should there be any suspicion of ideological involvement in violent offence.

Risk assessment for violence has two objectives. These are to evaluate an individual to determine the risk of future violent acts and to use the information obtained to design appropriate interventions (Borum, Swartz & Swanson, 1996; Borum et al., 1999, 2006; Borum, 2000, 2003). The risk assessment for a violent extremist obtains, incorporates and analyses information from a multi-disciplinary perspective to address these same two objectives. As Post summarised, 'to comprehend this complex phenomenon (terrorism) fully requires an inter-disciplinary approach, incorporating knowledge from political, historical, cultural, economic, ideological and religious scholarship' (Post, 2005). The VERA-2 contains 31 items for this multi-disciplinary analytical assessment of predictive risk of future violence. Of these, 25 are risk indicators and 6 are risk mitigating or 'protective indicators'. They are categorised into five domains: 'Beliefs and Attitudes', 'Context and Intent', 'History and Capability', 'Commitment and Motivation' and 'Protective Items'. The VERA-2 items appear in Table 9.1.

The use of the VERA-2 in a high-security correctional setting

The acceptance of the VERA-2 in an Australian high-security correctional setting illustrates the utility and value of the tool. Used with convicted and sentenced terrorist offenders, it provides information that was previously unavailable for this population. Before the VERA-2, there were no offence-specific, empirically validated risk assessments that could assist security and case management decisions for convicted extremist violence offenders.

TABLE 9.1 The VERA-2 indicators

VERA-2 Indicator Items (Pressman and Flockton)	Low	Moderate	High
BA. **BELIEFS AND ATTITUDES**			
BA.1 Commitment to ideology justifying violence			
BA.2 Perceived victim of injustice and grievances			
BA.3 Dehumanization/demonization of identified targets of injustice			
BA.4 Rejection of democratic society and values			
BA.5 Feelings of hate, frustration, persecution, alienation			
BA.6 Hostility to national collective identity			
BA.7 Lack of empathy, understanding outside own group			
CI. **CONTEXT AND INTENT**			
CI.1 Seeker, consumer, developer of violent extremist materials			
CI.2 Identification of target (person, place, group) for attack			
CI.3 Personal contact with violent extremists			
CI.4 Anger and the expressed intent to act violently			
CI.5 Willingness to die for cause			
CI.6 Expressed intent to plan, prepare violent action			
CI.7 Susceptible to influence, authority, indoctrination			
HC. **HISTORY AND CAPABILITY**			
HC.1 Early exposure to pro-violence militant ideology			
HC.2 Network (family, friends) involved in violent action			
HC.3 Prior criminal history of violence			
HC.4 Tactical, paramilitary, explosives training			
HC.5 Extremist ideological training			
HC.6 Access to funds, resources, organizational skills			
CM **COMMITMENT AND MOTIVATION**			
CM.1 Glorification of violent action			
CM.2 Driven by criminal opportunism			
CM.3 Commitment to group, group ideology			
CM.4 Driven by moral imperative, moral superiority			
CM.5 Driven by excitement, adventure			
P. **PROTECTIVE ITEMS**			
Note rating differences for protective items: high rating =more mitigation and less risk			
P.1 Re-interpretation of ideology less rigid, absolute			
P.2 Rejection of violence to obtain goals			
P.3 Change of vision of enemy			
P.4 Involvement with non-violent, de-radicalization , offence related programs			
P.5 Community support for non-violence			
P.6 Family support for non-violence			
SPJ **VER FINAL JUDGMENT**	Low	Moderate	High

As shown in Figure 9.1, the VERA-2 contributes to a multi-modal risk assessment process that is reliant on information initially obtained, analysed and validated by intelligence, security and law enforcement agencies. Following conviction, decisions are made for the security classification and initial placement of the offender within the correctional system. Standardised psychological and violence risk assessments with established validity and utility with non-terrorist offenders are then conducted to identify general criminogenic risks and needs, should any exist. Those criminogenic risks and needs that are identified through this process are then the focus of program interventions during the period of incarceration.

The addition of the VERA-2 to the field of potential risk assessment approaches enables a targeted assessment of risk specifically pertinent to extremist-based violence rather than general violence. The results can assist classification and placement reviews, program interventions and decisions relating to progression pathways to lower classification facilities and eventual release into the community. By using the VERA-2, security and case management considerations are better informed by the additional empirically supported information which enhances the validity and utility of the risk assessment process.

Critical to these decisions is the item and domain structure of the VERA-2. This provides for ongoing assessment of individual dynamic risk factors which include the response of the offender to the ongoing influence and association with other convicted 'terrorists', and exposure – for many for the first time – to a high-security

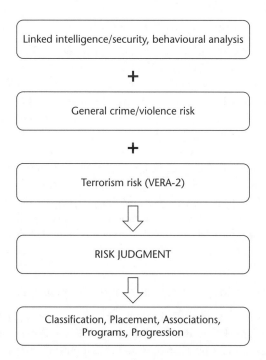

FIGURE 9.1 Risk assessment model for violent extremist high security offenders

prison environment. The impact of offence-specific 'de-radicalisation and disengagement' program interventions and any shifts in terrorist-related beliefs, attitudes and motivations can be systematically evaluated.

Evidence for the VERA-2 indicators

Beliefs, attitudes, ideology

Violent extremism has been described as the 'zealous adherence to a set of beliefs and values or ideology beyond the norm with a willingness to use violence' (Saucier et al., 2009). These attitudes and beliefs, socially developed and modified through direct contact (Halloran, 1967), are directed towards persons and objects and also towards ideas. Beliefs and attitudes are consistent with an individual's accepted ideology and may provide a foundation for extremism and motivate violent action. They relate to individual world view and shape goals. The FBI identifies ideological motivators as playing a role in violent extremism and terrorism (FBI, 2001, 2011). Commitment to an ideology that justifies the use of violence, while a pre-condition of unlawful violent extremism, does not alone fulfil the necessary and sufficient conditions for assessing risk of recidivism. Elements of intention and capacity are significant and are discussed in other sections below. Seven risk indicators are included in the Beliefs and Attitudes (Ideology) sector.

Commitment to an ideology justifying violence

Ideology, beliefs and attitudes are generally included in the stated reasons for terrorist attacks and for suicide terrorism (Kruglanski et al., 2009). They have been called the 'emotional fuel' for extremist attacks. They also provide justification for the use of violence to achieve the desired goals. An analysis of the written statements of 'militant-extremist'/terrorist groups that operated in seven regions of the world (Europe, the Middle East, Sub-Saharan Africa, East Asia, South Asia, Latin America, and North America) identified sixteen common themes (Saucier et al., 2009). Six of the identified themes involve aspects related to ideology, beliefs and attitudes of the terrorists. Intelligence analysts and researchers similarly support the fundamental role that ideology plays in justifying terrorist violence (Taher, 2011; Mullins, 2011). Ideology is the most commonly stated reason for terrorist attacks and suicide bombers in martyrdom video-tapes left behind to describe motivation (Kruglanski et al., 2009).

Perception of being the victim of injustice and grievances

Grievances are routinely identified as risk factors for terrorist actions and a key element in assessing risk of terrorism (Monahan, 2012). The perception of injustice and dominant grievances play a role in radicalisation (Silber & Bhatt, 2007) and support the final steps an individual takes in movement towards a terrorist act

(Atran, 2003; McCauley & Moskalenko, 2011). Grievances may be specific to an individual or be applicable to the group with which the individual identifies (Atran, 2003). They can result from actual or imagined circumstances. In communiqués to the world, terrorists cite these grievances and perceived injustices in their messages. This corresponds to the common terrorist theme identified, namely that 'one's own group is tragically obstructed' (Saucier et al., 2009).

De-humanisation of the identified targets of injustice

De-humanisation has been identified as one of eight stages in the process of genocide because it distances and demeans the target identified for killing and facilitates the psychological acceptance of the killing of humans (Stanton, 1996). De-humanisation was used in World War 2 to facilitate the Nazi extermination policy. It was used more recently in the 1994 genocide in Rwanda by the Hutu majority against the Tutsi minority. Used by terrorists, de-humanisation assists the psychological acceptance of the anticipated killing. It is consistent with the 'universal' terrorist theme described as 'de-humanising one's adversaries' (Saucier et al., 2009) and recent experiments illustrate that social connections enable de-humanisation (Waytz & Epley, 2012).

Rejection of democratic society and its values

The rejection of democratic society and its values is often used in statements of militant extremists as a motivation for their action. It is a universal theme of militant-extremist/terrorist groups across the world, labelled as 'the current civil government is illegitimate', or that 'modernity is disastrous' (Saucier et al., 2009). The leaders of the G-8 Summit in 2010 issued a statement to counter this rejectionist narrative and highlighted instead the benefits of a democratic society, its values, freedoms and the legitimacy of the rule of law (G-8 Summit, 2010). Terrorist groups promote the boycotting of democratic elections and have promoted right-wing and left-wing viewpoints that reject democratically legalised decisions. They have refused to recognise internationally accepted legitimate governments. Some terrorist groups reject all 'man-made' laws, only accepting what they consider to be the laws of a higher religious authority.

Feelings of hate, frustration, persecution and/or alienation

Moral emotions have been used to condemn others (Haidt, 2003) and feelings of hate, frustration and persecution can promote alienation from a society. These feelings may be exacerbated by anticipated calamities or perceived past or present calamities. Occupation of lands that are believed to belong to another group has resulted in terrorist activity in the Middle East, Africa and Europe due to frustration and moral outrage. Strong emotion can facilitate the willingness to use catastrophic violence even against 'fellow citizens'. Hate, anger and feelings of persecution over foreign policy decisions have been identified as motivating factors in terror plots in the United States, Canada, the United Kingdom and Australia. The theme labelled 'catastrophising', which is a focus on past, present or future calamities (Saucier et al., 2009), is known to have generated violent action.

Hostility to national collective identity

Post (2005, 2007) observed that collective identity can be a motivating factor in terrorist acts. Terrorists have been observed to subordinate their individual identity to the collective identity of their organisation or group. They view that whatever serves the terrorist group, organisation or network is of primary importance. This group allegiance can result in hostility to the national collective identity. Such hostility arises when personal and group values are incompatible with national values. In such cases, loyalty may transfer to the 'in-group' in place of the nation state in which one resides.

Lack of empathy to those outside one's own group

Members of an in-group may have empathy only for in-group members and a limited and selective group of others. Terrorists, unlike psychopaths, are generally social and bond to like-minded members of their group (Sageman, 2004, 2008). They are able to exhibit empathy albeit 'selective empathy' (Pressman, 2009). They are likely to have compassion for their 'brothers' and their in-group but not for those outside this group. Empathy with the in-group and valued membership in the in-group has been identified as a terrorism motivating factor by experts (Sageman, 2004, 2008; Post, 2005).

Context and intent

Having the intention to commit terrorist acts is an essential element of the risk assessment of violent extremists and terrorists. Belief in an ideology without the concomitant intention to use unlawful violence to achieve the desired goals diminishes risk. Elements pertinent to the conscious 'intention' to act with unlawful violence to support an ideology and contextual influences on intention are explored in this section of the VERA-2. Cultural and social contexts such as affiliations, personal contacts, family and friends may provide encouragement for the activation of intent. Intention differentiates adherents and sympathisers from those who aim to use violence to achieve ideological goals. Ideology and the intention to act with unlawful violence are precursors of violent extremism. Seven risk indicators comprise this section of the VERA-2.

Seeker, consumer, developer of violent extremist materials

The degree to which one is active in seeking out, consuming and developing violent extremist materials is a risk factor for radicalisation and for terrorist actions. The dynamic role of media and the internet in promoting terrorist acts was explored and active users and/or producers of terrorist-related material on the internet were found to be engaged in psychological warfare, publicity, propaganda production, fund-raising, information sharing, recruitment, mobilisation, and the planning and co-ordination of attacks (Weimann, 2004). The Institute for Strategic Dialogue (ISD) used case studies of terrorists to document the influence of the internet and other media on individual terrorists (ISD, 2011). Chatham House in the UK in a private roundtable conference on the impact of extremist materials on the internet concluded that such materials served as motivating influences on radicalisation and terrorism (Cornish, 2008). Many of the developers of internet materials have been terrorist leaders and ideologues, and violent extremists are known consumers who have sought out extremist websites and have consulted materials for both information and bomb-making directions. Maura Conway (2006, 2007) of the School of Law and Government at Dublin City University identifies five political uses made of the internet by terrorists and terrorist groups. These uses include information provision, financing, networking, recruiting and information gathering. Faisal Shahzad, who entered a guilty plea for the planned Times Square car bombing in New York City on May 1, 2010, is but one example of those influenced by the internet. He told interrogators that he was 'inspired by' Anwar al-Awlaki to take up the cause of Al Qaeda, that he had made contact over the internet with the Pakistani Taliban's Baitullah Mehsud, and that he had been in contact with a web of jihadists. Members of terrorist plots are often, when arrested, in possession of bomb-making directions, motivating terrorist materials and martyrdom video-tapes.

Identification of the target (person, place or group) for attack

A 2007 report for the United States Congress identified the importance of specificity of target identification in determining risk in terror attacks (Perl, 2007). From empirical experience and assassination research, The United States Secret Service identified this indicator as vital (Fein & Vossekuil, 1998). The more specific the target, in terms of person, place or group, the greater is the risk of attack.

Personal contact with violent extremists

Individuals who have engaged in terrorist acts often have some personal contact with other violent extremists. Personal contact influences attitudes and facilitates radicalisation and recruitment into groups. Extremist attitudes are socially developed and modified through direct contact (Halloran, 1967). Such contact can support the development of a sense of 'brotherhood'. This personal contact can shape intention to engage in violent extremist action (Sageman, 2008) and the actualisation of ideology (McCauley & Moskalenko, 2011). Although lone-wolf terrorists are not formal members of a group, contact via the internet has provided information and inspiration for terrorist action (Waytz & Epley, 2012).

Anger and the expressed intent to act violently

A relationship exists between emotion, the establishment of goals and the actualisation of goals, as extreme anger can function as a push factor to actualise goals and resort to violence as reflected in the writings of most terrorist groups (Saucier et al., 2009). Anger is often mixed with moral emotions which support the justification for violent action for the perceived greater good. This indicator refers to the expression of intention without concomitant action and represents the state where there is some indication of expressed intention but this is prior to active involvement.

Expressed willingness to die for cause

Post (2005) identified elements of what he refers to as the 'suicide production line' with the last stage being the production of a video. This indicator explores level of commitment in terms of a 'willingness' to die to further an ideology. Although such action may be constrained by situational constraints (incarceration), the willingness to die for the cause may be persistent. Post (2005) discusses the point from which an individual may find it difficult to back away from martyrdom. This risk indicator explores this status and is consistent with militant-extremists/terrorists theme of the 'glorification of dying for the cause' (Saucier et al., 2009).

Activation of intent through planning, preparing violent action

McCauley and Moskalenko (2011) and Atran (2010) identify differences between those individuals committed to radical or extreme beliefs who do not engage in unlawful violent action and those who do engage in such acts. The difference has been characterised as 'talking the talk' as compared to 'walking the walk'. This indicator assesses the presence of behavioural engagement involving participation in violent action. This status represents the critical progression from the expression of intention without concomitant action to action. In delineating the progressive stages of risk, expression of intent precedes action (Horgan, 2003, 2005, 2008, 2012; Taylor & Horgan, 2006).

Susceptibility to influence, authority, indoctrination by others

Some individuals are more susceptible to influence and indoctrination than others and such susceptibility can elevate risk. Charismatic leaders can persuade 'true believers' to carry out suicide attacks (Post, 2005) as demonstrated by secular terrorists such as the Tamil Tigers (LTTE), Kurdish separatists (PKK) and Al Qaeda. These influences are explored to determine who can exert influence on an individual. This information is significant both for the assessment of risk and to provide information useful in correctional interventions, disengagement initiatives and de-radicalisation programs (Weine et al., 2009; Sageman, 2008; Atran, 2008, 2010). Leaders are generally less susceptible to influence and indoctrination as compared to followers, which has implications within the correctional setting.

History and capacity

This section of the VERA-2 assesses indicators that are pertinent to the capacity of an individual to plan and carry out a violent extremist attack. It explores the experience, training, background and other skills related to capacity. This includes access to necessary individuals, resources and materials. Historical elements are investigated in this section that relate to previous exposure and involvement in militant-extremist/terrorist ideology. Prior activities, the skills possessed, training in militant-extremist tactics, and any kin involved in violent extremist activities are explored. Critical combinations of risk elements are observed.

Early exposure to pro-violence militant ideology

Exposure to militant extremism at a young age can be a predisposing factor to later violent acts of terrorism. This has been referred to as incipient radicalisation (Pressman, 2008) and as militant extremism that is 'bred in the bone' (Post, 2005). Early exposure supports familiarity and comfort with militant ideology. Just as language modelling in early childhood facilitates the development of language skills, so too does early exposure to militancy provide modelling for cognitive links that may facilitate future violent action. Piaget (1926), one of the most influential developmental psychologists of the past century, identified the importance of early concept associations on the development of thought. He concluded that early concepts and associations exert an influence on intellectual development, future behaviour and attitude development (Piaget, 1926). A child who is exposed to early violence, militancy, revenge and suicide bombing that is associated with family love, honour and duty will develop cognitive associations that can influence future behaviour (Piaget, 1926). This can facilitate radicalisation and subsequent terrorist activity (Pressman, 2008). Although some terrorists apparently become radicalised later in adolescence and adulthood without any apparent early exposure, and others who are raised in a militant environment may reject violence, this element should be explored. Grievances are known to have been developed through children's games, stories and the intentional retelling of history. In Northern Ireland, for example, children's books based on the lives of 'Catholic hunger strikers' and martyrs were intended to develop sympathy for the 'cause' from very early in life in nationalist families. Oral and written histories may be presented to children to inculcate moral emotions, anger and hostility while they are still youthful in order to instil a belief system conducive to fighting for the cause later in life. In the Palestinian territories television cartoon characters are used to promote hate of the 'enemy' and toddlers have been dressed-up as suicide bombers. Identification with victims at an early age can be pivotal as a predisposing risk factor (Horgan, 2008).

Network of family and friends involved in violent action

Atran (2008) estimated that 70 per cent of those affiliated with Al Qaeda join with friends and 20 per cent join because of kin. He observed that only humans fight to the death for friends and 'imagined kin', that is, for 'brotherhood' (Atran, 2010). This indicator refers to the familial and kin associations rather than superficial or limited contact with violent extremists. Family networks and close friends can exert a significant influence on future terrorist actors (Weine et al., 2009; Sageman, 2004, 2008; Atran, 2008, 2010). Horgan (2008) has identified the importance of kinship, friendship, romantic attachments and other personal affiliations in the development of the terrorists. This is supported by other researchers (Sageman, 2004, 2008; Goldson, 2011). Family members are recruited into terrorist groups because they are trusted. Zealous violent actors have been able to urge spouses and loved ones to become engaged in terrorism (McCauley & Moskalenko, 2011). McCauley and Moskalenko (2011) identified familial influence as one of six individual-level mechanisms of political radicalisation.

Prior history of criminal violence

Past offending is considered one of the strongest predictors for future violence (Borum et al., 1996; Borum, 2000; Douglas et al., 2002; Monahan & Stedman, 1994; Monahan et al., 2001). Although this characteristic does not generally apply to most terrorists (Nesser, 2004; Bakker, 2006; Sageman, 2004, 2008), it is included in order to explore the existence of any past history of violence. Bakker (2006) found some criminality in a subsection of his 242 subjects studied, but the majority of the terrorists analysed did not have a criminal history, and many of those with criminal histories were not of a violent nature. The absence of a criminal background in terrorists is supported by other studies (Pape, 2005; Silber & Bhatt, 2007; Merari, 2010; Taher, 2011; Mullins, 2011; Pressman & Flockton, 2012b). The FBI, which maintains a terrorist screening data base, has noted that without a criminal record or prior criminal activity, potential terrorists are difficult to detect. Reports of increasing radicalisation in prison may ultimately result in an increase in the number of ideologically motivated offenders with criminal backgrounds (Neumann, 2010).

Tactical, paramilitary, explosives training

The capacity to carry out terrorist attacks is enhanced by tactical, paramilitary and explosives training. The skill to build and develop bomb detonators, the knowledge of how to acquire and use weapons and ammunition and experience in the use of weapons are indicators that relate to risk. Risk is elevated when knowledge and training are combined with the intention to use unlawful violence. Tactical training, access to weapons and training in bomb making at camps run by militant factions is extremely pertinent to risk of future violence. It is known that many terrorists who have undergone training in the Waziristan region of Pakistan have advanced engineering education or other relevant skills.

Extremist ideological training

This indicator explores intensive ideological training designed to motivate the individual to progress into terrorist organisations or activities. Militant movements where ideological training occurs do not always escalate to terrorist action but the risk is present in ethno-nationalist, revolutionary and other radical politico-religious movements. Ideological training is available via the internet or 'in-groups', but this risk indicator refers to a structured intensive training program located domestically or abroad with the goal being the ideological indoctrination of trainees such as that undertaken by militant, revolutionary and terrorist movements such as Kosovar militants, Chechen rebels, Hamas, Hezbollah, Al Qaeda, the Taliban, or other groups with a militant focus. All militant ideological training, albeit less formalised, should be identified and described.

Access to funds, resources, organisational skills

Organisational capacity was identified as a key element of risk by the United States Secret Service (Fein & Vossekuil, 1998). This indicator refers to the 'capability' to carry out a complex plan. Terrorist plans require skills, funds, and organisation. Access to such resources is a constituent determinant of risk. An individual who is a member of a group or who is a 'lone-wolf' must have access to resources and/or persons with the organisational skills necessary to facilitate, plan, and carry out a terrorist attack.

Commitment and motivation

Post (2005) has highlighted the importance of distinguishing leaders from followers. He noted that leaders, who are also often ideologues, are able to draw together alienated and frustrated individuals or those looking for excitement through what he calls 'sense-making'. The leader provides a unifying message, identifies the external enemy as the cause, and draws individuals together into a collective identity (Post, 2005, 2007). The five indicators identified in this section delineate the potential drivers of a subject's commitment to violent action, for example, an individual may be a leader, an ideologue, a follower, criminal opportunist, seeker of excitement and adventure, or be motivated by a combination of many of these elements. This section permits a differential analysis of these components with a measurement of the importance of each. The weight of each of these commitment and motivational characteristics creates the individual composite analysis of the multi-faceted aspects of motivation. Information obtained from this analysis provides information on vulnerabilities, inspiration, and the motivational drivers that influence action, as well as an understanding of the impact that power and leadership exert on an individual. This information identifies how vulnerabilities may be utilised to influence individuals in a correctional setting. This knowledge is used to optimise the management of the offender. More difficulty would be anticipated to modify the attitudes of a leader or ideologue, for example, than for a follower, criminal opportunist, or a seeker of excitement and adventure. Commitment to the cause and the motivational drivers are known to be fundamental influences in acts of terrorism (FBI, 2011).

Protective indicators

This section includes indicators that represent mitigating influences on risk. These indicators include (1) the individual's re-interpretation of his or her ideology to a less rigid and less absolute position; (2) the rejection of the use of violence to achieve the desired goals; (3) a positive change in the offender's perception of who or what was 'the enemy' or a 'justifiable target' of grievances; (4) participation in non-violence-oriented interventions, de-radicalisation, or other offence-related programs; (5) community support for non-violence that can influence the offender; and (6) family (spousal, parental, and other kin) support for non-violence that has persuasive power on the offender. These indicators have been identified as exerting a mitigating influence on violent extremist action (Horgan, 2003; Sageman, 2004, 2008; Silber & Bhatt, 2007; Demant et al., 2008; Bjorgo & Horgan, 2008).

Summary and conclusion

The VERA-2 risk assessment protocol for violent extremists and terrorists is not a silver bullet of prediction. It is able to provide offence-specific supportive information on the risk of future violence of convicted and incarcerated violent extremist offenders. The information obtained from its use in a high-security correctional setting has been found to assist security and case management decisions for convicted violent extremists. In particular, the VERA-2 contributes to a multimodal risk assessment process that considers information from multiple sources. As such, the VERA-2 is being used in the risk assessment process in conjunction with other assessment approaches. The VERA-2 provides forensic psychologists and correctional staff in high-security correctional settings with previously unavailable and useful information. It has also provided relevant information to other officials. It is anticipated that the VERA-2 will have utility in other correctional facilities where violent extremists are incarcerated.

References

Andrews, D. A., & Bonta, J. L. (2000). *Manual for the Level of Service Inventory*. Toronto: Multi-Health Systems.

Atran, S. (2003). 'Genesis of suicide terrorism.' *Science*, 299, 1534–1539.

Atran, S. (2008). 'The making of a terrorist: A need for understanding from the field.' Testimony before the House Appropriations Subcommittee on Homeland Security. Washington, DC. Retrieved from http://sitemaker.umich.edu/satran/files/atran_congress_12march08.pdf

Atran, S. (2010). *Talking to the Enemy: Faith, Brotherhood, and the (Un)Making of Terrorists*. New York: HarperCollins.

Bakker, E. (2006). *Jihadi Terrorists in Europe their Characteristics and the Circumstances in Which They Joined the Jihad: An Exploratory Study*. The Hague: Netherlands Institute of International Relations. Retrieved from http://www.clingendael.nl/publications/2006/20061200_cscp_csp_bakker.pdf

Bjorgo, T., & Horgan, J. (2008). *Leaving Terrorism Behind: Individual and Collective Disengagement*. New York: Routledge.

Bonta, J., Law, M., & Hanson, R. K. (1998). 'The prediction of criminal and violent recidivism among mentally disordered offenders: A meta-analysis.' *Psychological Bulletin*, 123, 123–142.

Borum, R. (2003). 'Understanding the terrorist mind-set-perspective.' *FBI Law Enforcement Bulletin*, 72 (7), 7–10.

Borum, R. (2000). 'Assessing violence risk among youth'. *Journal of Clinical Psychology*, 56, 1263–1288.

Borum, R., Bartel, P., & Forth, A. (2006). *SAVRY: Professional Manual for Structured Assessment of Violence Risk in Youth*. Lutz, FL: Psychological Assessment Resources Inc.

Borum, R., Fein, R. A., Vossekuil, B., & Berglund, J. (1999). 'Threat assessment: Defining an approach for evaluating risk of targeted violence.' *Behavioral Sciences and the Law*, 17, 323–33.

Borum, R., Swartz, M., & Swanson, J. (1996). 'Assessing and managing violence risk in clinical practice.' *Journal of Practical Psychiatry and Behavioral Health*, 2, 205–215.

Conway, M. (2006). 'Terrorism and the Internet: New media-new threat?' *Parliamentary Affairs* 59(2), 283–298. *UK Politics and The Internet – The First Decade*, Oxford University Press, 2006.

Conway, M. (2007). 'Terrorist use of the internet and the challenges of governing cyberspace.' In M. Dunn, V. Mauer, & F. Krishna-Hensel (Eds.) *Power and Security in the Information Age: Investigating the Role of the State in Cyberspace*. London: Ashgate. 95–127.

Cornish, P. (2008). *Terrorism, Radicalisation and the Internet*. Chatham House, UK. Retrieved from: http://www.chathamhouse.org/sites/default/files/public/Research/International%20Security/0708terrorism_internet.pdf .

Crenshaw, M. (1981). 'The causes of terrorism.' *Comparative Politics*. 13, 379–399.

Crenshaw, M. (1995). 'Thoughts on relating terrorism to historical context.' In M. Crenshaw (Ed.), *Terrorism in Context* (pp. 3–24). University Park: Pennsylvania State University Press.

Crenshaw, M. (2000). 'The psychology of terrorism: An agenda for the 21st century.' *Political Psychology*, 21, 405–420.

Demant, F., Slootman, M., Buijs, F., & Tillie, J. (2008). *Decline and Disengagement: An Analysis of the Processes of De-radicalisation*. Amsterdam, Netherlands: IMES, University of Amsterdam.

Department of Defence (2010). *DOD Dictionary of Military and Associated Terms*. Retrieved from http://www.dtic.mil/doctrine/dod_dictionary/data/t/7591.html

Dolan, M. & Doyle, M. (2000). 'Violence risk prediction: clinical and actuarial measures and the role of the Psychopathy Checklist.' *British Journal of Psychiatry*, 177, 303–311.

Douglas, K., Webster, C. D., Hart, S., Eaves, D., & Ogloff, J. (2002). *HCR-20: Violence Risk Management Companion Guide.* Vancouver, BC: Mental Health Law & Policy Institute, Simon Fraser University.

FBI (2001). *Terrorism 2000/2001.* Federal Bureau of Investigation Publication #0308. Department of Justice, United States of America. Retrieved from: http://www.fbi.gov/stats-services/publications/terror/terror00_01.pdf

FBI (2011). *Federal Bureau of Investigation Counterterrorism Analytical Lexicon.* Department of Justice, United States of America. Retrieved 31 October, 2011 from: http://cryptome.org/fbi-ct-lexicon.pdf

Fein, R. A., & Vossekuil, B. (1998). *Protective Intelligence and Threat Assessment Investigations: A Guide for State and Local Law Officials* (NCJ No.170612). Washington, DC: National Institute of Justice, Office of Justice Programs.

Goldson, B. (2011). *Youth in Crisis? 'Gangs', Territoriality and Violence.* New York: Routledge.

G-8 Summit (2010). *Final Statement of the Leaders at the Muskoka G-8 Summit.* Accessed October 28, 2011 at http://www.canadainternational.gc.ca/g8/summit-sommet/2010/muskoka-statementterrorism-muskoka.aspx?lang=eng&view=d

Haidt, J. (2003). 'The moral emotions.' In R. J. Davidson, K. R. Scherer, & H. H. Goldsmith (Eds.), *Handbook of Affective Sciences* (pp. 852–870). Oxford: Oxford University Press.

Halloran, J. (1967). *Attitude Formation and Change.* Leicester: Leicester University Press.

Hanson, R. K. (2005). 'Twenty years of progress in violence risk assessment.' *Journal of Interpersonal Violence,* 20 (2), 212–217.

Hart, S. D., Cox, D. N., & Hare, R. D. (2003). *The Hare Psychopathy Checklist: Screening Version (PCL:SV).* Toronto: Multi-Health Systems.

Hart, S. D., & Logan, C. (2011). 'Formulation of violence risk using evidence-based assessments: The Structured Professional Judgment approach.' In P. Sturmey & M. McMurran (Eds.), *Forensic Case Formulation.* Chichester, UK: Wiley Blackwell. Retrieved from: http://www.sfu.ca/psyc/faculty/hart/Hart,_SFU_Website/Publications_files/Hart%20%26%20Logan,%202011,%20Sturmey%20%26%20McMurran,%20Formulation%20of%20violence%20risk.pdf

Horgan, J. (2003). 'Leaving terrorism behind: An individual's perspective.' In A. Silke (Ed.), *Terrorists, Victims and Society.* New York: John Wiley and Sons.

Horgan, J. (2005). *The Psychology of Terrorism.* London: Routledge.

Horgan, J. (2008). 'From profiles to pathways and roots to routes: Perspectives from psychology on radicalisation into terrorism.' *Annals of the American Association of Political and Social Sciences,* 618, 80–94.

Horgan, J. (2012). 'Interviewing the terrorists: Reflections on fieldwork and implications for psychological research.' *Behavioral Sciences of Terrorism and Political Aggression,* 4(3), 195–211.

ISD (2011). *Radicalisation: The Role of the Internet.* A Working Paper of the PPN. Institute for Strategic Dialogue: Retrieved from: http://www.strategicdialogue.org/allnewmats/idandsc2011/StockholmPPN2011_BackgroundPaper_FINAL.pdf

Kreuger, A. B. (2007). *What Makes A Terrorist: Economics and the Roots of Terrorism.* Princeton, NJ: Princeton University Press.

Kreuger, A. B., & Maleckova, J. (2002) 'Does poverty cause terrorism?' *The New Republic,* June 24, pp. 27–33.

Kruglanski, A., Chen, X., Dechesne, M., Fishman, S., & Orehek, E. (2009). 'Fully committed: Suicide bombers' motivation and the quest for personal significance.' *Political Psychology,* 30, 331–357.

Kruglanski, A., & Fishman, S. (2006). 'Terrorism: Between "syndrome" and "tool".' *Current Directions in Psychological Science,* 15, 45–48.

LaFree, G., & Dugan, L. (2004). 'How does studying terrorism compare to studying crime?' In M. DeFlem (Ed.), *Terrorism and Counter-Terrorism: Criminological Perspectives* (pp. 53–74). New York: Elsevier.

Marzuk, P. M. (1996). 'Violence, crime and mental illness: How strong a link?' *Archives of General Psychiatry*, 53, 481–486.

Merari, A. (2005). 'Social, organizational and psychological factors in suicide terrorism.' In T. Bjorgo (Ed.), *Root Causes of Terrorism: Myths, Reality and Ways Forward* (pp. 70–89). London: Routledge.

Merari, A. (2010). *Driven to Death: Psychological and Social Aspects of Suicide Terrorism*. New York: Oxford University Press.

Monahan, J. (1981). *Predicting Violent Behavior: An Assessment of Clinical Techniques*. Newbury Park, CA: Sage.

Monahan, J. (2012). 'The individual risk assessment of terrorism.' *Psychology, Public Policy, and Law*, 18(2), 167–205.

Monahan, J., & Steadman, H. J. (1994). 'Violence risk assessment: A quarter century of research.' In L. E. Frost & R. J. Bonnie (Eds.), *The Evolution of Mental Health Law* (pp.195–211). Washington, DC: American Psychological Association.

Monahan, J., Steadman, H., Silver, E., Appelbaum, P., Robbins, P., Mulvey, E., Roth, L., Grisso, T., & Banks, S. (2001). *Rethinking Risk Assessment: The MacArthur Study of Mental Disorder and Violence*. New York: Oxford University Press.

McCauley, C., & Moskalenko, S. (2011). *Friction: How Radicalisation Happens to Them and Us*. New York: Oxford University Press.

Mullins, S. (2011). 'Australian jihad: radicalisation and counter-terrorism – analysis.' *Eurasia Review*, October 2011. Retrieved from: http://www.eurasiareview.com/19102011-australian-jihad-radialisation-and-countre-terrorism-analysis/

Nesser, P. (2004). *Jihad in Europe: A Survey of the Motivations for Sunni Islamist Terrorism in Post Millennium Europe* (FFI Rapport 2004/01146). Kjeller, Norway: Norwegian Defence Research Establishment.

Neumann, P. (2010). *Prisons and Terrorism: Radicalisation and De-Radicalisation in 15 Countries*. London: ICSR Publication.

Ogloff, J. (2009). *The Violent Client: Advances in Violent Risk Assessment*. Melbourne, Victoria: The Australian Psychological Society.

Pape, R. (2005). *Dying to Win: The Strategic Logic of Suicide Terrorism*. New York: Random House.

Perl, R. (2007). *International Terrorism: Threat, Policy, and Response*. Congressional Research Service. Retrieved from: http://www.fas.org/sgp/crs/terror/RL33600.pdf

Piaget, J. (1926). *The Language and Thought of the Child*. First English translation from the French language. Originally published by Routledge, London. Reprinted by Routledge, NY, 2001 edition.

Post, J. M. (2005). 'Psychology: report of the Psychology Working Group.' In *Addressing the Causes of Terrorism: The Club de Madrid Series on Democracy and Terrorism, Volume 1*. The International Summit on Democracy, Terrorism and Security, 8–11 March, 2005. Available from Club de Madrid, Felipe 1V, 9–3 izqda, 28014 Madrid, Spain.

Post, J. M. (2007). *The Mind of the Terrorist: The Psychology of Terrorism from the IRA to Al Qaeda*. New York: Palgrave Macmillan.

Precht, T. (2007). *Home Grown Terrorism and Islamist Radicalisation in Europe: From Conversion to Terrorism*. Copenhagen, Denmark: Danish Ministry of Justice.

Pressman, D. E. (2008). 'Exploring the sources of radicalisation and violent radicalisation: Transatlantic perspectives.' *Journal of Security Issues*, 2, 1–20.

Pressman, D. E. (2009). 'Risk assessment decisions for violent political extremism.' Retrieved from http://www.publicsafety.gc.ca/res/cor/rep/_fl/2009-02-rdv-eng.pdf Available as *Risk Assessment Decisions for Violent Political Extremism 2009-02*. Public Safety Canada, Government of Canada, Ottawa. Cat. No. PS3-1/2009-2-1E-PDF

Pressman, D. E., & Flockton, J. S. (2010). *VERA-2. Violent extremism Risk Assessment, Version 2 Manual* (unpublished manuscript).

Pressman, D. E., & Flockton, J. S. (2012a). 'Calibrating risk for violent political extremists: The VERA-2 structural assessment.' *The British Journal of Forensic Practise*, 14 (4).

Pressman, D. E., & Flockton, J. S. (2012b). 'Applied risk assessment for violent political extremists and terrorists using the VERA 2.' Paper presented to the British Psychological Society: Division of Forensic Psychology Annual Conference Terrorism Symposium, Cardiff, Wales, 28 June, 2012.

Sageman, M. (2004). *Understanding Terror Networks*. Philadelphia: University of Pennsylvania Press.

Sageman, M. (2008). *Leaderless Jihad: Terror Networks in the Twenty First Century*. Philadelphia: University of Pennsylvania Press.

Saucier, G., Akers, L., Shen-Miller, S., Kne_evi_, G., & Stankov, L. (2009). 'Patterns of thinking in militant extremism.' *Perspectives on Psychological Science*, 4, 256–271.

Schmid, A. P., & Jongman, A. J. (1988). *Political Terrorism* (2nd edition). Oxford: North-Holland Publishing Company.

Silber, M. D., & Bhatt, A. (2007). *Radicalisation in the West: The Homegrown Threat*. New York: New York City Police Department. Retrieved from http://www.nypdshield.org/public/SiteFiles/documents/NYPD_Report-Radicalisation_in_the_West.pdf

Silke, A. (2003). 'Becoming a terrorist.' In A. Silke (Ed) *Terrorists, Victims and Society*. Chichester, UK: John Wiley & Sons Ltd.

Skeem, J., & Monahan, J. (2011). 'Current directions in violence risk assessment.' *Current Directions in Psychological Science, Virginia Public Law and Legal Theory Research Paper No. 2011-13*.

Stanton, G. H. (1996). *The 8 Stages of Genocide*. A briefing paper presented to the US State Department. Retrieved from: http://www.genocidewatch.org/aboutgenocide/8stagesofgenocide.html

Taher, A. (2011). 'The middle-class terrorists: More than 60pc of suspects are well educated and from comfortable backgrounds, says secret MI5 file.' *The Daily Mail* October 18, 2011. Retrieved from: http://www.dailymail.co.uk/news/article-2049646/The-middle-class-terrorists-More-60pc-suspects-educated-comfortable-backgrounds-says-secret-MI5-file.html

Taylor, M., & Horgan, J. (2006). 'A conceptual framework for addressing psychological process in the development of the terrorist.' *Terrorism and Political Violence*, 18, 1–17.

United Kingdom (2000). *Terrorism Act: 2000 (c.11)*. London, UK: Acts of Parliament, UK Government.

Waytz, A., & Epley, N. (2012). 'Social connection enables dehumanization.' *Journal of Experimental Social Psychology*, 48(1) 70–76.

Webster, C. D., Douglas, K. S., Eaves, D., & Hart, S. (1997). *HCR-20 Assessing Risk for Violence: Version 2*. Vancouver, BC: Mental Health Law & Policy Institute, Simon Fraser University.

Webster, C. D., Douglas, K. S., Eaves, D., & Hart, S. (2001). *HCR-20 Violence Risk Management Companion Guide:* Vancouver, BC: Mental Health Law & Policy Institute, Simon Fraser University.

Weine, S., Horgan, J., Robertson, C., Loue, S., Mohamed, A., & Noor, S. (2009). 'Community and family approaches to combating the radicalisation and recruitment of Somali-American youth and young adults: A psychosocial perspective.' *Dynamics of Asymmetric Conflict*, 2, 181–200.

Weimann, G. (2004). *www.terror.net How Modern Terrorism Uses the Internet.* Retrieved from: http://www.usip.org/publications/wwwterrornet-how-modern-terrorism-uses-internet, U.S. Institute of Peace.

Wong, S., & Gordon, A. (2000). *Violence Risk Scale – Screening Version.* Regional Psychiatric Centre (Prairies) and the University of Saskatchewan, Canada.

10

THE ISRAELI EXPERIENCE OF TERRORIST LEADERS IN PRISON

Issues in radicalisation and de-radicalisation

Sagit Yehoshua

Introduction

Since the 1967 war between Israel and its neighbours, many Palestinians have been convicted in Israeli courts for involvement in terror activities. They have come to be part of a unique group of prisoners incarcerated in Israeli prisons. In Israel these prisoners are defined as 'security prisoners'. This classification is determined by the prison governor and by regulations issued by the Israeli prison authority regarding the definitions of different types of prisoners. Its purpose is to differentiate these prisoners – usually by their identity, political attitude and offences – from regular criminal prisoners. This classification is an administrative policy and not a legal one, and allows the prison authorities a unique freedom in supervising this group of prisoners and in handling them in such a manner as to avoid a security risk when dealing with visits, phone calls and early releases. Furthermore, these prisoners are handled as a homogenous group posing a dangerous risk, rather than as individuals with unique backgrounds and specific needs (Rosenfeld, 2004; Nashif, 2008; Ajzenstadt and Ariel, 2008; Harel, 2011; Berda, 2011; Korn, 2011; Baker 2011).

The number of Palestinians detained and arrested in relation to security offences against the state of Israel was relatively high during the first Intifada (1987–1992). The Oslo accords signed in 1994 signalled a new era, during which Israel released a large number of prisoners and reduced the number of detentions and arrests. This trend lasted until the second Intifada broke out in 2000 (Isaac, 1989; Rosenfeld, 2011). Since then the dynamic has changed again, with the number of Palestinian prisoners in Israeli jails peaking in 2006 with nearly 10,000 inmates.

Since 2006, however, there has been a steady decline in prisoner numbers, with slightly more than 7,000 prisoners in 2009 and less than 6,000 in 2011.[1] In late 2011, Israel released 1,027 of these security prisoners as part of a deal with Hamas to free the Israeli soldier, Gilad Shalit, who was captured and held by Hamas for more than five years. This deal reduced the number of security prisoners in Israeli jails to less than 5,000.

Nashif (2008, p.72) described the Israeli prisons as "one of the major sites of Palestinian national movement" and Hajjar (2005, p.209) defined it as "part of the sociocultural bonds that unite Palestinians in the Occupied Territories as a community". Due to their quantity, Palestinian prisoners construct a whole new community inside the prisons, under a new social space, through the concepts of identity and collectivism, and into fully formalised institutions (Nashif, 2008; Shaked, 2008). Hajjar (2005, p.207) describes it as "a society within society". Rosenfeld (2011) details that the prisoners institutionalised themselves in the late sixties and early seventies, while their unique formation gained even further significance in the mid to late eighties up to the early nineties. These organisations took charge of handling every aspect of the prisoners' day-to-day lives, such as dealing with the prisoners' basic necessities, their education and their involvement in political discussions and political activism in general.

The organisations supply the prisoner with his basic needs as well as with information about the organisation itself and further education in relation to the conflict or general topics. The prisoner learns about the history of the conflict and the organisation's ideology, history, founders and conduct. Most prisoners report being more politically attuned and having a better understanding of the conflict and the struggle only after they have entered prison. Some prisoners even develop their leadership skills and abilities during their time in prison and others enhance their solidarity and sense of personal and social identity (Hajjar, 2005; Bornstein, 2001, 2010).

Accordingly, prison plays a significant role in affecting the life and conduct of security prisoners as well as forming a unique community and institution which shapes the life and identity of the prisoners as well as Palestinian society.

The following findings are based on research which was conducted in Israeli prisons and lasted more than a year. It includes interviews with eighteen leaders of the most active and audacious terrorist groups in Israel: Hamas, Fatah and Islamic Jihad. The interviews provided data regarding the life history, thoughts, mind-set, attitudes and social surroundings of the eighteen leaders. The findings emphasised the unique process this group of prisoners goes through while incarcerated, and the impact this process has on their conduct in prison and out of prison upon their release.

The process Palestinian prisoners go through in Israeli prisons

Criminology theories highlight the process that a prisoner goes through while in prison as a very traumatic and painful one, with the prisoner losing his total freedom along with his identity and personal safety (e.g. Sykes, 1958; Goffman, 1961). The findings of this research, however, illustrate that the interviewed prisoners go through a very different process, showing almost no signs of "pains of imprisonment"[2] such as desperation, loss of vitality or loss of self. Moreover, the Palestinian prisoners show a remarkable adjustment to prison at the very first stages of their incarceration, being active in daily life, taking on leadership roles and using their time effectively for gaining education and self-development.

The analysis of these interviews, as well as other resources such as personal files and statements by prison personnel, reveals that this process leads these prisoners to feel empowered rather than hopeless and despairing. Furthermore, it seems that the source of this unique mechanism of behaviour and attitude relies on the Palestinian – as well as the Arab – cultural perception of a prisoner in Israeli jails. This views being a prisoner as honourable and admirable, as being at the frontline of the struggle and as a metaphor for the Palestinian situation. For the prisoners themselves, this position of status allows them opportunities for self-improvement as well as an improvement of conditions for their families.[3]

Pain of imprisonment?

Planning for the future:

> When I entered prison I asked a veteran prisoner, who was already in prison for 25 years, how he sees the future, and he answered that there is no prisoner who does not plan his future and think of it every day. If a prisoner is convinced in what he has done, and what he is still doing, then he will always look forward, knowing that justice has to be done and that is what is holding him together and gives him strength. . . . When I look at myself and my future, sometimes I am worried but mostly I see a light at the end of the tunnel.
>
> *(Interviewee number 2)*

These are the words of a senior Hamas leader who was charged and convicted of multiple accounts of murder and terrorist acts and was sentenced to life imprisonment. His words reflect the thoughts of the majority of the leaders interviewed in this research in terms of anticipating their imminent release and hence planning their future carefully as well as feeling strong optimism towards it. In contrast to criminal prisoners, these prisoners entered prison with a sense of righteousness, belief in their acts, as well as their immediate honourable release (see also Qouta, Punamäki and El Sarraj, 1997; Shaked, 2008). Interestingly, interviewee number 2 was indeed released recently as part of the Gilad Shalit deal mentioned earlier in this chapter. The Shalit deal had ironically validated the prisoners' hopeful point of view and their anticipation that despite being convicted and sentenced to life imprisonment they would be free in the near future.

One more example to validate this argument can be gleaned from the words of interviewee number 5 who is a Hamas leader as well, charged and convicted of five counts of murder and other terrorist acts and sentenced to six life imprisonments. He declares: "I am not interested in looking back, only to the future. I want to plan my future carefully. I am working on it with my wife and believe there is a great chance that I will be released". This prisoner was also released following the Gilad Shalit deal.

Support from fellow prisoners and from the outside

Another aspect that contributes greatly to these prisoners' adjustment to imprisonment is the support and care they receive from sources outside prison, as well as from their fellow prisoners. The majority of interviewees were well aware of the support and respect that they receive from their social surroundings outside prison. Most of them declared their families to be very close and supportive, thus giving them strength, whether they are married and have children or are single and relying on their parents and siblings to be there for them. However, the majority of them prefer to ignore the pain that their acts can cause their families, and to instead place emphasis on the needs of their wider society, which indeed admires them for their acts. As can be seen from the words of interviewee number 13:

> We are ten people in the family, eight siblings and my parents. The relations in the family were always very good and we are very close . . . My dad wanted me to do other things, even though he was a Fatah member but forty years ago, he tells me to be careful to take care . . . They love me a lot, it was very hard for them when I went to prison but my mum is happy that at least she can see me and talk to me.

This interviewee is a Fatah member who was convicted of murders and different terrorist acts for which he was sentenced to twelve life sentences and fifty-five years in prison. Throughout his interview he describes the care and love he shares with his family, yet, whenever he was forced to choose between them and his activities in the organisation, as far as he was concerned, there was no question what was the right thing to do.

This pattern is quite consistent and appears in most interviews. Another example of it is shown in the case of interviewee number 15, a Fatah member who was sentenced to a life sentence for a murder and further terrorist acts he had committed.

> We are eight siblings in the family, I'm the youngest one. The situation in the family was very good, they gave me everything I wanted and the relationships in the family were very good . . . My family did not know about my involvement in the organisation but they have felt it and tried to warn me. It is difficult for them to see what is happening to our people but they still do not want me to get hurt or die . . . When I was arrested it was very hard, my mum was following me to the car crying, she could not believe I was being arrested. At the first visit she asked me, Why have I done that? And that I had everything I wanted. And I have told her that I just had to do it.

Correspondingly, these prisoners are part of a very strong group which gives them structure and support, teaches them everything they need to know about their incarceration and about the organisation, as well as other forms of knowledge they are interested in gaining, whether academic or vocational. During their time in prison the prisoners are exposed to substantial support offered by the organisation. Furthermore, they gain a degree of confidence and certainty with regard to their future, knowing they will be taken care of upon their release.

Interviewee number 18 explained it accurately by saying:

> I have no specific plans for when I will be released . . . but whenever I will be released I know that whatever I will ask for I will receive. I have a reputation outside and whatever I will want I will get, just like any other leader here in prison.

Education

According to data held by the Israeli Prison System (IPS), the security prisoner is entitled to study independently any subject he wishes to in accordance with the security limitations (Virtser, 2005; Shaked, 2008; Ben-Tsur, 2007). Most of the prisoners study to complete the Palestinian high school diploma exams called "Tawjiya", while many others are enrolled in higher education studies through the Open University and some are awarded academic degrees. However, the access these prisoners have to education and academic studies is rather controversial within Israeli society, where many think that they should not gain any benefits from their incarceration as a punishment for their acts. Recently, following the aforementioned Gilad Shalit deal, there was public outcry demanding a law to prohibit this "privilege" for prisoners convicted of terrorist activities, and indeed in the few years prior to Shalit release the prisoners were banned from acquiring any education while in prison (Ataeli and Bander, 2011; Bander, 2010; Vaysman, 2009).

This was emphasised by interviewee number 3, who said:

> After all the difficulties, I finished here in prison my degree in political science and international relations. I knew my family wanted to see me educated so when I received the diploma I gave it to my mum two weeks ago. It is an immense achievement to my family and a big step for me. I am planning on continuing to do a Master's and a Doctorate specialising in the media and diplomacy. I will have the title doctor in front of my name; I can make a difference and do important things.

This interviewee is a leader of Fatah; it is his first incarceration after being sentenced to twenty years on charges of committing various severe terrorist acts. He entered prison before finishing high school and developed himself in prison, achieved his first degree and is determined to continue further in higher education.

These aspects corroborate elements discussed previously, which suggest that prisoners imagine a hopeful future and will plan ahead, receiving massive support from their social surroundings as well as their organisations and their culture in general, gaining support and guidance from their fellow prisoners, and widening their horizons by further education. This is an altogether different and more intense process than the usual process that an "ordinary" criminal prisoner goes through (Sykes, 1958; Goffman, 1961; Dhami, Ayton & Loewenstein, 2007). Though none of them declare incarceration to be easy and enjoyable, the security prisoners interviewed do not show signs of "pain of imprisonment", and the research suggests that entering prison for the first time was relatively easy for them. Most of them have adjusted well to their circumstances and are even using it to develop themselves in the best way they can.

Radicalisation or de-radicalisation in Israeli prisons

The context in which de-radicalisation can occur is different from one place to another (Neumann, 2010; Gunaratna, Rubin and Jerard, 2011). Nonetheless, the Israeli case is unique in the sense that the government cannot initiate any programmes of rehabilitation or de-radicalisation to apply to the prisoners, unlike in the cases of other examples detailed in this book such as Saudi Arabia, Singapore or Yemen (e.g. Braddock, 2013; Porges, 2013; Ramakrishna, 2013). This is due to the fact that the majority of these prisoners do not even recognise Israel's existence and therefore will never cooperate with such initiatives.[4] However, according to the findings of this research, it seems that some of the variables that influence the de-radicalisation processes in these other countries still have some effects on the security prisoners in Israeli prisons as well. These variables, which will be analysed below, are: the attainment of education, the assumption of leadership roles and communication with the "others", meaning the Israeli authority, as well as the length of time spent in prison.

Acquiring education

As detailed previously, gaining education in prison is a very high priority for the security prisoners. This has a major effect on the process they go though in prison and in easing their adjustment to imprisonment. However, gaining education, especially higher education, while in prison, also has a significant influence on the process of de-radicalisation. The prisoners deliberately choose topics that relate to Israeli society, history and culture for strategic reasons, but by learning about these topics they inadvertently open their minds to a better understanding of Israeli society, which allows them to become more pragmatic towards the conflict and its conduct.

There are no studies on this subject in Israeli prisons (Ben-Tsur, 2007), but the data which is available shows that while the majority of prisoners are studying to complete their high school diplomas, many others are studying academic degrees in prison via the Open University. However, in the years leading to the Shalit deal, the prison authorities banned any kind of formal education in prison except for non-formal means such as family visits and television privileges (Lis, Kobovitch and Shtul-trauring, 2011). This was originally done as a part of an attempt to put pressure on the organisations to release Shalit, but the policy has continued in the aftermath of Shalit's return and is still in place at the time of writing.

In terms of the educational status of the eighteen interviewees in this research, only two did not finish high school, while two others are still minors and thus had not finished high school. Of the other fourteen interviewees, seven did finish high school, three of them while in prison, but did not continue their studies to higher education, although three of them were keen on doing so in prison but were refused by the IPS. Seven other interviewees have gained degrees – most at undergraduate level – and two have gained a Master's degree. Four of these seven acquired their degrees while serving their time in prison.

Nevertheless, all the interviewees stressed the importance of their studies, whether academic or not, and the massive impact it has on their perceptions and conduct relating to every aspect of their lives, mainly their perception of the Israeli-Arab conflict and their role in it. Moreover, most of them, especially the ones who completed their studies while in prison, testify that these studies opened their minds towards understanding the conflict better, particularly the motives and conduct of Israeli society. To some extent this has even led to a change in their attitude regarding their methods and past behaviour towards a more pragmatic approach of dialogue and open-mindedness.

As interviewee number 5 explained:

> Since I entered prison I think before I decide, I count to ten and only then act – it was not like that before I entered prison. In prison we learn a lot from the Jews and also from the Open University – it changed me – I learn a lot about Israeli society and its history. In prison we live in a democracy, we always consult with each other. Outside I was not familiar with the concept of democracy and could not relate it to Islam. After I entered prison and started my studies I understood that it does not collide – I can say whatever I think and even fight for my opinion but also understand when my opinion is not accepted.

This interviewee is a senior Hamas leader who had been convicted of murders and other violent acts and was sentenced to six life terms. He is currently studying for his first degree at the Open University in prison.

Taking leadership roles – communication with the "others"

Prisons can also be places that allow communication with other groups and individuals, who normally do not have the opportunity or will to interact with each other. Such a channel of communication can open up minds and provoke thought on issues that gained limited consideration before (Ashour, 2007, 2008). In the Israeli prisons, the security prisoners are not allowed by their leadership to individually approach the guards and the prison authority; this option is possible only for prisoners who take up leadership roles. Communicating with the prison authorities has become one of the most influential elements of this process of de-radicalisation. Indeed, the leaders in prison have constant communication with the prison authority regarding the needs of the prisoners as well as regarding political and social decisions. Therefore, they all declare that their perceptions about Israelis have changed since becoming leaders, as this entailed getting to know the Israelis with whom they had to work, which was not an option before.

This is illustrated by a statement made by interviewee number 12:

> When I entered prison for the first time, I could not understand at all how the prisoners were communicating and cooperating with the guards, but now I understand that it is different here, that this is a different battlefield and there are different rules and different ways of conduct. Whoever enters prison goes through a positive change and becomes more moderate. Leaders that are released from prison are more pragmatic because they know that there is also another side, that not everything is black and white. In prison a leader deals constantly with compromises and many times he has to put himself in the place of the other side to be able to solve the matter.

This prisoner is the veteran interviewee in this research; he was sentenced to five life sentences for the murder of Israeli civilians and by the time of the interview he had already been in prison for almost thirty years.

Length of time spent in prison

Another important aspect identified in this study is the length of time prisoners spend in jail. Most of the prisoners when they were interviewed had already served more than ten years in prison, while the vast majority of them had been sentenced to, at least, a life sentence. Based on the analysis of the interviews, records and documents such as their personal files supplied to the researcher by the IPS, as well as prison staff reports, it appears that these prisoners are going through a unique process. Upon entering prison and for the first few years, they are radical in their views, hostile and angry towards the prison and Israeli authorities and society in general. They do everything they can to enhance their knowledge and practices relating to the organisations and the extremist agenda and conduct, to the extent that they become quite educated in every aspect relating to it. After this initial period and upon reaching the peak of their knowledge and proficiency, they feel confident enough to search for general knowledge, to open their minds to options that they had little exposure to before. In addition, the routine in prison is comfortable and relaxed so they are able to think more clearly and rationally and they become much more pragmatic towards the conflict and practical ways to deal with it.

This is a slow process, and is more likely to occur with the fulfilment of the other elements already mentioned such as gaining higher education and taking leadership roles. The first phase of amplified hostility usually takes place during the first four to five years of imprisonment, followed by another four to five years of the transitional phase characterised by mind opening and the broadening of horizons. Thus, it can take a prisoner at least eight to ten years to reach the phase characterised by pragmatic thinking. However, for many of the leaders in prison it might take even more time than that, depending on whether the other elements detailed previously are implemented, completely, partially or not at all. Other important factors relate to whether the organisations to which they belong are more radical in their agenda or are more religious, elements which might limit their views and their ability to compromise.

As interviewee number 15 expressed:

> I was not politically attuned, I did not have a solid political stance that will guide me to what is right or wrong and how to do things or not to do them at all. That has all changed since I entered prison where I had time to think and find my political way. Outside it's different, the leaders are playing a game which is different than what we want, there is a rivalry between people at the organisation and among the organisations and the people in general and it does not help our cause. Everyone believes in a different way and there is no cooperation. In prison it is different; there is an understanding between the people and the organisations as well, we do have different opinions but we debate and discuss the options and then decide together. I was twenty-one when I entered prison, I was young and hot blooded, and did things without thinking them through. That was the hardest lesson I have learned here. Today I have changed, I am more confident and have the strength to act accordingly.

This interviewee was sentenced to life in prison for a murder he committed and other terrorist acts. He had a history of holding radical views and extremist behaviour during his first twelve years in prison, but this pattern changed and in the three years prior to the interview the records indicate a more moderate prisoner and a pragmatic leader. The longer period of time that it took for him to go through the process of de-radicalisation may be linked to the fact that he only started his involvement in higher education later in his incarceration which he had not completed at the time of the interview. Furthermore, as a leader he initially refused to cooperate with the prison authority and began to do so only in the last three years of his confinement.

Another important aspect linked to the length of time the leaders spend in prison relates to their perceptions of what they conceive of as a sacrifice made by them. The vast majority of them have been imprisoned for more than ten years. As a result, they feel as though they have sacrificed enough and hence earned the privilege to think for themselves from this point on and to let others continue what they have started. Only eight out of the eighteen interviewees state that they will continue their involvement in relation to the struggle, though most of them distinguish between the military wing of the organisations and the political wing. They consider that by joining the political wing of the organisation and being part of the decision making (in contrast to continuing to be in the military wing) changes their whole involvement in the fighting, to the extent that they are not violent any more, that they have chosen a different path, in spite of the fact that it is the same organisation and whatever the leadership board decides, the operational wing executes.

As interviewee number 9 explains:

> I would not leave my political involvement but the way will change, the means will change. I believe I did what I had to do, since the beginning it was not something I specialised in, I am not qualified for it but I did it because I had to. Now I need to do what I am right for, what I am good at, I did enough. When I will be released I see myself raising my family, finishing my doctoral degree and having a distinguished position in the organisation but only on the political side.

This is an Islamic Jihad leader who was sentenced to twenty-one life terms. This is his second incarceration. In total he has been in prison for more than eight years and since his last incarceration he has been known to be cooperative and pragmatic in his decisions.

Summary

It seems that these prisoners' adjustment to incarceration is relatively easy and that they suffer from fewer symptoms of "pain of imprisonment" in comparison to other criminal prisoners. This can be verified by their conduct in prison, through their determination to plan for their near future despite their long-term sentences, and their persistent self-development via higher education and developing wider knowledge and skills. Furthermore, they are well aware of the strong support they receive from their family and social surroundings outside prison, as well as from their fellow prisoners who guide them throughout their first days in prison in every basic need. This patronage from both sources influences their self-esteem and allows them to perceive the incarceration as an essential task in reaching ideological and personal goals.

The results relating to the analysis of radicalisation or de-radicalisation of the leaders in Israeli prisons are not definite, or indeed similar, to the formal de-radicalisation programmes used in other countries and described elsewhere in this volume (e.g. Braddock, 2014; Porges, 2014). They do however show some real resemblance with the processes seen with paramilitary prisoners in Northern Ireland as described in chapters 6 and 19 (Morrison, 2014; Ferguson, 2014). It can be argued that due to the length of time spent in prison and by gaining education and general knowledge and taking on leadership roles, these Palestinian prisoners are all going through a process of self-development and mind opening. However, it is difficult to state whether it has been an actual de-radicalisation process due to the fact that most of them still believe in their organisation's agenda and some of them even declare they will be happy to go back to work in the organisation upon their release, although not in the military side of it but the political side. For this reason, there is a need to also consider other aspects such as the strong support of the organisations and their social surrounding towards the struggle and fighting for the noble cause of releasing their people and land from deprivation. This social context prevents them from abandoning entirely the agenda, and in adjusting to their prison experiences, they still see themselves as fighters but ones who are more pragmatic about solutions and more open minded to dialogue and communication.

Notes

1 The details and statistics are from the Israeli Prison Service website: http://www. shabas.gov.il/Shabas/TIPUL_PRISONER/Prisoners+Info/prisoners_bithahoni.htm, which was updated in June 2011. For more information see also Baker (2011, p.101–102).
2 "Pains of imprisonment" referred to the prisoner's loss of sovereignty and freedom of movement. For more regarding this concept see Johnson and Toch (1982); Haney (2006); Riley (2002).
3 For information regarding the attitude towards prisoners in the Palestinian society see Bornstein (2001, p.559); Nashif (2008, p.96); Marcus and Zilberdik (2011).
4 This attitude can be verified by a significant document written, in 2006, by the leaders of the main terrorist organisation in Israeli prisons, called "the prisoners' document", which was aimed at forming a reconciliation between Hamas and Fatah based on eighteen principles that both organisations should agree upon. Even though there was no acknowledgement of Israel's right to exist, the document was eventually accepted by all parties. See National Conciliation Document of the Prisoners, June 28, 2006, the original document translated to English and a revision: http://www.mideastweb. org/prisoners_letter.htm. For an analysis of the document by Israeli Ministry of Foreign Affairs see http://www.mfa.gov.il/MFA/About+the+Ministry/Behind+the+Headlines/ Palestinian+Prisoners+Document-+Stepping+away+from+peace+29-Jun-2006.htm.

References

Ajzenstadt, M. and Ariel, B. (2008). 'Terrorism and risk management.' *Punishment & Society*, 10/4, pp.355–374.
Ashour, O. (2007). 'Lions tamed? An inquiry into the causes of de-radicalization of armed Islamist movements: the case of the Egyptian Islamic Group.' *The Middle East Journal*, 61/4, pp.596–625.
Ashour, O. (2008). 'Islamist de-radicalization in Algeria: Successes and failures.' *The Middle East Institute Policy Brief*, 21, pp.1–10.
Ataeli, A. and Bander, A. (2011). 'The families' victims are furious – the security prisoners' conditions is outrageous.' *Maariv*, June 15, 2011, sec. News. http://www.nrg.co.il/ online/1/ART2/250/510.html.
Baker, A. (2011). 'Palestinian political prisoners.' In Nadim Rouhana and Areej Sabbagh-Khoury (Eds.), *The Palestinians in Israel: Readings in History, Politics and Society*, pp.100–109. Haifa, Israel: Mada al-Carmel Arab Center for Applied Social Research.
Bander, A. (2010). 'The ministers committee certify worsening the conditions of Hamas prisoners.' *Maariv*, May 25, 2010, sec. Military and security. http://www.nrg.co.il/ online/1/ART2/109/846.html.
Ben-Tsur, D. (2007). 'Political conflict confronted through prison education: a case study of Israeli teachers working with Palestinian prisoners.' *Journal of Correctional Education*, 58/2, pp.108–128.
Berda, Y. (2011). 'The security risk as a security risk: notes on the classification practices of the Israeli Security Service.' In Abeer Baker and Anat Matar (Eds.), *Threat: Palestinian Political Prisoners in Israel*, pp.44–56. London: Pluto Press.

Bornstein, A. (2001). 'Ethnography and the politics of prisoners in Palestine-Israel.' *Journal of Contemporary Ethnography*, 30/5, pp.546–574.

Bornstein, A. (2010). 'Palestinian prison ontologies.' *Dialectical Anthropology*, 34, pp.459–472.

Braddock, K. (2014). 'The talking cure? Communication and psychological impact in prison de-radicalisation programmes.' In A. Silke (Ed.), *Prisons, Terrorism and Extremism*. London: Routledge.

Dhami, M., Ayton, P. and Loewenstein, G. (2007). 'Adaptation to imprisonment.' *Criminal Justice and Behaviour*, 34/8, pp.1085–1100.

Ferguson, N. (2014). 'Northern Irish ex-prisoners: the impact of imprisonment on prisoners and the peace process in Northern Ireland.' In A. Silke (Ed.), *Prisons, Terrorism and Extremism*. London: Routledge.

'Full text of the Palestinian prisoner's national conciliation document.' (2012). *Mideastweb.org*, February 24, 2012. http://www.mideastweb.org/prisoners_letter.htm.

Goffman, E. (1961). *Asylums: Essays on the Social Situation of Mental Patients*. Harmondsworth, UK: Pelican.

Gunaratna, R., Rubin, L. and Jerard, J. (2011). *Terrorist Rehabilitation and Counter-Radicalisation: New Approaches to Counter-Terrorism*. London: Taylor & Francis.

Hajjar, L. (2005). *Courting Conflict: The Israeli Military Court System in the West Bank and Gaza*. University of California Press.

Haney, C. (2006). *Reforming Punishment: Psychological Limits to the Pains of Imprisonment*. Washington, DC: American Psychological Association.

Harel, A. (2011). 'Who is a security prisoner and why? An examination of the legality of prison regulations governing security prisoners.' In Abeer Baker and Anat Matar (Eds.), *Threat: Palestinian Political Prisoners in Israel*, pp.37–43. London: Pluto Press.

IPS (2011). 'The total sum of "security prisoners".' *Israeli shabas*. http://www.shabas. gov.il/Shabas/TIPUL_PRISONER/Prisoners+Info/prisoners_bithahoni.htm.

Isaac, J. (1989). 'A socio-economic study of administrative detainees at Ansar 3.' *Journal of Palestine Studies*, 18/4, pp.102–109.

Johnson, R. and Toch, H. (1982). *Pains of Imprisonment*. New York: Sage.

Korn, A. (2011). 'Prison policy and political imprisonment in Northern Ireland and Israel.' In Abeer Baker and Anat Matar (Eds.), *Threat: Palestinian Political Prisoners in Israel*, pp.68–82. London: Pluto Press.

Lis, J., Kobovitch, Y. and Shtul-trauring, A. (2011). 'Prime Minister Benyamin Netanyahu delayed for a year the legislation of worsening the conditions of security prisoners.' *Ha'aretz*, June 26, 2011. http://www.haaretz.co.il/news/politics/1.1178361.

Marcus, I. and Zilberdik, N. (2011). 'Abbas glorifies terrorist prisoners.' *PMW- Palestinian Media Watch*, November 1, 2011. http://www.palwatch.org/main.aspx?fi=157&doc_id=5794.

Morrison, J. (2014). 'A time to think, a time to talk: Irish Republican prisoners in the Northern Irish peace process.' In A. Silke (Ed.), *Prisons, Terrorism and Extremism*. London: Routledge.

Nashif, E. (2008). *Palestinian Political Prisoners: Identity and Community*. London: Taylor & Francis.

Neumann, P. (2010). *Prisons and Terrorism- Radicalisation and De-Radicalisation in 15 Countries*. London: ICSR Publication.

'Palestinian "Prisoners' Document": Stepping Away from Peace 29-Jun-2006', June 29, 2006. http://www.mfa.gov.il/MFA/About+the+Ministry/Behind+the+Headlines/Palestinian+Prisoners+Document-+Stepping+away+from+peace+29-Jun-2006.htm.

Porges, M. (2014). 'Saudi Arabia's "soft" approach to terrorist prisoners: a model for others?' In A. Silke (Ed.), *Prisons, Terrorism and Extremism*. London: Routledge.

Qouta, S., Punamäki, R. and El Sarraj, E. (1997). 'Prison experiences and coping styles among Palestinian men.' *Peace and Conflict: Journal of Peace Psychology*, 3, pp.19–36.

Ramakrishna, K. (2013). 'The "Three Rings" of terrorist rehabilitation and counter-ideological work in Singapore: a decade on.' In A. Silke (Ed.), *Prisons, Terrorism and Extremism*. London: Routledge.

Riley, J. (2002). 'The pains of imprisonment: exploring a classic text with contemporary authors.' *Journal of Criminal Justice Education*, 13/2, pp.443–461.

Rosenfeld, M. (2004). *Confronting the Occupation: Work, Education, and Political Activism of Palestinian Families in a Refugee Camp*. Stanford: Stanford University Press.

Rosenfeld, M. (2011). 'The centrality of the prisoners' movement to the Palestinian struggle against the Israeli occupation: a historical perspective.' In Abeer Baker and Anat Matar (Eds.), *Threat: Palestinian Political Prisoners in Israel*, pp.3–24. London: Pluto Press.

'Shahada (Death for Allah) Promotion | PMW', n.d. http://www.palwatch.org/main.aspx?fi=110.

Shaked, R. (2008). 'The security prisoners in Israeli prisons.' *Roim Shabas*. 26–29.

Sykes, G. (1958). *Society of Captives: Study of a Maximum Security Prison*. Princeton University Press.

Vaysman, L. (2009) 'The government decided: worsening the conditions of security prisoners in Israel.' *Globes*. 29 March. Available from: http://www.globes.co.il/news/article.aspx?did=1000438687.

Virtser, A. (2005) *Security Prisoners Incarcerated in the Israeli Prison System*. Available from: http://www.ips.gov.il/NR/rdonlyres/64FFF90C-4D22-43EE-A87B-7318EAE7048D/0/bitchoneemnet.pdf.

PART IV
Key case studies

11

TERRORISM, EXTREMISM, RADICALISATION AND THE OFFENDER MANAGEMENT SYSTEM IN ENGLAND AND WALES

Richard Pickering[1]

Introduction

The offender management system in England and Wales is familiar with the challenges posed by terrorism, extreme violence, criminal behaviour and dissocial attitudes. The questions and challenges raised by "new" types of terrorism, in particular Al Qaeda-influenced terrorism and the broader social phenomenon of radicalisation, play to a wider audience than those traditionally interested in prison, probation and offender management. Alongside wide-ranging speculation, academic and operational learning has increasingly begun to identify the drivers and stages of radicalisation as manifested in the offender population. A range of organisations, agencies and bodies who have responsibilities for delivering national security, are now looking to the offender management system as a potential area of vulnerability, risk, opportunity and learning. The challenge is to capture the learning so as to manage those risks.

Against this background, what is striking is that whilst there is agreement that there are a set of what might broadly be described as risks with an extremist flavour within the offender population, there is relatively little hard evidence. Instead, we have significant speculation and a degree of disagreement on both the extent and shape of this risk and the appropriate response.

Within government, CONTEST (the government's counter terrorism strategy) and the revised PREVENT strategy (which sets out the government's approach to identifying and countering radicalisation) both reference prisons and offenders as areas of concern (see HM Government, 2011a,b). The recent Home Affairs Select Committee (2012) report into the roots of violent radicalisation acknowledged the focus of these strategies but, after investigating, took a slightly different interpretation of the importance of institutions in the radicalisation process (see paras 36 and 37 of the report).

Discussion within pressure groups and think tanks, including RUSI (Clarke and Soria, 2010) and the Quilliam Foundation (Brandon, 2009) has in large part speculated on the diffuse question of radicalisation, the extent to which it may be taking place in the prison system and the adequacy and appropriateness of the operational response. This narrative is echoed in extensive press coverage which has recently started to address the risks posed in the community by terrorist offenders who have served the custodial part of their sentence (e.g. Gardham, Hutchison, Bingham and Savill, 2010; Firth, 2009).

These are all legitimate viewpoints and add to the discussion taking place around this range of topics. They echo the considerations and debates which took place within the prison service following the attacks of 9/11, and which then gathered pace and direction following the London bombings of 7/7 in 2005.

Where prisons come in – the Extremist Prisoners Working Group (EPWG)

The prison system in England and Wales has significant experience in the management of terrorists. The escape from HMP Whitemoor of IRA prisoners and the subsequent report by Sir John Woodcock (1994) was the single most influential incident of the last 50 years in shaping the delivery of secure prisons. But the emergence of what appear to be new, more covert, extreme and complex forms of terrorism has raised legitimate concerns about the ability of prisons to manage risk effectively, with particular concerns around radicalisation. It was against this background that the then Deputy Director General convened, in 2006, a series of seminars involving a wide range of practitioners, to consider these questions.

The report produced from these seminars recommended that there should be:

- written briefing materials to senior operational staff about the role of the Muslim chaplain within the Prison Chaplaincy Team and the establishment;
- a support network for Muslim chaplains that envelops their role both within the Prison Service and within their local communities;
- tools to help staff identify and counter the radical extremist;
- counter-radicalisation measures dovetailed into existing security systems and policies and priorities, to avoid impinging on core-business;
- Prison Service IT security intelligence systems (SIS) developed and networked;
- protocols to regulate how the Prison Service interacts with other agencies;
- policies on the strategic management of Islamist extremist prisoners, taking into consideration the comparative risks of dispersal and concentration and the long-term impact of extremism, as well as the resources available within the prison estate;
- dedicated training for establishment security managers, training managers and intelligence analysts on Islamist extremism and radicalisation;
- ongoing analysis of the extent of extremism across the prison estate as intelligence data is received;

- proposals should form a part of the Prison Service's commitment to the decency agenda;
- resettlement projects; and
- international learning to ensure best practice.

These recommendations were grouped into an action plan focusing on training, intelligence systems, intelligence and information analysis, facilitating deradicalisation and policy and procedure.

The Prison Service was at the same time dealing with the consequences of another seminal event – the racist murder at HMYOI Feltham of Zahid Mubarek, a young Asian man who was killed by his violent, racist cellmate in which the risks were neither identified nor actioned by the organisation. In its wake the then Director General acknowledged that the Prison Service was institutionally racist. This event, together with two subsequent Commission for Racial Equality (CRE) investigations and a public inquiry (Keith, 2006) became a watershed in the management of race issues and, alongside the conclusions of the EPWG, was critical in shaping the overall approach to extremism that followed.

How do things look now?

There have been significant developments since the EPWG reported. Many of these developments are as foreshadowed by the report There is increased and enhanced connectivity with operational partners; a range of training and briefing materials has been produced and continue to be refined; guidance on reporting and enhanced intelligence infrastructures are in place, with a new intelligence infrastructure commissioned and in its final stages of testing; there has been significant investment in and development of Muslim chaplains and the broader chaplaincy; and as discussed in chapter 7 in this volume, there has been a major drive in the development, evaluation and operationalisation of new and innovative interventions and other offender management tools.

The EPWG was, though, an exercise in crystal ball gazing. It speculated on the potential impact of a small but growing number of terrorist prisoners on the wider prisoner population and the implications for the configuration of service delivery and risk management. Discussion focused on the potential growth of these numbers with continuing prosecutions of large and complex conspiracies. The prospect of hundreds more such offenders, extrapolated from the public discussion of a speech by the Director General of the Security Service in November 2007 (BBC News, 2007) was not lost on the National Offender Management Service (NOMS) and was a matter of significant discussion.

In the event, the numbers current at the time of the EPWG report remained remarkably static. What did change over time was the mix and profile of prisoners held under Terrorism Act (TACT) powers. There have been fewer of what have been characterised as "goal line clearances" (arrest and prosecutions of well-developed plots shortly before their activation) and more "upstream" prosecutions of preparatory acts, fundraising and other "lesser" offences. This has meant a more diffuse population, receiving a wider range of sentences, with a small but significant number who have acted alone.

With passage of time, those who receive finite sentences progress through the system towards release. As a result, a significant and growing number of terrorist offenders have completed the custodial part of their sentence and have now spent time under licence in the community. There are currently a total of around 120 terrorist prisoners, just over 20 of whom are on remand and just under 20 held under extradition or immigration powers, with the balance convicted. Ninety are identified as Al Qaeda influenced, with the remaining 30 including animal rights, separatist and other domestic extremists. Since 2007, around 70 terrorist prisoners have progressed through the prison system; some have completed their sentence, some have been removed from the country and others remain under supervision in the community.

In terms of risk management, a set of behaviours have emerged that are progressively less conceptual and more the focus for active management. They include continuing extremist activity, criminal behaviours, threats to order and control, violent acts, bullying and radicalisation.

Development and implementation of a strategy

Whilst the initial focus of the extremism strategy was on taking forward the findings and recommendations of the EPWG, other operational, political and organisational developments have shaped the work further.

The impact of Mubarek has been significant. With hindsight it is noteworthy that many of the key players directly involved in formulating the extremist strategy had been closely associated with Mubarek and its aftermath. Whilst security and intelligence have been to the fore, key players in implementing the strategy have been the Muslim and Equalities Advisers, operational practitioners and, increasingly, developers and deliverers of interventions and public protection colleagues. The need for effective inter-agency work, a key conclusion of the EPWG, has been clear and is being realised. There has been increasingly close working with police, Home Office and other agencies, with a strong focus on formalising ways of working, structures and intelligence sharing.

The re-configuration of NOMS as an integrated organisation delivering end-to-end management of offenders has supported this holistic approach. Progressive developments in the demographics of the terrorist population, improving understanding of the impact of broader social pressures and radicalisation, and improved intelligence reporting have shaped the approach further. Resources have been allocated, including funds secured from the Home Office, to strengthen and develop key areas in intelligence, development of chaplaincy capacity, training, interventions and co-ordination of these activities.

Security and Intelligence have sought to define what we know about offender dynamics in custody. There has been a significant investment of time and effort in the security infrastructure, most notably of the High Security Estate with enhanced intelligence functionality. A wider infrastructure of regional counter terrorism co-ordinators provides an interface with external partners to facilitate joint working and assist operational colleagues in, for example, awareness raising and threat profiling.

Alongside a range of awareness raising, training (both internal and external) and briefings, a range of behaviours of potential concern have been identified and formalised to help front-line staff understand the complexities of radicalisation and produce assessments of threat, both of quantitative and qualitative natures.

One of the most critical areas of work has been attempting to look below the surface behaviours to understand the risk factors and the most appropriate response to them. The ability of NOMS staff to engage directly with extremists who not only have undergone a process of radicalisation but have gone to the extreme of acting on their ideology is a privileged one, not readily available to any other sector of government. A programme of activity, led by forensic psychologists, undertook extensive fieldwork to understand the dynamics and drivers behind the radical-isation and criminal acts of a number of terrorist offenders. This work became the basis for the development of bespoke interventions and a framework for the formulation of case management.

From the digest of learning, which captured some of the drivers and the phenomena which distinguish the fully formed terrorist from the disaffected and dissocial, emerged the Extremism Risk Guidance (ERG22+) which groups by engagement, intent and capability the key drivers observed in terrorists. This guidance, which is progressively being rolled out to practitioners in prisons and probation, provides a basis for screening offenders, identifying risk factors and signposting appropriate interventions.

At the same time, innovative approaches to intervention have been formulated, including the development of the Healthy Identity Intervention (HII), the Healthy Identity Intervention + (HII+) and explicitly faith-based approaches including Al Furqan (see Chapter 7 this volume). These new interventions sit alongside the existing suite of interventions and resettlement pathways whose relevance and applicability to extremist/radicalised offenders can be determined through the findings of the ERG and other risk screening tools such as OASys.

The role of the chaplaincy and specifically of Muslim chaplains and imams in responding to the risks posed by extremism and radicalisation has been much discussed. It was a key focus of the EPWG and is one of the areas of greatest divergence in terms of the scale and nature of provision between England and Wales and other administrations where provision of spiritual and pastoral support can be patchy and uncoordinated.

There has been a Muslim Adviser post in NOMS since the late 1990s and progressively a drive for greater multi-faith provision within the chaplaincy function specified in legislation. A negative Commission for Racial Equality report in 2003 commented that the faith needs of non-Christian religions, particularly Muslims (most of whom were members of minority ethnic groups), were not adequately met and, progressively, these deficits have been addressed through regime, diet and spiritual provision.

There are now in excess of 200 Muslim chaplains in prisons in England and Wales (as opposed to fewer than 100 in 2008). This increase has taken place against a background of careful recruitment in which religious credentials are checked and tested, backgrounds vetted and staff bolstered by training, support and networking opportunities. Muslim chaplains have been progressively integrated, through the multi-faith chaplaincies, into the management of prisons, providing a source of advice to governors on the appropriate provision of faith, pastoral support and advice. Muslim chaplains now run one-on-one sessions and Islamic classes, including formalised courses such as Tarbiya, to enhance prisoners' knowledge of Islam and provide support and help. Doing so helps to address issues of identity, faith and purpose and to counter the single narrative and distorted version of Islam used by radicalisers. Most recently, the development of the Al Furqan intervention has looked to do this explicitly where concerns exist about the risk posed by individual terrorist offenders.

In terms of demographics, one of the most striking developments of recent years has been the variation in sentences given by the courts to terrorist offenders. Whilst lengthy sentences continue to be handed down, as discussed above, the nature and variety of offences committed has also resulted in a wide range of sentences, some of which are relatively short. This, allied to the passage of time, has placed an increasing focus on preparing for the inevitable return to the community of convicted terrorists.

Against a background of a desire for de-radicalisation and counter-radicalisation tools, in part taken forward through the work on interventions referenced above, a framework for risk management has also developed, using as a starting point existing Multi Agency Protection Panel Arrangements (MAPPAs). Terrorist offenders have been brought within MAPPAs, with probation, police and other resources configured around this structure, aligned to the demographic of known and anticipated releases.

One challenge to this process has been the ability to engage effectively with released terrorists through the provision of interventions and resettlement activities within the multi-agency supervisory framework of MAPPAs, as well as the specific licence conditions available for the management of terrorist offenders. There is an unequal distribution of releases of terrorist offenders across the country, with high concentrations in a small number of urban areas. Local provision varies and questions of public acceptability are to the fore in working with local partners. Part of multi agency management of offenders in the community can include onward referral from NOMS providers to our Channel partners. Compliance with licence conditions has been closely monitored and enforcement action has been taken in discussion with MAPPA partners when concerns have been raised.

And as approaches and tools are developed for identifying and managing extremist risk in the broader population, structures are progressively being created to match risk to capability. A new pathfinder initiative requires action to be taken on receipt of information suggesting concerns about possible sympathies with extremist ideologies, specifically looking at the case for onward referral to intervention providers, both in the scope of offender management and, potentially, into areas of police primacy.

So what have we learned?

First, the terrorist population is not homogenous. Whilst initial concerns (possibly grounded in the experiences of the 1970s and 1980s) focused on co-ordinated and sophisticated terrorist plots being disrupted, with key players transplanted from the community into prisons, the current picture is much more nuanced. Numbers have not increased as significantly as initially feared or expected. The large, complex and multi-handed trials which created a significant operational challenge a few years ago (such as the dirty bomb and airline plots) have been followed by the arrest and prosecution of individuals for much more diverse behaviours, including self-starters, fund raisers and proselytisers. The resultant demographic, including women and teenagers as well as adult male offenders and with a range of challenging presentations including mental health deficits and significant public profiles, creates further challenges around estate configuration and infrastructure.

As a consequence, some of the theoretical discussions rehearsed in the EPWG and more widely about appropriate managerial responses now seem simplistic. For example, discussions of a dispersal policy premised on offence type as opposed to risk presentation have proved to be fundamentally misconceived given the actual demographic and risk profile of the terrorist population.

Second, the broader demographic of prisons is challenging and changing, and radicalisation, though much discussed, is hard to quantify. A lot of discussion has focused on risk factors including, for example, the role of charismatic individuals, grievances, conversion to Islam and the roles of various schools of faith. Yet many of these factors apply, in varying degrees, across the broad offender population. Much has been made by some of the apparently disproportionate number of Muslims in prisons. Distinguishing cultural identify from religious practice, from religiosity and from inappropriate behaviour is enormously challenging and can throw up a number of false positives, potentially generating actions that can deepen grievances and make things worse. Such analysis requires an in-depth understanding of concepts, custodial environments, individuals and group dynamics before a real understanding can be reached.

What is clear from reporting and research is that there are a multiplicity of behaviours and motivations in play which revolve around identity and manifestations of identity. Crudely, these can include ways of coping with imprisonment, techniques of self-protection, opportunities to exploit the custodial environment for personal or criminal gain and attempts to create power bases potentially for criminal purposes which may extend into extremist behaviour. The role of "moments in time", exploited by individuals including those who employ charismatic or violent personal characteristics, can be significant.

Third, the prison environment is a heightened and different version of that present in the community. Coping strategies reflect the specific pressures faced by individuals and vary from offender to offender, from location to location and from prison to prison, and may very well be only temporary. Challenges exist in understanding the very personal question of how an offender deals with the deprivation of liberty, the pressures and opportunities created by others and the impact of friendships, allegiances, bullying and criminal endeavour which all play out in a constrained environment. The extent to which these dynamics can also be positively influenced by location, regime, friendships and intervention also depends on the individual. Critically, the fluidity of these factors, the readiness of individuals to adapt and our lack of knowledge around the persistence of what may be temporary behaviours and affiliations all represent a major challenge in identifying and managing possible risk.

Fourth, risk management in this area is emergent and dynamic. The progression of terrorist/extremist offenders through the system requires careful mapping. The case for multi-agency activity is self evident and clear articulation of respective roles and responsibilities essential. The most obvious points of transition – remand into prison custody, conviction, sentence, release into the community on licence and sentence expiry – all represent points where the respective agency roles and responsibilities shift. This is no less true for terrorists or radicalised individuals than for other offenders and is a principle which shapes the work of all the various agencies that operate in this space.

Current and future challenges

Offender management is and remains a critical part of the government's overall counter terrorism strategy. It deals with the aftermath of the radicalisation process in the event that the state is unable to prevent it proceeding to terrorist activity. But it also has a role to play in managing those who may be vulnerable to radicalisation by diverting or protecting them from radicalising influences, or by identifying and reversing pathway influences. Where individuals remain resistant to these efforts and continue to seek to draw others to their world view and/or actively seek to engage in planning terrorist and other criminal acts, then intelligence gathering becomes a crucial aspect of good offender management.

But these are not activities which take place in a vacuum. The demographics of prisons are challenging in terms of age, health, learning and skill deficits, racial, social and ethnic tensions, disaffection and criminal activity. They are also changing as discussed in Liebling, Arnold and Straub's (2011) study of staff–prisoner relations at HMP Whitemoor. The HM Chief Inspector of Prisons (2010) thematic inspection of Muslim prisoners highlighted the further dangers of conflating risk with race or faith. The management of these complexities is challenging enough in itself, together with the ongoing priorities of delivering safe and decent regimes, rehabilitation, diversity, decency and effective work with partners, without the introduction to this mix of the difficult concept of radicalisation.

The operational culture within which this agenda develops is similarly complex. In one analysis, the aftermath of the CRE investigations following the murder of Zahid Mubarek created a dynamic of staff being fearful of getting it wrong, of being accused of being racist and hesitant to engage with certain groups of prisoners as a result. Yet at the same time, many of the improvements set in train following the investigation – equality impact assessments, improved equality monitoring, clear policies and auditable standards and better provision for minority groups, support the conclusions of the learning drawn from engagement with extremists – that an environment that respects ethnic and religious difference and actively promotes racial harmony is incompatible with divisive radicalising narratives and can protect against their influence or prompt their undoing. The acknowledgement of detriment and the honest promotion of remedial actions can go a significant way in protecting against both criminogenic and radicalising influences.

This is an emerging area of learning both for NOMS and government more broadly. The importance of the counter terrorism agenda has meant that funding streams have been available to develop capability at a time when other sources of income are reducing. The challenging agendas of delivering the rehabilitation revolution (Ministry of Justice, 2010), addressing the risks posed by organised crime (HM Government, 2011c) and maintaining public protection exist alongside this work.

The ability to integrate both tactically and strategically work on extremism and radicalisation into NOMS' broader responsibilities without losing focus on accountability is challenging. Future funding cannot be taken for granted and dependencies with partners may become progressively strained as, post Olympics, budgets and priorities are reassessed.

Conclusion

One of the challenges to any strategy is defining success. Narrowly, a counter terrorism strategy will be judged on its ability to prevent terrorist attacks but simply delivering a negative is hard to evidence. CONTEST through its 4 Ps (Protect, Prepare, Pursue and Prevent) articulates this challenge well. But in the specific setting of offender management the challenge is more nuanced. The starting point of risk management is to stop criminal activity. The offender management process seeks to do this but also to rehabilitate, and within this the extremism strategy looks to integrate into the broader offender management strategy specialist approaches to the identification and management of risk. We have made some progress but this is an area where ongoing dialogue, reflection and analysis remain crucial. NOMS remains a potential area of vulnerability, risk, opportunity and learning.

Note

1   An earlier version of this chapter was published as Pickering, R. (2012). 'Terrorism, extremism, radicalisation and the offender management system – the story so far.' *Prison Service Journal*, 203, pp.9–14.

References

BBC News, (2007). '"Thousands" pose UK terror threat.' http://news.bbc.co.uk/1/hi/uk/7078712.stm

Brandon, J. (2009). *Unlocking Al-Qaeda. Islamist Extremism in British Prisons.* London: Quilliam.

Clarke, M. and Soria, V. (2010). 'Terrorism: the new wave.' *RUSI Journal*, 155/4, pp.24–29.

Firth, N. (2009). 'Five freed terrorists sent back to prison after breaching parole.' *Daily Mail*, 1 October 2009. http://www.dailymail.co.uk/news/article-1217384/Five-freed-terrorists-sent-prison-breaching-parole.html

Gardham, D., Hutchison, P., Bingham, J. and Savill, R. (2010). 'Christmas bomb plotters were radicalised in jail.' *The Telegraph*, 22 Dec 2010. http://www.telegraph.co.uk/news/uknews/terrorism-in-the-uk/8218219/Christmas-bomb-plotters-were-radicalised-in-jail.html

HM Government, (2011a). *CONTEST: The United Kingdom's Strategy for Countering Terrorism.* London: The Stationery Office.

HM Government, (2011b). *Prevent Strategy.* London: The Stationery Office.

HM Government, (2011c). *Local to Global: Reducing the Risk from Organised Crime.* http://www.homeoffice.gov.uk/publications/crime/organised-crime-strategy?view=Binary

HM Chief Inspector of Prisons (2010). *Muslim Prisoners' Experiences: A Thematic Review.* http://www.justice.gov.uk/downloads/publications/hmipris/thematic-reports-and-research-publications/Muslim_prisoners_2010_rps.pdf

Home Affairs Select Committee (2012). *Roots of Violent Radicalisation.* London: The Stationery Office.

Keith, B. (2006). *Report of the Zahid Mubarek Inquiry.* London: HMSO.

Liebling, A., Arnold, H. and Straub, C. (2011). *An Exploration of Staff–Prisoner Relationships at HMP Whitemoor: 12 Years On.* Cambridge: Cambridge Institute of Criminology.

Ministry of Justice (2010). *Breaking the Cycle: Effective Punishment, Rehabilitation and Sentencing of Offenders.* London: The Stationery Office.

Woodcock, J. (1994). *Report of the Enquiry into the Escape of Six Prisoners from the Special Security Unit at Whitemoor Prison, Cambridgeshire, on Friday 9th September 1994.* London: HMSO.

12

SAUDI ARABIA'S "SOFT" APPROACH TO TERRORIST PRISONERS

A model for others?

Marisa Porges

Over the past decade, Saudi Arabia has taken a leading role in the global effort to develop new methods to tackle the significant difficulties inherent in holding terrorist prisoners. Faced with an extremist prisoner population numbered in the thousands,[1] Saudi officials wanted tools that addressed concerns for a prisoner's potential further radicalisation while in custody, for the threat posed when an alleged or convicted terrorist is released, and for larger domestic political issues surrounding the detention of extremists. What emerged was the Saudis' unique, comprehensive, and highly tailored approach to terrorist prisoners, a strategy rooted in the concept of "reform and transformation."[2] Embedded within a new counter terrorism policy introduced by the Saudi Ministry of Interior (MoI) after a series of deadly domestic terrorist attacks struck the country in May 2003, this strategy established a central role for "soft" tactics – including a focused government effort to de-radicalise and rehabilitate terrorist prisoners. By 2012, this initiative had been offered to hundreds – and, for particular sub-components of the program, thousands – of the country's extremist prisoners, including some of the most notorious Al Qaeda members in captivity.

The Saudi experience thus provides myriad points of reference for academics studying extremism in prisons, policymakers handling detention and counter-terrorism, and practitioners working to mitigate the threat of terrorists in their custody. However, to appreciate the nuances of the Saudi strategy – and, most importantly, to gauge the impact of Saudi Arabia's approach and to determine whether it serves as a model for other countries – one must understand both the program's core components and how they emerged within a framework of broader governmental security efforts. With this in mind, the following chapter explains how Saudi efforts to de-radicalise terrorist prisoners developed as part of a new counterterrorism strategy introduced by the Saudi Ministry of Interior in 2004. It will outline key components of the government's engagement with terrorist prisoners, highlight how the program has grown and changed over time, and briefly note the geo-political and security context within which this specialised form of terrorist rehabilitation was implemented. Saudi de-radicalisation efforts will also be evaluated in terms of their successes and failures with individual prisoners and as part of the kingdom's wider counterterrorism strategy, thereby highlighting critical lessons for other countries detaining terrorist prisoners.

Ultimately, this chapter demonstrates that Saudi Arabia's three stage approach to extremist prisoners – as defined by tailored programming in Ministry of Interior prisons and in prisoner rehabilitation centres, followed by "aftercare" initiatives for recently released prisoners – is both highly individualised and very context specific. The Saudis maintain that they have been successful with a large subset of their terrorist prisoner population, relying on religious and non-religious programming, family involvement, and financial support, as well as a robust aftercare program that includes security-oriented elements. While not perfect, the "Saudi model" provides elements that other countries might modify to address their own terrorist prisoner problem.

Program origins and overview

Between 1995 and 2006, twelve major terrorist incidents occurred in Saudi Arabia that killed at least 110 and injured approximately 800 more. The targets were initially U.S. and Western interests, like the attacks at the Riyadh National Guard Building in 1995 and on Khobar Towers in 1996. However, from 2003 onward, the targets were more often Saudi citizens or the kingdom itself. In May 2003, a compound in Riyadh was bombed and 26 people were killed, including both Saudis and Americans. In November of the same year, bombs in a Riyadh complex killed 18 people and left more than 122 injured; many of the victims were Saudi, and nearly all were Muslims (Ashraf, 2007, p.104). These, along with five additional terrorist incidents in 2004, concerned Saudi security officials who saw terrorism becoming a serious domestic security risk – a threat to Saudi citizens, the royal family, and the country's critical infrastructure facilities.

Rather than combat this threat solely with the operational tactics that had been central to Saudi security forces to that point – tools like arrests, interrogations, and targeting efforts by Saudi Ministry of Interior officers – the Saudis wanted to try a different strategy. In the words of one official, they began to "assess the experiences of countries hit by terrorist operations – such as Egypt, Algeria and others – to confront and address the intellectual deviation and terrorist operations taking place" (al-Abdallah, 2010). The result was a focus on alternative approaches that fought terrorism in two ways: "with guns, and with ideas."[3] The Saudi Ministry of Interior, the government agency responsible for the country's internal security and counterterrorism operations, began developing a strategy that used both "hard" and "soft" tools, and that relied upon a dual-pronged approach balancing traditional tactics with social, religious, and psychological programming. The Saudi regime thus announced its support for a "'war of ideas,' which aim[ed] to instil the concepts of moderation and tolerance, and to undermine any justifications for extremism and terrorism on an intellectual level" (Royal Embassy of Saudi Arabia Information Office, 2011, p.6).

To manage and implement this strategy, the Saudi Ministry of Interior established four internal organisations with mutually supportive roles and responsibilities: the Religious subcommittee, the Psychological and Social subcommittee, the Security subcommittee, and the Media subcommittee. The first, the Religious subcommittee, was staffed with approximately one hundred scholars, clerics, and religious studies professors who were responsible for countering extremist ideology and for clarifying interpretations of the Holy Qur'an and the sayings of the Prophet Muhammad. The Psychological and Social subcommittee included psychologists and social scientists who focused on a prisoner's mental and emotional conditions, aiming to address "the psychological problems within the [prisoner]."[4] This group also aimed to address any family issues at play, particularly through direct and tailored social service support that was offered to a prisoner's immediate family. Ministry of Interior officers handled the work of the Security subcommittee, which reviewed prisoners' files to evaluate potential security risks. They also oversaw post-release monitoring of former prisoners. Finally, the Media subcommittee was responsible for producing literature, TV shows, and the like for schools, mosques, or other community groups with the aim of combating radicalisation and terrorist recruitment at the local level.

With regard to programming for terrorist prisoners, this strategy originally included three core components: prevention efforts in the form of the *al Munasah* (Advice) program, efforts to rehabilitate terrorist prisoners at the Mohammed bin Nayef Centre for Counselling and Care, and social work programs for released terrorist prisoners. De-radicalisation quickly emerged as a key element of each, and thus became a focus of a broader MoI strategy called Prevention, Rehabilitation, and Aftercare (PRAC). As a result, de-radicalisation-related programs received significant attention, funding, and support from the Ministry of Interior. Ultimately, this effort expanded to include numerous additional programs and four additional "departments," to include offices handling research, technology, and public relations. As of summer 2012, twenty-three different programs were offered to terrorist prisoners and their families as part of this PRAC initiative.[5]

Prevention through counselling

What do these programs involve? How did the Ministry of Interior implement their PRAC strategy? From the start, the focus was religious and psychological counselling offered to terrorist prisoners in custody at MoI prisons. Called the *al Munasah* (Advice) initiative, this program sought to engage prisoners "who hold extremist thoughts . . . through healing programs,"[6] and to help them "realize their errors and make positive change in their minds without extremism" (al-Abdallah, 2010). This reflected a core principle of the overall program, which was to treat "the detainees as 'beneficiaries' who are seen as having been 'misled' and in need of 'advice,' rather than as criminals requiring punishment" (Chowdhury-Fink and El-Said, 2011, p.13).

The first application of this counselling approach was in late 2003, in Ministry of Interior prisons that housed thousands of individuals for national security-related crimes.[7] Religious scholars and psychologists or social workers were sent in teams of three to "sit with prisoners to answer questions."[8] Prisoners could voluntarily participate in individual counselling sessions, where each prisoner had the chance to talk with counsellors without pressure from other inmates. Group counselling was also offered, in which lectures were given to groups of 20 to 24 detainees for 4 to 5 hours over the course of multiple weeks; discussions covered "topics related to suspect intellectual [notions], such as *takfiri* thought among the detainees, with the goal of rectifying their ideas" (al-Abdallah, 2010). This early effort was therefore mainly religious in nature, using a combination of religious and psycho-social techniques to encourage detained terrorists to change their beliefs.

Over time, this initiative expanded to include preventative counselling beyond the prison walls – for the families of detainees and, eventually for the wider Saudi public – through programs at mosques, schools, sport venues, and other public meeting places. The aim became broader counter-radicalisation, and the goal was "to prevent the society from misguided and deviant thoughts and extremism."[9] It was thus designed to address "if not the roots, then at least the sprouts of terrorism in the country" (Crossroads Arabia, 2009), with a focus on those groups deemed most vulnerable to terrorist radicalisation and recruitment.

As of December 2011, over 5,590 terrorist prisoners had participated in the counselling program, including 17 women. In addition, 26 preventative sessions occurred outside prison, in no less than nine different provinces.[10]

Rehabilitation for terrorist prisoners

Another central element of the PRAC program – and one that has received significant attention, both from international press and from counterterrorism officials worldwide – are Saudi efforts to de-radicalise and rehabilitate some terrorist prisoners prior to release in a special, halfway-house-like setting.

The idea to add such a program as a "next-step" to counselling in MoI prisons dates to early 2007, when a Saudi Sheikh took it upon himself to work with a soon-to-be released terrorist prisoner in Jeddah. The Sheik spent one month devising a rehabilitation and reintegration-oriented curriculum based outside the confines of the prison, using one-on-one discussions, lectures, and TV programs to engage the prisoner. The goal was "to know whether [the prisoner's] thoughts were sound or not and at the same time to rehabilitate him to take part in the daily life."[11] When they discussed issues outside prison, the prisoner appeared more relaxed, more open to and accepting of new ideas. For the entire month, the Sheikh lived with this prisoner in a Jeddah hotel – eating, swimming and sitting with him in the lobby, and writing up reports on his programs every night. He also took the prisoner to Friday prayer at his mosque. After one month, they met with Prince Mohammed bin Nayef, then the Saudi Deputy Minister of Interior in charge of counter-terrorism, and explained the prisoner's changed thinking. The prisoner was subsequently released.

As the Sheikh described it, though the man spent four years in prison, he changed more in one month of focused programming than he did while sitting in prison. Saudi officials claim that because of this, the Islamic calendar year 1428 was a "new year [that] brought new vision [and] new era."[12] It was the start of the Mohammed bin Nayef rehabilitation program for terrorist prisoners.[13]

The Mohammed bin Nayef Centre for Counselling and Care, located in the suburbs of Riyadh, formally opened in 2007 as a modified "half-way house" that combined elements of a detention centre with those of a social services institution. Its launch coincided with the return of eighteen detainees from U.S. custody at Guantanamo Bay, Cuba.[14] This was intentional, as priority was placed on first receiving – and rehabilitating – detainees returning from abroad, either those held at Guantanamo or in other Islamic countries (e.g., Iraq), and then on rehabilitating terrorist prisoners held by the Saudi Ministry of Interior. The primary goal was to "re-integrate [these national security prisoners] in society as persons with sound orientation and thoughts." The Centre also aimed to:

- spread the "concept of moderation and rejection of extremism and deviant ideas";
- help the prisoners achieve "intellectual, self, and social balance"; and
- highlight the government's role in "fighting terrorism, addressing the perverse and misguided ideas and provide care and education to its children [sic]."[15]

With this in mind, the program intended to build upon the ideologically oriented initiatives of prison-based counselling while also providing disengagement-oriented programming to help "beneficiaries" reintegrate back into society after release.

The opportunity to participate in this program was offered to select Ministry of Interior prisoners who had responded well to prison-based programming (i.e., the *al Munasah* initiative described above), and who had completed their prison sentence. Before being released,[16] these prisoners transferred to the Mohammed bin Nayef Centre for Counselling and Care, and take part in lessons and training centred on four core areas; there were religious, psychological, social, and educational programs. For each theme, staff – who numbered approximately ninety and represent a variety of Saudi academic faculties, universities, and government ministries, and a variety of regions[17] – held classes, group discussions, or one-on-one sessions to promote dialogue with the beneficiaries. Topics ranged from *sharia* law and Saudi history, to culture, politics, and art therapy. Saudi officials insist these sessions were not just lectures but active discussions with students; as described by Centre staff members in October 2009, "listening is a policy in the centre . . . [because] we believe in [the] Kingdom that thought has to be fought with thought."[18]

A core component of the Centre's effort is a religious program that attempts to correct misunderstandings of Islam and remove ideological sources for terrorist activity. Because, as the Centre's religious director explained, "beneficiaries [i.e. the prisoners] who misunderstand ideas of Islam . . . this gives the motives to be terrorists."[19] To tackle this problem, lectures and classes are offered that aim to correct prisoners' religious misconceptions, to answer their questions about specific elements of the Qur'an, and to underscore notions of peace and respect as central tenets of Islam. Specific emphasis is placed on "atonement and its guidelines, jihad and its guidelines, loyalty and innocence, misguided books and how to react on it, protected blood and its regulations."[20] For this portion, the MoI underscores the need to select credible interlocutors to engage with the prisoners; Saudi officials state that the Centre has a team of highly respected sheiks who maintain some level of independence from the Saudi regime, thereby avoiding problems wherein "detainees do not sit down with religious figures who lack credibility in the eyes of fundamentalists and their admirers" (Boucek, 2008).

The psychological portion of the program is intended to address a detainee's psyche and self-esteem, using lectures, seminars, and interviews to develop his sense of self and, in some cases, to improve his anger management skills. According to Centre staff, "no one wakes up in [the] morning wanting to be a terrorist."[21] This portion of rehabilitation includes approximately five hours of weekly sessions for each beneficiary; it approaches each prisoner as an individual, intending to "help [him] think positively about himself and about his society where he is going to live after he leaves the centre."[22] Prisoners at the Mohammed bin Nayef Centre for Counselling and Care also undergo regular psychological evaluations to assess their state of mind and evaluate their progress in the program. This element has been expanded since the Centre's inception, as Saudi Ministry of Interior officials have tried to improve the tools used to gauge a prisoner's mental condition and his potential security threat prior to release.[23]

In order to help a detainee successfully reintegrate into society after release, Saudi officials also offer social service support for both the detainee and his family. The intention is to help "develop [detainees'] social aptitudes to be compatible with their society," while minimising any social stigma toward ex-detainees or terror-ists.[24] This part of the program includes family visits, phone calls, and "furlough vacations" with family members. It also can include government support for weddings or other family celebrations, and financial support for family members. Originally intended primarily to help the detainee, this initiative has also developed into a mechanism for Centre officials to connect with the detainee's family – those individuals most likely to spend time with the detainee after release, to notice if his behaviour changes or if he seems likely to return to dangerous activity.[25] This component thereby dovetails with after-care efforts described in forthcoming sections, establishing both a support system for the detainee and a network by which Saudi officials can indirectly observe a program beneficiary after release.

In contrast to the heavily religious tone of early counselling efforts, the education portion of Saudi rehabilitation programs has evolved over time to include more and more secular elements. For example, history and cultural lessons were intro-duced in 2009, in response to increased concern by Centre staff over Al Qaeda's efforts to manipulate Arabian Peninsula history to recruit followers. These classes were intended to help clarify Islamic history for the detainees and demonstrate that "fighting is not the history of the prophet."[26] Toward this end, the teachers produced documentaries of Islamic history for the students and also focused on discussing contemporary historical issues, like the Palestinian problem. There is also art therapy that "gives [detainees] a way of expressing . . . [of] communicating to release tension [and] anger," computer training, and sports programs.[27] Of note, these sports program are intended not just to "to get *Shabab* (the youth) to release energy," but also to help staff monitor the level of aggression a detainee demonstrates while playing in order to evaluate his mental state during rehabilitation.[28] This provides another level of input for the aforementioned psychological assessment techniques. Finally, there is a professional rehabilitation program intended to provide each prisoner with skills that will help him find employment after release. This program includes computer training, classes on English writing and speaking, vocational training (e.g., training on "cooling mechanics"), and general instruction on the job market. These programs are supported by other government agencies (e.g., the Saudi Ministry of Social Affairs), universities (e.g., the University of King Saud), and also the private sector.[29]

Due to space constraints, the primary rehabilitation centre – the Mohammed bin Nayef Centre for Counselling and Care, located on the outskirts of the Saudi capital of Riyadh – can accommodate approximately 125 prisoners at one time. However, a new facility is expected to open near Riyadh in fall 2012 that will increase the program's capacity to 300. Plans are underway to open additional rehabilitation centres, including in Dammam, so that Saudi Arabia will eventually have five separate centres for the rehabilitation of extremist prisoners.[30] The extra facilities will house prisoners whose families are not in the Riyadh area, to encourage greater family involvement in the program.

As of summer 2012, approximately 1,175 "beneficiaries" had graduated from the Mohammed bin Nayef Centre,[31] approximately 120 of whom were formerly held at Guantanamo.[32] A newer facility in Jeddah had released three groups of "beneficiaries" by August 2012.[33] The MoI contends that a small number of all these individuals returned to terrorist activity after release, with one official estimating that, as of summer 2012, at least 25 former terrorist prisoners were designated as recidivists – including 11 former beneficiaries who fled to Yemen to join Al Qaeda groups there.[34] The MoI also states that select prisoners did not graduate from the program and remain in custody, though data on this aspect is unclear. The Saudi government spent over $30 million (USD) on this program from 2004 to 2007, including for the post-release social services described below (Stracke, 2007); however, this figure was calculated prior to the opening of new facilities, which increased the number of program participants – and related costs – significantly.

Aftercare programming

The final element of this PRAC strategy – and a key component of the Saudi approach to terrorist prisoner de-radicalisation – is a post-release or "aftercare" program that aims "to realize self-security for the [rehabilitation] graduate . . . [to] make him able to deal with his daily problems and to adapt to problems and adapt with life pressure."[35] Saudi officials have said that this element of de-radicalisation may be the most critical aspect. It must mitigate the most common problems facing terrorist prisoners after release, when "these guys will face many problems in life" and they will be tempted to re-join previous terrorist associates or return to terrorism activity.

Aftercare programming is based upon a dual-pronged approach that uses both social service provision and security monitoring to mitigate the threat of a former terrorist prisoner once released from custody. Regarding social service elements, Saudi officials consider three elements for re-socialisation and successful reintegration: a detainee's willingness to get married and re-join his wife and family; his participation in university or other continuing education; and his re-joining the workforce. With this in mind, the Ministry of Interior actively helps former detainees on all these fronts by providing financial assistance, helping him find a job, or providing other necessary social services. Prince Mohammed bin Nayef has even attended ex-detainees' weddings in order to show support for their post-release life and to encourage their settling down with a family.[36]

This approach also underscores the critical role that a beneficiary's family plays in Saudi de-radicalisation efforts. Ministry of Interior officials consider family critical in processes of both radicalisation and de-radicalisation, and they call the prisoner's family "a cornerstone of [the] program."[37] As a result, the Saudi program has expanded over the years to include a more central role for a beneficiary's extended family – during both rehabilitation and after release. Early in PRAC implementation, family engagement typically focused on family visits at the Mohammed bin Nayef Care Centre and having the beneficiary participate in family meals during holidays. This still plays a key function during the rehabilitation stage, though family members now also play a significant role designing post-release programming – helping security services prevent former prisoners from becoming a threat again. In 2009, family members started to provide input to Centre staff, helping design specialised programs for their relatives, both before and after release. The Centre also began sequenced trial releases for beneficiaries, in order to observe the terrorist prisoners with their parents and family, to assess how each party responds to the other, and to determine what type of aftercare support might be needed.[38] Though extremely time consuming and difficult to implement for more than small groups at a time, security officials point to the potential long-term benefits of this approach – particularly as regards supporting efforts to combat radicalisation in broader Saudi society.

Former detainees and their families also receive a range of financial incentives, from salaries, housing and cars to medical support or educational opportunities.

For example, graduates from the Mohammed bin Nayef Centre for Counselling and Care are given 10,000 Saudi Riyal ($2,650 USD equivalent) upon release. Following that, they are provided a monthly salary of 2000 to 3000 Saudi Riyal ($535 to $800 USD equivalent) for one year, or until they no longer need government financial assistance. This form of economic co-optation is "intended to create a set of interlocking responsibilities which make it difficult for an individual to revert to illicit violent activities" (Chowdhury-Fink and El-Said, 2011). This element of the Saudi approach also raises some questions with both policymakers and the public, especially insofar as it appears to create financial incentives for radicalisation and extremism. While a viable option in the Saudi context, this approach would not be appropriate in all countries, both because of the financial resources it requires and because of the questions that arise when former extremists receive monetary support from government sources.

Finally, Saudi officials acknowledge that their aftercare programming includes a clearly defined security element as a safeguard against former terrorist prisoners returning to dangerous activity. Post-release support therefore includes not just counselling, financial incentives, and family programs but also "consistent and sustained monitoring . . . to determine who the person keeps company with and who is his spiritual guide and mentor at the neighbourhood mosque" (Wagner, 2010). Security officials ask for reports on a former detainee's behaviour from his wife, school, and workplace.[39] They also set up a probation-like reporting system, do covert monitoring, and have staff from the Centre periodically phone or visit former students to assess their state of mind and reintegration progress.

As of September 2011, 402 detainees were given financial rewards for graduating from rehabilitation,[40] 18 were given money to fund a wedding, 25 were given local jobs, and over 200 were provided medical services. In addition, 127 were given university-level education, 3 were given cars, and over 300 were taken to Mecca for Hajj.[41]

A success? A model for other countries?

For scholars studying de-radicalisation, policymakers handling national security, and practitioners working with terrorist prisoners, the central question remains whether the Saudi approach is effective and whether it provides a model that can be used in other places. What parts of the Saudi program are most important and could be used in other contexts? How might the Saudi experience provide a roadmap for other countries?

On these questions, a close inspection of Saudi efforts paints a mixed picture. Saudi officials have developed an innovative and comprehensive program that, despite some public failures, has helped them mitigate the threat of terrorist prisoners when pursued alongside other security-related initiatives. However, it is also a program that is highly culturally and contextually specific, that relies heavily on social, familial, and economic support, and that may be hard to replicate in other places.

To date, the primary metric for evaluating Saudi efforts has been measuring recidivism – that is, the rate at which beneficiaries of the Saudi de-radicalisation and rehabilitation program return to terrorist activity after release. Using this point of reference, the Saudis claimed to be 100 percent successful for the first few years of the program (e.g. Henry, 2007) – until January 2009, when the Saudi Ministry of Interior confirmed that eleven former Guantanamo detainees had graduated from its Riyadh-based de-radicalisation program and subsequently fled to Yemen to join Al Qaeda in the Arabian Peninsula, Al Qaeda's regional affiliate (Worth, 2009; Boucek, 2011). Since then, Saudi officials have been more circumspect in evaluating the program's success. In December 2011, Saudi officials overseeing de-radicalisation reported that more than 5,000 terrorist prisoners had participated in some aspect of the program and been released, and they estimated an 80 to 98 percent success rate with this group. In June 2012, when specifically discussing the rehabilitation centre, a Saudi official reported that approximately 25 individuals have returned to violence.[42] Other Ministry of Interior officials have privately conceded that the most committed terrorists, particularly those with ideological motivations, are not likely to respond to their program.[43]

These fluctuating reports underscore the inherent difficulty in definitively assessing, with quantitative analysis, the impact of de-radicalisation efforts – in Saudi Arabia or anywhere around the world. Even the Saudi program, which benefits from the Ministry of Interior's significant support for research on the program's progress and an extensive internal security service to monitor released prisoners, suffers from a dearth of information. There are also critics within Saudi society who contest the validity of public reporting on the program; "nobody out of jail knows what the program is," argued one Saudi woman, "I don't think the program for *Munasah* is doing anything."[44] Furthermore, though the program has been active in some form since 2004, it may not have been operational long enough to determine whether behavioural changes in program graduates are lasting. This is particularly a concern since many of the newest initiatives were not introduced until 2009 or 2010; those prisoners released most recently have had the benefit of a much more extensive rehabilitation program and may therefore provide the most useful subjects for measuring effectiveness in the years ahead. However, in the interim, the program's long-term impact remains unclear.

Nonetheless, Saudi de-radicalisation and rehabilitation programs provide valuable points of reference for other countries and suggest central elements to consider when holding terrorist prisoners. It underscores the usefulness of having a broad and comprehensive engagement program, as well as the importance of including prisoners' families and the benefits of "relationship building" between prisoners and program staff. It also highlights the need to continually modify any strategy in response to both positive and negative feedback, and to the needs of individual prisoners, stressing the need for a highly tailored and contextually specific approach.

First and foremost, the Saudi experience has demonstrated the usefulness in offering a broad range of programming to its prisoners – including the religious and non-religious classes, vocational training and reintegration-focused programming, and psychological and social counselling described earlier in this chapter. While each program must be tailored to the individual country involved and the individual prisoners who participate, a broad range of engagement helps ensure the program meets two, mutually supportive goals: helping to shape the thoughts and behaviour of its "beneficiaries," and ultimately helping them reintegrate into Saudi society. Given that the pathways of radicalisation are different for different terrorist prisoners, this also helps ensure that programming tries to address ideological root causes along with a variety of other sources of radicalisation.

Since PRAC's inception, Saudi officials have also greatly expanded the role played by a prisoner's extended family. As one Saudi official stated, "if families are part of the problem, they need to be part of the solution."[45] Early rehabilitation efforts focused primarily on a family's engagement with the detainee during visits and meals, hoping to use familial support as a secondary tool for encouraging a prisoner to change. While this is still a focus, family members now play a much more active role. As described earlier in this chapter, they provide input on designing specialised programs for each detainee and inform how his progress is evaluated. They also participate in group sessions at the Centre, including new initiatives like the "Family Connection" program which is designed to ensure that a prisoner's family is prepared to help him reintegrate – into his family and into broader Saudi society – after release. Ultimately, this focus on family is to prevent both the prisoner and his family from having problems in the future, and to ensure that security officials have the trust of the family in the future.[46]

A third lesson learned from Saudi efforts is the important role played by interpersonal relationships and prisoner mentorship – a factor that Saudi officials think promotes both lasting change in individual prisoners and, also, improves their ability to assess the progress of each beneficiary throughout the program. Toward this end, staff at the Mohammed bin Nayef Centre for Counselling and Care encourage "beneficiaries" to build relationships with the social workers, psychologists and other staff members; they even ensure departing prisoners have their personal phone numbers, so that they can contact a staff member after release if they need help or advice. Anecdotal reporting demonstrates that, in fact, former prisoners do stay in contact with individual Centre staff and that, on occasion, it has prevented certain individuals from returning to illicit activity.[47] The Saudis contend it is likewise important to have strong public leadership for any terrorist rehabilitation program; in Saudi Arabia, this support has come from the Deputy Minister of Interior Prince Mohammed bin Nayef, who one Saudi local called "charismatic, generous, and determined" in his advocacy for the care and counselling effort.[48]

Finally, the Saudi experience underscores the need to ensure any program for imprisoned terrorists is culturally specific and tailored to the needs of individual prisoners, but is also able to actively adapt to new challenges and potential problems as they arise. In the face of public failures that could have derailed the program entirely, including aforementioned incidents when program graduates joined Al Qaeda forces in Yemen, Saudi officials have instead responded by modifying the program over time; they use successes and failures, and even feedback from detainees and their families to continually expand and adjust their strategy. Though extremely time consuming and difficult to implement for more than small groups at a time, security officials point to potential long-term benefits in this approach – particularly as regards broader efforts to combat radicalisation in Saudi society.

Conclusion

There is no perfect strategy for handling terrorist prisoners or reducing the risks if they are released. However, by adapting a variety of innovative approaches to prisoner rehabilitation, Saudi authorities have taken major steps to develop a comprehensive program for their own sizeable population of extremist prisoners. In the process, they have used both research and trial and error to explore what works and what doesn't within their own system.

The resulting "Saudi model," which relies on combining elements of prevention, rehabilitation, and after-care, cannot be systemically replicated in other countries with any hope of similar levels of success. It has worked for the Saudis within the context of Saudi society, with the support of a robust and well-financed security service. However, as this chapter demonstrates, the Saudi experience suggests key components that other countries should consider and underscores potential problems that both practitioners and policymakers may face in the course of developing and implementing their own program. The Saudi experience thus provides an imperfect albeit useful model, laying the groundwork for future terrorist prisoner programs in and out of prison.

Notes

1 In late 2011, the Saudi Ministry of Security held almost 6,000 prisoners with terrorist or extremist ties.
2 Author's interview with Saudi Ministry of Interior (MoI) official, Riyadh, June 2012.
3 Author's interview with Saudi official, Riyadh, June 2012.
4 Author's interview with Saudi official, Riyadh, June 2012.
5 Author interview with Saudi MoI official, Riyadh, June 2012.
6 MoI Report on Efforts of Mohammed bin Nayef Centre for Counselling and Care, provided by Saudi official, Sept 2011.
7 Author's interview with British official, Riyadh, Saudi Arabia, October 2009. In late 2009, MoI prisons held over 4,000 individuals in security detention.
8 Author's meeting with Saudi MoI official, Riyadh, Saudi Arabia, October 2009.
9 Brief from Saudi MoI official, The Hague, the Netherlands, December 2011.
10 Brief from Saudi MoI official, The Hague, the Netherlands December 2011.
11 MoI report on Efforts of Mohammed bin Nayef Centre for Counselling and Care, provided by Saudi official, September 2011.
12 As told to author by Saudi Sheikh, Riyadh, Saudi Arabia, October 2009. Note: According to the Islamic calendar, the year 1428 occurred 1428 years after the *Hijrah*. 1428H began in mid-January 2007.
13 As told to author by Saudi MoI official, Riyadh, Saudi Arabia, October 2009.

14 MoI report on Efforts of Mohammed bin Nayef Centre for Counselling and Care, provided by Saudi official, September 2011.
15 MoI Report on Efforts of Mohammed bin Nayef Centre for Counselling and Care, provided by Saudi official, September 2011.
16 Saudi officials note that "Any individual who has committed or participated in a violent crime, constituting murder, will not be released following completion of the course." See Royal Embassy of Saudi Arabia Information Office (2011).
17 Author's interview with Saudi MoI official, Riyadh, Saudi Arabia, October 2009, and again June 2012.
18 Author's interview with Saudi MoI officials, Riyadh, Saudi Arabia, October 2009.
19 Author's interview with Saudi MoI official, Riyadh, June 2012.
20 MoI Report on Efforts of Mohammed bin Nayef Centre for Counselling and Care, provided by Saudi official, September 2011.
21 Author's interview with Saudi MoI officials, Riyadh, Saudi Arabia, October 2009.
22 Report on Efforts of Mohammed bin Nayef Centre for Counselling and Care, provided by Saudi official, September 2011.
23 Author interviews with Saudi MoI officials, Riyadh, Saudi Arabia, October 2009. For additional details, see Porges (2010).
24 Report on Efforts of Mohammed bin Nayef Centre for Counselling and Care, provided by Saudi official, September 2011.
25 Author interview with Saudi MoI officials, Riyadh, Saudi Arabia, June 2012.
26 Interview with Saudi MoI officials, Riyadh, Saudi Arabia, October 2009.
27 Interview with Saudi MoI officials, Riyadh, Saudi Arabia, October 2009.
28 Interview with Saudi MoI official, Riyadh, Saudi Arabia, October 2009. As described in Porges (2010). For additional details, see Chowdhury-Fink and El-Said (2011).
29 MoI report on Efforts of Mohammed bin Nayef Centre for Counselling and Care, provided by Saudi official, September 2011.
30 Brief by Saudi MoI official, Riyadh, June 2012.
31 Interview with MoI officials in Riyadh, June 2012. (Note the difference between this number and the 650 number used in the September 2011 Saudi CT report.) Note also that the Saudi MoI states that "only a very few people did not graduate" (Saudi CT report, 2011).
32 GTMO number from brief by Saudi MOI official, The Hague, the Netherlands, December 2011.
33 Saudi Ministry of Interior press release, August 14, 2012, found at: http://www.moi.gov.sa/
34 Author's interview with Saudi MoI officials in Riyadh, June 2012.
35 Brief by Saudi MOI official, The Hague, the Netherlands, December 2011.
36 Author's interview Riyadh, Saudi Arabia, June 2012.
37 Author's interview with Saudi researcher, Riyadh, Saudi Arabia, June 2012.
38 Author's interview with Saudi MoI officials, Riyadh, Saudi Arabia, October 2009.
39 Author's interview with KSA MoI officials, Riyadh, Saudi Arabia, October 2009.
40 Brief by Saudi MOI official, The Hague, the Netherlands, December 2011.
41 MoI report on the Efforts of Mohammed bin Nayef Centre for Counselling and Care, provided by Saudi official, September 2011.
42 Brief by Saudi MOI official, Riyadh, June 2012.
43 Ref author's interviews with Saudi MoI officials, Riyadh, Saudi Arabia, October 2009. Also see Boucek (2008).
44 Author's interview, 2012.
45 Saudi MoI official, in brief to The Hague, December 2011.
46 Author's interview with Saudi researcher, Riyadh, June 2012.
47 Author's interviews, October 2009 and June 2012.
48 Author's interview, Riyadh, June 2012.

References

al-Abdallah, S. (2010). 'Saudi Munasaha programme rehabilitates extremists through dialogue and scientific methods.' *Al Shorfa*, December 27, 2010. Found at http://al-shorfa.com/en_GB/articles/meii/features/ main/ 2010/12/27/feature-01

Ashraf, A. (2007). 'Transnational cooperation on anti-terrorism: a comparative case study of Saudi Arabia and Indonesia.' *Perceptions: Journal of International Affairs*, 12/3, pp.91–121.

Boucek, C. (2008). *Saudi Arabia's "Soft" Counterterrorism Strategy: Prevention, Rehabilitation, and Aftercare*. Carnegie Papers, Middle East series 97. Washington, DC: Carnegie Endowment for International Peace.

Boucek, C. (2011). *Carnegie Guide to the Saudi Eleven*. Available at http://carnegieendowment. org/2011/09/07/carnegie-guide-to-saudi-eleven/519s

Chowdhury-Fink, N., & El-Said, H. (2011). *Transforming Terrorists: Examining International Efforts to Address Violent Extremism*. New York: International Peace Institute.

Crossroads Arabia (2009). "'Munasaha' Program Takes to the Road." http://xrdarabia. org/2009/10/29/munasaha-program-takes-to-the-road/ Posted October 29, 2009.

Henry, T. (2007). 'Get out of jihad free.' *The Atlantic Magazine*, June. Available at http://www.theatlantic.com/magazine/archive/2007/06/get-out-of-jihad-free/305883/

Porges, M. (2010). *The Saudi Deradicalisation Experiment. US Council on Foreign Relations*. Expert Brief, 22 January; available at http:///www.cfr.org/publication/21292/saudi_deradicalisation _experiment.html

Royal Embassy of Saudi Arabia Information Office (2011). *Kingdom of Saudi Arabia – Initiatives and Actions to Combat Terrorism report*. Washington, DC: Royal Embassy of Saudi Arabia. http://www.saudiembassy.net/files/PDF/Reports/Counterterrorism.pdf

Stracke, N. (2007). 'Arab prisons: a place for dialogue and reform.' *Perspectives on Terrorism*, 1/4.

Wagner, R. (2010). *Rehabilitation and Deradicalisation: Saudi Arabia's Counterterrorism Successes and Failures*. Peace and Conflict Monitor special report; available at http://www.monitor. upeace.org/innerpg.cfm?id_article=735

Worth, R. (2009). 'Saudis issue list of 85 terrorist suspects.' *New York Times*, February 3, 2009.

13

DE-RADICALISING THE LIBERATION TIGERS OF TAMIL EELAM (LTTE)

Some preliminary findings

Arie W. Kruglanski, Michele J. Gelfand, Jocelyn J. Bélanger, Rohan Gunaratna and Malkanthi Hettiarachchi

In the Fall of 2009, our team conducted a psychological study on detained members of the Liberation Tigers of Tamil Eelam (LTTE) in various Sri Lankan centres where they were held following the LTTE defeat at the hands of the Sri Lankan army. Our purpose was to carry out research designed to evaluate the de-radicalisation/rehabilitation programs administered to the detainees. To our knowledge, this is the first instance of primary research involving a systematic, quantitative assessment of a de-radicalisation program; we are grateful to the Sri Lankan government for granting us unrestricted access and complete freedom in our inquiries. In the pages that follow, we describe our research and report our preliminary findings. As an advance organiser, we discuss detainee de-radicalisation from a broader perspective, followed by a description of the specific work we carried out and our data.

Detainee de-radicalisation: The big picture

The detention of members of terrorist organisations is a fact of life, an inevitable part and parcel of the war on terror. "You cannot kill them all," Bruce Hoffman, recently quipped. Nor do you want to. As a civilised society it is incumbent to conduct one's dealings with detained terrorism suspects in a legally appropriate manner, in accordance with the law. More importantly, from a moral perspective, it is unacceptable to take human lives, other than in an act of self-defence, no matter who they are. In this sense, the asymmetric conflict between states and terrorists is so in the moral sense, not only in terms of relative might: We, members of the international community are morally prohibited from the slaughter of unarmed civilians; they, the terrorists feel free to perpetrate mayhem on innocents. Finally, in many cases, the ultimate goal of counterterrorism is to make peace with the community that the terrorists came from. Indiscriminate killing of militants would only create bitterness and a desire for revenge detrimental to peace and reconciliation efforts.

On the other hand, leaving militants at large is dangerous, hence not an option, as it may enable further attacks resulting in deplorable loss of life of civilians and others. For all these reasons, detention of terrorism suspects is well-nigh inevitable. But it creates its own problems. Some of these are legal, and in the United States, for example, a discussion raged about the lawful status of the detainees. Should they be considered criminals; are they entitled to habeas corpus; are they to be prosecuted in criminal courts? Or are they to be considered soldiers, "enemy combatants"; can they be kept without trial, sentenced by military courts, subjected to "enhanced interrogation techniques." There are also multiple problems associated with the detainees' maintenance: How to prevent their escape and re-engagement in the fight? How to prevent prison riots?

Beyond these short-term, mundane, worries, there is the long-term, strategic concern. How to prevent the inmates from radicalising further, how to help them de-radicalise, and how to plant in their hearts and minds the seeds of reconciliation? Intriguingly, whereas some aspects of the custodial situation are conducive to detainee radicalisation, others afford the conditions for de-radicalisation. We examine both next.

Radicalisation in prisons

There are well known examples of jihadists who converted to Islam while in custody. Richard Reid, the infamous "Shoe Bomber" converted in a British prison. Also, Jose Padilla, the so-called "Dirty Bomber," was exposed to radical Islam in an American prison. Christian Ganczarski, a German convert who coordinated logistics for the Djerba bombing in April 2002 off the coast of Tunisia, and Pierre Richard Robert, implicated in terrorist attacks in Morocco, were recruits with criminal backgrounds. Further instances of radicalisation in prisons are depicted in the Rand Report by Hannah, Clutterbuck, & Rubin (2008).

The psychology of prison radicalisation

What factors lead incarcerated individuals to convert to militancy and violence? Consider the psychological state of a newly entered inmate. Typically, it is a state of fear, a sense of disempowerment and humiliation. In psychological terminology we refer to it as a *loss of personal significance* (Kruglanski et al., in press; Kruglanski, Chen, Dechesne, Fishman, & Orehek, 2009). The individual feels weak, insignificant, reduced to a child's status, overpowered by an external force, and divested of control over her or his fate. For most individuals, this is a highly upsetting experience that they are anxious to be rid of. This anxiety renders people vulnerable to an ideology that promises a restoration of significance and empowerment. These can be obtained through attachment of self to a powerful organisation that strikes at one's oppressors. Identification with a group that promises to bring one's enemy to its knees restores one's sense of significance by levelling the playing field, and presumably getting respect from the party who inflicted on oneself the dishonour. In short, identification with a group and its ideology confers significance on the individual members; the ideology prescribes actions that lend one considerable importance in eyes of the community (e.g., self-sacrifice and martyrdom while striking at the enemy).[1]

De-radicalisation in prisons?

Even as prisons could constitute petri dishes for radicalisation, they also set the conditions for de-radicalisation and, ironically, they do so for psychologically similar reasons. These have to do with the *cognitive openness* induced by the novel and disempowering incarceration context. In the same way that individuals may open their minds to a radical ideology that promises a restoration of their dishonoured personhood, others, who have tried the terrorist route and found it wanting, may open their mind to a constructive, pro-social, way of significance restoration, devoid of violence.

Two likely conditions may promote detainees' readiness to de-radicalise while in custody: (1) disaffection with the terrorist ideology, often induced by the trials and tribulations of their lives as terrorists, and (2) the ability to independently think and reflect, free from the paralysing peer pressure, that the incarceration situation may afford.

Pursued by government forces, deprived of normalcy and stability, and in the constant risk of annihilation, terrorists may lose their appetite for struggle over time, and their resilience and resolve may wear thin. This may prompt a serious reassessment of their organisation's activities and sharpen their vigilance to their comrades' possible corruption and their departures from the ideological "straight and narrow."

We (AK & MG) recently interviewed in Manila Mr. Abu Hamdi (nom de guerre) a major figure in the Abu Sayyaf Group (ASG), a terrorist organisation in Southern Philippines affiliated with the Indonesian Jemmah Islamiyah, and who presently is collaborating with the government. He recounted how he had originally joined the organisation for ideological reasons and with the idea of improving the lot of his people, Fillipino Muslims in Mindanao; yet in time he realised that what actually he was doing (kidnapping civilians and tourists for ransom) did not clearly serve any lofty purpose and actually amounted to simple banditry.

Leading an exasperating life on the run, unable to pursue his professional career (as a teacher) and to support and spend time with his family, he finally had enough and decided to leave the ASG. Significantly, he came to his decision while in prison, away from the everyday normative reality of the ASG, and free to contemplate independent ideas and possibilities.

Mosab Hassan Yousef, son of Sheikh Hassan Yousef, a founding member of the Hamas organisation in the West Bank, recounts in his recent autobiographical volume (2010) *Son of Hamas* how cruel and sadistic interrogation and torture of other

Palestinians by Hamas detainees in the Megido penitentiary prompted his disenchantment with the movement and led to his (stunning) decision to cooperate with the Israeli Shin Beth (Sherutei Bitachon, or Security Services).

Disaffection with a terrorism-supporting ideology may often occur in the context of the perception that the organisation's activities may bring about defeat and failure, and hence shame and ignominy, rather than pride and significance. We recently interviewed in Cairo Mr Makram Mohamed Ahmad, a senior editor of the Egyptian daily the *Al Ahram* and former editor-in-chief of the weekly *Dar El-Hial*. Mr Makram had played a significant role in mediating the de-radicalisation of the Al Jihad group (responsible among others for the assassination of Egypt's President Anwar Sadat, and whose erstwhile member was Ayman al Zawahiri, the present commander in chief of Al Qaeda). Mr Makram reported that Al Jihad's leader's (Dr Falk) decision to abandon violence occurred only after the Egyptian security apparatus effectively demolished the organisation's operational capability, with its major figures under arrest, its weapons caches confiscated, and its public support dwindling.

Fernando Reinares (2011) carried out interviews with former ETA members (Euskadi Ta Askatasuna),[2] the longstanding Basque terrorist organisation, who left the movement and now cooperate with the government. Several formed their decision to break with ETA while in prison. In some cases, this had to do with the perception that violence against civilians is immoral and against one's religious principles. In other cases, it had to do with the perception that violence is unlikely to accomplish much beyond what had been already attained (the autonomy to the Basques ratified by the Spanish Parliament in 1979). And in part it had to do with the notion that one had contributed enough to the cause, hence earning one's claim to significance, and the right to turn to one's own personal affairs (for discussion see Kruglanski et al., in press).

The possibility that time in prison may cool the detainees' enthusiasm about re-joining the fight is also suggested by Yehoshua's (2013) research with 18 incarcerated Palestinian terrorists, members of the Hamas, Fatah, and Palestinian Islamic Jihad (PIJ) organisations and held in an Israeli custodial facility (see also Chapter 10 in this volume). Specifically, Yehoshua carried out extensive interviews with these detainees and found that they are loath to re-join the fight upon their release and consider assuming political roles in their movement or leaving the field of struggle altogether.[3]

Whatever their specific reasons for de-radicalising, it is of interest to consider whether the prison situation as such might have contributed to detainees' re-assessment of their violent pursuits, and if so why. There are good psychological reasons to believe that it should. Primarily, this has to do with the fact that it often (though not invariably) removes individuals from their group's sphere of influence. In other words, the immediate social reality defined by the group's norms may recede in its accessibility to imprisoned individuals, especially if they find themselves isolated from other, highly committed, members of the group. Such separation, if it occurred may allow the individuals to think for themselves and distance themselves from the social pressures that the group may exert on its members. There is ample anecdotal evidence that such extrication from the "clutches" of the organisation whether afforded by the incarceration or otherwise (e.g. through military service) often constituted the prelude to individuals' reorientation and ultimate separation from a terrorist organisation.

De-radicalisation programs

In recent years, the possibility of using the incarceration situation to effect de-radicalisation of detained terrorism suspects has been exploited in several programs carried out in Muslim nations, or countries with significant Muslim populations (Saudi Arabia, Yemen, Singapore, Indonesia, Iraq). In the main, these programs aimed to persuade detainees, members of extremist Islamic organisations (such as the Jemaah Islamiyah, Al Qaeda, Abu Sayaaf, and others), that violence against unarmed civilians is contrary to the teachings of Islam, and is explicitly prohibited by the Qur'an. Generally, this message has been delivered by Islamic clerics (ulama) who engaged the detainees, over months and years, in a religious dialogue concerning the prohibition (vs. permission) of violence against civilians.

The Sri-Lankan rehabilitation program

Unlike the latter, Islamic, programs, which contained a significant dose of theological argumentation, the Sri Lankan rehabilitation program, described later, incorporated no religious argumentation, for the simple reason that at the heart of the struggle there was an ethno-nationalist dispute rather than a religious ideology.

Historical background

The historical background in this case has been a 26-year war that the Liberation Tigers of Tamil Eelam (LTTE) waged against the Sri Lankan government in their quest for a separate Tamil state on parts of this South Asian island. The LTTE has been known as one of the most vicious and ruthless terrorist organisations ever. They deserve the (dubious) credit for having invented the suicide belt, and having assassinated heads of state (India's prime minister Rajiv Ghandi, Sri Lankan President Ranasinghe Premadasa), as well as numerous politicians, high-ranking military figures, journalists and academics among others.

Following many failed agreements, in 2007 the Sri Lankan government decided to launch a decisive campaign against the LTTE. By then, this organisation had evolved into a formidable foe. It boasted its own navy (the feared Sea Tigers), air-force (the Air Tigers) and a considerable intelligence capability used to plan sophisticated attacks and assassinations. The Sri Lankan government under the leadership of the Secretary of Defence Gotabaya Rajapaksa doubled the size of the army through a massive recruitment effort and commenced an all-out offensive against the LTTE that by May 19, 2009 decisively demolished that organisation.

Its cult-like leader, Velupillai Prabakharan, was killed in battle, and around 12,000 LTTE cadres surrendered to the Sri Lankan forces.

In light of the heavy casualties the LTTE caused the Sri Lankan army, and their history of ruthless violence, many of the detainees feared harsh and punishing treatment by the army. They were in for a surprise, however! President Mahinda Rajapaksa ordered the army "to treat them as your children." So, rather than being imprisoned or punished, a vast majority of the LTTE cadres were put in rehabilitation centres where they were offered a variety of activities designed to promote their de-radicalisation.

Characteristics of the program

The Sri Lankan rehabilitation program contained a number of ingredients that are highly consistent with the psychological analysis of detainees' states described earlier. These ingredients were (1) separation of the moderate LTTE members from the hard-core militants highly committed to the cause, an important consideration because in the confusing and humiliating circumstances of incarceration, the extremists might have been able to sway the moderates and radicalise them; (2) restoration of the detainees' sense of significance in various ways including calling them "beneficiaries," rather than "prisoners," or "detainees"; (3) setting up the conditions that encourage them to focus on their *individual* persons rather than on their *collective* group membership in the LTTE, through spiritual programs like yoga, and arts activities that afford individual expression. Most importantly, perhaps, (4) the Sri Lankan rehabilitation program contained vocational education courses designed to prepare the detainees/beneficiaries for integration in the society at large upon their release. These courses included a range of offerings from electronics, to carpentry, and construction as well as training in cosmetics and the garment industry intended for female detainees.

Our team was fortunate to be granted access to those detainees and to administer to them a variety of questionnaires. These included personality and demographic questionnaires, as well as attitudinal measures tapping the respondents' support for armed struggle against the Sinhalese. Our instruments were translated into the Tamil language and appropriately back-translated into English. They were then finalised in Tamil and administered to thousands of detainees by a Tamil-speaking team. A large body of these data has yet to be analysed. In what follows, we are pleased to present some preliminary findings pertinent to the success of the rehabilitation effort that we were aiming to assess.

The sample

Our rehabilitation sample included 1,906 individuals (169 women and 1737 men). They were assembled from six rehabilitation samples in North Eastern (Tamil-populated) parts of Sri Lanka. These centres included (1) Pompemadu Peace Village Zone, (2) Dharmapuram, (3) Maradamadu, (4) Pompemadu, (5) TEC

Technical College and (6) Tamil Primary College. To assess possible attitude change, we administered to detainees in these centres a series of questionnaires early on in the incarceration period (December, 2009) and then nine months later (September, 2010).

The research questions

Our main research questions were (1) whether the beneficiaries changed in the course of their participation in the rehabilitation program, (2) whether the change was uniform for beneficiaries assumed to be more versus less involved with the LTTE organisation, and (3) what may have produced the change if it indeed occurred. To that end, we administered to beneficiaries a (1) measure of organisational embeddedness (assumed to tap their degree of personal involvement with the LTTE), (2) measure of their perceived friendliness on the part of the centres' personnel, and (3) their degree of support for armed struggle against the Sinhalese. A more detailed description of these measures is given below.

Organisational embeddedness

Detainees' embeddedness in the LTTE organisation was measured using six items derived from Mitchell and colleagues' Job Embeddedness Scale (Mitchell et al., 2001). The items were selected and adapted to the present context. Different types of items were included to reflect the construct's multidimensionality. They variously tapped (1) the extent to which one had strong attachments to the group or organisation (e.g., "I felt a strong sense of belonging to the armed group"); (2) the extent to which they perceived themselves to have good fit with the organisation's goals (e.g., "The armed group valued my contribution to its goals"); and (3) the degree to which they would have to give up benefits or make sacrifices should they lose their role in the organisation (e.g., "I had a lot of influence in the armed group/LTTE"). The scale yielded acceptable internal consistency (Cronbach's $\alpha = .72$).

Positive attitude toward the personnel

Beneficiaries' positive attitudes toward staff members of the rehabilitation program was measured using the following five items: (1) Staff are trustworthy, (2) The staff have been fair towards me, (3) The staff treat me with dignity and respect, (4) The staff has been helpful, and (5) The staff are understanding of the problems we faced with the armed group. Detainees rated the extent to which they agree or disagree with each of these statements using a 7-point Likert scale ranging from 1 (strongly disagree) to 7 (strongly agree). The scale had acceptable internal consistency (Cronbach's $\alpha = .88$).

Support for armed struggle

Detainees' attitudes and willingness to take up arms against the Sinhalese was measured using a 10-item scale developed especially for that purpose. Its items tapped into detainees' attitudes toward military means as ways of advancing the Tamils' cause for a separate state. Sample items were: "Armed fight is a personal obligation of all Tamils today", "Suicide bombers will be rewarded for their deed in the afterlife." Responses to these items were recorded on 7-point scales ranging from 1 (strongly disagree) to 7 (strongly agree). Responses were highly inter-correlated (Cronbach's α of sample = .81).

The results

We were first anxious to find out whether the detainees have changed during the course of their incarceration. Figure 13.1 plots the detainees' attitude change as a function of time. As can be seen, their support for struggle declined from December 2009 ($M = 2.32$, $SD = .78$) to September 2010 ($M = 2.15$, $SD = .66$). This change is statistically significant $F(1, 1904) = 70.10$, $p = .001$.

We further inquired whether individuals' tendency to change their attitudes in a conciliatory direction is related to the degree of their embeddedness in the LTTE organisation. We expected that the more embedded individuals would be less likely to exhibit an attitude change of this sort than the less embedded individuals. In fact, the opposite turned out to be the case. As shown in Figure 13.2, the greater one's embeddedness, the greater the attitude change, $\beta = -.33$, $p = .001$. This finding should be regarded with caution, because of a possible regression to the mean artefact. At least, however, it suggests that the more embedded individuals did not change any less (!) than the less embedded individuals.

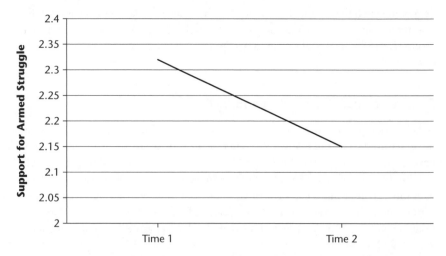

FIGURE 13.1 Support for armed struggle in the rehabilitation group as a function of time

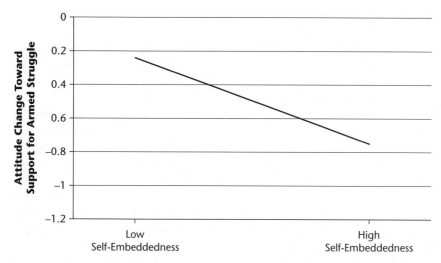

FIGURE 13.2 Attitude change toward support for armed struggle as a function of detainees' self-embeddedness in the LTTE organisation (lower numbers indicate greater de-radicalisation)

The fact that detainees' scores exhibited change does not tell us whether the change was authentic or whether it reflected socially desirable responding on the detainees' part. Nor does it reveal whether it was the rehabilitation program that produced the change, or whether the change was effected by the mere effects of time (that "heals all wounds") and/or by historical events that transpired in the interim (e.g., the realisation that the Tamils' military option has been eliminated for all intents and purposes, or that the government is channelling substantial efforts into reconstruction of the Tamil populated areas). It was also possible that the change was effected by the psychological distance from the heat of the battle and, from the pressing, and ruthlessly enforced, influence of the LTTE organisation upon its members. Further consideration was needed to address these possibilities.

On reflection, concern about socially desirable responding as a possible alternative explanation of the observed attitude change seems somewhat implausible. Given what we could gather from our interviews, at the time of their surrender the detainees were quite fearful of their captors, anxious about the fate that awaited them, and frightened about the strange and severe punishments that likely would befall them. As time went by, however, they realised that nothing terrible was likely to happen. Consequently, detainees' anxiety largely dissipated and gave way to calm (that we amply observed on our visits to the rehabilitation centres). If anything, socially desirable responding should have been more likely early on in the custodial term, when the detainees were highly concerned about their fate, rather than subsequently when their fears were allayed. This suggests that if socially desirable responding was to occur, it should have occurred early on in the incarceration period rather than later. This, in turn, suggests that the detainees' early responses should have been more conciliatory to the Sinhalese than the later responses, and yet the opposite was the case.

Of greater concern is the possibility that the observed attitude change, though possibly authentic, was nonetheless due to something other than the rehabilitation programs as such, instead having to do with the mere passage of time, and/or the time-bound psychological processes that may have occurred in the interim as noted earlier. To investigate these possibilities, one needs a control group assessed at the same points in time as the rehabilitation group without, however, being afforded the rehabilitation programs. Ideally, detainees would be randomly assigned to the rehabilitation and control groups to statistically control for the possibility that these groups systematically differed in some meaningful ways.

Unfortunately, obtainment of such random assignment is unlikely in real-world contexts. Few, if any, governments or custodial authorities would allow research priorities to dictate the assignment of detainees to conditions or agree to a with-holding of rehabilitation treatments from some detainees while extending it to others. Field research, however, represents the "art of the possible" and we were able to identify a control group that, while not exactly ideal, constitutes a close enough approximation that allows one to draw meaningful comparisons.

The control group in question consisted of a sample of 152 detainees ("bene-ficiaries") in a centre at Omanthai in Northern Sri Lanka who for logistic reasons were not offered the rehabilitation programs (except for yoga and meditation) during the relevant time period, that is, between December 2009 and September 2010. The following features of the Omanthai sample rendered it a reasonable control group. First and foremost (1) it was tested at the same times as the rehabilitation group, that is, in December 2009 and September 2010. Furthermore, when initially tested it was equal on the average to the rehabilitation group on several relevant variables, specifically on (2) support for armed struggle, (3) negative attitudes toward the Sinhalese, (4) sense of meaning in life, (5) specific emotions (anger, shame, sadness), (6) embeddedness in the LTTE organization, (7) social-dominance orientation, and (8) need for cognitive closure.

The Omanthai control group did differ from the rehabilitation group slightly in the average age of its members: Whereas the average age of the rehabilitation detainees was 27.54 years ($SD = 6.66$), that of the Omanthai control was 30.22 years ($SD = 6.48$), $F(1, 2053) = 22.81$, $p < .001$. Additionally, the rehabilitation sample was on the average slightly more educated than the control sample. Forty-nine percent of the rehabilitation sample had at least the equivalent of a high-school degree compared to 28.6% in the control sample ($\chi^2 = 22.58$, $p = .001$). Neither of these differences appears particularly relevant to the main issue of present interest: the detainees' degree of support for an armed struggle against the Sinhalese.

Somewhat more problematic is the fact that members of the Omanthai group were given a medium risk classification by the Sri Lankan army, meaning that they were involved to some extent in anti-social crimes, and in recruitment to the LTTE. In contrast, members of the rehabilitation group were involved in more peripheral activities on behalf of the organisation. Bearing this concern in mind, it is still of interest to see that whereas a statistically significant change occurred in the rehabilitation group (as already noted), there was hardly any change in the control group. This is reflected in the statistically significant interaction (see Figure 13.3), $F(1, 2055) = 3.88$, $p < .05$, which indicates that support for armed struggle was at its lowest in the rehabilitation group at Time 2.

We further inquired whether the relations of the detainees to the centres' personnel mattered in producing the positive attitude change toward the Sinhalese that obtained in the rehabilitation group. The answer appears to be affirmative. As shown in Figure 13.4, positive change in attitudes toward the centres' personnel moderated the positive change toward the Sinhalese, in that those who changed in a positive direction in their liking for the centres' personnel also reduced to a greater extent their support for violent struggle against the Sinhalese. In contrast, in the Omanthai control group, the degree of positive change toward the centre's personnel did not predict the degree of their support for struggle against the Sinhalese.

A possible interpretation of this finding is that liking for the camp personnel is not enough to foster change and that in addition one needs the various programs in place for de-radicalisation to occur. The logic of this interpretation is that if liking and positive rapport with the personnel were sufficient, both our groups would have exhibited a relationship between positive change in attitudes to the personnel and reduced support for armed struggle. As we have seen, however, such a relationship occurred only in the rehabilitation group but not in the control group.

Nonetheless, one must be cautious in drawing such a conclusion because it is possible that the Omanthai detainees were simply more committed to the LTTE cause and hence were less likely to change as a function of their attitudes toward their centre's personnel as well as less likely to reduce their support for violent struggle. So the open question remains whether the rehabilitation programs (versus

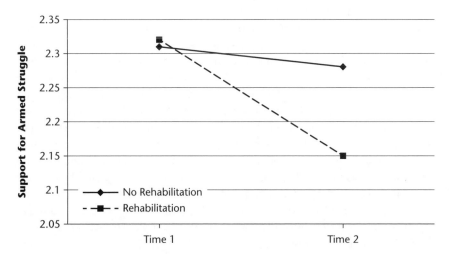

FIGURE 13.3 Support for armed struggle across time for detainees in the rehabilitation and the no rehabilitation groups

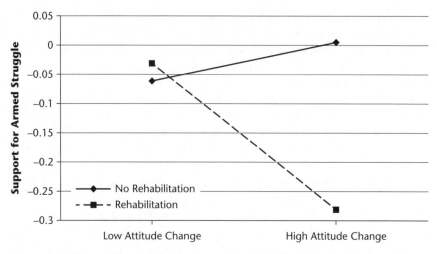

FIGURE 13.4 Support for armed struggle as a function of attitude change toward the staff members for detainees in the rehabilitation and the no rehabilitation groups

other factors) account for the change observed in the rehabilitation group, and whether the absence of change in the control group is attributable to the absence of exposure to the rehabilitation programs or to this group's higher risk classification. Perhaps it is the less committed (lower risk) individuals who would change regardless of whether they received the rehabilitation programs, whereas the more hard-core members (higher risk) would not change even if they had received such programs. This possibility is addressed next.

Among the facilities to which we had access was also the Boossa facility in the town of Galle on the southernmost tip of Sri Lanka. What made this centre of particular interest was a conjunction of two factors: (1) it held the most hard-core detainees, those in the highest risk category, (2) it implemented the full-fledged panoply of rehabilitation programs including the vocational education courses and so on. We administered our measures to Boossa detainees at two points in time: In the month of December of 2010, and in the month of December in 2011. The preliminary findings at this moment appear promising. As of now, we have observed a declining trend (although not yet significant) in support for violence from December 2010 to 2011. Perhaps more importantly, replicating the findings found with the rehabilitation group found earlier, positive change in attitudes to the personnel significantly predicts decline of support for armed struggle. These results are intriguing given that the detainees of Boossa are amongst the most determined and convinced members of the (former) LTTE. Clearly, several additional hypotheses await further investigation and greater sample sizes will enable us to clarify these preliminary results.

These findings bear on our concern about the difference described earlier between the rehabilitation group and the control group at Omanthai. That concern related to the possibility that the decline in support for violence in the rehabilitation sample, but not in the control sample, was due to the effect of time that reduced the militancy of the rehabilitation detainees but had no appreciable effect on the more hard-core, committed, members of the control detainees. But if this was so, and if the rehabilitation programs were ineffectual, then surely no effect of time should be observed for the Boossa detainees who were even more hard core, higher risk class than the Omanthai detainees. The fact that these Boossa detainees, exposed to the full panoply of the rehabilitation programs, did appear to manifest change suggests (though not yet conclusively) that the rehabilitation programs did work, and that they produced a salutary change not only for the low-risk detainees in our original rehabilitation group but also for the high-risk, committed Boossa detainees.

Concluding remarks

The above results imply that rehabilitation efforts of the kind implemented in Sri Lanka can be effective. Specifically, our findings indicate that the observed attitude change in our rehabilitation and Boossa samples wasn't merely due to the passage of time, nor (in the rehab sample at least) due to the mere friendliness of the centres' personnel; nor, apparently, was the conciliatory change in attitudes restricted to low-risk detainees, or to ones less embedded in the LTTE organisation. Rather, these preliminary data suggest that the change was authentically effected by the rehabilitation programs that were implemented. At the time of writing, we are carrying out additional analyses, looking at developmental trajectories of change in individual detainees and at other issues of interest. What we have found so far, however, is encouraging.

Can the present rehabilitation model be applied to other samples of detained terrorism suspects, in other cultures, and different socio-political circumstances? Only comparative empirical research may be able to answer this question definitively. It is possible, however, that the Sri Lankan case is indeed unique. Of greatest potential significance is the fact that the rehabilitation effort occurred in the aftermath of the LTTE's complete defeat and demolition. In such conditions, engagement in armed struggle appeared no longer an option that could succeed and offer an avenue to a significant gain to those who participated in it. As with the Egyptian terror-using organisations (the Egyptian Jemaah Islamiyah and Al Jihad groups) that de-radicalised after they had been devastated on the ground, it could be that the LTTE members' readiness to disengage from violence and embrace an alternative, peaceful, route to a meaningful existence was strongly influenced by the elimination of the militancy option as a route that could succeed. This possibility should be kept in mind while investigating alternative de-radicalisation attempts carried out in the shadow of a continuing struggle.

Notes

1 Elsewhere (Kruglanski et al., in press, 2009), we point out that occasionally the dishonour and humiliation can stem from an individual's personal circumstances (e.g., the shame of infertility, divorce or extramarital affair) unrelated to any action by one's group's enemy. In those conditions too, the individual may attempt to erase the ignominy by embracing a group's cause and acting on the group's behalf.
2 *Basque Freedom and Homeland.*
3 Though Yehoshua felt that her interviewees were reporting their authentic attitudes while in custody, this is no guarantee that these may not re-radicalise upon release, once they are back in a terrorism-supporting community.

References

Hannah, G., Clutterbuck, L. and Rubin, J. (2008). *Radicalisation or Rehabilitation: Understanding the challenge of extremist and radicalized prisoners*, RAND Europe (TR-571).

Kruglanski, A. W., Bélanger, J. J., Gelfand, M., Gunaratna, R., Hettiarachchi, M., Reinares, F., Orehek, E., Sasota, J., & Sharvit, K. (in press). 'Terrorism: A (self) love story. Re-directing the significance quest can end violence.' *American Psychologist.*

Kruglanski, A. W., Chen, X., Dechesne, M., Fishman, S., & Orehek, E. (2009). 'Fully committed: suicide bombers' motivation and the quest for personal significance.' *Political Psychology*, 30, 331–357.

Mitchell, T. R., Holtom, B. C., Lee, T. W., Sablynski, C. J., & Erez, M. (2001). 'Why people stay: Using job embeddedness to predict voluntary turnover.' *The Academy of Management Journal*, 44, 1102–1121.

Reinares, F. (2011). 'Exit from terrorism: A qualitative empirical study on disengagement and de-radicalisation among members of ETA.' *Terrorism and Political Violence*, 23, 780–803.

Yehoshua. S. (2013). 'The social-psychology profile of terrorist leaders in Israeli prisons.' Unpublished doctoral dissertation. Kings College, London.

Yousef, M. H. (2010). *Son of Hamas: A Gripping Account of Terror, Betrayal, Political Intrigue, and Unthinkable Choices.* Tyndale Momentum.

14

THE "THREE RINGS" OF TERRORIST REHABILITATION AND COUNTER-IDEOLOGICAL WORK IN SINGAPORE

A decade on

Kumar Ramakrishna[1]

> I would like to make a strong statement that what the JI did was wrong. Muslims must be aware that violence advocated by the JI and like-minded groups has no place in Islam.
>
> *"M" – former Singapore Jemaah Islamiyah*

In the decade since the September 11, 2001 terrorist attacks in the United States, considerable scholarship has been generated on the so-called religiously inspired "new terrorist" threat and ways of countering the real-time threat posed to free societies. In recent years, however, much analysis has moved beyond a focus on law enforcement and military-kinetic strategies to embrace softer counterterrorism measures, in particular terrorist rehabilitation. Much of the discussion on rehabilitation has oscillated between the pros and cons of terrorist "de-radicalisation" as opposed to "disengagement." By "disengagement" we mean the process by which an individual disengages physically from "terrorist activity" – without necessarily demonstrating a "concomitant change or reduction in ideological support" or displaying full autonomy from the "social and ideological control that the particular ideology exerts on the individual" (Horgan, 2008). On the other hand "comprehensive de-radicalization" occurs when an individual "de-legitimizes the use of violent methods to achieve political goals, while also moving towards an acceptance of gradual social, political and economic changes within a pluralist context" (Ashour, 2009, pp.5–6). This chapter seeks to analyse Singapore's terrorist rehabilitation and counter-ideological program – an effort that has been designed to reduce the risk of convicted terrorists' potential re-engagement in terrorism post-release (Qatar International Academy for Security Studies, 2010).

The rationale for such a program dates back to December 2001, just a few months after the September 11 Al Qaeda strikes in New York and Washington DC. The Singaporean Internal Security Department (ISD) – the functional equivalent of MI5 in the United Kingdom or the FBI in the United States – arrested 13 Singaporean Muslim militants of a previously unknown, Al Qaeda-linked terrorist network called Jemaah Islamiyah (JI). In so doing, ISD disrupted a plot to mount six suicide truck bomb attacks on US, British, Australian, and Israeli diplomatic missions, US naval facilities, as well as commercial buildings housing US entities (Ministry of Home Affairs, 2003). A second major ISD operation in September the following year led to the detentions of 18 more persons, 17 of whom were confirmed to be current or former JI members, as well as one individual who was in fact a member of the Moro Islamic Liberation Front (MILF) in the southern Philippines. The second JI group had been conducting surveillance of Singapore's Changi International Airport as well as key water pipelines (Ministry of Home Affairs, 2003). Over the following months it was established that the original aim of JI leaders, who had emerged from the older Darul Islam (DI) separatist movement in Java, was to set up an Islamic State in Indonesia. However, following the participation of some Indonesian JI fighters in the campaign against the occupying Soviet forces in Afghanistan in the 1980s and the ensuing contact with individuals who later formed Al Qaeda, a more global jihad orientation developed. Thus senior JI leaders, especially after splintering from Darul Islam in January 1993, began to seek, through armed jihad, to create a Southeast Asian caliphate – inspired by the Al Qaeda vision of restoring the glorious Islamic caliphate of old (Hammond, 2006). This transnational outlook of the Indonesian-based JI leadership led it to set up regional commands or *mantiqi* governing the operations of cells in different Southeast Asian countries, including Singapore.[2] Following the thwarted Singapore plot of December 2001, JI regrouped and struck again – this time all too successfully – on the Indonesian tourist island of Bali on October 12, 2002. The twin suicide bombings of two popular nightspots frequented by Western tourists, the Sari Club and Paddy's Bar, killed 202 people, mainly Australian tourists. The Bali attack drove home JI's resolve in pursuing its deadly agenda (Ramakrishna and Tan, 2003). This greatly alarmed Singaporean authorities and Muslim community leaders, who by 2002 had already understood the need to find ways of countering the dangerous JI ideology that seemed to have such insidious appeal to elements within the Muslim communities in Singapore and the region. By "ideology" here we adopt the perspective of Swidler (1986), who sees ideology as "a highly articulated, self-conscious belief and ritual system, aspiring to offer a unified answer to problems of social action."

The rest of this chapter will be divided into four sections. The next section situates the analysis by sketching out the wider historical, geopolitical and socio-cultural milieu within which Singapore's Muslim community – from which the JI detainees have emerged – is embedded. The section after that tightens the analytical focus on what is known publicly about the backgrounds of the Singapore JI detainees to better understand their aims and motivations. Against this backdrop, the origins and evolution of the Singaporean terrorist rehabilitation and counter-ideological program is then analysed. Finally, an assessment of the entire program to date is attempted.

The operational context: Singapore's Muslim community

The former British colony of Singapore, a regional financial and manufacturing hub heavily dependent on global trade and open markets, is home to a population of 5.35 million people. Ethnic Chinese form more than three-quarters of the population. Ethnic Malays, who are virtually all Muslims, comprise 13.9 percent of the population. Ethnic Indians comprise about 7.9 percent of the population. English is the language of administration, while Malay, Chinese, and Tamil are all official languages. In addition, Christianity, Buddhism, Taoism, Hinduism and of course Islam are all officially recognised and constitutionally protected faiths.

The practical necessity from the 14th century CE onward of expediting commercial transactions within and beyond the bustling, cosmopolitan Malay trading world, as well as the powerful appeal of the mystical Sufism of south Indian Muslim traders, helped ensure that over the centuries Southeast Asian, including Singaporean, Islam developed an accommodating and moderate hue (McAmis, 2002). To be sure, the waves of Islamic revivalism that swept through Southeast Asia from the 1980s onward resulted in noticeably increased personal piety levels amongst Muslims throughout the region (Azra, 2003). Nevertheless, significant numbers of Singaporean Muslims, even if more religiously observant, have nevertheless remained politically and socially moderate in being willing to practice their faith within the multi-cultural, secular, democratic political framework in Singapore.[3]

That said, the Singapore government, acutely conscious of Singapore's status as a Chinese-majority city-state located at the heart of a periodically unstable Malay/Muslim archipelago,[4] as well as how racial and religious tensions have exploded into domestic violence in the past, has always been interventionist in the religious sphere.[5] Hence, apart from introducing legislation aimed at tackling threats to racial and religious harmony, such as the Maintenance of Religious Harmony Act,[6] the government has kept an eye on the regulation of Muslim socio-cultural and educational affairs in Singapore, through the Islamic Religious Council of Singapore or MUIS (Majlis Ulama Islam Singapura), a statutory board formed in 1968. MUIS oversees the sermons in the 70 Singapore mosques serving Singapore's half a million Muslims (MUIS, 2012; Kong, 2007). Balancing somewhat this careful official oversight of Muslim affairs is an independent Muslim civil society presence. Key organisations in this category include the Association of Muslim Professionals (AMP), representing the secular Muslim professional class; the Association of Adult Religious Class Students (Perdaus); and perhaps most significantly for the purposes of our analysis, Pergas, the Singapore Islamic Scholars and Religious Teachers Association.

To keep things in perspective, it must be observed that the Singaporean Muslim community, well before the September 11 2001 attacks in the United States and the emergence of the JI threat, have had concerns about their relative status in the Singaporean pecking order. First, Singapore's Malay Muslims have always felt a certain natural kinship with their brethren in the wider Malay/Muslim world –

particularly Malaysia and Indonesia – and resent the ensuing suspicions toward them by the Chinese majority as well as the government, which has long been keen on promoting an overarching, multi-racial Singaporean national identity (Kahn, 2006). Local Muslims feel that such latent official distrust explains a number of policies that have appeared to go against the interests of the community over the years: first, the perceived lack of representation of proportionate numbers of Muslims in sensitive appointments in the Singapore Armed Forces (SAF) (Mamat, 2007; Yong, 2009); the decision by the government to introduce compulsory national education for all children of primary school age, thereby impacting Muslim religious school (*madrasah*) education;[7] more recently, the ban of the wearing of headscarves or *tudung* by Muslim schoolgirls attending national schools; and finally, the penchant of a number of employers in Singapore to require Mandarin proficiency as a job requirement, something which some Muslims feel unhappy about.[8] Second, the Muslim community has tended to lag behind the Chinese and Indian communities in terms of educational and economic attainment, as well as living standards, although the gap began to close with the setting up, with government support, of the community self-help group Yayasan Mendaki in the 1980s (www.mendaki.org.sg/). Up to the present, however, there remain generalised sentiments amongst a number of Singaporean Muslims that they have to put up with a sort of unwarranted "least favourite child" existence within the country (Suhaimi, 2008), although Chinese-majority Singapore itself represents a minority within a wider Malay/Muslim world.

Reinforcing such generalised if latent misgivings have been geopolitical factors. While the global Islamic revival since the 1980s as noted did have an impact on the overall piety levels of many local Muslims, this never fully translated into a more pronounced consciousness of the transnational unity of the global Muslim community or *ummah*. There existed, however, a certain long-running muted resentment towards Israel for its occupation of the Palestinian territories and the United States for its support of Tel Aviv.[9] However, the Bush administration's war on terrorism after the September 11 2001 attacks and in particular, the ill-conceived 2003 Iraq invasion intensified local Muslim unhappiness with US foreign policy missteps – and generated a more acute awareness on the part of the average Singaporean Muslim of his wider, transnational Islamic identity. These factors taken together help explain why the emergence of JI at the end of 2001 was met initially by a sense of scepticism within the Muslim community. There were dark murmurings in some quarters of a Singapore government "conspiracy" to undermine the image of Islam in the country.[10] Government ministers felt compelled to meet Muslim community leaders behind closed doors to assure them that the Singapore JI "arrests were not targeted against the Singapore Muslim community or Islam" (Tong, 2004). All notions of an official conspiracy were quickly dispelled, however, when two respected independent Muslim religious leaders, Ustaz Haji Ali Haji Mohamed, Chairman of the influential Khadijah Mosque, and Ustaz Haji Muhammad Hasbi Hassan, President of Pergas, were invited by ISD to talk face-to-face to the JI detainees in 2002. Meeting and talking to the detainees had a profound effect on both *asatizah*.[11] First, they came away utterly persuaded not only that JI was not a figment of some bureaucrat's fevered imagination. Second they were alarmed by the dangerous ideology that had been sketched out for them first-hand by the JI detainees themselves.[12]

The Singapore Jemaah Islamiyah detainees: an overview

It should be noted that in Singapore, access to the JI detainees is heavily restricted. Hence much of the information about them is available mainly from press reports, official government statements and certain religious clerics with access to them as part of or in association with the Religious Rehabilitation Group (RRG – to be discussed below). Of particular importance to researchers is the Singapore Ministry of Home Affairs White Paper that was released on January 7, 2003 and provides much valuable and authoritative information about the JI network in Singapore and Southeast Asia. At the time the White Paper was being prepared in 2002, 31 JI detainees, largely Malay but including a small number of Indian Muslims as well, were in custody (Ministry of Home Affairs, 2003). From a close reading of the White Paper, some idea of the typical background of the average JI detainee can be discerned. As the paper notes, these men were "not ignorant, destitute or disenfranchised outcasts," and held "normal, respectable jobs" (Ministry of Home Affairs, 2003). The range of occupations was very diverse, running the gamut from businessmen, managers, engineers and project co-ordinators, to more blue-collar jobs such as technicians, delivery men, dispatch clerks, canteen operators, drivers, used-car salesmen, a butcher, and even a part-time foot reflexologist! A number were unemployed at the time of their arrests. Most detainees had received a secular education (although one had obtained an Islamic Studies degree in Malaysia) (Ministry of Home Affairs, 2003).

To be sure, according to knowledgeable religious clerics, some of whom have been in direct contact with the detainees, several of the latter, like some in the wider Muslim community in Singapore, had been unhappy about certain policies and practices that appeared to be discriminatory. These included *inter alia*, the government ban on the wearing of the *tudung* by Muslim schoolgirls in national schools and the compulsory education policy mentioned earlier.[13] Moreover, in a much more pronounced manner in comparison with the average Singaporean Muslim, the detainees possessed what one informant considered a "feeling of hatred toward America" and had been upset with the Singapore government for allying too closely with the United States.[14] However, these issues were not decisive elements. They were rather "cumulative" and "links in a chain" of factors leading to the eventual radicalisation of the detainees.[15] On closer analysis, it seems that what held these varied individuals together in a common trajectory towards radicalisation was a desire for "spiritual revival." Not particularly well versed in the fundamentals of Islam, the majority of the JI detainees were seeking to atone for past sins and wished to turn over a new leaf. This led them to seek out religious teachers who would guide them in the right path. This is how they came into contact with the Singapore

JI leaders who "presented an extremist interpretation of Islam imbibed from Afghanistan that included a strong, anti-American, jihadist streak" (Ramakrishna, 2002a). Moreover, the atrocity propaganda employed by JI ideologues depicting graphic Muslim civilian casualties in the conflicts against non-Muslim forces in Palestine, Bosnia, Chechnya, and Ambon and Poso in eastern Indonesia had a powerful effect as well.[16] The detainees generally found that the compelling JI worldview provided structure and justification for whatever individualised resentments they each harboured and why extreme measures needed to be taken to rectify perceived wrongs. They withdrew from the mainstream Singaporean Muslim community and re-imagined themselves as members of an exclusive, secret Islamic vanguard, unafraid to wage armed jihad against apostate governments and other infidels and establish the "true" Islam in Singapore and the region (Ramakrishna, 2002a; Ministry of Home Affairs, 2003). Hence, on interrogation the detainees articulated the view that they had in fact regarded themselves as "doing good" and engaged in jihad for the righteous cause of setting up an "Islamic State."[17]

The "Three Rings" of the Singapore terrorist rehabilitation and counter-ideological program

The Inner Ring: The detainees

Following the realisation by Ustaz Ali, the Chairman of the Khadijah Mosque, and Ustaz Hasbi, the President of Pergas, that the JI threat was real, they gathered together other Muslim scholars to discuss ways and means of correcting the virulent, adversarial worldview of the JI detainees through a rehabilitation process driven chiefly via a counter-ideological approach. There was apparently no blueprint at that point to refer to and everything had to be done from scratch.[18] Eventually the program developed three rings of activity: an inner ring involving the detainees; an outer one targeting detainee families and friends; and an outermost ring involving the wider community. At any rate, the Religious Rehabilitation Group or RRG, an unpaid, all-volunteer grouping of Islamic scholars and teachers serving in their personal capacities was formed quietly by both *asatizah* by April 2003. RRG counsellors possessed formal Islamic educational credentials from both local *madrasahs* as well as respected foreign institutions such as Al Azhar University in Cairo, the Islamic University of Medina in Saudi Arabia and the International Islamic University in Malaysia (Hassan, 2007). In addition, the RRG counsellors, who were a mix of younger and older scholars and clerics, were put through a seven-month diploma course in counselling skills to supplement their religious knowledge. Thus each RRG counsellor received a certified Specialist Diploma in Counselling Psychology (Hassan and Mostarom, 2011). It was felt that such formal training in counselling skills was essential, as conducting one-to-one counselling with a detainee was quite different from speaking in a mosque with 200 people listening.[19] By January 2004, the RRG boasted 16 male and 5 female counsellors (Hassan, 2007). By April, a full year after the formation of the RRG, and armed with a Religious Rehabilitation or so-called "Jihad Manual" to alert each RRG counsellor to JI ideological deviations from Islamic teaching, the actual counselling sessions with the JI detainees began in earnest. Typically, one RRG counsellor worked in a three-man team assigned to each detainee. The other two members of the team included an ISD case officer and a Home Affairs Ministry psychologist. The RRG counsellor confined himself solely to religious matters, though he was kept informed by the case officer on other issues pertaining to the detainee's state of mind and relevant personal circumstances. JI detainees were never jointly counselled and they were kept apart from one another in detention.[20] They underwent religious counselling between two and four hours each day (Qatar International Academy for Security Studies, 2010, p.14).

Initially the RRG counsellors were viewed with great suspicion by the JI detainees who were abusive, accusing them of being nothing more than *munafiq* (hypocrites) and "puppets of the government."[21] Over time, the RRG counsellors realised that most of the JI detainees, despite outward appearances, possessed a very superficial understanding of Islamic jurisprudence, and had a very narrow understanding of jihad. Whatever little knowledge of Islam they had came not from a formal Islamic education in a *madrasah* but relatively simple and basic ad hoc part-time classes organised by the likes of Pergas and Perdaus.[22] This rudimentary, fragmented knowledge had rendered them intellectually susceptible to the ideological blandishments of determined JI ideologues. In fact, it became clear that a number of simplistic and overly literal JI themes needed "extricating" and "negating" from detainee minds, as the RRG likes to put it (Ali, n.d.). These were: the notion that Muslims must hate and disassociate themselves from non-Muslims and Westerners; that jihad only means perpetual warfare against infidels; that the *bai'ah* or oath to the JI leadership was inviolable; that martyrdom through suicide operations was to be sought after and celestial virgins awaited them in the afterlife; and that Muslims can practice an authentic faith only within an Islamic State (Hassan, 2007). Between April 2004 and September 2006, the RRG conducted more than 500 counselling sessions with the JI detainees (Hassan, 2007).

To be sure, the "hard core" detainees such as Singapore JI spiritual leader Ibrahim Maidin and others "deeply involved in the movement for more than a decade" apparently remain unmoved by RRG counselling efforts. In this category was the former operational leader of the Singapore JI cell, Mas Selamat Kastari. Following the ISD crackdown at the end of 2001, he escaped from Singapore but was arrested by Indonesian authorities and sentenced to 18 months' jail in 2003 for immigration violations. Because of the lack of an extradition treaty between Indonesia and Singapore, Kastari was not deported upon release. He was, however, rearrested by the Indonesians in January 2006 for possession of a fake identity document and this time was handed over to the Singaporeans, who detained him under the Internal Security Act in March 2006. However, Kastari sensationally escaped from Whitley Detention Centre – where all JI detainees are interned – in February 2008, sparking a massive island-wide manhunt. He was arrested yet again – this time by the Malaysian Special Branch, in April 2009, and sent back to

Singapore in September 2010 where he remains under detention under the ISA at the time of writing. Nevertheless, other less ideologically committed detainees, between six months to a year after the RRG sessions began, evinced discernible changes in beliefs and behaviour (Ali, n.d.). These were, according to RRG assessments, typically the "normal members" who were "not really serious" but had decided to take the *bai'ah* or oath of allegiance to the JI leaders because their friends asked them to. They eventually showed remorse for their involvement with JI, were "receptive" of RRG efforts to instil in them more balanced Islamic teachings and were appreciative of government efforts to rehabilitate rather than prosecute them outright. Some of these detainees were later released on Restriction Orders (ROs)[23] but were still required to attend mandatory counselling with the RRG to prevent theological backsliding.[24] The existence of the RRG was made public by the Singapore government in October 2005 (Hassan, 2007). RRG members also began to venture abroad, paying study visits to Saudi Arabia and Egypt to pick up ideas from rehabilitation programs in those countries (Qatar International Academy for Security Studies, 2010).

The Outer Ring: detainee families

By 2005, RRG counsellors had begun shifting attention to the families of the detainees as it was understood that the spouses of the detainees were likely either radicalised themselves due to exposure to their husbands' ideas, or confused and vulnerable to radicalisation. It was thus vital as part of the overall rehabilitation and counter-ideological effort to help "sustain and or facilitate family stability during and after detention" (Qatar International Academy for Security Studies, 2010, p.16). Observers in this regard acknowledge that the aftercare assistance is strategic because if this support to the families of detainees is lacking "then it is possible that extremist elements will move in to provide it".[25] The RRG thus dispatched female counsellors to talk to detainee spouses who were willing to voluntarily subject themselves to counselling.[26] RRG family counselling efforts in this respect were greatly aided by the formation of the Interagency-After Care Group (ACG), which focused "on the welfare of the families of detainees" (Yong, 2007). The ACG was initiated in 2002 by five groups: the aforementioned Yayasan Mendaki and AMP, as well as the voluntary organisation Taman Bacaan, the Khadijah Mosque and En Naeem Mosque (Hassan, 2007). The ACG gradually overcame the initial suspicions of detainee spouses in very practical ways, for example, by providing financial assistance as the "detainees were all sole breadwinners and the families" needed "financial support to stay on their feet" (Nirmala, 2007). The ACG helped the wives find work as "clerks, cleaners and other blue-collar jobs," taught them to read "utility bills or pay property taxes," and, importantly, ensured that the education of the detainees' children continued uninterrupted, through various means such as enrolling them in tuition programs, securing school fee waivers and providing pocket money (Nirmala, 2007).

The Outermost Ring: the wider Muslim community and society

Also since 2005, the RRG has expanded its efforts to mitigate religious extremism in the wider Muslim community as well as promote inter-religious tolerance (Qatar International Academy for Security Studies, 2010). RRG clerics have addressed schools, youth clubs and community organisations and have "conducted and participated in a series of talks, workshops, seminars and conferences discussing issues on the global terrorism phenomenon, misconstrued ideology, counter-terrorism and radical ideology responses" (Gunaratna and Hassan, 2011, p.44). RRG also has an active website so as to reach an audience beyond the borders of Singapore, as well as published newsletters for its members, articles to the mass media and journals, and booklets and brochures for the public (Gunaratna and Hassan, 2011). The RRG website, in particular, serves as a useful tool for public education as it provides readers access to a wide range of scholarly publications, news articles and media interviews that focus on effective responses to extremism (Hassan, 2007). The ultimate aim of the website is to help "immunize" the wider Singaporean Muslim community against JI or similarly violent radical Islamist ideologies.[27] The Islamic Religious Council of Singapore or MUIS also set up websites to counter extremist ideology and warn young Muslims about dubious websites (Hassan and Mostarom, 2011).

It should be noted that the wider counter-ideological program in Singapore has undergone further evolution beyond the RRG and similar efforts by the likes of MUIS. It was recognised in official quarters that it was very important to create additional societal mechanisms aimed at undermining the appeal of violent extremist ideologies by creating and encouraging a united and tolerant community. In this regard the institution from 2002 onwards of Inter-Racial (later renamed Inter-Racial and Religious) Confidence Circles and Harmony Circles "at community levels, schools and workplaces promotes better inter-racial and inter-religious understandings between different communities and [provides] a platform for confidence building among the different communities as a basis for developing, in time, deeper friendships and trust" (Ministry of Home Affairs, 2003, p.23). By June 2006, there were 84 IRCCs comprising more than a thousand Singaporeans of various ethnic backgrounds (Kwek, 2007). By September 2007, 80 percent of all Singaporean religious organisations were IRCC members (Selvaretnam, 2007). In a similar vein, though pegged at a more ambitious scale, the Ministry of Home Affairs spearheaded from 2006 a Community Engagement Program (CEP). The CEP aims to strengthen the bonds between Singaporeans of diverse faiths, as well as augment community preparedness during emergencies. According to recent research conducted by Hassan and Mostarom (2011), the CEP currently comprises the involvement of multiple support groups, such as "religious groups, ethnic-based organisations, educational institutions, the media, businesses and unions as well as grassroots organisations," which are each organised into categories and supported by a relevant ministerial body. One of the key aspects of this program is the sense that both the government and the public at large have roles to play in building a society resilient to the communal stresses and strains following a terrorist attack. Since its inception, the CEP has grown to produce a compilation of anti-terrorism and counter-extremist ideology speeches and articles, which are subsequently distributed to educational institutions, community organisations and libraries. Such government-initiated counter-ideological programs have since been supplemented by similar efforts by individuals and civil society groups apart from the RRG. One excellent example is Muhammad Haniff Hassan, a respected religious scholar involved with the well-known International Center for Political Violence and Terrorism Research (ICPVTR) at the S. Rajaratnam School of International Studies, Nanyang Technological University. Haniff runs a well-liked counter-ideology blog. The energetic civil society group *Simply Islam*, meanwhile, while seeking to educate Singaporean Muslims on how the faith can continue to help them navigate life in a globalised, fast-paced society, also speaks out against violent extremist ideologies.

Assessment and observations

Ten years since the discovery of the JI network in Singapore, how should one assess terrorist rehabilitation and counter-ideological work in Singapore? By November 2009, more than 1,200 counselling sessions for the detainees and 150 sessions for the family members had been held. At the time of writing the RRG has grown to include 26 male and female counsellors, supported by an 8-person Secretariat and guided by a resource group of 3 eminent scholars.[28] More to the point, there is much evidence of the effectiveness of the RRG-led detainee rehabilitation and counter-ideological effort. First and foremost, observers point to the lack of substantive "JI activity" in Singapore since the major ISD swoops in 2001 and 2002.[29] Importantly, by 2010, of the 60 individuals arrested since 2001, three-quarters were released after participating in the rehabilitation program (Qatar International Academy for Security Studies, 2010). More precisely, 40 former detainees were released on Restriction Orders, and approximately another 15 remained incarcerated at Whitley Detention Centre (Qatar International Academy for Security Studies, 2010). Rohan Gunaratna's assertion made in 2008 that Singapore's detainee rehabilitation program is "working" and that the "rate of recidivism is exceptionally low" (Hussain, 2008) appears to still hold at the time of writing. This appears true even with the emergence in the past five years or so of the so-called "lone wolf" or "D.I.Y. radical" with no necessary institutional linkages to JI – but who has rather been radicalised partly by imbibing violent ideological material online (e.g. Chieh, 2010; Ramakrishna, 2007, 2010). Little wonder then that observers generally concur – to be candid, justifiably so – that the "Singapore program is probably the most comprehensive of all disengagement or deradical-isation programs" and its terrorist rehabilitation program "comes as close as any program can to the ideal type" (Rabasa, Pettyjohn, Ghez and Boucek, 2010).

Nevertheless, there remain a few issues that deserve further reflection. At a 2009 International Conference on Terrorist Rehabilitation held in Singapore, it was noted that there is a severe lack of "fool-proof measures" to determine whether a terrorist has been objectively and measurably de-radicalised. A similar view was offered by the authors of a RAND study who concurred that "it is difficult to assess the level of success achieved by the Singapore programme" (Hannah, Clutterbuck and Rubin, 2008, p.36). While some observers have been pushing for "more objective 'benchmarks' [that could] be used to improve the program over time," others, such as the then ISD Director, "expressed concern about any effort to 'objectively' measure what he sees as an inherently subjective and highly individualised process" (Qatar International Academy for Security Studies, 2010, p.17). In any case, Singapore is not alone. One 2010 study confirmed that "objective and systematic evaluation" of terrorist rehabilitation and counter-ideology programs is a "critical deficiency" in many countries (Qatar International Academy for Security Studies, 2010, p.52). Certainly at the time of writing, whether Singapore JI and other similar detainees have their detention orders terminated basically depends on the outcome of a subjective joint risk assessment by the RRG counsellor, ISD case officer and the psychologist in attendance.[30] There is no empirical basis for specifying a particular threshold or standard as the rehabilitation program is based on qualitative as opposed to quantitative measures. At present the status of detainees is reviewed every two years, in accordance with the Internal Security Act, by an Advisory Board composed of a High Court judge and two private citizens appointed by the President (Qatar International Academy for Security Studies, 2010). The Home Affairs Minister and the Cabinet, based on the Board's advice, ultimately decide whether a detainee is released (Rabasa et al., 2010).

Even more challenging is the task of assessing the extent to which the broader counter-ideological work of the RRG and other bodies is effective in "immunizing" detainee families and the wider Singaporean Muslim community against the "us-versus-them" ideological narratives promoted by the likes of Al Qaeda and JI. To be sure, the government has tried to foster closer ties between Muslims and non-Muslims so as to ensure that a sufficiently robust social resilience exists to weather the fall-out of an actual terrorist strike. It has done so through such instruments as the aforementioned CEP, IRCCs and Harmony Circles in neighbourhoods, the workplace and schools (Hassan and Pereire, 2006). Despite these commendable efforts, it has to be conceded, however, that a residual conspiracy mind-set still afflicts elements of the Muslim community in Singapore, much like in neighbouring Malaysia and Indonesia.[31] This is because – adopting a term from the insightful young Singaporean Malay-Muslim journalist Nur Dianah Suhaimi – "the least-favoured child syndrome" continues to afflict segments of the Singaporean Muslim community. Broader counter-ideological efforts have to thus operate against a wider sub-cultural canvas. Moreover, while some local observers laud the attempts by Muslim community leaders to develop a uniquely "Singapore Muslim Identity" as one possible antidote to foreign extremist ideological appeals (Hassan and Pereire, 2006, p.465), others cast doubt on such a measure. These more conservative commentators caution that "Singapore Muslims and Islam in Singapore are inextricable from the wider Islamic world," and that if Singapore's Muslim leaders press too hard in redefining local Islam to expedite greater Muslim integration into mainstream Singapore society, "Singapore would likely isolate herself, and the flock, bewildered, might seek an overseas shepherd," including foreign "terrorists" (Alwi, 2008). Dealing with the least-favoured child syndrome of segments of the wider Singaporean Muslim community requires generational change, and must involve attitudinal adjustments on the part of Muslims and non-Muslims alike, the Singapore authorities and businesses. Moreover, given how Singapore is so wired through the Internet to the outside world, a much more politically calibrated US foreign policy toward the Muslim world would somehow have to be part of the mix as well (Hassan and Pereire, 2006). In this connection, US Republican presidential candidate Mitt Romney's comments in July 2012 about the lack of Palestinian economic vitality in comparison with Israel and, more significantly, his observation that the hotly disputed city of Jerusalem should be regarded as the Israeli capital, would merely fuel virulent Islamist narratives of the type that have animated the Singapore JI. Perhaps it was just electoral rhetoric, but that makes no difference to determined JI and associated extremist propagandists (Abdalla, 2012).

Nevertheless, creative ways have recently been explored to further enhance the impact of the rehabilitation and counter-ideological effort. One potentially important approach in this regard is to deploy reformed JI detainees to support RRG efforts in undermining violent extremist ideological appeals to vulnerable elements in the community. Seasoned analysts have opined in this regard that the "power to convince the public of the danger of JI ideology is greater if it comes from former JI members," and their participation would "greatly enhance the credibility of the RRG's substantive argument" (Hassan and Pereire, 2006). Essentially "a measured employment of carefully selected ex-detainees" makes sense as they "possess a certain 'street cred' by virtue of actually having been within the movement," and they are far more familiar than ordinary scholars of "the problems and real-world contradictions within JI ideology" (Ramakrishna, 2012). Daniel Freedman (2010) makes a supportive point, arguing that "reformed terrorists will encourage other group members to abandon the cause," and that "having served time for the group, released terrorists have a credibility among members that's hard to challenge." In any case, employing former terrorists in rehabilitation and counter-ideological work is hardly a new departure in the Singaporean policy context. During the Malayan Emergency from 1948–60, surrendered Communist Party of Malaya (CPM) guerrillas were extremely effective in undermining the faith of active Communists in the Cause, while warning the ordinary Chinese public of the contradictions within CPM propaganda (Ramakrishna, 2002b). Furthermore, the Indonesian police in more recent times have been making active use of so-called "reformed" Indonesian JI militants such as Nasir Abbas to undercut the network's recruitment efforts (Mydans, 2008; Ramakrishna, 2009), with some tangible results, though it is equally obvious that the program has not been a comprehensive success (Ramakrishna, 2012).

This, however, does not imply that there is *ergo* no role for former JI detainees in rehabilitation and counter-ideological activities. It does suggest that some circumspection must accompany the selection of former detainees for such work. While moderate scholars such as those that lead the highly effective RRG must continue to exercise overall strategic guidance of rehabilitation and counter-ideological efforts, the judicious use of carefully selected willing former detainees could potentially further enhance the effectiveness of the overall program (Ramakrishna, 2012). In this respect, it is timely that former Singaporean JI militants – such as "M" whose quote started off this chapter – are gradually being brought into the counter-ideological effort (Hussain, 2012).

By way of conclusion, is there a broader lesson of the Singaporean approach to terrorist detainee rehabilitation and broader counter-ideology work that is worth further exploration? Perhaps it is the conviction that "capture and detention are just tools" and "not long-term solutions" and that a "fully developed, multi-faceted, resource-intensive risk reduction program for militant detainees" (Qatar International Academy for Security Studies, 2010) – involving not just measures undertaken within prison walls, but indeed, the policies beyond – is quite simply the way forward.

Notes

1 This chapter revises, expands and updates arguments and material drawn from the author's "A Holistic Critique of Singapore's Counter-Ideological Program," *CTC Sentinel*, 2/1 (January 2009), pp. 8–11; and "'Counter-Ideological' Work in Singapore: A Preliminary Assessment," *Journal of Policing, Intelligence and Counter Terrorism*, 4/2 (November 2009), pp. 4–52. The author thanks Elaine Coates for assistance in the research for the current chapter.

2 The *mantiqis* and their subdivisions have usually been described as a territorially based administrative structure. Thus, the *mantiqis* were equivalent to regions, *wakalah* to districts, down to the *fiah* or cells. See Ministry of Home Affairs (2003, p.10).

3 In Singapore, as in the rest of the Malay world in Southeast Asia, to be ethnic Malay is largely to be of the Muslim faith as well (McAmis, 2002, p. 47). In addition, while most ethnic Indians in Singapore are Hindus, a significant minority are Muslims as well.

4 Singapore and Malaya (later Malaysia) were embroiled in a long-running counter-insurgency campaign against the Communist Party of Malaya from 1948 to 1960. In August 1965, after a short-lived political union, Singapore found itself expelled from Malaysia while both countries were at the time on the receiving end of Indonesian President Soekarno's so-called *Konfrontasi* policy. Soekarno had sought to undermine the expanded Malaysian Federation, comprising Malaya, Singapore, Sabah and Sarawak, as he considered this a neo-colonial creation to preserve British influence in Southeast Asia. For details on the Communist insurrection, see Short (1975); for an analysis by a Singaporean elder statesman of the painful exit from Malaysia and *Konfrontasi*, see Lee Kuan Yew (1998).

5 In particular, the 1950 religiously motivated Maria Hertogh riots, the 1955 Communist-inspired Hock Lee riots and the 1964 violence between Malay/Muslims and Chinese, have all been said to have had a profound effect in shaping Singapore leaders' assumptions about the need for a firm hand in dealing with internal matters of race and religion.

6 This legislation allows the Singapore authorities to deter and restrain religious leaders and groups from inciting anti-government sentiments or fostering inter-religious ill will. See Bureau of Democracy, Human Rights, and Labor, US Department of State, "Singapore: International Religious Freedom Report 2004," available online at http://www.state.gov/g/drl/rls/irf/2004/35427.htm (accessed August 1, 2012).

7 The Compulsory Education Act came into effect in 2003 and required all Singaporean children – including those attending the city-state's six *madrasahs* – to pass the standardised Primary School Leaving Examination (PSLE). This move by the government generated concerns in some Malay/Muslim circles that the traditional independence of *madrasahs* in Singapore – for decades an important "identity marker" – would be constrained somewhat. See Kassim (n.d.).

8 Interview with Muhammad Haniff Bin Hassan, Oct. 25, 2007. Ustaz Haniff is a trained Islamic scholar who is engaged in counter-ideological work in Singapore. He is the author of *Unlicensed to Kill: Countering Imam Samudra's Justification for the Bali Bombing* (Singapore: Peace Matters, 2006).

9 Haniff interview, Oct. 25, 2007.

10 Interview with Mohamed Bin Ali, Oct. 25, 2007. Ali, a trained Islamic scholar, has been personally involved in counselling JI detainees as part of the Religious Rehabilitation Group.

11 Plural for "*ustaz*" or religious teacher.

12 Mohamed Ali interview; also Religious Rehabilitation Group, "An Understanding of Islam," presentation at the Religious Harmony Gathering, organised by Geylang Serai Inter-Racial and Religious Confidence Circle (IRCC) and Masjid Khalid (Khalid Mosque), Singapore, September 17, 2006.

13 Haniff interview, Oct. 25, 2007; Mohamed Ali interview.

14 Mohamed Ali interview.

15 Haniff interview, Oct. 25, 2007.

16 Mohamed Ali interview; Haniff interview, Oct. 25, 2007.

17 Mohamed Ali interview.

18 Mohamed Ali interview.

19 Mohamed Ali interview.

20 Mohamed Ali interview.

21 Mohamed Ali interview; Mohamed Bin Ali, "Rehabilitation of Extremists: The Singapore Experience," n.d.

22 Mohamed Ali interview.

23 A person released on Restriction Orders must abide by several conditions. He must seek ISD clearance in order to change his residence or employment, or travel out of Singapore. He also cannot make "public statements, address public meetings or print, distribute, contribute to or be involved in any publication, duplicate or disseminate any audio or video recording, hold office in, or be a member of any organisation, association or group without the prior approval of Director ISD." He is also required to report to ISD at specified times and dates, and present himself for counselling and/or interviews. See http://www.singaporeunited.sg/cep/index.php/web/Our-News/Detention-Imposition-Of-Restriction-Orders-And-Release-Under-The-Internal-Security-Act (accessed August 2, 2012).

24 Mohamed Ali interview.

25 In this respect similar assumptions apparently undergird the well-studied Saudi approach to rehabilitation e.g. Boucek (2007).

26 Mohamed Ali interview; Ali (n.d.). While detainees themselves were generally required by the authorities to submit themselves to counselling, their spouses were not required to, but could do so if they wished.

27 Mohamed Ali interview.

28 http://www.rrg.sg (accessed July 28, 2012).

29 Haniff interview, Nov. 27, 2008.

30 Haniff interview, Nov. 27, 2008.

31 Haniff interview, Oct. 25, 2007.

References

Abdalla, J. (2012). 'Romney riles Palestinians with digs at culture, economy.' *Reuters*, July 30, 2012, available online at http://www.reuters.com/article/2012/07/30/us-romney-israel-palestinians-idUSBRE86T0JV20120730 (accessed August 1, 2012).

Ali, Mohamed Bin (n.d.) "Rehabilitation of Extremists: The Singapore Experience."

Alwi, S. (2008). 'Islam in Singapore: Where to from here?' *The Online Citizen*, May 1, 2008, available online at http://theonlinecitizen.com/2008/05/islam-in-singapore-where-to-from-here/ (accessed August 1, 2012).

Ashour, O. (2009). *The De-Radicalization of Jihadists: Transforming Armed Islamist Movements*. London: Routledge.

Azra, A. (2003). 'Bali and Southeast Asian Islam: Debunking the myths.' In Kumar Ramakrishna and See Seng Tan (Eds.) *After Bali: The Threat of Terrorism in Southeast Asia*. Singapore: World Scientific/Institute of Defence and Strategic Studies.

Bureau of Democracy, Human Rights, and Labor, US Department of State (2004). 'Singapore: International Religious Freedom Report 2004,' available online at http://www.state.gov/g/drl/rls/irf/2004/35427.htm (accessed August 1, 2012).

Boucek, C. (2007). 'Extremist re-education and rehabilitation in Saudi Arabia.' *Jamestown Foundation Terrorism Monitor*, 5/16, available online at http://www.jamestown.org/single/?no_cache=1&tx_ttnews%5Btt_news%5D=4321 (accessed August 1, 2012).

Chieh, L. (2010). 'The D.I.Y. radical,' *My Paper*, July 7, 2010, available online at http://news.asiaone.com/News/AsiaOne%2BNews/Singapore/Story/A1Story201007 07-225618.html (accessed August 1, 2012).

Freedman, D. (2010). 'What (reformed) terrorists told me,' *Forbes*, December 15, 2010, available online at http://soufangroup.com/news/details/?Article_Id=27#.UBOSk-azT_E.email (accessed July 30, 2012).

Gunaratna, R. and Hassan, M. (2011). 'Terrorist rehabilitation – The Singapore experience.' In Rohan Gunaratna, Jolene Jerard and Lawrence Rubin (Eds.) *Terrorist Rehabilitation and Counter-Radicalisation: New Approaches to Counter-Terrorism*. London: Routledge.

Hammond, A. (2006). 'Islamic Caliphate a dream, not reality, say experts.' *Reuters*, Dec. 13, 2006, available online at http://uk.reuters.com/article/2006/12/14/lifestyle-islam-caliphate-dc-idUKL0427547720061214 (accessed August 1, 2012).

Hannah, G., Clutterbuck, L. and Rubin, J. (2008). *Radicalization or Rehabilitation: Understanding the Challenge of Extremist and Radicalized Prisoners*. Santa Monica: RAND Corporation.

Hassan, U. (2007). 'The roles of the Religious Rehabilitation Group (RRG) in Singapore.' In Abdul Halim bin Kader (Ed.) *Fighting Terrorism: The Singapore Perspective*. Singapore: Taman Bacaan.

Hassan, M. and Mostarom, T. (2011). *A Decade of Combating Radical Ideology: Learning from the Singapore Experience, 2001–2011*. Singapore: S. Rajaratnam School of International Studies Monograph.

Hassan, M. and Pereire, K. (2006). 'An ideological response to combating terrorism – The Singapore perspective,' *Small Wars and Insurgencies*, 17/4.

Horgan, J. (2008). 'Deradicalization or disengagement? A process in need of clarity and a counterterrorism initiative in need of evaluation.' *Perspectives on Terrorism*, 2/4, available online at http://www.terrorismanalysts.com/pt/index.php/pot/article/view/32/html (accessed March 24, 2012).

Hussain, Z. (2008). '5 JI terror members released'. *Straits Times*, September 15, 2008.

Hussain, Z. (2012). 'What Jemaah Islamiyah did was wrong, convicted terrorist says.' *Jakarta Globe*, January 7, 2012, available online at http://www.thejakartaglobe.com/home/

what-jemaah-islamiyah-did-was-wrong-convicted-terrorist-says/489696 (accessed July 30, 2012).

Kahn, J. (2006). *Other Malays: Nationalism and Cosmopolitanism in the Modern Malay World.* Singapore: Singapore University Press.

Kassim, Y. (n.d.). 'Remodelling the madrasah in Singapore: Past, present and future.' *Karyawan,* available online at http://www.amp.org.sg/edisi/data/Publications/Karyawan %20%2D%20Vol%209%20Issue%201/Vol9%20Iss1%20%2D%20ME%20Crossroads %20%2D%20Remodelling.pdf (accessed August 1, 2012).

Kong, L. (2007). 'New worry: Homemade extremists,' *Today* (Singapore), June 2, 2007, available online at http://www.rrg.sg/index.php?option=com_content&view=article& id=181:todayonline-new-worry-homemade-extremists-saturday-2-june-2007&catid= 20:june-2007-today&Itemid=17 (accessed August 1, 2012).

Kwek, K. (2007). 'Challenge for IRCCs: Rope in more religious leaders, build ties.' *The Straits Times,* January 14, 2007.

Mamat, K. (2007). 'Beyond tokenism, Malays, integration and the SAF,' *The Online Citizen,* Nov. 6, 2007, available online at http://theonlinecitizen.com/2007/11/beyond-tokenism-malays-integration-and-the-saf/ (accessed July 30, 2012).

McAmis, R. (2002). *Malay Muslims: The History and Challenge of Resurgent Islam in Southeast Asia.* Grand Rapids, MI: William B. Eerdmans Publishing Company.

Ministry of Home Affairs (2003). *The Jemaah Islamiyah Arrests and the Threat of Terrorism.* cmd. 2 of 2003. Singapore: Ministry of Home Affairs.

MUIS (2012). 'About us'. http://www.muis.gov.sg/cms/aboutus/default.aspx (accessed July 30, 2012).

Mydans, S. (2008). 'Nasir Abas, terrorist defector, aids Indonesian police.' *New York Times,* Feb. 29, 2008.

Nirmala, M. (2007). 'JI detainees: Taking care of family matters.' In Abdul Halim bin Kader (Ed.) *Fighting Terrorism: The Singapore Perspective.* Singapore: Taman Bacaan.

Qatar International Academy for Security Studies (2010). *Risk Reduction for Countering Violent Extremism: Final Report of the QIASS Countering Violent Extremism (CVE) Risk Reduction Project.* Qatar International Academy for Security Studies.

Rabasa, A., Pettyjohn, S., Ghez, J. and Boucek, C. (2010). *Deradicalizing Islamist Extremists.* Santa Monica, CA: RAND.

Ramakrishna, K. (2002a). 'Jemaah Islamiah: Aims, motivations and possible counter-strategies,' *IDSS Commentaries, 21/2002,* October 2, 2002, available online at http:// dr.ntu.edu.sg/bitstream/handle/10220/4029/RSIS-COMMENT_196.pdf?sequence=1 (accessed August 1, 2012).

Ramakrishna, K. (2002b). *Emergency Propaganda: The Winning of Malayan Hearts and Minds 1948–1958.* Richmond, UK: Curzon.

Ramakrishna, K. (2007). 'Self-radicalisation: The case of Abdul Basheer Abdul Kader.' *RSIS Commentaries* 61/2007, June 11, 2007, available online at http://www.rsis.edu.sg/ publications/Perspective/RSIS0612007.pdf (accessed August 1, 2012).

Ramakrishna, K. (2009). *Radical Pathways: Understanding Muslim Radicalization in Indonesia.* London: Praeger Security International.

Ramakrishna, K. (2010). 'Self-radicalisation and the Awlaki connection,' *RSIS Commentaries* 75/2010, July 7, 2010, available online at http://www.rsis.edu.sg/publications/ Perspective/RSIS0752010.pdf (accessed August 1, 2012).

Ramakrishna, K. (2012). 'Engaging former JI Detainees in countering extremism: Can it work?' *RSIS Commentaries,* 3/2012, January 4, 2012, available online at http://www.rsis. edu.sg/publications/Perspective/RSIS0032012.pdf (accessed July 30, 2012).

Ramakrishna, K. and Tan, S. (2003). 'Is Southeast Asia a 'terrorist haven'?' In Kumar Ramakrishna and See Seng Tan (Eds.) *After Bali: The Threat of Terrorism in Southeast Asia.* Singapore: World Scientific/Institute of Defence and Strategic Studies.

Selvaretnam, S. (2007). 'Religious groups roped into IRCCs.' *The Straits Times,* September 7, 2007, available online at http://www.singaporeunited.sg/cep/index.php/cluster/News-Room/Religious-groups-roped-into-IRCCs/(cluster)/MCYS (accessed August 1, 2012).

Short, A. (1975). *The Communist Insurrection in Malaya.* London: Frederick Mueller.

Suhaimi, N. (2008). 'Feeling like the least favorite child,' *The Straits Times,* August 17, 2008, available online at http://www.sgpolitics.net/?p=467 (accessed August 1, 2012).

Swidler, A. (1986). 'Culture in action: Symbols and strategies.' *American Sociological Review,* 51/2, p. 279.

Tong, G. (2004). 'Beyond Madrid: Winning against terrorism,' speech at the US Council on Foreign Relations, May 6, 2004, available online at http://www.cfr.org/taiwan/beyond-madrid-winning-against-terrorism/p7004 (accessed August 1, 2012).

Yew, L. (1998). *The Singapore Story: Memoirs of Lee Kuan Yew.* Singapore: Times Editions.

Yong, J. (2007). 'Care group for families of JI detainees lauded.' *The Straits Times,* November 14, 2007, available online at http://counterideology.multiply.com/journal/item/104?&show_interstitial=1&u=%2Fjournal%2Fitem (accessed August 1, 2012).

Yong, N. (2009). 'SAF's first Malay general,' *The Straits Times,* June 26, 2009, available online at http://news.asiaone.com/News/AsiaOne+News/Singapore/Story/A1Story2009 0626-151072.html (accessed July 30, 2012).

15

RADICALISATION, RECIDIVISM AND REHABILITATION

Convicted terrorists and
Indonesian prisons

Sulastri Osman

Introduction

Over ten years after the Bali bombings of 2002 killed over two hundred people – most of them foreign tourists to the Indonesian holiday resort island – the threat of terrorism posed by Islamist militants continues to hang over the country. The men behind the devastating attacks had belonged to Jemaah Islamiyah (JI), a clandestine militant group with local roots but a globalist agenda and extensive personal ties to individuals from other armed militias in the region, even to Al Qaeda. JI's far-reaching transnational links, the group's strong ideological foundations that were as much shaped by the country's history and socio-political environment as they were built on an extremist interpretation of religious commandments, as well as its meticulous organisational arrangement that made it all at once highly structured but amorphous, made it a formidable entity to take down (Osman, 2010). The major attacks JI was considered responsible for included the bombing of the J.W. Marriott Hotel in 2003, the bomb attack on the Australian embassy in 2004, the (second) Bali bombings of 2005, and the twin luxury hotel bombings in Jakarta in 2009. Smaller-scale terrorist activities and operations also took place in various spots across the country and many were traced back to individuals who could be linked in one way or another to JI.

But over the decade, while JI and its evolving web of affiliated groups continued to reorganise, plan and carry out sporadic terrorist operations, Indonesian authorities did make concurrent and crucial inroads into the militant network. With help from its international partners in counterterrorism, namely the United States and Australia, Indonesia's elite counterterrorist task force Detachment 88 led the way in police raids across the country which resulted in the arrests or deaths of many high-profile terrorists and terrorist suspects.[1] Many operational successes at dismantling the JI network and other terrorist cells followed through the years; there has been marked progress, too, with wider counterterrorism efforts aimed at stemming recruitment into terrorist groups and support for their activities.

However, recent concerns over recidivism among released terrorist convicts have led to a reassessment of the hard-won achievements thus far. In particular, many have started to question the effectiveness of Indonesia's prison service because, evidently, the deterrent function of being placed behind bars has proved to be insignificant for some. While it is difficult to precisely disentangle the impact of prison time, or the lack thereof, on different recidivists, their prison experience remains an important factor that warrants closer examination. Prisons, after all, exist as the space that contemporary societies commit to the punishment and the rehabilitation of its more criminal elements. That some inmates should upon release continue with their old ways demonstrate that either such individuals are incapable of change, or that the prison system is inadequate at fulfilling its function.

More often than not, the reason lies somewhere in between. Accordingly, the increasing number of terrorist inmates in Indonesian prisons since 2002 brings to light two separate but related issues,[2] as this chapter will show. The first revolves around the terrorist inmates themselves: what are the kinds of problems they pose to prison management and how do they affect the way the facility is run on a day-to-day basis? In this regard, more micro-level analyses that document their activities in prison as well as assess the dynamics of their relations with other inmates, with prison administrators and amongst themselves help demonstrate their impact on the prison system. But because terrorist convicts do not enter into a system that is devoid of a long-standing organisational culture, politics, or simply a way of going about things, a concurrent examination of the state of Indonesian prisons is also in order. There are already systemic problems with the country's prisons, including lax enforcement of prison rules and regulations, chronic corruption, gang violence and overcrowding – extant problems that the presence of terrorist inmates only further exacerbates. In recognising that the interaction between terrorist inmates and the wider prison environment they inhabit is oftentimes two-way – a reality that tends to be overlooked as terrorist inmates habitually become the assumed singular problem in the equation – this chapter seeks to present a comprehensive analysis of the topic at hand. It is crucial to get as clear a picture as possible regarding the issue of terrorist inmates in prisons in order to gain a proper understanding of the challenges they pose and to appropriately address them.

With that in mind, this chapter examines the nature and extent of prisoner radicalisation in Indonesia. Are the prisons 'incubators' for extremism, serving to further harden terrorist convicts who go through the system as well as generate new ones? A former terrorist inmate once said: 'You go in a normal jihadi, you come out Al Qaeda'.[3] So, to what extent does a terrorist inmate's experience in prison lead him down the path of recidivism and/or make terrorists out of other kinds of inmates? How have the authorities tried to arrest the radicalising effects of time in prison on the inmates? At the same time, how have they attempted to constrain the activities of terrorist inmates that can radicalise just the same, and how do they try to limit the influence of such men on others around them? These are some of the questions this chapter will address. Additionally, this chapter will also assess the current 'de-radicalisation' initiatives and terrorist rehabilitation efforts spearheaded by the police and those in civil society.

Inside Negara Cipinang[4]

There are close to 400 prisons and detention centres peppered across Indonesia, but only about 20 hold inmates convicted under charges of terrorism (Ministry of Justice and Human Rights, 2012; International Crisis Group, 2007). Jakarta's Cipinang Prison holds the largest concentration of terrorist inmates, and at the time of writing, the official tally within Cipinang walls stands at 64.[5] Many in the current batch were part of the Islamist militant camp that was discovered operating out of Aceh in early 2010, the aptly dubbed *lintas tandzim* (cross-organisation) cell – formally *Tandzim al Qaeda Serambi Mekkah*, or al Qaeda in Aceh – as it was made up of individuals from different armed groups in what is a yet unparalleled attempt to create a broader-based struggle (International Crisis Group, 2010). Others were variously charged with the 2009 bomb attacks on the J.W. Marriott and the Ritz Carlton in Jakarta or other cases of terrorist violence in Indonesia, or for abetting terrorism.

Among the men are those serving their second stints in prison. Oman Rochman a.k.a. Aman Abdurrahman, for example, a notorious hard-line cleric highly regarded within Indonesian jihadi circles, was previously arrested in March 2004 for arranging a bomb-making class for his followers in Cimanggis, just outside Jakarta. Barely two years after his release in 2008, he was rearrested for playing one of the central roles in the establishment of the militant camp in Aceh and is now serving a 9-year prison sentence. Similarly serving a long sentence, and for the second time in the very same Cipinang prison, is Abdullah Sunata, a former KOMPAK leader in Ambon. First arrested in June 2005 for helping terrorist fugitive Noordin Top when Top was on the run, Sunata was sentenced to 7 years in prison; remissions saw to his early release in March 2009, but his involvement in the militant camp in Aceh led to his rearrest in June 2010. Luthfi Haidaroh, a.k.a. Ubaid, who was also rearrested in 2010 and sentenced to 10 years in prison for his part in the same militant camp, had previously served time between 2004 and 2007 for helping terrorist fugitive Noordin Top after the 2003 J.W. Marriot Hotel bombing. Yet another terrorist inmate also arrested for his involvement in the Aceh militant camp had served time for 'anti-Pancasila activities' prior to his current 8-year sentence.[6]

For these men, their previous stints in prison have evidently not deterred them from returning to the old network. There are admittedly many intricate and highly dynamic factors involved in their decisions to return to or turn away from violence, but it nevertheless remains important to extricate as many prison-related factors as possible by examining what goes on behind prison walls.

Under the spotlight: 'Narapidana kasus teroris'[7]

For many of the terrorist inmates, time in prison is largely considered as being in an *istana uzlah* – a 'palace of isolation' – which they regard as a period away from active fighting and where they can concentrate on deepening their Islamic knowledge and bettering their everyday religious observances like praying and fasting.[8] Such activities, of course, do not contribute to a further hardening of their militant stance.

But how their stints in prison are framed and internalised – thanks to an understanding, according to the militant jihadi narrative, that they are not serving time for having done something wrong but for being morally right in opposing a hegemonic *thogut* (un-Islamic) political system that is determined to not only quell their way of life but Islam too – does affect the impact of their punishment.[9] For many, being behind bars is a consequence they are more than willing to bear and a likelihood they have come to accept as inevitable, fully aware that their activities are against the law. Also, in perceiving the laws as those imposed upon them by an un-Islamic authority and therefore illegitimate, they understand being imprisoned as simply part and parcel of their jihad experience, even something to be proud of as it reflects a high level of dedication to the cause.[10] In fact, imprisonment often serves as further proof that the authorities are simply afraid that they may actually succeed in turning the masses against the existing status quo, which in turn boosts their commitment to the fight.

Further contributing to them staying firm to their militant cause despite imprisonment is the fact that they are able to congregate among themselves, mingle with the rest of the inmate population and continue almost unabated with their pre-detention activities. This is largely because of lax enforcement of prison regulations, although this is something that is slowly changing. Up until a couple of years ago, one of the terrorist inmates would usually be the *imam* at the prison mosque and lead the daily prayers, deliver sermons and run religious discussion groups. Widely perceived as pious men whose commitment to religion was irrefutable – considering they are willing to lay down their lives for it – they are often respected if only for their unyielding religious devotion. The kinds of advice sought of them from other prisoners often extend beyond routine issues of religious piety and into the realm of political behaviour; if there are opportunities to preach the necessity of taking to arms as a religious duty, they often will.[11] But now, with the recently instated regulations regarding acceptable activities in the prison mosque, terrorist inmates can no longer congregate beyond the stipulated prayer times. Neither can they lead in prayers or deliver sermons to the wider prison population because only vetted and approved *ustadz* are allowed to.[12]

Still, prison-based sermons and discussion groups persist, albeit on a smaller scale. Many of the meetings now take place during visiting hours in the visitors' hall, an area of constant movement hardly supervised or monitored. This is where the students and followers of Aman Abdurrahman, for example, gather almost daily to spend a few hours with their highly revered cleric. At times they come singly, at times they come in groups of up to 10 or more; their admittance into prison remains largely unregulated, allowing Abdurrahman, as do some others, to freely receive a flock at any one time.

The problem with unregulated visitors is not just about the number a terrorist inmate receives but about who exactly comes to visit. The administrative processes associated with the daily visitor log has been increasingly computerised in recent years but many of the steps within the registration procedure are done manually, and this usually means the staff at the tail end of the lengthy process, including the ones who physically check the visitors and their belongings and the ones who designate the tables they should occupy in the visitors' hall, are not alerted to the identity or the category of inmate they are coming to see. This approach means that terrorist inmates can continue to interact with their supporters and followers and even fellow militants with whom they persist in engaging in clandestine activities, even if in limited forms. Such activities can range from something as low-key as translating extremist Arabic-language literature to Bahasa Indonesia to something that has the potential to pose grave security threats such as discussing and planning future operations. Abdurrahman's in-prison translation works from Arabic to Bahasa was what propelled him to a higher standing among the jihadi circles, and it was in prison that both he and Sunata had separately conceptualised and fleshed out the idea of setting up the militant camp in Aceh, all the while keeping in regular contact with each other from their respective cells (International Crisis Group, 2010).

While prison staff are observably stricter today regarding the kinds of things visitors can get through prison doors and thoroughly check for forbidden goods and objects like weapons and mobile phones, they continue to be largely oblivious to the considerably less illegal but still unsavory items like extremist literature and other inciting materials. It is largely through the supporters and followers who come to visit that terrorist inmates continue to spread their extremist messages as their writings find their way into radical mosques and onto the Internet.

It is at the same visitors' hall where the terrorist inmates themselves also congregate. Their movements are largely unencumbered during visiting hours and this time allows them the chance to reconnect and, for those who have not had the chance to meet, to forge new relations. Not all of the men who were involved in the militant camp in Aceh knew one another until they were put in the same prison;[13] networking opportunities are ample behind bars. Ubaid, for example, only got close to Abu Bakar Ba'asyir, widely considered JI's spiritual leader, when his first prison sentence overlapped with that of the elderly cleric's. Ubaid later went on to join Ba'asyir's *Jamaah Anshorut Tauhid* outfit upon release and they went on to work together in Aceh.

Part of the reason terrorist inmates have relative freedom to move around the compound is because the prison staff are said to be afraid to stop them from doing so, largely owing to the fact that they are, simply, 'terrorists'. The inmates have a reputation for being fearless and loathful of any worldly authority and they are quick to employ religious rhetoric to denounce those working for the state as perpetuating a *thogut* system.[14] For many prison staff, of whom the majority are Muslims, it is at times easier to just leave the terrorist inmates to themselves than be at the receiving end of a verbal religious tirade or a possible fist. Some of the prison staff may be cowed into submission; some others, however, become furious when their Muslim-ness is called into question and incidences over being called '*thogut*' or '*syaitan*' (devil) can quickly become heated.

Between the individual and the environment: a dynamic interface

Apparent bravado appears to accord some degree of freedom of movement, but there are other wider dynamics at work that warrant some appreciation. For one, everyday corruption inside the prison in no small way contributes to the hardening of terrorist inmates. Upon entry, they, like every other prisoner, are expected to pay fees for their daily upkeep including for food and cell space and even access to their own visitors, technically all that they have a basic entitlement to as inmates (MacDougall, 2008). To get to the visitors' hall from their respective blocks, for example, they have to get past four gates and at each point they have to pay a fee to the guard stationed there. Those who can afford the fees are able to move easily; those who cannot, however, simply have to get used to being even more restricted than is usually the case when behind bars.[15] The terrorist inmates, however, leveraging on their supposed reputations as both pious men and violent men, have collectively refused to pay, and their lack of aversion to challenge the system in place as well as to start an altercation have paid off in that regard.[16] Compared to others, they are able to walk in and out of the visitors' hall during visiting hours as they wish even if they are not receiving visitors of their own.

Nevertheless, having money remains important for the terrorist inmates because money does equate to power and influence in prison. Imprisoned terrorist leaders have in fact had their influence eroded because they lacked money in prison (International Crisis Group, 2007). As collectives tend to have a larger pool of resources to draw on, inmates naturally band together as much for access to better 'services' in prison as for protection in numbers, particularly in light of overcrowded conditions and greatly limited resources. Ganging up also ensures access to means of making money whether by way of dealing in the internal narcotics trade, extortion rackets, or selling groceries, all businesses that require to varying degrees the collusion of some within the prison staff (MacDougall, 2008). Even if the more popular extremist figures among the terrorist inmates tend to have a more or less constant supply of money because they receive a lot of different visitors, the necessity to be able to earn their keep has resulted in some selling traditional herbal medicines and food supplies.[17] Some also get money translating extremist Arabic-language literature which is then published and sold as books by one of the country's radical publishing houses. Abdurrahman and Ubaid, for example, are prolific writers and have had a number of their writings published while behind bars.

But defending access to the money supply often gives rise to turf wars, and gang fights become normal occurrences that can quickly turn fatal as poorly trained prison staff either deliberately stay out of the way or are incapable of bringing order when violence spirals out of control (International Crisis Group, 2007). The usual gang configuration is by ethnicity, but those charged on cases of terrorism generally tend to stick together. In spite of very real ideological divisions among them – differences in ideology that, however nuanced, do affect the cohesion of the group in many ways – a united front in a precarious prison setting does bring more benefits. Other inmates, in fact, have chosen to align themselves with the terrorist group because they feel that the men can offer security and often have better access to resources (International Crisis Group, 2007).

The prison environment, as Cipinang shows, is harsh and dangerous; it is a fair assumption that no one will want to go through the experience twice. Yet the same prison experience helps expand and reinforce militant networks and buttress extremist sentiments, particularly in light of the extant system of economic inequity and corruption that inmates have to confront on a daily basis.

That said, recidivism among terrorist inmates cannot solely be attributed to the state of the prisons in Indonesia, even if the conditions do have some contributory role. There are wider dynamics at play beyond the confines of prison walls. The reasons for recidivism are as multiple and as varied as the kinds of motivations that spur some individuals to want to engage in terrorism in the first place. Familial pressures and culture, for one, remain a big factor affecting an individual's decision to continue along the militant path. Islamist militants have long been a part of the contemporary Indonesian political landscape – when fighting against colonialists, at independence and during subsequent phases of nation-building (van Bruinessen, 2002) – and for the convicted terrorists who have had fathers, grandfathers and uncles variously involved in contesting and literally fighting the state over the way it went about governing, the 'tradition' of taking to arms in defence of their way of life and practise of religiosity is a hard one to break.[18]

Another group of factors that is important to keep in mind is the constantly evolving militant jihadi ideology and tactical shifts on the ground. In recent years, there has been increasing emphasis on *jihad fardiyah* (individual jihad) over *jihad tandzim* (organisational jihad) among those active in the militant circles, i.e., lone operations are increasingly favoured over those led by established jihad organisations like JI. At the same time, the targets of attacks have shifted from Western ones to the local law enforcement as the militants increasingly perceive the police to be the perpetuator of a repressive system and therefore the more immediate enemy. Also, *ightiyalat* (secret assassination) are increasingly considered more effective compared to indiscriminate large-scale operations that also kill Muslims. These adjustments in theory and practice became most evident after the July 2009 suicide bombings on the Ritz Carlton and the J.W. Marriott, and were essentially in response to increasingly lethal police raids and in light of the difficulties new militant operatives face in planning and executing major attacks because of crumbling networks and an ever-tightening police dragnet. The very establishment of the militant camp in Aceh was in actuality a direct result of anger among the militant circles over the deaths of fellow jihadis in heavy-handed police raids, and it was to serve, in part, as a place where militants can learn the arts of self-defence.[19] Further, the gamut of terrorist attacks that were carried out either individually or by small cells in 2011 on police personnel – from targeted 'book bombs' in Jakarta, to a suicide bombing at a police mosque in Cirebon, and a fatal stabbing of a police officer in Bima, West Nusa Tenggara – also reflect an evolving threat trend that makes it operationally easier for those who have spent years behind bars to jump back on the wagon (Osman, 2012).

The non-recidivists: a necessary exploration

However, despite prison conditions and other dynamics beyond, not every convicted terrorist returns to violence after their release from prison. In fact, the majority of those who have been released over the years have kept out of trouble. While accounting for the experiences of the recidivists and examining why their time in prison did not lead to a revision of their take on armed jihad, equally important to note are the prison experiences of those who *have* chosen to move away from violence.

Despite imprisonment having long been framed in a positive light, being in prison does unfavourably affect terrorist inmates when it comes to their imagining of the armed struggle. As many only meet in person in prison, they no longer operate on the notion of an imagined united brotherhood that they all belong to and are a part of. Now they are confronted with very real issues of differing ideologies and clashing personalities. Different understandings regarding armed jihad, particularly when it comes to greatly subjective concerns of time, location and targets of attack, create rifts among the terrorist inmates, especially when their specific operation of choice gets critiqued. Relationship is strained, for instance, between one of the terrorist inmates who is critical of the attempt to set up a militant base in Aceh and the men who were part of the camp; the former thinks it should have been obvious that Aceh was a bad idea whereas the latter do not think much of the former's so-called Internet jihad.[20] The brashness of some of the younger and comparatively more belligerent militants also rubs others in the group the wrong way.

Also, many do not want to risk being back in prison for reasons that span practical and ideological spectrums. For example, one former inmate and militant who was active in Mindanao in the early 2000s, being imprisoned for many years angered him as he felt betrayed because he was ultimately arrested for doing a favour for a respected militant cleric. He now prefers to not have anything to do with people from his old network.[21] For more than a few others, being behind bars means they cannot provide for their wives and children and therefore they are not fulfilling their social and religious responsibilities as husbands and fathers.[22] For some others – including a number who played roles in the first Bali bombings – they have taken the fact that they were arrested and imprisoned as a sign that their fellow Muslims in Indonesia are not yet ready for their kind of *amaliyah* (operation), which means that they were wrong in their strategic calculations. Now they believe that the *ummah* has to be united on issues of jihad or else the controversies that arise in the aftermath of attacks will only fragment the community and bring more harm than good to Muslims in general.[23]

Prisons do, therefore, have a deterrent effect in one way or another and on some more so than others. And while the prison environment appears to contribute to decisions to return to or turn away from violence as much as the activities of the terrorist inmates themselves, it is evident that they are ultimately greatly personal decisions. Recognising the factors behind them nevertheless helps shed light on how best to carry out 'de-radicalisation' and rehabilitation efforts that necessarily will have to be tailor-made.

'De-radicalisation' and rehabilitation efforts

Over the years, Indonesia has realised that counterterrorism means more than just dismantling militant networks. The processes of law enforcement have moved ahead in leaps and bounds when it comes to detecting and catching terrorist suspects and building up cases based on sound evidence. The country's judicial process has also been widely lauded; terrorists and suspected terrorists are all tried publicly in fair and (very) open trials.[24]

The prison service, however, has yet to catch up when it comes to dealing with terrorist individuals. As highlighted in the previous section, poor enforcement of in-house regulations and everyday corruption remain major issues, as does prison staff lacking the necessary training to deal with terrorist inmates. Further, over-crowded facilities means there is simply not enough space to ensure that terrorist inmates are sufficiently separated from others to stem radicalisation and recruit-ment, with not enough personnel to keep watch over all inmates, their activities and interactions.

Police 'de-radicalisation' programme

With this in mind, the police have taken it upon themselves to hold some terrorist inmates. The detention facility at the police headquarters in central Jakarta currently has ten to twelve men convicted of various cases of terrorism in its holding cells. Among them are Ali Imron and Utomo Pamungkas, a.k.a. Mubarok, both serving life sentences for their roles in the first Bali bombings; high-ranking JI leader Ainul Bahri, a.k.a. Abu Dujana, serving a 15-year sentence for protecting terrorist fugitives Noordin Top and Azahari Husin after the 2003 J.W. Marriot bombing; and Lilik Purnomo, a.k.a. Haris, a militant who masterminded the October 2005 beheading of three Christian high-school girls in Poso.

The main reason for their being at the police headquarters is so that they are separated from the rest of the prison population. On one hand, it makes it easier for the police to keep a closer eye on them and their activities as well as to prevent them from influencing other inmates with their extremist ideology. On the other hand, and in some cases more on point, it is to prevent them from getting *re-*

radicalised considering they had confessed to their terrorist activities, shown some degree of remorse for their actions and had been cooperative on one level or another with the police during the course of their investigations.

Keen to harness the nascent relationship, and in exchange for information, the police reward them with perks such as better detention conditions, reduced sentences and economic assistance for them and their families. This 'soft' counter-terrorism approach has garnered results and the police consider it central to its so-called 'de-radicalisation' programme. 'De-radicalisation' remains tricky to define, but the police commonly use it to refer to a wide-ranging array of efforts aimed at getting convicted terrorists to turn away from violence. The programme thus also includes countering the violent extremist aspect of the jihad ideology by getting such terrorist inmates and other former militants who once held key positions within their various networks to get those within their spheres of influence to rethink armed struggle. Ali Imron and Nasir Abas have proved constructive in this regard.[25] Since their arrests, both men have separately published books that essentially draw attention to the futility of indiscriminate violence (Imron, 2007; Abas, 2005), and when the police arrest known terrorists or new suspects, the men are called upon to establish first 'friendly' contact based on considerations of prior personal relationships and joint experiences in the field.

Intrinsic to such a 'de-radicalisation' endeavour is the debating of ideology among those considered part of the movement. The arguments of reputed militants who have revised their use of violence often leave a deeper impact on supporters of violent jihad than appeals for peace from moderate religious figures ever can. Counter-ideology efforts in Indonesia are unlike, for example, neighbouring Singapore because the focus is less on programmes like religious re-education or psychological counselling. Such programmes are essentially based on the assumption that if one can be radicalised, one can then be *de*-radicalised and the ultimate goal is the unconditional renunciation of the use of violence. In Indonesia there appears to be tacit acknowledgement that such an ideological reversal is, in most cases, impossible and this is as much shaped by history and socio-political context as it is informed by a familiarity with the doctrines of Islam. For Imron and Abas, as with many others, the military defense of Islam remains a tenet of religion; armed jihad is essentially based on the concept of just war, and the central contention for the likes of them is more over issues of proper time, place and targets of attack than of kind. Consequently, they are not exactly renouncing the use of violence; they are simply advocating disengagement for now. Islamist militant activities where inter-sectarian clashes had taken place, for example, in Ambon and Poso, or in Mindanao and Afghanistan where fellow Muslims are historically embroiled in the fighting, have consistently proven to be less contentious than the indiscriminate bombings in Bali and Jakarta where no physical conflict and/or repression are evident. Practical applications of the concept over the years have led to a range of opinions among those in the jihadi circles – and even the wider Muslim community too – regarding what kinds of activities they can possibly condone and what they will entirely reject.

The nuances are understood by the police, or at least the ones who have a say over counterterrorism policies. Understanding the fine distinctions among the different kinds of motivations that had spurred different inmates as well as forging rapport and building trust requires much patience and resources, and there are simply not many within the police force who are ready or willing to dedicate their time. The issue of not having enough trained personnel still stands, and as such, there are not many inmates the police can afford to continually engage with at any one time. One would, moreover, have to wonder if all the terrorist inmates who do decide to cooperate with the police are in actuality the more committed ones in the first place who will make a significant shift in the landscape of violent jihadi should they ever revise their views on violence. Counterterrorism success in this fashion is not always guaranteed; some terrorist inmates have accepted help from the police but later rejoined their old network. For many among them, the issues underlining extremist actions are not a matter of economics but of clashing ideologies; financial assistance will not chip away at the core of the problem.[26]

Further, while the police are keen to develop close relations with terrorist inmates in order to gather information that can be of use to their investigations, managing them is not essentially under the purview of the police. Continued police involvement in this regard will mean dedicating resources to areas outside their operational jurisdiction and can mean potential institutional clashes with the prison service.

Terrorist rehabilitation and wider counter-radicalisation efforts by civil society

Technically free of bureaucratic politics are programmes run by those in civil society. In recent years, independent indigenous non-state actors have been proving increasingly useful in the fight against terrorism in Indonesia. Yayasan Prasasti Perdamaian (YPP, or the Institute for International Peace Building), for example, a Jakarta-based non-profit organisation established in 2008, attempts to plug the 'gaps' present within an Indonesian prison service that is largely unsure of how to deal with terrorist inmates (Osman, 2011). Among its projects, the YPP, in collaboration with another non-governmental organisation, Search for Common Ground, conduct workshops in prisons on anger management for high-risk individuals, including terrorist inmates. The programme started in 2009 and has reached out to about 300 inmates from eight prisons across Indonesia (Search for Common Ground, 2011). Thus far, 300 prison officers have also been trained and standard operating procedures for dealing with high-risk inmates have been developed.[27] The YPP also extends a hand to the wives of current terrorist inmates by coaching them to be self-sufficient and guiding them to run their own home-based businesses to help make ends meet while their husbands serve out their prison time. A recent cooking course conducted by the YPP in Jogjakarta for the women in the network served the dual function of encouraging their entrepreneurial spirit as well as of outreach as it is important the women know that there are people they can turn to outside their closed circle if they ever needed to. Helping set former inmates up economically through small trade start-ups like food stalls or selling herbal medicinal products in order to get them back on their feet post-detention also works to prevent them from reengaging in violence.[28] The YPP chooses not to debate or contest convicted terrorists' life-long ideological beliefs but rather engages them on more worldly concerns that will leave them with as little time as possible to get involved in clandestine activities again. The men, despite their concerns for spiritual salvation, are all essentially 'part-time jihadi' as they still need to earn a living to feed their families.[29] The YPP's rehabilitation programme entails engaging and supporting the entire family unit, providing new social relationships outside the network and constructive, meaningful employment.

Beyond a focus on the individual terrorists, there are concurrent efforts within civil society on wider counter-radicalisation endeavours targeting the larger community in an attempt to marginalise extremist elements and stem the spread of violent extremism within the Muslim mainstream. The Wahid Institute, for example, is active at critically examining and refuting the extremist message through different types of printed mass media including books, reports and news articles.[30] The outputs are also disseminated over the Internet, recognising that the potential for radical change and for political discontent converge in the urban youth. Lazuardi Birru also reaches out to Indonesian youths and promotes constructive debates regarding radicalism and terrorism, and among its more novel endeavours to shed light on such issues include a graphic comic book that portrays the 2002 Bali bombings from the points of view of the wife of a bomb victim as well as of one of the bombers himself who subsequently regretted his actions.[31]

Such counter-radicalisation activities, however, while highly commendable, are difficult to evaluate, particularly in terms of reach and effectiveness. Also, because there is no evident national-level strategic coordination among the different initiatives, whether the pockets of people most at-risk of radicalisation are effectively engaged remains in question. Further, the attempt to directly rehabilitate terrorist individuals has similar shortfalls to the police's 'de-radicalisation' endeavour. For instance, some individuals helped by the YPP, monetarily and otherwise, had returned to violence.[32] While the YPP devote great amounts of time forging good relationships with the individuals they work with, there is no systematic method in place to measure either readiness to disengage, or subsequently, levels of disengagement. To determine a 'successful' case in this regard is greatly subjective. There is nothing to stop former inmates if they choose to partake in future fighting. Renewed clashes in Ambon, for example, is one of the instances many convicted terrorists say would get them to pick up arms again.[33] Also, considering the time dedicated to each of those the YPP engage with, there is a very limited number that it can effectively work with at any one time.

Both rehabilitation and counter-radicalisation are long-term projects and the results are never immediate; funding thus remains an issue for civil society organisations. However, sources of money and project collaborations need to be properly thought through because they can essentially work against such initiatives.

Collaborations with state agencies, for example, can affect perceptions of independence which can adversely impact outreach, particularly considering the individuals they want to reach out to are either staunchly anti-establishment or already highly suspicious of the state.

Conclusion

The issue of terrorist inmates in prisons is a multifaceted one, and the Indonesian case goes to show that as much as such individuals have an impact on the system, so does the system on them. Accordingly, 'de-radicalisation' and rehabilitation efforts in Indonesia need to take into account both sides of the equation in order to be effective, and broader prison reform, too, is necessary to curb the problem of radicalising inmates. Recidivism continues to be a great concern because it remains a reality that some individuals exit prisons more radical than before they entered and have gone on to plan and carry out terrorist attacks. That said, the majority of terrorist inmates have not reengaged in violent activities since their release and it is as important to understand the factors that have appeared to discourage them from rejoining their old militant network as to understand the factors that spur the recidivists. Every convicted terrorist will inevitably experience life behind bars, and it is here where much counterterrorism energy and resources should be focused. Prisons, as the tightly controlled, highly monitored, quarantined environment they are intended to be, serve as the most opportune setting to affect positive changes in terrorist inmates to ensure that they do not re-enter the world of violence.

Notes

1 Among them, Azahari Husin, an explosives expert tied to the attacks on Bali in 2002, the J.W. Marriott in 2003 and the Australian embassy in 2004, was killed in a police raid November 2005; Bali bombers Imam Samudra, Ali Ghufron and Amrozi, based on a judgement that was passed five years prior, were executed November 2008; Noordin Top, linked to both the J.W. Marriott bombings of 2003 and 2009, the Australian embassy bombing of 2004 and the second Bali bombing of 2005, was killed in a police raid September 2009.

2 There were individuals charged with terrorism prior to the Bali bombings, but the numbers soared in the aftermath. Several JI members were arrested for the series of coordinated Christmas Eve bombings of December 2000 and the Atrium shopping mall bombing in 2001.

3 Interview with former inmate, Jakarta, June 2009. By 'normal' jihadi, the former inmate meant a supporter of military jihad but not necessarily one who would advocate the use of indiscriminate terrorist attacks on soft targets.

4 *Negara Cipinang* means "Cipinang Country", as described by an inmate who is currently serving his second stint in Cipinang Prison. He explained that Cipinang was really a microcosm of the state of affairs in Indonesia and showcased all that was wrong with the country. Interview with inmate, Jakarta, June 2012.

5 The numbers constantly change with new arrests, or as inmates are released or transferred.

6 The inmate said he was arrested for being involved in jihadi activities that ran counter to the *Pancasila*, the Indonesian largely secular constitution, but because there were no

anti-terrorism laws in the mid-nineties, he was not charged with terrorism. Interview with inmate, Jakarta, June 2012.

7 *Narapidana kasus teroris*, or 'inmates charged with cases of terrorism', are how the inmates refer to themselves; they also use *ikhwan* (Arabic for brothers) and *jihadi*.

8 Various interviews with inmates and former inmates between 2010 and 2012.

9 There are numerous books published by radical publishing houses that lionise the position of those imprisoned for defending their religious beliefs. For example, Az-Zahrani (2007) details the stories of popular scriptural figures including Moses and Joseph who had bravely faced imprisonment when they opposed their respective oppressive regimes, as well as of Muhammad's leave of Mecca to avoid persecution.

10 Various interviews with inmates and former inmates between 2009 and 2012.

11 Various interviews with inmates and former inmates between 2009 and 2012. In Muslim-dominated Indonesia, while there is hardly support for indiscriminate terrorist attacks, there nevertheless remains widespread empathy for militants who had fought in conflict areas like Ambon and Poso where local adherents, in the popular Indonesian Muslim imagination, had faced persecution.

12 Interviews with inmates, Jakarta, June 2012.

13 Interview with inmate, Jakarta, June 2012.

14 Various interviews with inmates and former inmates between 2009 and 2012. The scuffle that broke out between inmates and prison wardens on June 13, 2012 provides a recent illustration of the inmates' aversion to figures of authority. The fight started when one of the inmates reportedly refused to allow a warden to go through the things a visitor brought in for him; the actual spark behind the incident remains disputed. For an account as reported in the local news, see Pertiwi (2012); the account as shared by the inmates included details of petty corruption in the prison.

15 Interview with terrorist inmate, Jakarta, June 2012.

16 Various interviews with inmates and former inmates between 2009 and 2012.

17 There has been no talk or reports of terrorist inmates involving themselves in the lucrative internal drug trade; in fact, they are often contemptuous of those who do and those who use, considering drugs *haram* (forbidden) in Islam. A terrorist inmate had once detailed the social hierarchy among prison inmates, and occupying the lowest levels were the sex offenders and, just slightly ahead, the drug addicts; according to him, the most respected inmates were the convicted terrorists, particularly those who had fought in Ambon and Poso. Interview with former inmate, Jakarta, June 2009.

18 Various interviews with inmates and former inmates between 2009 and 2012. Also see Osman (2010).

19 The individuals who formed the militant camp in Aceh were largely unhappy with existing jihadi organisations, particularly JI, for not doing enough for the cause, but at the same time they were against the kinds of blanket attacks carried out by the more militant splinters. In their minds, Aceh was to be a base for the formation of a proper Islamic community, but more tactically, it was also where jihadis could gather and train to defend themselves against the police.

20 That Aceh should serve as a militant base was a bad idea was a particular critique shared by many within the jihadi circles; that 'jihad of the pen' was a 'lower' sort of jihad compared to 'jihad of the sword' was an opinion largely shared by those of the more militant kinds. Various conversations with inmates and former inmates, June 2012.

21 Interviews with former inmate between 2009 and 2012. The former inmate was helping an acquaintance he knew from his old network in the southern Philippines keep some of his belongings in his house; he did not know that among them was a cache of firearms.

22 Various interviews with inmates and former inmates between 2009 and 2012.

23 Various interviews with inmates and former inmates between 2009 and 2012.

24 However, one of the critiques regarding such a process is that trials often become a media circus. Trials involving terrorist suspects would attract many of their supporters as well as hardline Muslim groups from all over Indonesia who might not exactly support terrorist individuals but would take the opportunity to protest against the largely secular

state and its apparent discrimination against Islam; they would camp themselves outside the courts and try to disrupt proceedings or intimidate by mere loud presence.

25 Ali Imron, Afghan veteran, JI member and the brother of executed Bali bombers Ali Ghufron, a.k.a Mukhlas and Amrozi, is currently serving a life sentence for his extensive role in the first Bali bombings. Nasir Abas, released from prison in 2004, is a former high-ranking JI militant trainer based in Mindanao; a number of those involved in the Bali attacks had been part of his training camp.

26 Various interviews with inmates and former inmates 2010 to 2012.

27 Interview with YPP research director Taufik Andrie, Jakarta, November 2011.

28 Conversations with YPP executive director, Noor Huda Ismail, between 2009 and 2012. Noor Huda, himself a former student at *Pesantren Al-Mukmin* in Ngruki, the Islamic boarding school in Central Java that came under scrutiny soon after the 2002 Bali bombings, initiated the programme largely based on personal impetus; when he found out that a former schoolmate with whom he had shared a boarding room with was also involved in the attack, he was struck by their very different life trajectories and sought to understand why his childhood friend became engaged in violence, and then subsequently, how he can constructively address some of the factors that underline such extremist actions. The *pesantren* Noor Huda and his former schoolmate attended was founded by radical cleric Abu Bakar Ba'asyir and the school quickly gained infamy in the aftermath of the Bali attacks as it came to be known that a number of the men involved in the attacks were graduates of the school. The developing situation then not only made the authorities increasingly concerned over the kinds of curriculum being taught at the school and the apparent spread of religious extremism but also the lack of control they have over such *pesantrens* which receive funding from private donors, particularly those from the Middle East. The *pesantren* has been described as a militant hub; it has also been understood as a pulse of political Islam in Indonesia. See also International Crisis Group (2002) and Noor (2007).

29 Conversations with Noor Huda Ismail between 2009 and 2012. Over and above the programmes run by the YPP, Noor Huda runs his own sideline projects, and one of them is *Dapoer Bistik* (Bistik Kitchen), a diner that employs former terrorist inmates as well as troubled youths. One of the two *Dapoer Bistik* in Semarang is currently managed by a former inmate, as is the one in Solo that very recently opened. Both managers are today no longer employees; they have been made stakeholders too because it is important that they feel invested in the project.

30 The Wahid Institute, founded in 2004, is named after late Indonesian president Abdurrahman Wahid, also known as Gus Dur, an Islamic scholar in his own right who was known for his tolerant and pluralistic take on Indonesian Islam. See official website http://wahidinstitute.org/.

31 See *Ketika Nurani Bicara* (When Conscience Speaks), *Yayasan Lazuardi Birru*, September 2010. See official website http://www.lazuardibirru.org/.

32 Conversations with Taufik Andrie, Jakarta, November 2011 and June 2012.

33 Various interviews with inmates and former inmates between 2009 and 2012.

References

Abas, N. (2005). *Membongkar Jamaah Islamiyah: Pengakuan Mantan Anggota JI* (trans: *Uncovering Jamaah Islamiyah: Confessions of a Former JI Member*). Jakarta: Grafindo Khazanah Ilmu.

Az-Zahrani, F. (2007). *DPO: Buronan dalam Lintasan Sejarah Islam Klasik* (trans: *List of Wanted Individuals: Wanted Persons in Classic Islamic History*). Solo: Jazera.

Imron, A. (2007). *Ali Imron: Sang Pengebom* (trans: *Ali Imron: The Bomber*). Jakarta: Republika.

International Crisis Group (ICG) (2002). *Al-Qaeda in Southeast Asia: The Case of the 'Ngruki Network' in Indonesia*, available at: http://www.unhcr.org/refworld/docid/3de746c62.html

International Crisis Group (ICG) (2007). '"Deradicalisation" and Indonesian prisons.' *Report No. 142*. International Crisis Group.

International Crisis Group (ICG) (2010). 'Indonesia: Jihadi surprise in Aceh.' *Report No. 189*. International Crisis Group.

MacDougall, J. (2008). 'Prison cum hostel?', *Inside Indonesia No. 93*. http://www.inside indonesia.org/feature-editions/prison-cum-hostel.

Ministry of Justice and Human Rights (2012). Corrections directorate website. http://www. ditjenpas.go.id/pas2/.

Noor, F. (2007). 'Ngruki revisited: Modernity and its discontents at Pondok Pesantren Al-Mukmin of Ngruki, Surakarta.' *RSIS Working Paper No. 139*. Singapore: S. Rajaratnam School of International Studies.

Osman, S. (2010). 'Jemaah Islamiyah: Of kin and kind.' *GIGA Journal of Current Southeast Asian Affairs*, 29/2, pp. 157–175.

Osman, S. (2011). 'Radicalisation in prisons and new de-radicalisation initiatives in Indonesia.' Paper presented at the *ARC Linkage Project on Understanding Terrorism in an Australian Context: Radicalisation, De-Radicalisation and Counter-Radicalisation*. Monash University, September 2011.

Osman, S. (2012). 'Freelance fighters and "do-it-yourself" terrorism: What lies ahead for Indonesia.' *RSIS Commentaries*, No.011. Singapore: S. Rajaratnam School of International Studies.

Pertiwi, A. (2012). '*Narapidana Terorisme Keroyok Sipir Lapas Cipinang*' (trans: *Terrorist Inmate Fought Warden at Cipinang Prison*). *Tempo*, June 14, 2012. Available at: http://www.tempo. co/read/news/2012/06/14/064410562/Narapidana-Terorisme-Keroyok-Sipir-Lapas-Cipinang.

Search for Common Ground (2011). *Program Evaluation Report: Countering and Preventing Radicalization in Indonesian Prisons.* Jakarta: SFCG. http://www.sfcg.org/sfcg/evaluations/indonesia.html

van Bruinessen, M. (2002). 'Genealogies of Islamic radicalism in post-Suharto Indonesia.' *South East Asia Research*, 10/2, pp. 117–154.

16

THE RED ARMY FACTION PRISONERS IN WEST GERMANY

Equal treatment or unfairly tough?

Gisela Diewald-Kerkmann

It is widely recognised that the Red Army Faction prisoners in the 1970s were held under unusual and extreme conditions. The strict solitary confinement conditions that most male and female RAF members were held under had not previously been used in Germany. The prisoners were also distinctive through having to spend several years in detention before trial, e.g. Ulrike Meinhof from 1972 to 1976, Gudrun Ensslin, Andreas Baader and Jan-Carl Raspe, 1972 to 1977 or Monika Berberich from 1970 to 1974. Ensslin, Baader and Raspe had still not been convicted before their suicides on 18th October 1977 (the judgement of the higher Court of Stuttgart, 28 April 1977, was not yet legally valid). Technically, they should not have been held for more than six months before trial – the normal legal upper limit. Exceptions are only possible for special reasons, such as having problems making inquiries. Undoubtedly, the police and public prosecution had difficulties in the face of the conspiratorial activities of the RAF, complicated by the fact that there were very few confessions. However, not only the defence criticised the long time in prison and the "baseless and arbitrary delay of the investigation."[1] Tougher prison treatment was also mentioned in the study by Blath and Hobe, published by the Federal Ministry of Justice in 1982. They made it clear that of all defendants – who were convicted in the years from 1975 to 1979 – only 4.5 percent were taken into custody. In contrast, 65.7 percent of "the alleged terrorist offenders and their supporters were in prison on remand in the same period" (Blath and Hobe, 1982, p. 60). Taking the period from 1971 to November 1980, the percentage increased to 70.6 percent. Even though not all of their acts could be classified as criminal offences, the alleged terrorist offenders were held in detention although custody was usually only for serious crimes. The average length of pre-trial detention was unusually high, too. Although only 3.4 percent of those sentenced had to spend a year in custody, among the RAF-members and their supporters it was 52.1 percent. Further, the RAF-members received higher prison sentences and – according to Blath and Hobe (1982) – the penalties were less often changed to probation.

Differences in prison conditions

It is necessary to distinguish the prison conditions for different people, places and time periods. As an example, for the period 1971 to 1974 we can use the conditions of imprisonment of Astrid Proll, Ulrike Meinhof and Gudrun Ensslin, who were serving a part of their remand in the "dead section" of the Cologne-Ossendorf prison. There were no other prisoners in this wing. Proll was the first RAF member who was here for a long time and she spent various months in complete isolation as the only inmate. From her arrest on 6th May 1971 she was exposed to conditions "which some called insulating prison conditions, others called isolation torture" (Hannover, 2001, p.149). These conditions were responsible for her severe circulatory disease. She described her time in the "dead section" with the words:

> It was incredibly shocking here. I heard no sounds except the ones I created myself. Nothing, absolute silence. I became nervous, I was haunted by visual and auditory hallucinations. Extreme difficulty concentrating, fainting spells. I did not know how long this would go on for. I was terribly afraid of going crazy.
> *(Proll, 1998, p.11).*

One consequence was that Proll was not fit for the criminal proceedings and the trial was stopped for this reason on the 32nd trial day. The defendant, who was released from prison on 1st February 1974, was – according to a doctor on 12th February 1974 – seriously ill. Her health had improved since her release, but not as fast as he had initially expected.[2]

Meinhof was the second remand prisoner in the "dead section" in Cologne-Ossendorf. In her case, the Federal Prosecutor General had decided on 14th April 1971 to "bring the journalist into pre-trial detention".[3] The reason was the suspicion of an offence pursuant to §129 of the Penal Code. She was strongly suspected of having founded an association together with Mahler, Baader, Ensslin and various other persons. The purpose of this group involved the commission of criminal acts. But their ultimate goals were "actions" to eliminate the "system of class domination and oppression". They were willing to use any means to reach this aim. Ulrike Meinhof – in the opinion of many people – was the "ringleader". She was arrested on 15th June 1972. Her defender had written in a letter of complaint to the investigating judge of the Federal Court that they had taken X-rays for the purpose of identification against her will. In total, she spent nine months in the "dead section" in Cologne-Ossendorf, from 16th June 1972 to 9th February 1973, from 21st December 1973 to 3rd January 1974, and February 1974 again. Meinhof described her first experience in this prison as follows:

> The feeling, one's head would explode (the feeling that the skull would crack, crack open) – the feeling that one's spinal cord was being pressed into the

brain . . . the feeling one was continuously and imperceptibly under stress controlled by others . . . One wakes up, opens his eyes: the cell moves – in the afternoons when the sun was shining in – it stopped suddenly. You could not lose the feeling of driving . . . the feeling that one becomes dumb – you can no longer identify the meaning of words, only guess.

(Stuberger, 1977)

At the request of the Federal Prosecutor General, Ensslin was held in the same prison from 5th February 1974, too. The defence criticised this relocation and demanded that the two women be moved into normal cells. The justice legitimised the special conditions of detention with the argument of safety. The RAF members wanted to "politicise" the prisons. Ensslin had tried this again and again during her imprisonment in the detention centre in Essen/NRW. Further he stressed that "the current accommodation of Meinhof and Ensslin – contrary to the untruthful and malicious allegations – should neither affect them physically nor psychologically."[4]

Special security measures were arranged for the prisoner Irmgard Möller in the penal institution in Offenburg. The accused, her property and prison space were intensively searched. All personal belongings and utensils were confiscated and she was not allowed to use her own clothes and underwear. The aim of the administration of the prison was to make sure that all possibilities for contact between Möller and other prisoners were prevented. She was excluded from participation in all community events and had only solitary prison yard walks (Einzelhofgang), which were supervised by two staff. Before beginning each walk and after it had ended, the local police station was called by telephone to do an extra check of the surroundings of the prison. During her single bath, which was also supervised by two staff, all other prisoners had to be locked in their cells. Any time, day or night, a male prison warden had to be present in the institution. Möller's cell was checked thoroughly every day. A special form was filled out noting when and by whom each cell check was done.[5]

The security measures in prisons were legitimised – especially for Meinhof – with the opinion that she was the "hard core of the Baader-Meinhof gang".[6] Arguing that as she was one of the ringleaders, the investigating judge ordered on 20th June 1972 that she should only receive visits and post from her family. Also, she could only get official post, newspaper or magazines through the head of the prison.[7] In contrast to this practice a "normal prisoner" had the right to controlled but otherwise unrestricted oral and written communication with the outside world and visits. The defender of Meinhof, Heinrich Hannover, made clear that this isolation contradicted all the constitutionally guaranteed rights of his client (e.g. Article 4 of the German Constitution). But according to the legal authorities there was a suspicion that the RAF members wanted to liberate their "comrades imprisoned with all means at their disposal, including the use of firearms".[8] The head of the prison in Cologne-Ossendorf had ordered on 20th June 1972 that visits for Meinhof must be controlled by officials of the Federal Criminal Police Office. Visitors or their belongings had to be searched, too. Excerpts of the prison rules show the special arrangements for Meinhof. Under the headline "strict solitary confinement", it was explained that the neighbouring cells may not be occupied. An additional lock was installed. After work the key should be given to the staff member who has overall surveillance. This transfer had to be noted in a special book. A male staff member had to be permanently present in the corridor outside the cell. The opening of the cell was only possible in the presence of one female and one male staff member. There was daily monitoring of the cell, the personal belongings of the prisoners and body searches. According to the administration of the prison it was necessary to observe her every 15 minutes and therefore there was permanent illumination, day and night. The results of this observation and any unusual occurrences were noted in the report book. The solitary prison yard walk was closely guarded by two male and one female prison warden. Any contact with other prisoners (and especially Astrid Proll) was prohibited. Visits were only allowed after notification of the security inspector, the director of the prison and the warden on duty. Only one person was admitted per visit. Before and after each visit, the prisoner was physically searched and had to change clothes. During the visit nothing was allowed to be exchanged. All visitors had first to be checked, including the lawyers. She was not allowed to leave her cell without prior permission from the judge. He could order special safeguards in agreement with the head of the prison. Meinhof had to be excluded from all social events in the prison.[9]

Meinhof's lawyer demanded that the warrant of arrest be cancelled in December 1972. According to him, the pre-trial detention of his client was psychological terror. She was absolutely isolated in the prison. He argued that the absence of any sound in the cell and the continuous lack of communication with other people was intolerable and could lead to serious mental disorders. Even convicted criminals – according to the lawyer – were entitled to respect for and protection of human dignity, even more so those prisoners still awaiting trial. The presumption of innocence according article 6.2 of the Convention on human rights should not be forgotten.[10] This application was refused because of strong suspicion of criminal acts and risk of escape attempts. The petitions by the defence on easing the special security measures were also rejected. The Federal Prosecutor General wrote in a letter to the investigating judge in February 1973: "Meinhof has shown through her intensive activities for the aims of the RAF in the prison in Cologne . . . that she has not reduced her involvement in criminal acts and is still dangerous."[11]

Solitary confinement rules

Meinhof had been on hunger strike since 19th January 1973. Her aim was to improve her prison conditions. The prison authorities had arranged to watch her every 10 minutes during the day and night because of the risk of suicide or self-harm. The head of the prison informed the Federal Prosecutor General on 7th February 1973 that the prison psychiatrist had come to the following conclusion:

> I have briefly examined Mrs Meinhof twice and I believe that the breaking point has now been reached. I think the current practice of isolation in this

form is no longer acceptable. The reason for this tolerance limit is her bad general condition, a result of the stress of her illegal situation before.[12]

The head of the prison wrote on 17th February 1973, that:

> the measures e.g. the limited social contacts with wardens and doctors, special feeding have already improved the condition of Mrs Meinhof . . . but according to medical opinion this is not sufficient. In the case of Miss Proll – who has been in custody much longer – an increase of social activity is more important than in the case of Mrs Meinhof, who is still active. . . . She has a lot of energy and speaks to us in her aggressive way every day. We expect that this will have a negative affect for other prisoners. She entirely lives in these ideas and will not distance herself from them.[13]

The defence pointed out that Meinhof had spent nine months in the "dead section". This condition was changed only in March 1973 when she was moved into a male prison building in Cologne-Ossendorf. The fact that this was a male section expressed – in the opinion of her lawyer – yet another special discrimination against her. Meinhof's defender requested a transfer to a normal prison wing for women. Although his client was no longer in an isolation cell in the "dead section", she still did not have the same conditions as other pre-trial prisoners. The neigh-bouring cells were not used, she did not see or hear any other prisoners and she still had a solitary walk.[14]

These hard solitary confinement conditions were not only in place for the "leaders of the gang" like Ulrike Meinhof and Gudrun Ensslin. More marginal people such as Marianne Herzog and Margrit Schiller often had comparable conditions. For example, Herzog was arrested on 2nd December 1971 because she was suspected of having connections to the Baader-Meinhof group. During her arrest, she had neither resisted nor carried a weapon. After a year of detention she was physically and mentally close to breakdown. She had lost a lot of weight (107 pounds at 5 feet 7 inches). According to the evangelical theologian Dorothee Sölle – "she had increasingly often bouts of weakness and dizziness and had heart attacks and permanent visual problems. Since 11th December 1972 she was not able to leave the bed in her cell."[15] Margrit Schiller, who was arrested in Hamburg on 22nd October 1971, was "isolated", too. This happened although the Federal Prosecutor General said that she was a marginal figure in the Baader-Meinhof group. Nevertheless, the guarding of the prison was intensified and the court of Hamburg had ordered all restrictions possible according to the rules of pre-trial imprisonment. For example, the hands of the accused must be bound when she was outside her cell and during her solitary walk. Her defender pointed out that she was not sentenced and that the "statutory of innocence" was also relevant for pre-trial prisoners.[16] According to §119.5 code of criminal procedure (StPO) a remand prisoner should be only handcuffed if there is a danger that he will use violence against persons or property, or if he resists. This was not true in the case of Margrit

Schiller. Further he criticised the decision of the district court, that Schiller's cell was illuminated by day and night. She was checked at intervals of 30 minutes, in the night, too. The behaviour of Schiller had given no reason to treat her so cruelly. Only the suspicion written in "the arrest warrant that she belonged to a RAF-group"[17] that was not sufficient.

The turning point: 1974/1975

The detention conditions of the RAF members changed – for example for Meinhof and Ensslin – when they were relocated to Stuttgart-Stammheim in 1974/75. Ensslin moved to the JVA Stuttgart-Stammheim on 28th April 1974 so that the main trial could be held against the five founding members in Stuttgart. The changed conditions can be seen by the fact that Meinhof and Ensslin could now have a "prison yard walk" with other female remand prisoners. But this walk depended on a physical search before and after the walk. Further, Meinhof and Ensslin got the opportunity to watch TV with other prisoners outside their cells, but not together.[18] Therefore, Horst Bubeck, the former warden in Stammheim was right that the prison conditions for the RAF-members were now different. For example, Meinhof was neither in a "quiet section" nor did she have to be in total solitary confinement. She was in normal prison conditions.

The former Federal Prosecutor Peter Zeis argues too, that there were detention benefits which were extremely unusual. Men (Baader/Raspe) and women (Ensslin/Meinhof) were permitted to spend eight hours a day together – a novelty in a male prison. After Meinhof's suicide, two female RAF prisoners (Brigitte Mohnhaupt and Ingrid Schubert) were specially transferred to Ensslin in Stammheim. Contact offers, e.g. in a "prison yard walk" with normal prisoners, were strictly rejected by the prisoners because they felt they were being spied on. The RAF prisoners had television, radio, record player, books and magazines. Also the European Commission on Human Rights rejected in two decisions the complaints of the prisoners as unfounded in May 1975 and July 1978. Their argument was: "The special prison conditions of Baader, Ensslin and Raspe do not constitute inhuman treatment" (Oesterle, 2003, p.79).

After 1974/75 these conditions were changed insofar as that individual isolation – not least because of the medical opinions and public debate – was cancelled in favour of group isolation. This transfer was closely linked with the question of being fit for trial, because their health problems had emerged more and more as a fundamental difficulty for the trial. While the defence blamed the health problems on the prison conditions, the court believed that the hunger strikes (January to February 1973, May to June 1973 and September 1974 to February 1975) were responsible.

Overall, it should not be overlooked that these defendants presented the penal institutions with challenges it had not faced before. The RAF prisoners were given "privileges" (cell equipment, etc.) and "detention facilities" that – according to the Federal Prosecutor – "were generally not granted to their accomplices". However, the fundamental question was in which way the prison conditions for the RAF members were changed through these "privileges"? For example communication between the pre-trial prisoners was controlled rigorously. They were isolated from normal or quasi-normal interactions and lived outside the informal infrastructure of the institution through which prisoners generally have some psychological support. The Federal President Gustav Heinemann pointed out the poor health of the RAF-members in December 1974. He noted in a letter to Meinhof:

> I have great concern. You and some of your friends, who participating in the hunger strike are in great danger of dying . . . If you continue the hunger strike, you will come to the inevitable end of your life. The complaints against prison conditions, which you have linked with your hunger strike, are – at least today – largely irrelevant. We are looking into your remaining complaints. So therefore there is no reason to continue the life-threatening hunger strike any longer at all.[19]

After the suicide of Ulrike Meinhof, on the 9th May 1976 at 2 a.m., the conditions of detention for the other RAF members would be changed again. The presiding judge ordered that the RAF prisoners (Andreas Baader, Gudrun Ensslin, Brigitte Mohnhaupt, Jan-Carl Raspe and Ingrid Schubert) should come together for four hours a day. In the remaining hours the men, Baader and Raspe, and the women, Ensslin, Mohnhaupt and Schubert, should be in one cell. Medical examinations of Ensslin, Baader and Raspe were the reasons for this decision in April 1977. There was – from a medical point of view – a deterioration in their health. According to the expert this was especially true for Gudrun Ensslin, where her depletion was extreme. Her ability to concentrate and emotional ability to sympathise were greatly reduced. Ensslin was in a very poor state and she had "aged" before her time. The expert believed that the deterioration of her health was a direct result of the special detention conditions she was being held under.[20] The doctors in Stuttgart had reached a similar assessment and judged that Ensslin's health had suffered the most both mentally and physically. Physically, she seemed greatly reduced; most noticeable was her low blood pressure and weight loss, which had already been pronounced before the beginning of her hunger strike. Taken as a whole, all of the RAF prisoners showed a marked deterioration and increased vegetative instability.[21]

The challenge for prison institutions

The German prison institutions were confronted with prisoner behaviour for which they were simply not prepared. Many observations show that the "anarcho-terrorists in custody and imprisonment" constituted a problem (Nass, 1973, p.37). The criminologist Gustav Nass explained in March 1973 that not much was known about the behaviour of this new type of "anarcho-terrorist" but he thought that you could not deny that "some fanatics among the terrorists had a certain personality format" (Nass, 1973, p.36). In his opinion the "terrorist does not mix with other categories of prisoners. He feels different from thieves, defrauders and sexual assault perpetrators. He wants to be treated as an offender with political convictions" (Nass, 1973, p.37). Even the former head of the prison in Bruchsal wrote that the imprisonment of the RAF members had initially challenged not only those prisons which directly held RAF members, but over the years this became a problem for all prisons. From the institutions' perspective the main point was the discussion about security. All other issues were secondary. As Preusker (1997) noted this "partly exaggerated and extremely expensive focus on security characterized the entire prison system, even today – long after the end of the RAF."

The expert Wilfried Rasch recognised that the prison authorities were faced with an unusual task. "The new prisoners were of another format: They belong to a different class than most other prisoners, they are intellectuals and feel that they are political prisoners who are not willing to give up the pursuit of their goals and the belief in final success" (Rasch, 1976, p.62). For the authorities, these prisoners changed the concept of dangerousness. It now had a different meaning and the function of security gained a new dimension. The "battle of the prisoners with their own body" against the prison conditions added a further new element to the situation.

Some investigations show that the controversies surrounding the prison conditions had a substantial impact on RAF members and sympathisers living in freedom. According to the former officer of the Federal Criminal Police Office, Dieter Schenk, the prison situation created a strong impetus towards action. In particular, the death of Holger Meins – following a hunger strike on 9th November 1974 – was a key factor behind the expansion of the "second-generation of the RAF" (Schenk, 2000, p.164). The head of the Hamburg Constitutional Protection (Verfassungsschutz), Christian Lochte, argued that the harsh prison conditions themselves were responsible for the fact "that many prisoners do not come to their senses . . . (Their) struggle stance against the state was thereby stabilized".[22] He added that the solitary confinement of the RAF prisoners had helped to win them new supporters.

The year 1977, "The German Autumn", proved to be the climax of the confrontation between the RAF and the state. 1977 witnessed another big change in prison conditions because the Federal Prosecutor General Siegfried Buback, his driver Wolfgang Göbel and bodyguard Georg Wurster, the banker Jürgen Ponto and the President of the Confederation of German Employers' Associations Hanns Martin Schleyer were all killed by the RAF. When Schleyer was abducted on 5th September 1977, his driver Heinz Marcisz and the policemen Reinhold Brändle, Helmut Ulmer and Roland Pieler were shot. Due to this abduction the legislative responded with the "contact ban law" on 30th September 1977.[23] This was the fastest law in West German legal history, "passed within three days of the parliament and Federal Council of Germany, signed by the President and published in the Journal of Laws. It usually takes a year" (Wesel, 2002, p.278). The law was approved with four votes against and 17 abstentions by MPs of the coalition of SPD and FDP in the second and third reading. According to the lawyer Erich Schmidt-Leichner, the "contact ban law" was a "pronounced emergency law" which constituted a serious interference of the Executive with the rights of the Judiciary, the third power. Through this law, prison conditions were radically changed for the RAF members: the time together in the cell was cancelled, radio, television and newspapers were taken away and the prisoners were isolated indefinitely from the outside world.[24] Further, even the prisoners' lawyers could be denied access to their clients, if the latter were on the list of those RAF members wanted in exchange for Schleyer. The MP Herta Däubler-Gmelin (SPD) argued that calling a state of emergency §34 of the Criminal Code (StGB) was problematic and not necessarily legal (Däubler-Gmelin, 1987, p.100).

It is clear that the conflict concerning the prison conditions for the RAF members determined the public debate about terrorism. While the persons affected and their lawyers spoke about the increased isolation conditions and of "torture in the Federal Republic of Germany" (Eschen, Lang, Laubscher and Riemann, 1973), the authorities claimed that these were normal prison conditions for common criminals (Presse-und Informationsamt der Bundesregierung, 1977, p.9). According to officials, the RAF pre-trial prisoners were not worse but actually *better treated* than other suspects. This opinion obviously does not hold water if we bear in mind the descriptions already provided in this chapter.

Recognition that the RAF prisoners were held under special conditions came from within the prison system itself. For example, the head of the Cologne-Ossendorf prison believed that there were special prison conditions. He drew attention to Meinhof, who like Proll and Ensslin, was held in a detention room of the psychiatric wing for female prisoners, which was not occupied by any other prisoners. All the prison doctors, psychiatrists and psychologists agreed that Meinhof's breaking point had been reached and that these conditions were no longer acceptable.

It should be noted that not all the RAF members were treated the same. Stricter regulations and controls were directed against Astrid Proll, Ulrike Meinhof, Gudrun Ensslin (Cologne-Ossendorf penal institution), Irmgard Möller (Offenburg penal institution), Marianne Herzog (Frankfurt/Main penal institution) and Margrit Schiller (Hamburg penal institution). In contrast, the conditions for the male members differed greatly. Although Andreas Baader (Schwalmstadt penal institution), Horst Mahler (Berlin penal institution), Jan-Carl Raspe and Gerhard Müller (Cologne penal institution) were in normal detention houses or in the normal prison system, the special arrangements for Ronald Augustin (Hannover penal institution), Holger Meins (Wittlich penal institution), Wolfgang Grundmann (Hamburg penal institution) and Henry Jansen (Berlin-Moabit penal institution) demonstrate the strictest conditions of prison. Their situation included strict solitary confinement, being chained outside the prison cells, entering the cell only with two officials, and solitary prison yard walks. They were excluded from all community events and were only allowed to wear prison clothing.[25] The same was true for Klaus Jünschke (Zweibrücken penal institution) and Siegfried Hausner (Pforzheim penal institution).

The measures of protection ordered by the Federal Prosecutor General were for all RAF members, but the real embodiment of the detention conditions through the prisons was different. Thus, the degree of isolation was more dependent on the special prison institution and where it was, rather than on issues specific to the prisoners. Ultimately, a very important factor was the role the specific federal state (e.g. North Rhine-Westphalia) played in determining the prison conditions.

Conclusion: stricter prison conditions – a myth?

Despite the fact that the controversies about the conditions of detention were exploited by the RAF members and sympathisers for their own purposes, doubts about the hypothesis of equal treatment are justified. The same applies to arguments that the strict solitary prison conditions were only propaganda and myth (Peters, 2006, p.224). It is true that the female and male members of the RAF continued their "anti-imperialist struggle"[26] in the prisons. That is shown by their "cells reports", the process explanations and the "info-system". With the help of a distribution system, discussion papers and programs, newspaper reports and analyses reached the prisoners as lawyers post. The imprisoned RAF leaders decided which of the other RAF prisoners received material. According to the former federal prosecutor Peter Zeis, the RAF prisoners followed their revolutionary goals even from their cells. Written material, which had fallen into the hands of the investigating authorities, show that the RAF priorities, for example, now included the broadening of the revolutionary base and the "politicization" of prisons.[27]

The RAF ran a campaign to publish and scandalise their prison conditions. According to Horst Mahler, a former RAF member, there was only one aim for this "pity campaign", to recruit sympathisers and new members for the terrorist group.[28] The hunger strike reflected the continuation of the confrontation between the state and the RAF. For example Andreas Baader said about the consequences of hunger strikes in a "cell-report" from 22nd October 1974:

> This is a matter of consequence and escalation to exert pressure in prisons, because they are no longer able to cope with the pressure. Because they will see that they cannot succeed with force-feeding. They cannot prevent an RAF prisoner from dying slowly – or quickly – whatever that means, this will stick to them . . . This public murder (and it will run publicly) will remain their problem."[29]

Whether or not the RAF tried to scandalise their prison conditions, the special security measures cannot be ignored: for example, the orders for the monitoring of pretrial prisoners, the searches of their cells in July 1973, February 1974, December 1974 and January 1975, the checking of the post from their lawyers and the recording of their conversations with the lawyers in the Stuttgart-Stammheim prison. The reason for these special prison conditions – according to the arguments of the law enforcement authorities and the courts – was the danger posed by the RAF members. It was – according to the Federal Prosecutor General – the aims of the accused to "politicise" the prisons and to encourage other inmates to revolt. Thus, equality with other prisoners was not possible, because they were dangerous.[30]

In stark contrast, the director of the women's prison, Helga Einsele, and the editor Nele Löw-Beer assessed that the isolation from other prisoners proved to be a failure. The elite attitude of the terrorist group was reinforced in catastrophic dimensions, and led to a situation where hardly anyone could escape the RAF peer pressure (Einsele and Löw-Beer, 1978, p.33).

Notes

1 Frankfurter Allgemeine Zeitung, 14.04.1974.
2 Vermerk des BKA, 12.02.1974; Bundesarchiv (BArch), B 362/3415. (Endorsement from the Federal Criminal Police Office, 12.02.1974; Federal Archive Coblenz, B 362/3415).
3 Schreiben des GBA an den Ermittlungsrichter II des BGH, 14.04.1971; BArch, B362/3168, Bd. V, Bl. 1. (Letter from the Federal Prosecutor General to the investigating judge II of the Federal Court of Justice of Germany, 14.04.1971; Federal Archive Koblenz, B362/3168, Bd. V, Bl. 1).
4 Schreiben des GBA beim BGH an den Untersuchungsrichter bei dem OLG Stuttgart, 10.04.1974; BArch, B 362/3171, Bd. VII, Bl. 219 (Letter from the Federal Prosecutor General to the investigating judge from the Higher Regional Court Stuttgart, 10.04.1974; Federal Archive Coblenz, B 362/3171, Bd. VII, Bl. 219).
5 Dienstanweisung an die Dienststellenleiterin der Außenstelle Bühl, 12.07.1972; BArch, B 362/3219, C 89, Bl. 70 (Prison-Regulations, 12.07.1972; Federal Archive Coblenz, B 362/3219, C 89, Bl. 70).
6 Schreiben des Leiters der Untersuchungshaft- und Aufnahmeanstalt Berlin-Moabit an den BGH, 13.12.1972; BArch, B 362/3168, Bd. V, Bl. 244 f (Letter from the director of the prison Berlin-Moabit to the Federal Court of Justice, Germany, 13.12.1972; Federal Archive Coblenz, B 362/3168, Bd. V, Bl. 244 f).
7 Beschluss des Ermittlungsrichters des BGH, 20.06.1972; BArch, B 362/3166, Bd. III, Bl. 7 (Order of the investigating judge of the Federal Court of Justice, Germany, 20.06.1972; Federal Archive Coblenz, B 362/3166, Bd. III, Bl. 7).
8 Schreiben des Verteidigers an den Ermittlungsrichter des BGH, 21.07.1972; BArch, B 362/3166, Bd. III, Bl. 7 (Letter from the defender to the investigating judge, 21.07.1972; Federal Archive Coblenz, B 362/3166, Bd. III, Bl. 7).
9 Beschluss des Ermittlungsrichters, 20.06.1972 (Order of the investigating judge, 20.06.1972).
10 Beschluss des Ermittlungsrichters des BGH, 14.08.1972; BArch, B 362/3166, Bd. III, Bl. 153 (Order of the investigating judge, 14.08.1972).
11 Schreiben des Leiters der JVA Köln (Ossendorf) an den Ermittlungsrichter beim BGH, 20.06.1972; BArch, B 362/3168, Bd. V, Bl. 85 ff (Letter from the director of the prison Cologne-Ossendorf to the Federal Prosecutor General, B 362/3168, Bd. V, Bl. 85 ff).
12 Schreiben des Leiters der JVA Köln an den GBA beim BGH, 07.02.1973; BArch, B 362/3168, Bd. V, Bl. 278 (Letter from the director of the prison Cologne-Ossendorf to the Federal Prosecutor General, 07.02.1973; Federal Archive, B 362/3168, Bd. V, Bl. 278).
13 Schreiben des Leiters der JVA Köln an den GBA beim BGH, 17.02.1973; BArch, B 362/3168, Bd. V, Bl. 284 (Letter from the director of the prison Cologne-Ossendorf to the Federal Prosecutor General, 17.02.1973; Federal Archive, B 362/3168, Bd. V, Bl. 284).

14 Schreiben des RA Hannover an den Ermittlungsrichter des BGH, 12.11.1973; BArch, B 362/3169, Bd. VI, Bl. 38 (Letter from the lawyer Heinrich Hannover to the investigating judge of the Federal Court of Justice, Germany, 12.11.1973; Federal Archive, B 362/3169, Bd. VI, Bl. 38).

15 Quoted from Sölle, Blick in die *Zeit*, 03.06.1973; Federal Archive Coblenz, B 362/3170, Bd. VIII, Bl. 70 f.

16 Schreiben des RA Groenewold an das AG Hamburg, 24.10.1971; StA Hamburg, Bd. I, Bl. 36 (Letter from the lawyer Kurt Groenewold to the district court Hamburg, 24.10.1971; prosecution Hamburg, Bd. I, Bl. 36).

17 Ibid, p.41.

18 Beschluss des OLG Stuttgart, 16.08.1974; BArch, B 362/3171, Bd. VII, Bl. 253 (Order of the Higher Regional Court, 16.08.1974; Federal Archive Coblenz, B 362/3171, Bd. VII, Bl. 253).

19 Brief von Dr. Dr. Gustav W. Heinemann an Meinhof, 11.12.1974; StA Hamburg (Akz. 141 Js 71/74), Bd. 52., Band: Vorgänge hins. Zwangsernährung (Letter from Dr. Dr. Gustav W. Heinemann to Ulrike Meinhof, 11.12.1974; prosecution Hamburg (Akz. 141 Js 71/74), Bd. 52).

20 Schreiben an den Vorstand der JVA Stuttgart-Stammheim, 06.04.1977; BArch, B 362/3481, Bl. 281 (Letter to the administration of the prison Stuttgart-Stammheim, 06.04.1977; Federal Archive Coblenz, B 362/3481, p.281).

21 Schreiben des Prof. Müller, Chefarzt am Zentrum für Innere Medizin Robert-Bosch-Krankenhaus Stuttgart und Prof. Schröder, Ärztlicher Direktor der Medizinischen Klinik II des Bürgerhospitals Stuttgart an den Regierungsmedizinaldirektor der JVA Stuttgart, 08.04.1977; BArch, B 362/3481 (Letter from Prof. Müller, chief physician of Robert-Bosch-hospital Stuttgart to the prison Stuttgart-Stammheim, 08.04.1977; BArch, B 362/3481).

22 Frankfurter Rundschau, 18.08.1990, p.4.

23 Gesetz zur Änderung des Einführungsgesetzes zum Gerichtsverfassungsgesetz, vgl. BGBl. I, S. 1877 (Law for change of the Introductory Act to the Gerichtsverfassungsgesetz, see German Civil Code, p. 1877).

24 Verfügung des Vorsitzenden Richters des OLG Stuttgart, 06.09.1977; BArch, B 362/3161, Bd. VII, Bl.3/109. (Order of the chief judge of the Higher Regional Court Stuttgart, 06.09.1977; Federal Archive Coblenz, B 362/3161, Bd. VII, Bl.3/109).

25 Schreiben des AG Hamburg an die Verteidiger, 11.04.1972, in Kursbuch 32, S. 22 (Letter from the district court Hamburg to the lawyers, 11.04.1972, in Kursbuch 32, S. 22).

26 Hungerstreikerklärung der RAF, 13.09.1975, in Rote Armee Fraktion. Texte und Materialien, p.190 f.

27 The prosecutor Peter Zeis in conversation with the author on 17.09.2007.

28 Mahler am 14.10.1978 in einem Brief an Peter-Paul Zahl, in Zahl, Die Stille und das Grelle. Aufsätze, Frankfurt/Main 1981, S. 142 (Letter from Horst Mahler to Peter-Paul Zahl, 14.10.1978, in Zahl, Die Stille und das Grelle. Aufsätze, Frankfurt/Main 1981, p.142).

29 Ibid, p.111.

30 Schreiben des GBA beim BGH an den Untersuchungsrichter bei dem OLG Stuttgart, 10.04.1974; BArch, B 362/3171, Bd. VII, Bl. 219 (Letter from the Federal Prosecutor General to the investigating judge of the Higher Regional Court, 10.04.1974; Federal Archive Coblenz, B 362/3171, Bd. VII, Bl. 219).

References

Blath, R. and Hobe, K. (1982). *Strafverfahren gegen linksterroristische Straftäter und ihre Unterstützer, hrsg.* Bonn: vom Bundesministerium der Justiz.

Däubler-Gmelin, H. (1987). 'Im Zweifel für die Grundrechte oder Kontaktsperre im Parlament.' In Michael Sontheimer and Otto Kallscheuer (Eds.), *Einschüsse: Besichtigung eines Frontverlaufs*. Berlin: Deutschen Herbst.

Einsele, H. and Löw-Beer, N. (1978). 'Politische Sozialisation und Haftbedingungen.' In Susanne von Paczensky (Ed.), *Frauen und Terror. Versuche, die Beteiligung von Frauen an Gewalttaten zu erklären*, pp.24–36. Hamburg: Reinbek bei Hamburg.

Eschen, K., Lang, J., Laubscher, J. and Riemann, J. (1973). *Folter in der BRD. Dokumentation zur Lage der Politischen Gefangenen, zusammengestellt von Verteidigern in Politischen Strafsachen.* Berlin.

Hannover, H. (2001). *Die Republik vor Gericht 1975–1995*. Berlin: Erinnerungen eines unbequemen Rechtsanwalts.

Nass, G. (1973). 'Anarcho-Terroristen in Untersuchungs – und Strafhaft.' *Zeitschrift für Strafvollzug*, März, pp. 36–40.

Oesterle, K. (2003). *Stammheim. Die Geschichte des Vollzugsbeamten Horst Bubeck*. Tübingen.

Peters, B. (2006). *Der letzte Mythos der RAF*. Berlin: Ullstein Verlag.

Presse-und Informationsamt der Bundesregierung (1977). 'Wie inszeniert man Sympathie-Kampagnen?' *Kommentarübersicht Fernsehen/Rundfunk*. Nachrichtenabteilung.

Preusker, H. (1997). 'Reform-Entzug?' *Neue Kriminalpolitik*, 2, pp.34–36.

Proll, A. (1998). *Hans und Grete: Die RAF 1967–1977*. Göttingen.

Rasch, W. (1976). 'Die Gestaltung der Haftbedingungen für politisch motivierte Täter in der Bundesrepublik Deutschland.' *Monatsschrift für Kriminologie und Strafrechtsreform*, 2/3, pp.61–69.

Schenk, D. (2000). *Der Chef. Horst Herold und das BKA*. Munich: Spiegel.

Stuberger, U. (1977). *In der Strafsache gegen Andreas Baader, Ulrike Meinhof, Jan-Carl Raspe, Gudrun Ensslin wegen Mordes u.a. Dokumente aus dem Prozeß*. Syndicate: Frankfurt/Main.

Wesel, U. (2002). *Die verspielte Revolution: 1968 und die Folgen*. München.

17

PRISON POLICY AS AN ANTI-TERRORIST TOOL

Lessons from Spain

Manuel R. Torres Soriano

Background of Spain's counter-terrorism experience

Historically the main terrorist threat in Spain has come from ETA (Basque Homeland and Freedom), which began its activities in 1959. The terrorist group's ideology combines extreme left-wing revolutionary components and ultra-radical Basque nationalism. Its ultimate goal is the creation of 'Euskal Herria', an 'independent socialist state' comprising the Spanish regions of the Basque Country, Navarre and part of neighbouring French areas known as the 'French Basque Country' (Elorza, 2000). The commencement of ETA's activities coincided with the decline of the dictatorship of General Franco (1939–1975). The organisation's actions were aimed primarily at elements representing the regime, such as the security forces and senior military chiefs, and included the assassination of the prime minister and number two in the regime, Admiral Carrero Blanco (1973). At the time ETA enjoyed considerable international legitimacy and support within the community given that its discourse included references to the need to bring about the democratisation of the Basque Country. Moreover, the disproportionate response by the dictatorship, which attempted to stifle the growing terrorist threat through mass raids, torture of detainees and death sentences, ultimately served to broaden recruitment and support for the organisation. The organisation's strategy was grounded on the Maoist principle of action-reaction-action designed to trigger an excessive reaction by the regime in order to mobilise Basque support for ETA and trigger a guerrilla war which would eventually see the Spanish state defeated.

Far from bringing about an end to terrorism, the return to democracy (1977) and the granting of several full amnesties for ETA prisoners prompted an increase in the organisation's activities and the deadliness of its strikes. ETA aimed to topple Spain's weak, fledgling democracy and thus cause a political involution to support its discourse and widen its support base (Reinares & Jaime-Jiménez, 2000). When the strategy failed, ETA continued its activities with a new objective: to force political negotiation with the state in order to secure its goals (Sánchez-Cuenca, 2001). It resorted to threats, blackmail, kidnappings and indiscriminate attacks in a bid to wear down the state's resistance. The failure of early negotiation attempts, the state's powerlessness to curb the terrorist offensive and the scant anti-terrorist cooperation received from France (where the ETA rearguard was based) facilitated the emergence of a new form of terrorism linked to certain state sectors and the police and which used violence to target members of ETA and its support network. However, the outcome of the actions of these groups was not only ineffective but also hampered the fight against terrorism by undermining the legitimacy of the state and bolstering the discourse of ETA, which was able to argue that it was fighting the state with the same methods used by the enemy (Domínguez Iribarren, 2003).

Over time, Spain's anti-terrorist response gradually gained in sophistication and effectiveness (Jaime Jiménez, 2002). Improved police action, better intelligence gathering, more appropriate criminal legislation and judicial and penitentiary systems, actions aimed at delegitimising terrorism, and increased involvement by society have progressively weakened ETA and its political and social environment, although without achieving its total elimination.

Terrorist action by jihadist networks and groups constitute Spain's most recent threat. During the 1980s and 1990s, these groups used the country for logistical purposes although their actions were carried out elsewhere. The mid-1990s brought the first arrests of GIA (Armed Islamic Group) and GSPC (Salafist Group for Call and Combat) jihadists as part of anti-terrorist cooperation between Spain and France to curb the wave of attacks suffered by the latter. The same period saw the commencement also of systematic surveillance of the activities of such networks and the creation of the first counter-terrorist units set up to deal specifically with the threat. Anti-terrorism chiefs believed that these groups sought to use the country as a logistical base or transit point for actions carried out in other countries but did not represent a direct threat to national security in Spain or its allies. The approach focused on vigilance and increasing available knowledge on the networks (Jordán & Horsburgh, 2005). Following the 9/11 attacks, all the information gathered during this time was put to use and Al Qaeda's infrastructure in Spain was dismantled. More resources were allocated to tackling terrorism of this type. However, the main terrorism threat against Spain was still believed to come from ETA. The strategy against jihadist networks was to ensure they did not turn Spain into a logistics base or 'refuge'. The Madrid train bombings of 11 March 2004 altered this approach dramatically (Jordán & Horsburgh, 2006). The bombings demonstrated that the support cells could be transformed into strike cells very rapidly. Since then Spain has viewed jihadist terrorism as a main threat to its security and has increased the resources to combat it, while also implementing a series of organisational reforms aimed at increased effectiveness (Reinares, 2009).

The need of a prison policy to fight ETA

The basic principle governing the prison system is Article 23 of the Spanish Constitution, which stipulates that the aim of custodial sentences is to re-educate prisoners and reinsert them in society. This fundamental norm implies not only that life imprisonment is excluded but also that the length of prison terms is limited in order to ensure that they do not become de facto life sentences. The aforementioned principle also sets out a series of restrictions concerning the treatment of inmates, which must be consistent with the re-education and reinsertion objective. Accordingly, certain punitive or preventive measures inside prison are limited.

Since the 1980s, prison policy has been used as an anti-terrorist instrument and its importance is reflected in the fact that powers for the running of prisons were transferred from the Ministry of Justice to the Ministry of the Interior in the mid-1990s (Reinares, 2008).

The two main measures of this strategy are prisoner 'dispersal' and 'reinsertion'. Both are a response to the strategy adopted by ETA, which has attempted to retain control over its incarcerated prisoners. Its prisoners are a crucial part of the organisation's discourse since they are held up as political prisoners of the Spanish state and heroes who are subjected to torture and humiliation of all kinds (Domínguez Iribarren, 1998). ETA has put in place an elaborate support network for its prisoners consisting of amnesty pressure groups ('Gestoras Pro-Aministía'), help organisations that ensure permanent contact with prisoners and facilitate contact with their families, and even payment of a small financial contribution to the prisoners to improve their quality of life while in jail.

The reinsertion scheme seeks to encourage ETA members to give up their terrorist activities and foster dissent within the organisation, propitiating the emergence of a sector in favour of ending the terrorist fight. The scheme facilitates the release of ETA prisoners not convicted of blood crimes who agree to break their ties with ETA and show remorse. In 1983–84 around 230 ETA prisoners benefited from the scheme (Warnes & Hannah, 2008).

Likewise, dispersal seeks to eliminate the tight control exercised by ETA over its incarcerated members. The discipline imposed by the organisation is helped greatly by the fact that a large number of ETA prisoners are housed in the same prison. As a general rule in Spain, the decision to distribute prisoners among different jails aims to allow them to be as close to their home or place of origin in order to facilitate contact with relatives and friends. This principle was applied also in the case of convicted ETA prisoners. Consequently, a large number of ETA inmates – the vast majority of whom were from the small Basque Country region – were concentrated in a handful of prisons.[1] This not only facilitated ETA control over its members behind bars but also made it difficult for prisoners to disengage from the group, given the peer pressure inside the jail and group conduct reaffirmation processes.

In order to break the hold of the organisation, in 1989 Spain adopted a dispersal policy, splitting ETA members up among different prisons across the country.[2] This policy is approved by the Interior Ministry and is implemented according to the profile of each prisoner, their behaviour in prison, developments in the fight against terrorism, and the political context of the country. The measure helps:

- Prevent a large number of terrorists in the same prison facilitating the planning and execution of mutinies and pressure/protest measures against the state.
- Facilitate disengagement by prisoners wishing to give up terrorist militancy but who were prevented from doing so by the pressure and coercion exerted by their colleagues in prison.
- Impede control by the network of support organisations set up legally by ETA to 'assist' the terrorist prisoners. Housing the prisoners in jails hundreds (and at times thousands) of kilometres from such persons hampered the logistics and the actions of the organisations and individuals.
- 'Isolate' jailed terrorist leaders or the most radical members who exercised authority over their colleagues or were acknowledged as leaders in the prison. The individuals entrusted with applying the ETA 'line' in prisons lost this capacity when imprisoned in jails where very few or no other members of the organisation were held.

Dispersal also offered an added advantage for the state in that it could be used to encourage dissent within the terrorist organisation. For example, moving prisoners closer to home could be used as a reward for senior figures or members willing to break the discipline imposed by the leadership and to advocate an end to terrorist actions. Conversely, prisoners who were keen to continue to support new terrorist attacks could be 'punished'. Indeed, dispersal has been used as leverage in the different negotiations down the decades between various governments and the ETA leadership. For instance, the state has taken advantage of the possibility to move some ETA prisoners closer to home as a goodwill gesture in negotiations. The measure was fully reversible if the talks failed and it did not carry such a high political cost as the release of the prisoners.

The jihadist dilemma

The Spanish government lacks a similar approach to tackle the jihadist terrorism phenomenon in the country's prisons. The dispersal and reinsertion measures are a response to the specific characteristics and methods of ETA rather than a general approach applicable to all prisoners incarcerated for terrorist activities. Dispersal is the prison system's response to a terrorism which is based on the existence of a clearly defined organisation with its own hierarchies and chain of control, designed to exert permanent control over its members in prison. This approach is totally at odds with the reality of jihadist terrorism in the country (Jordán, 2008). The operations against this kind of terrorism in Spain show that it bears little resemblance to the fully institutionalised organisations capable of surviving the loss of members (Jordán, 2007; Jordán, Mañas & Horsburgh, 2008). There is no identifiable organisation or social network whose control over prisoners must be neutralised; moreover, the prisoners themselves deny having links with jihadist terrorism activities and networks.

Jihadist terrorists in prison not only deny having any part in the crimes they are accused of but also deny links with other prisoners jailed for the same crimes.

Consequently, there is no clear criterion as to how to manage such prisoners, not to say confusion as to the possible outcomes of potential measures. One of the main problems (unlike with ETA prisoners) is the radicalisation and recruitment of common prisoners. Spain has a total prison population of 70,392 (January 2012)[3]; 24,144 are foreign prisoners, of whom approximately 10,000 (14% of the total) are from predominantly Muslim countries. This sizeable sector of the prison population constitutes a fertile ground for those seeking to capitalise on loss of liberty to facilitate the terrorist radicalisation of other Muslims (Alonso, 2012). The existence of the threat has been confirmed, for example, by the NOVA operation undertaken by police in October–November 2004 against a jihadist network which had been partially created in prisons. The network was made up of former GIA militants who recruited common prisoners to carry out a series of terrorist strikes on their release to mark the first anniversary of the 11 March bombings in Madrid (Gutiérrez et al., 2007).

This kind of terrorism throws up a number of paradoxes:

First, the prisoners who radicalise other prisoners are not necessarily those serving time for terrorist activities. Indeed, those jailed for terrorist offences have a vested interested in not being associated with jihadist radicalism so as not to jeopardise their possible release. Common Muslim prisoners occasionally agree to act as precursors for radicalisation and terrorist recruitment or have themselves been radicalised while in jail.

The second paradox is what to do with radical prisoners. Under Spanish law, isolating prisoners from their peers is a temporary measure, a specific punishment for a breach of prison regulations. Radical proselytism is not listed as a breach of the regulations and, moreover, is extremely difficult to detect by prison staff. Jihadist inmates must be in permanent contact with common prisoners. The large number of inmates from Muslim countries makes it impossible to separate the radicals from other Muslims. If they are concentrated in one jail, a dangerous core could form consisting of radical prisoners with the power to control other Muslim inmates. If they are dispersed, the 'fire' of terrorist radicalisation could spread throughout the country's prisons.

The lack of a de-radicalisation approach

For decades, the bulk of the terrorist threat faced by Spain came from a single source: ETA. The specific characteristics of this terrorism meant that a de-radicalisation approach was unnecessary. ETA itself had sought to gain legitimacy as an armed political organisation which was fighting to defend the interests of the Basque Country and people (Llera Ramo, 2003). ETA sporadically targeted common criminals and drug traffickers in the Basque Country as a strategy to increase its standing in the community. To avoid the possible damage which links with the world of crime would cause to its image, ETA has endeavoured to resolve certain logistic problems such as weapons and explosives procurement and fundraising outside criminal networks. Consequently, ETA members have not engaged in proselytism in prison nor have they tried to radicalise common prisoners. Incarcerated members of the organisation consider themselves to be 'political prisoners', with no links to other incarcerated criminals. They have endeavoured to maintain this status by avoiding mixing with common prisoners and refusing prison privileges of any kind (such as access to day-release schemes etc.) that might suggest implicit acknowledgement that their crimes were 'ordinary'.

The absence of a de-radicalisation approach can also be explained by factors arising out of the political context. For decades, overtures by the state to ETA have been based implicitly on the premise that ETA is a rational political player that has chosen terrorism as the most effective strategy to secure its objectives. Thus, the state's approach has been to persuade/force ETA to give up the armed struggle after weighing up the costs and benefits and realising that democratic political activism is the most appropriate strategy to achieve its goals. Indeed, for many years the official state discourse amounted implicitly to the negation that ETA terrorism was the product of a violent radicalisation of a group of individuals. It argued further that all ideology (including that advocated by ETA) was legitimate and could be accommodated in the politics of democracy provided it did not resort to violence. The premise was strengthened also by the existence of non-violent Basque nationalist parties (vital on several occasions to enable the mainstream Spanish parties to form a governing majority) which have been able to exert considerable influence on the formulation of the state's counter-terrorism policies. The approach of such parties has been to foster the integration in the political system of ETA and its support base, not by de-radicalising its members but by establishing negotiation processes that will lead the members to give up terrorist activism in favour of participation in the democratic process.

The debate on the need for a de-radicalisation approach is a recent phenomenon, triggered by the presence of prisoners with links to jihadist terrorism and the growing numbers of Muslim prisoners in Spanish jails. However, the prevailing approach is prevention-focused and aims to avoid the radicalisation of common Muslim prisoners. No need has been felt thus far for measures to de-radicalise jihadist prisoners for the following reasons:

a   In numerical terms, prisoners convicted of jihadist-inspired terrorism offences represent a very small proportion of the overall prison population: 74 members (July 2009). In a context of finite resources, the small numbers are a constraint on the establishment of specific programmes. These prisoners are treated within the broader framework of cultural integration and vocational training programmes, which are followed also by prisoners from gipsy backgrounds, sub-Saharans etc.

b   Jihadist prisoners categorically deny they are radicals and even that they are in any way linked to the offences for which they are prosecuted. They refuse to take part in any activity or action that entails an implicit assumption that they are jihadists (for example, granting interviews to journalists, researchers, etc.).

These prisoners usually have a good knowledge of how the legal system and Spanish prison rules operate. They are aware that release and access to privileges such as passes or day-release schemes are dependent on their behaviour in prison and on the perception that they are not a threat once outside. Hence, they keep a 'low profile' inside jail, and even tone down their religious practices or lifestyles to avoid conveying any visible hint of radicalisation.

c   According to Spain's prison legislation, prisoner participation in any training, leisure or other activity is voluntary. Consequently, the establishment of terrorist de-radicalisation programmes in no way guarantees that prisoners will sign up to them. Although participation may have beneficial repercussions on access to privileges, in terms of cost-benefits and with a view to release it may prove more beneficial to deny the charges, avoid any implicit recognition of them and assume the role of a victim of a miscarriage of justice or of state persecution against Muslims.

Successes and failures of the Spanish prison policy in the fight against terrorism

Any assessment made must first draw a distinction between the effects on ETA and the effects on jihadist terrorism.

In the case of ETA, prison policy is, broadly speaking, viewed as a success. The prison policy based on reinsertion and dispersal has contributed to weakening control by the terrorist organisation over its incarcerated members, has encouraged dissent between active members and those in prison, and has allowed some prisoners to break their ties with terrorism on their release, thus affording the government an important bargaining advantage over ETA.

The best indicator of the success of the approach can be gauged from ETA's own behaviour. The organisation reacted swiftly to try and neutralise the government's offer of 'reinsertion' for its prisoners. Its propaganda machine denounced those who accepted the offer, branding them as traitors and cowards. In order to stem the flow of desertions, ETA went as far as to murder Yoyes (in 1986), a former woman leader who had signed up to the measure.

The impact of the prison policy measures on ETA prompted the organisation to add Spanish prison staff and senior officials to its list of 'targets'. In 1996, for example, the organisation kidnapped prison officer José Antonio Ortega Lara, who was held for 532 days until he was freed by the Civil Guard. ETA set as a condition for his release the transfer of all its prisoners to Basque jails. ETA responded to the police operation to free Ortega Lara by kidnapping Miguel Angel Blanco, a local politician from the Basque Country, and gave the authorities 48 hours to move the prisoners to jails in the region. The government refused to bow to blackmail and the councillor was murdered.

These and other actions demonstrate that the terrorist organisation has established the neutralisation of the dispersal policy as a top priority. It has been one of its main demands in recent years in all negotiation or ceasefire attempts.

ETA has also sought to hamper implementation of the measures through vigorous denunciations of Spain's prison policy. It has used its propaganda capabilities and organisational network to undermine the legitimacy of the dispersal policy, which is held up as a manifestation of state torture and a systematic violation of the human rights of the Basque people. One of the most frequently used arguments is, for example, that dispersal is an instrument to extend the punishment to the Basque prisoner's family and social environment. Accordingly, ETA's network has not hesitated to present as further victims of state violence any relatives and friends who suffer road accidents when travelling to jails to visit Basque prisoners.

The assessment is very different in the case of jihadist terrorism. The mainstream feeling among many political quarters, heads of prisons and members of the police and intelligence services is that there is no clear idea with respect to how best to tackle the presence of jihadists in Spanish jails. The belief exists that the policies put in place to combat ETA terrorism in prisons have not only proven ineffective against jihadist terrorism but may even be counterproductive. The prison system is not managing to neutralise the dangers posed by these individuals and prisons have become a fertile ground for a worsening of the phenomenon, generating more terrorist radicalism.

If we focus on mistakes, in the case of ETA, the main error is the excessive use made of the policy as a tool in negotiations with the group. Far from considering suspension of the policy as an exceptional measure, different governments have opted for 'partial regroupings' of ETA prisoners, moving them to Basque jails, in return for concessions from the terrorist organisation. The willingness to suspend the approach temporarily has undermined the legitimacy of the policy because it implicitly acknowledges that ETA prisoners are discriminated against and that this exceptional situation could be ended if certain conditions are met. The constant moving back and forth on this issue conveys an impression of temporariness and allows the terrorist organisation to assume that the battle for control of its prisoners is not lost and this effective instrument can be neutralised through various coercion and negotiation measures.

In the case of jihadist terrorism, the absence of a clear and explicit policy on how to address the phenomenon has led to many errors and dysfunctions caused by:

a   Legal constraints. The reinsertion and rehabilitation principles that underpin the functioning of the Spanish prison system have been viewed as a constraint on the segregation of terrorist prisoners from common prisoners. Isolation is applied only as a temporary punishment for breaches of prison regulations. Consequently, jihadist prisoners live side by side in the same wings as the other inmates, many of whom are from predominantly Muslim countries and are therefore targets for recruitment and radicalisation by these prisoners.

b   Insufficient financial and human resources. Monitoring prisoners with links to jihadist terrorism (and their potential victims inside jail) requires extra resources but this requirement has not been addressed appropriately. The main problem is the need to understand the Arabic used by the prisoners, as well as its different dialects. Prison staff are not equipped to understand the oral communications between these prisoners. Despite increased recruitment of translators in Spanish prisons, there are still too few (in 2008, approximately 35 translators for 6,000 Arab-speaking inmates (Gutiérrez *et al.*, 2007)) to cope with the sheer volume of information generated not just by this sector of the prison population. Moreover, translators are not allowed to enter prisoners' living quarters and their role is restricted to translation of some communications with the outside world and letters. As a result, much oral communication by these prisoners goes unmonitored and control is restricted to observation and an intuitive reading of their behaviour. The low staff-prisoner ratio (1:160) makes continuous and detailed observation of prisoner conduct extremely difficult (Trujillo *et al.*, 2009). Another consequence of material constraints is a lack of staff who are specialised in dealing with and monitoring these prisoners. Constant staff rotations means that experience gained by officers in dealing with the jihadists is not capitalised on fully and specific training programmes have not been set up for managing prisoners linked to jihadist terrorism.

c   Insufficient control of prisoners' links with the outside world. Certain material limitations and legal restrictions such as the inability to carry out full body searches of persons visiting the prisoners means that it is impossible in practice to prevent the prisoners from having access to banned substances and items such as drugs or mobile phones. In the case of jihadist terrorism, the problem extends also to the introduction of cassettes, CDs, books and magazines with radical content. Moreover, not enough control is exercised with respect to the identity and motivations of the persons and organisations visiting Muslim prisoners. Some temporary imams are completely unknown to the authorities and there is no database on either them or their backgrounds. The problem is compounded by the lack of a common database of visits to prisoners in Spanish jails, which hampers efforts to prevent the same individual acting as a communications link between prisoners in different jails (Gutiérrez *et al.*, 2007).

d   Insufficient coordination between prison staff and the members of the security forces and intelligence services responsible for combating terrorism. There is no institutionalised system to provide a smooth and continuous flow of information generated inside and outside prisons.

Conclusions

The long dictatorship suffered by Spain (1939–1975), the late return to democracy and the experience of a short-lived 'dirty war' against terrorism have had a major influence on the approach to and implementation of anti-terrorist policy in prisons (Reinares & Jaime-Jiménez, 2000).

On the one hand, the desire to demonstrate democratic credentials similar to other western countries has led to the drawing up of criminal and prison legislation which affords excessive guarantees. Democracy came about through a system of transition, as opposed to a clean break, and a large part of the repressive state apparatus remained in place. The desire to avoid any hint of suspicion outside Spain as to the sincerity of the democratic change undergone by the country led to the adoption of a criminal legislation that catered excessively for the rights and freedoms of the accused, which in turn implicitly cast a shadow of structural suspicion over the police's actions, a situation which has constituted an important restriction in the fight against terrorism. The tendency was reinforced by the rhetoric employed by ETA, which claimed to be fighting to 'democratise the Basque Country' and free it from the remnants of an oppressive Spanish regime which had been forced to wear the 'mask' of a false democracy. The brief period of 'state terrorism' exacerbated the situation and partly legitimised the terrorist discourse, in turn increasing the desire for a legal and criminal justice system that would remove all shadow of a doubt concerning the nature of Spain's democracy.

This 'inferiority complex' in terms of democracy has been particularly evident in the shaping and functioning of the modern prison system, where the memory of political prisoners and of the abuses committed in jails was still alive.

The above accumulation of historic and political factors has played a major role in shaping Spain's anti-terrorist approach. Indeed, the formulation and adjustment of the country's response to terrorism has been based not just on the calculations of its effectiveness but also on its impacts on citizens' rights and freedoms and the external image of Spanish democracy.

Prison policy as a tool to fight terrorism is considered successful on account of its ability to weaken control by ETA over its incarcerated members and to foster dissent between its leaders and ideologists in jail and those who are not in jail. According to former Justice Minister Juan Fernando López Aguilar, dispersal 'has been useful to weaken ETA' and 'will continue until ETA is definitively defeated'.[4] The main obstacle has been the need for broad political consensus among the different parties to implement the measure. The use of a policy that might be interpreted demagogically as a discrimination or curtailment of fundamental rights could be seized on by some political parties to obtain electoral advantages or the support of other parties. For example, the dispersal policy has been denounced publicly by all the Basque nationalist parties, including those who have been in power in the regional government. The campaign has even seen formal complaints lodged with leading international courts and human rights bodies that the policy breaches human rights. In some cases, the bodies in question have been receptive to the complaints, which can be detrimental to the political credit and capital of the government.

Regarding the policy for 'reinserting' ETA prisoners, the main obstacle was the response by the organisation, which managed to neutralise the measure by threatening all members who signed up to them and even murdered a prominent terrorist leader who did sign up. The measure was rendered unusable as a result. For ETA prisoners the main attraction of the offer was a possible transfer to their home towns to get on with their lives (Reinares, 2001). However, coercion by ETA made this impossible. Self-esteem among ETA prisoners was largely conditional upon recognition and acceptance in their social and family environments and this was impossible if the prisoner was dubbed a 'traitor to the Basque people' by ETA. For ETA prisoners the only possibility of returning home and getting on with their lives with dignity was if they adhered to the rules of the organisation and gave up prison privileges of any type,[5] serving out their sentence or waiting for ETA to secure the release of all its prisoners through its 'armed struggle'.

If we talk about which elements of this policy can be described as country specific, the main influencing factor has been the complex Basque political scenario, which is deeply divided between nationalists and non-nationalists (Shabad & Llera, 1995). The existence of nationalist political forces in the Basque Country who sympathise with the independence aims of ETA but not the methods used to secure them has influenced the design of policies to tackle the terrorist organisation. Since the legitimacy of ETA's goals could not be undermined – to do so would have led to the alignment of all the democratic nationalist parties – the anti-terrorist discourse has centred on the rejection of violence. Hence, the guiding principle has been to neutralise the pro-violence components within ETA and facilitate the incorporation of ETA members and the organisation's community support into the democratic system. To that end, anti-terrorist measures have aimed to weaken the control of the organisation over its members and propitiate the emergence of dissenting factions in favour of non-violent political activism.

The key lessons to be learned from the Spanish's experience are:

a   Prison policy can be a very important instrument in the fight against terrorism, but these measures require a high degree of consensus among all political forces, otherwise they run the risk of being seized on to strengthen terrorist discourse and undermine the legitimacy of the state.

b   It is necessary and possible to weaken the control of terrorist organisations over their incarcerated members. Disengagement is very difficult to implement due to the presence of strong terrorist organisations willing to use extreme violence to neutralise such measures. The fact that the terrorist groups are willing to make members who sign up to the measures their new enemies can render the measures non-viable.

c   In the case of terrorist organisations with a clear structure and hierarchy, avoiding the concentration of prisoners in the same jail can prove a useful tool for weakening the control of the organisation over its members.

d   Prison legislation can be an obstacle to the adoption of prison policies appropriate to the new reality of jihadist terrorism. The main problem is the lack of an explicit and clearly articulated approach to address the phenomenon of jihadist terrorism in prisons appropriately.

Notes

1   In October 2011, Spain's prison system had 529 ETA prisoners.
2   Spain's prison system comprises 82 prisons, which are managed by the Interior Ministry (Directorate General for Penitentiaries) except those in Catalonia, which are run directly by the Catalan regional government.

3   Source: Ministry of Interior Website: http://www.institucionpenitenciaria.es/web/portal/documentos/estadisticas.html
4   See: *El Pais* newspaper: "López Aguilar states prisoner dispersal will continue until ETA is definitively defeated", *El País*, 30/09/2004.
5   ETA's official stance was set out in a directive issued to all its prisoners in April 1991 ordering them not to apply for privileges. The ETA leadership and prisoners who share its views consider that 'to accept that the policy is inevitable is to accept that the enemy has won the dispersal fight . . . acceptance effectively means that we are, in terms of prison practice, placed on an equal footing with common prisoners; it means abandoning to their fate those who have suffered retaliation; it will encourage applications for day release and bail, as well as encouraging personal solutions'. (Elorza, 2000: 374).

References

Alonso, R. (2012). 'The spread of radical Islam in Spain: challenges ahead', *Studies in Conflict & Terrorism*, 35:6, 471–491.
Domínguez Iribarren, F. (1998). *ETA: Estrategia Organizativa y Actuaciones 1978–1992*. Bilbao: Universidad del País Vasco.
Domínguez Iribarren, F. (2003). *Las raíces del miedo. Euskadi, una sociedad atemorizada*. Madrid: Aguilar.
Elorza, A. (2000). *La Historia de ETA*. Madrid: Temas de Hoy.
Gutiérrez, J.A., Jordán, J. & Trujillo, H. (2007). 'Prevention of jihadist radicalization in Spanish prisons. current situation, challenges and dysfunctions of the penitentiary system', *Athena Intelligence Journal*, 1, 1–12.
Jaime Jiménez, O. (2002). *Policía, terrorismo y cambio político en España, 1976–1996*. Valencia: Tirant lo Blanch.
Jordán, J. (2007) 'Las redes yihadistas en España. Evolución desde el 11-M', *Athena Intelligence Journal*, 3, 79–102.
Jordán, J. (2008). 'Anatomy of Spain's 28 disrupted jihadist networks', *CTC Sentinel*, 11, 10–11.
Jordán, J. & Horsburgh, N. (2005). 'Mapping jihadist terrorism in Spain', *Studies in Conflict & Terrorism*, 28, 169–191.
Jordán, J. & Horsburgh, N. (2006). 'Spain and Islamist terrorism: Analysis of the threat and response 1995–2005', *Mediterranean Politics*, 2, 209–229.
Jordán, J., Mañas, F. & Horsburgh, N. (2008). 'Strengths and weaknesses of grassroot jihadist networks: the Madrid bombings', *Studies in Conflict & Terrorism*, 1, 17–39.
Llera Ramo, F. (2003). 'La red terrorista: subcultura de la violencia y nacionalismo en Euskadi'. In Robles Egea, A. (Ed.). *La sangre de las naciones. Identidades nacionales y violencia política*, Granada: Universidad de Granada.
Reinares, F. (2001). *Patriotas de la muerte: quiénes han militado en ETA y por qué*, Madrid: Taurus.
Reinares, F. (2008). 'Tras el 11 de marzo: estructuras de seguridad interior y prevención del terrorismo global en España'. In Powell, C. & Reinares, F. (Eds.). *Las democracias occidentales frente al terrorismo global*, Madrid: Ariel.
Reinares, F. (2009), 'After the Madrid bombings: Internal security reforms and prevention of global terrorism in Spain', *Studies in Conflict & Terrorism*, 32:5, 367–388.
Reinares, F. & Jaime-Jiménez, O. (2000). 'Countering terrorism in a new democracy: the case of Spain'. In Reinares, F. (Ed.). *European Democracies Against Terrorism: Governmental Policies and Intergovernmental Cooperation*. Ashgate: Aldershot.
Sánchez-Cuenca, I. (2001). *ETA contra el Estado. Las estrategias del terrorismo*, Barcelona: Tusquets.

Shabad, G. & Llera, F. (1995). 'Political violence in a democratic state: Basque terrorism in Spain'. In Crenshaw, M. (Ed.). *Terrorism in Context*, University Park: The Pennsylvania State University Press.

Trujillo, H., Jordán, J., Antonio Gutiérrez, J. & González Cabrera, J. (2009). 'Radicalization in prisons? Field research in 25 Spanish prisons', *Terrorism and Political Violence*, 4, 558–579.

Warnes, R. & Hannah, G. (2008). 'Meeting the challenge of extremist and radicalized prisoners. The experiences of the United Kingdom and Spain', *Policing*, 4, 402–411.

PART V

Post-release experiences

18

DO LEOPARDS CHANGE THEIR SPOTS?

Probation, risk assessment and management of terrorism-related offenders on licence in the UK[1]

Benedict Wilkinson

The UK's counter-extremism doctrine, notoriously enshrined in the 'Prevent' workstream of CONTEST, has tended to divide opinion. Under the Labour Government, the strategy received vociferous criticism that 'through its unbelievably stupid belief that non-violent extremists can be used as the antidote to violent extremists, [it was] actually radicalising a new generation of Muslims, sometimes with the very funds that are supposed to be countering radicalisation' (Phillips, 2009). Others, in contrast, argued that it was precisely these constituencies which are best placed to identify and challenge violent extremism, warning that 'without the active engagement of Muslim communities the long-term risks will be much higher' (Briggs, Fieschi and Lownsbrough, 2006, p.84). More recently, the subsequent Coalition government has responded to these claims and counter-claims by instituting an in-depth review with the result that the Prevent Strategy has been extricated from the related process of promoting community integration. It has also seen a substantial broadening of the targets of Prevent so that it now includes non-violent extremists of all ideological backgrounds.

Despite these developments, the strategy remains heavily geared towards countering extremism by challenging radical ideology in communities. The related but distinct processes of de-radicalising and rehabilitating individuals who have committed terrorist offences for which they have been tried and convicted is all but overlooked.[2] Where the strategy does touch on terrorism-related offenders, the focus tends to be on those who remain in prison and are seen to pose a threat of radicalising fellow offenders (Neumann, 2010). The issue of how the UK manages the threat posed by convicted terrorists completing their sentences on licence in the community remains under-examined. By the same token, there is comparatively little understanding of the risk management of terrorist offenders on licence in the community, and investigation of the process of rehabilitating and/or de-radicalising terrorist offenders on licence is limited.

Despite the dearth of literature, offenders on licence do present a substantial (if as yet unrealised) threat. In the first place, if an offender, convicted under counter-terrorism legislation and completing their licence in the community, were to commit further terrorist acts, the media backlash would be inevitably damaging and would undoubtedly cause substantial loss of public trust in the police and Probation Service. In the second place, although the number of Terrorism Act offenders on licence is small, it is increasing and likely to continue to do so exponentially.[3] According to the Prevent strategy paper, by February 2011 there were 36 offenders completing their licences in the community, with a further 34 due to reach their release dates in the next four years. From September 2010 to September 2011 alone, 29 terrorism-related offenders were released from UK prisons on licence.[4] It is likely that these numbers will grow as a consequence of increasingly short sentences for lesser non-violent offences such as 'possession of terrorist literature' or 'possessing records likely to be useful in terrorism'.[5] Between 2009 and 2010, for example, 13 of the 23 individuals convicted of terrorism-related offences received a sentence of between only 1 and 4 years (Policing Statistics Team, 2012, p.12). In the third place, although these offenders are few in number, they present a particularly concerning threat. They have the potential not only to be more embittered against their perceived enemies in the West as a consequence of their sentences, but also to be more deeply embedded in extremist networks encountered in prison.

Bearing all this in mind, this chapter seeks to examine the way in which the UK manages those convicted under terrorism-related offences on licence. The following section describes the primary channel through which the risk of a terrorism offender on licence is assessed: Multi-Agency Public Protection Arrangements (MAPPAs). The second section examines the licence conditions which MAPPAs seek to impose upon an offender in order to manage the risk they present. The third and final section aims to ascertain whether MAPPAs are an appropriate and fit-for-purpose risk management tool. This final, analytical section identifies five issues in the use of MAPPAs which range from the difficulties of heavy resource consumption in a bleak financial climate, to operational problems in service culture mentality and the sharing of secret intelligence between responsible agencies. It is the final two issues, however, which are seen to present the greatest problem. MAPPAs are too unwieldy and resource heavy to deal with the ever-growing numbers of non-terrorist offenders who acquire radical views while in prison and yet no other mechanism has been developed to manage this (perhaps greater) risk. Second, there has been an identifiable shift of priorities away from the rehabilitation and de-radicalisation of both terrorist and non-terrorist offenders with extremist views, to containment and control through MAPPA licence conditions. In short, MAPPAs are increasingly used solely to manage risk rather than coupling it with reducing that risk through de-radicalisation.

MAPPAs and risk assessment

The process for dealing with Terrorism Act offenders after their release currently revolves around MAPPAs. To date, little work has been done on MAPPAs and a full description of their inner workings is necessary to fill this gap. Historically, MAPPAs were designed to manage sex offenders and violent offenders who pose a risk to public safety and were adopted (but not adapted) to deal with terrorist offenders in the years after 9/11. Offenders fall into three categories: Category 1 encompasses those sexual offenders who are 'registerable' and Category 2 includes violent and/or sexual offenders. Terrorist offenders fall under Category 3, "Other Dangerous Offenders" – that is, they have a previous conviction which shows they have the capacity and potential to cause serious harm to the public. Different levels of response, graded according both to the risk offenders pose to the public and the level of management required (particularly if management involves considerable participation of agencies other than the Probation Service), are applied to these categories.

BOX 18.1: LEVELS FOR RISK MANAGEMENT

Level One: Ordinary Agency Management

This level is used in cases where the risks posed by the offender can be managed by the Probation Service. It only applies to Category 1 or 2 offenders. Although this is not a formal MAPPA, other agencies can be involved and in general offenders will be assessed as presenting a low or medium risk of harm. In 2008/09 about 89% were managed at this level.

Level Two: Active Multi-Agency Management I

Requires the active involvement and co-ordination of interventions from other agencies to manage the risks identified in Multi-Agency Public Protection Meetings (MAPPMs). Offenders are normally those who were assessed as high or very high risk but they may have been managed at level 3 before being downgraded. In 2008/09, approximately 10% of offenders were managed at this level.

Level Three: Active Multi-Agency Management II

This level of management is used where it is determined that the management issues require active conferencing and senior representation from the lead agency (Probation or Youth Offending Team) and their partners. There may be a need to commit significant resources at short notice because of significant media and public interest. These offenders often pose the highest risk of causing serious harm and in 2008/09 only 1% of offenders were managed at this level.

Source: NOMS (2009)

In much the same way as Terrorism Act offenders always fall into Category 3, they are always managed at Level 2 or 3 (National MAPPA Team National Offender Management Service Public Protection Unit, 2009, p.158). The particular level is negotiated between the police, probation and prison services six months before release and a Risk Management Plan devised. The Offender Assessment System (OASys) is the primary platform under which an offender's risk assessment is conducted, supported by intelligence from the Violent and Sexual Offenders Register (ViSOR) (Home Office, 2002; HM Prison Service, "Prison Service Orders 2205," http://www.justice.gov.uk/offenders/psos; Mehta, 2008; National Police Improvement Agency, 2010). As with non-terrorist-related offenders, it is through OASys and, to a lesser extent, ViSOR, that the potential risk posed by a terrorism-related offender – based on collated information from the Probation Service, Prison Intelligence, Police Counter-Terrorism Units and Special Branches and the Security Service – to the public is assessed. Hand in hand with MAPPAs' clearly defined operational process goes a rigid oversight structure. All three responsible agencies have a steering group who report on the success (or failure) of MAPPAs at ministerial level. Beneath that, each of the 42 police and probation regions has its own Strategic Management Board made up of senior members of the three responsible agencies (the police and probation and prison services), typically at Assistant Chief Constable and Assistant Chief Officer level.

MAPPAs and risk management

Risk Management Plans are constructed through negotiation in the MAPPM and employ a number of measures to mitigate the risk that offenders pose to the public. The chief method for risk managing offenders is found in the licence conditions to which the offender must adhere in order to complete his or her sentence in the community; the decision to apply particular licence conditions is based on negotiation in the MAPPM, but final responsibility resides with the Probation Service. The content of these licences is standard for Level 1 and Level 2 offenders, consisting of conditions which appear on every licence. The offender must a) keep in touch with their supervising officer as directed, b) agree to receive visits from the supervising officer at home, c) permanently reside at an approved address, d) undertake only approved work, e) not travel outside the UK without express permission, and f) must be of good behaviour.

However, the risk to the public posed by those convicted under terrorism-related offences (e.g. Level 3 offenders) can require the MAPPAs to adopt further licence conditions (see NOMS, 2011a,b). The imposition of additional licence conditions must be both necessary for the effective management of the offender and proportionate with the index offence. Typically, additional licence conditions were targeted at those sexual and violent offenders whom MAPPAs were originally designed to manage, but further conditions have been provided for terrorism and terrorism-related offenders. These include but are not limited to[6] a) prohibitions on particular activities (including restrictions on the use of computers and mobile phones); b) prohibitions on contact with those who have been charged or convicted of any terrorism-related offence; c) a requirement 'not to attend or organise any meetings or gatherings other than those convened solely for the purposes of worship without the prior approval of the supervising officer'; d) restrictions on particular activities, including only attending places of worship agreed by a supervising officer and not delivering any lecture, talk or sermon without the approval of the super-vising officer; e) further requirements to avoid possession of material that might 'promote the destruction of or hatred for any religious or ethnic group or that celebrates, justifies or promotes acts of violence, or that contain information about military or paramilitary technology, weapons, techniques or tactics'; and f) in the case of ideologues, a similar requirement not to attempt to recruit other individuals to extremist or radical groups can be introduced.

The purpose of these additional licence conditions is clear: they are designed to prevent offenders not only from becoming more deeply embedded in extremist movements (particularly if involvement in terrorist attacks is possible), but also to preclude the recruitment of others. Thus, there is clear emphasis on preventing association with individuals who 'hold what could be identified as extreme religious and or political views which could be associated with offending behaviour' (National MAPPA Team National Offender Management Service Public Protection Unit, 2009, p.159). Of similar concern is the potential for accessing extremist material online or disseminating it to others through lectures and seminars. The logic of MAPPAs is clear: they are designed to remove the risk of an offender returning to their previous ways by pre-empting and preventing particular situations, activities and relationships which are perceived to encourage terrorist behaviour.

To date, MAPPAs have been reasonably successful in preventing serious recidivism amongst terrorism offenders. Nevertheless, recidivism does occur. At the time of writing, there have been a number of minor breaches involving the failure to comply with licence conditions, normally resulting in warnings. There has been one case of a Terrorism Act offender committing further terrorism-related offences while on licence and one case of a Terrorism Act offender returning to the index offence after the completion of his licence. For minor breaches, a warning, then a final warning is given after which further breaches will see the return of the offender to prison to serve out the remainder of their term. For major breaches, particularly those that indicate a risk of committing offences of a terrorist nature (such as possession of terrorist literature, attempting to buy chemicals for manufacturing a bomb), the licence can be immediately revoked.

For those offenders who abide by the licence conditions, which remain in force from a few months to several years, the termination of the MAPPA is followed by far weaker Notification Orders (which can continue for up to 30 years). Notification Orders require a former offender to provide details of their residency and their National Insurance number at a police station once a year. Other legislation – Terrorism Prevention and Investigation Measures (TPIMs) – is in existence for managing the *potential* risk of (re-)offending, but has not, at the time of writing, been used. TPIMs, which contain elements similar to MAPPA licence conditions such as a curfew, limited use of the internet and mobile telephones, restrictions on associating with particular individuals and so on, could theoretically be used if there were reasonable suspicion of involvement in terrorist activity, but a lack of evidence to gain a conviction.

Limitations in the MAPPA model

Having provided a detailed account of the way in which MAPPAs work, and how they function differently to other forms of risk management of terrorism-related offenders, it is worthwhile examining whether this model is appropriate and proportionate not only to the current situation, but for the future.

Requirement for considerable resources

To date, MAPPAs have been largely successful in preventing re-offending amongst Terrorism Act offenders on licence. But part of the reason for this success is the sheer volume of resources that need to be allocated in order for MAPPAs to work. Beyond the three main partners – the police and probation and prison services – a diverse range of agencies, from the Security Service to the Housing Association and Job Centre Plus also play a part in managing the risk posed by terrorism-related offenders, contributing to a significant use of resources. Currently, the Probation Service is stretched, dealing with only a small number of individuals convicted of terrorism-related offences. Not surprisingly, these offenders require very close monitoring and probation officers have a 'protected' case load which limits the number of offenders with which they are tasked. Added to this, officers supervising Terrorism Act offenders have to undergo extensive further training and require particularly close supervision when dealing with these offenders. By much the same token, terrorism offenders are a drain on police resources; officers are required not only to undertake multiple risk assessments, but to monitor offenders throughout their licence period. Bearing in mind recent cuts to both the police and Probation Service, it seems inconceivable that there is scope for increasing this capacity.

Lack of centralised MAPPA process

Despite the hierarchical structure and clear operational protocol, MAPPAs for terrorism-related offenders are run differently across the 42 regions. In London, for example, both the Probation Service and police have centralised units for dealing with Terrorism Act offenders. These centralised units run MAPPMs across all London boroughs and comprise police and probation officers, some of whom have undergone developed vetting (DV) level security clearance in order to facilitate the process of information sharing. In other regions, however, informal structures are used to disseminate appropriate information in the risk assessment, often bypassing security concerns. It is not surprising, perhaps, that London Probation and the Metropolitan Police, who have responsibility for more terrorism-related offenders than any other region, have established centralised units dedicated solely to this relatively small number of individuals. These services both have greater financial resources available to devote to risk managing these offenders, but it remains to be seen what will happen when other regions begin to acquire significant numbers of terrorism-related offenders.

Service mentalities

MAPPAs, by their very nature, require substantial interaction and cooperation between law enforcement and criminal justice agencies. These authorities, unsurprisingly, have different service cultures or 'mentalities'. For the police, their primary duty in MAPPAs is to assess the risk posed by terrorist offenders in the context of protecting the public. For the Probation Service, their duty is to manage the risk presented by these offenders in the context of their statutory duty to aid rehabilitation and create a relationship of trust. The differences between these service cultures are particularly heightened in the case of terrorist offenders because of the risk they pose to the community by supporting or committing acts of violence with the potential for causing significant loss of life. Although, to date, co-operation has been managed with some success, the significant differences in service culture are likely to cause problems in the future, particularly under the growing pressure of increased numbers of terrorist offenders.

One area in particular has caused issues: a good deal of intelligence material available to Police Counter-Terrorism Units present at MAPPMs is provided by confidential sources of information (e.g. the Security Service, the Secret Intelligence Service, GCHQ, confidential police sources) which often cannot be passed onto MAPPA partners when they conduct their risk assessment. This presents genuine problems: probation officers cannot make a fully informed judgement about the best way to manage the risk presented by an offender on licence without this information and yet, very few probation officers hold the appropriate levels of clearance to enable sharing of the information. Under these circumstances, the police have to resort to a simple assertion of their preferred method for dealing with an individual, in particular over their licence conditions, without being able to provide an evidence-based rationale for that assessment.

To date, this difference in service mentality, which has the potential to cause broader conflict between MAPPA partners, has been navigated through well-established, if informal, ties between the responsible agencies. In the longer term, future ownership of counter-terrorism policing is uncertain. There are indications to suggest that these powers might be transferred to the National Crime Agency. Whatever the merit or otherwise of this move, it is clear that it will require a time-consuming re-establishment of similar ties between agencies that have no history of working in co-operation. This has the potential to cause delays in conducting risk assessments and disrupt the process so significantly that terrorism-related offenders may be managed at the wrong level, that opportunities for gaining the trust of these offenders are lost, and that intelligence opportunities are overlooked.

Non-terrorism offenders

Thus far, this chapter has focused exclusively on the potential threat posed by terrorism-related offenders on lesser, often non-violent, charges after their release. As suggested, the threat is limited but concerning: these offenders tend to have a proven history of at least marginal involvement in violent extremist networks, hold a deeper grudge against the West as a consequence of their imprisonment which they often perceive to be ill-deserved and, on occasion, have acquired a deeper familiarity with extremist networks during their time in prison. The threat is limited, however, because the number of offenders is – just – manageable using existing resources. Earlier, it was suggested that these resources have been stretched to breaking point and further risk management of terrorist offenders is likely to tip the balance.

However, there is now increasing evidence that prisons are acting as radicalising centres (e.g. Neumann, 2010). This affects not only those individuals convicted for lesser offences in the Terrorism Act, where it might drive them to increased participation and commitment to the cause, but also to those convicted for non-terrorism related offences who can buy into extremist philosophy. One 2010 report estimated that 800 newly radicalised violent extremists could be released in the next five to ten years, although these figures are probably an over-estimate and were rejected as such by the Ministry of Justice (Clarke and Soria, 2010). Others have avoided putting the issue into numerical terms, stating that "It is difficult to find firm evidence or to quantify the impact, [and] it does appear that being recruited to a self-identified Muslim grouping within prison is more about association and personal safety than about radicalisation, but the authorities would do well to work closely with Muslim organisations to understand what is happening within the prison community and its links with the outside world" (House of Commons Home Affairs Committee, 2012).

Whatever the precise level of radicalisation in prisons (a topic addressed in far more detail elsewhere in this book), they are environments in which individuals can often feel vulnerable and embittered. This combination is ripe for radicalisation – not only for bringing new members into extremist ideology, but for concretising those with partial or incomplete commitment to radical causes. The problem for the police and Probation Service is that it is extremely difficult to identify whether an individual is genuinely caught up in extremist beliefs or whether they have joined radical factions in prison for other reasons (e.g. protection). To put it another way "the formation of temporary and opportunistic alliances between offenders is a commonly observed behaviour in prisons" and even if views espoused in prison are radical, it is not clear to what extent they are genuinely absorbed by offenders (House of Commons Home Affairs Committee, 2012).

During the writing of this chapter, initiatives to risk manage non-terrorist offenders radicalised in prison were beginning to be rolled out in a number of pilot studies. Risk assessment is based on a number of intelligence sources that are analysed in multi-agency extremism meetings and risk management, and where deemed necessary, can take the form of imposing further licence conditions or finding appropriate interventions to change behaviour. Although the approach is to be fully tested and it is too early to produce a full evaluation, it is important to note that this is not a formal MAPPA. The implications are three-fold: non-terrorism-related offenders are not managed by those probation officers specifically trained to deal with terrorism-related offenders, although they will undoubtedly act in an advisory role; second, there are difficulties identifying to what extent the offender is genuinely radical, and this can influence risk management options; third, the majority of interventions take place while the offender is in custody, and there are few targeted options for challenging an offender's extremist views after their release.

In light of this, it seems all too easy for those radicalised in prison, particularly those who have acquired extremist views whilst serving their sentence, to fall through the cracks after their release. Although the pilot study is in its early stages, it does appear that it lacks the specialist knowledge and expertise found in MAPPAs, which would seem to provide a better framework for risk management. And yet, the MAPPA partners are too stretched to address the issue of a substantial number of non-violent offenders who have developed radical views as a consequence of their time in prison. It remains to be seen how effectively the police and Probation Service will manage the risk of radicalised non-terrorism-related offenders, but it is concerning that those with the expertise remain minor players in the process.

The failure to rehabilitate

Rehabilitation interventions, in the case of terrorism offenders perhaps more accurately described as de-radicalisation programmes, are only occasionally used as primary elements in managing the risk of terrorism-related offenders on licence. Despite the fact that the Coalition government has been decidedly in favour of rehabilitation schemes for violent and sexual offenders in prison and on licence, the political debate over the relative merits of de-radicalisation seems to have superseded this preference. Prisoners with other problematic behaviours – notably, drug addictions and anger management issues – are addressed through well-established, often effective, interventions.[7] At the heart of the issue is the fact that Prevent has long been criticised for using non-violent extremists to counter those who espouse the need for violence. It is along this critical fault-line that Prevent has been re-structured in the aftermath of the 2011 review.

As it is, terrorism-related offenders with entrenched ideological beliefs which are inextricably linked to the nature of their violent behaviour are rarely provided with dedicated bespoke programmes which challenge both their attitudes and actions. This is not to say that such programmes do not exist: in the past, terrorism offenders have attended programmes which target precisely the ideology-driven behaviour that is linked to the original offence. At the time of writing, a new intervention called Healthy Identity Intervention was about to be piloted for offenders with extremist beliefs who were suitable candidates for the programme (see Chapter 7 in this volume for much more on this). Once again, it is too early to provide an evaluation, but early indications suggest that the scheme is narrow in scope and will be used in the risk management of those offenders who have shown some inclination to relinquish their views. It remains to be seen how the government will address those with deeply entrenched views and commitments, other than resorting to resource heavy licence conditions.

In short, there seems to be an attitude, held in government rather than in the responsible agencies, that leopards do not change their spots – once a violent extremist, always a violent extremist. The corollary of this logic is the assertion that risk management through monitoring and limiting behaviour is a better option in terms of cost, security and the offender, than risk reduction which changes that behaviour. But imprisonment and probation both provide critical opportunities for intervention and for preventing further ideological commitment in the future. If MAPPAs are to work, not only by managing risk, but by reducing it, rehabilitation schemes which challenge extremist ideology will be critical elements which can contribute significantly to UK Security.

Notes

1   This chapter could not have been written without the help of the police and Probation Service, to whom I am very grateful.
2   It is worthwhile picking up on a definitional issue here. There are significant differences between the overlapping processes of rehabilitation and de-radicalisation (which seek to initiate a cognitive shift manifest in a change of behaviour) and the broader concept of counter-extremism, which is the attempt to prevent violent extremist views taking hold in communities or to dilute the effect of those already present; it is the drive to "challenge the ideology behind violent extremism and support mainstream voices" and "to increase the resilience of communities to violent extremism" (Home Office, 2009, p.14).
3   In October 2010, the Probation Service estimated that by April 2011 more than a hundred terrorism-related offenders would have been released from prison (see Travis, 2010).
4   2011 saw a 15% increase in arrests in comparison to the previous year (see Policing Statistics Team, 2012, p.7).
5   For example, Samina Malik, the so-called "lyrical terrorist", was convicted of possessing records likely to be useful in terrorism, but received only a suspended sentence. See Truscott (2007).
6   The licence conditions are too numerous and lengthy for full description here. For more see NOMS (2011b).
7   Although access to these schemes is becoming increasingly difficult in the face of cuts. See HM Inspectorate of Probation and HM Inspectorate of Prisons (2012).

References

Briggs, R., Fieschi, C. and Lownsbrough, H. (2006). *Bringing It Home: Community Based Approaches to Counter Terrorism.* London: Demos.

Clarke, M. and Soria, V. (2010). "Terrorism: The New Wave." *The RUSI Journal*, 155/4, 24–31.

HM Inspectorate of Probation and HM Inspectorate of Prisons (2012). *Second Aggregate Report on Offender Management in Prisons.* Manchester: HM Inspectorate of Probation.

HM Prison Service (n.d.). *Prison Service Orders 2205*. http://www.justice.gov.uk/offenders/psos.

Home Office (2002). *OASYS Guidance*. London: The Stationery Office.

Home Office (2009). *The United Kingdom's Strategy for Countering International Terrorism*. London: The Stationery Office.

House of Commons Home Affairs Committee (2012). *Roots of Violent Radicalisation: Nineteenth Report of Session 2010–12, Vol. 1: Report, Together with Formal Minutes, Oral and Written Evidence*. London: The Stationery Office.

Mehta, A. (2008). "Fit for Purpose: Oasys Assessments and Parole Decisions – a Practitioner's View." *Probation Journal*, 55/2, 189–94.

National MAPPA Team National Offender Management Service Public Protection Unit (2009). *Mappa Guidance 2009*. London: Ministry of Justice.

National Offender Management Service (2009). *Public Protection Manual*. London: Ministry of Justice.

National Offender Management Service (2011a). "Prison Service Instructions 2011." http://www.justice.gov.uk/offenders/psis/prison-service-instructions-2011.

National Offender Management Service (2011b). "Probation Instruction 07/2011." http://webarchive.nationalarchives.gov.uk/20101216070244/http://www.probation.homeoffice.gov.uk/output/page31.asp.

Police Improvement Agency (2010). *Visor Standards 2.0*. London: National Police Improvement Agency.

Neumann, P. (2010). *Prisons and Terrorism: Radicalisation and De-Radicalisation in 15 Countries*. London: International Centre for the Study of Radicalisation.

Phillips, M. (2009). "Persistently Validating Extremism." *The Spectator*.

Policing Statistics Team (2012). *Operation of Police Powers under the Terrorism Act 2000 and Subsequent Legislation: Arrests, Outcomes and Stops and Searches: Quarterly Update to September 2011*. London: The Stationery Office.

Travis, A. (2010). "Terror Warning over Radicalised Prisoners." *The Guardian*.

Truscott, C. (2007). "'Lyrical Terrorist' Sentenced over Extremist Poetry." *The Guardian*.

19

NORTHERN IRISH EX-PRISONERS

The impact of imprisonment on
prisoners and the peace process in
Northern Ireland

Neil Ferguson

The "Troubles" in Northern Ireland (as the political violence in the North of the island of Ireland is colloquially and euphemistically known) began over 40 years ago when a banned march of approximately 400 people on 5 October 1968 to demand electoral, employment and housing reform were confronted by the Royal Ulster Constabulary (RUC) who blocked their route at Duke Street in Londonderry and baton-charged the demonstrators. This event proved to be the point when Northern Ireland crossed its Rubicon, and began a destructive spiral to near civil war in the following years (Purdie, 1990).

The Troubles are widely perceived as a primordial ethnic or religious conflict between Protestants and Catholics; however, these religious labels are used as badges of convenience in what is effectively a political struggle between those who wish to see Northern Ireland remain within the United Kingdom and those who desire a reunification of the island of Ireland (Darby, 1983). The majority of Unionists who wish to remain within the UK are also Protestants, while the majority of Nationalists who desire to reunify Ireland are Catholic, so the religious labels reflect these political aspirations, but are by no means exclusive, with as many as 52% of Catholics holding pro-union attitudes (see Darby, 1997; Northern Irish Life and Times, 2010).

The political violence in Northern Ireland continued for decades without either side gaining any clear advantage or achieving military domination of the others. Then during the early 1990s secret dialogue between the British and Irish governments and the IRA began to lay the foundations for a peace process. The IRA and Loyalist ceasefires in 1994 built on these foundations. Bill Clinton's visit to and interest in Northern Ireland, coupled with the election of Tony Blair's Labour party in 1997 energised the stalling peace process and in 1998 after protracted negotiations chaired by Senator George Mitchell the Belfast (or Good Friday) Agreement (Agreement, 1998) was reached and accepted by a large majority in an all-Ireland referendum.

This period of political violence led to the deaths of over 3,600 people and the injury of an additional 40–50,000. These injuries and fatalities were caused by approximately 36,000 shooting incidents and 16,000 explosions which took place during the Troubles (CAIN, 2012). The majority of people killed and injured during the conflict were victims of Northern Irish paramilitary groups (80% of all deaths), whether Republican (56% of all deaths) or Loyalist (24%; Smyth & Hamilton, 2004). Given the small population of 1.68 million and the small geographical area of 5,456 square miles, it is clear that this conflict had a substantial impact on the population (Fay, Morrissey & Smyth, 1998).

As a result of perpetrating these injuries and fatalities, it is estimated that 20,000 to 32,000 people were incarcerated for politically motivated offences (Conflict Transformation Papers, 2003; McEvoy, 2001) during the Troubles. Indeed, Jamieson, Shirlow & Grounds (2010) estimate that former politically motivated prisoners now make up a sizable proportion (between 5.4% and 30.7%) of the Northern Irish men aged between 50 and 64. Political prisoners and the nature of imprisonment in Northern Ireland have made a huge impact on the intensity of the conflict, the politics of Northern Ireland and the peace process. For example, the hunger strikes in the early 1980s produced a rise in widespread violence outside the prison, and resulted in the election of hunger striker Bobby Sands as an MP to Westminster. Then in January 1998, during the negotiations which produced the Good Friday Agreement, the then Secretary for State for Northern Ireland, Mo Mowlam visited prisoners in the Maze to sell the Agreement to disaffected political prisoners. Additionally, many former prisoners were involved in the negotiations of the Agreement, employing skills which they honed from their negotiations with the prison staff while imprisoned. This chapter will explore the impact of imprisonment on Northern Irish politically motivated prisoners and the role of prisoners in maintenance and transformation of conflict in Northern Ireland post-release. Research[1] conducted in Northern Ireland with former Ulster Volunteer Force (UVF) and Red Hand Commando (RHC) prisoners will be incorporated to illustrate how imprisonment impacts on the prisoners and how the former prisoners impact on peace and stability in Northern Ireland.

The history of imprisonment in Northern Ireland is dynamic, and characterised by changes to British policy impacting on prison conditions and resulting in violent and non-violent resistance by the prisoners and their colleagues outside the prison walls. Operation Demetrius in August 1971 brought about the (re) introduction[2] of internment without trial in response to the spiralling violence on the streets of Northern Ireland. Internment lasted for a period of 4 years and almost 2,000 people were interned at Long Kesh during this period. During internment the internees had rights of free association, wore their own clothes, made their own rules, were recognised as political prisoners and housed by paramilitary grouping.

The initiation of Special Category Status (SCS) for all prisoners convicted of terrorism-related offences in 1972 and the establishment of a system of Diplock courts in 1973 were both a response to an international backlash against internment and a new method of dealing with the Republican offenders more effectively.

Special-category prisoners were effectively treated as political prisoners, while Diplock courts were used to try 'scheduled' or terror-related offences, with the trials taking place in front of a single judge in a juryless court. The introduction of Diplock courts and the removal of internment marked the beginning of a new approach to imprisonment, during which acts of terrorism and terrorist offenders were to be 'criminalised' and have their rights as political prisoners eroded, an erosion which was completed with the removal of SCS in 1976 as a result of the Gardiner Report (1975).

From March 1976 anyone convicted of a scheduled offence was to be treated as an ordinary criminal and would have to wear a prison uniform, engage in prison work and serve their sentence in the Maze prison which had been constructed alongside Long Kesh. This move to criminalise politically motivated prisoners led to years of resistance and conflict within and outside the Maze prison (McEvoy, 2001). Notably, the change led to the hunger strikes by Republican prisoners in 1980–81 which resulted in the death of 10 prisoners, while 21 prison officers were also murdered between 1976 and 1981.

While the British government and press initially hailed the handling of the hunger strikes as a victory over Irish Republicanism, the strikes had reinvigorated the Republican Movement, propelled Sinn Fein into electoral politics, garnered huge international support for Irish Republicanism and paved the way for the signing of the Anglo-Irish Agreement. Also, in a matter of days after the second hunger strike finished, the political prisoners had the majority of their demands met in an announcement by James Prior, the then Secretary for State for Northern Ireland, meaning a return to political status in all but name.

The Belfast Agreement made provision for the release of prisoners who were part of paramilitary groups on ceasefire within two years of the ratification of the Agreement. There was to be the 'normalisation' of security arrangements, which included the removal of military bases and installations and a reduction in troop numbers to garrisoned peacetime levels, in addition to the reform of the militarised police force and the removal of emergency powers legislation. The Agreement also acknowledged that the decommissioning of all paramilitary weapons was an 'indispensable' (1998: 20) part of peace-building; the Independent International Commission on Decommissioning (IICD), staffed by international observers, indicated that all illegal armed groups should aim to achieve decommissioning of their weapons within two years.

However, while the Agreement included provision for decommissioning, security normalisation and the release of politically motivated prisoners, it did not include a detailed strategy or plan for these processes to reach completion. The first step in this process saw the early release of prisoners within two years of their group's officially recognised ceasefire; this process led to the eventual release of 452 prisoners; of these 197 were Loyalist, 242 Republican and 13 non-aligned (Northern Ireland Prison Service, 2010). It must be remembered that this final release of prisoners is only a small proportion of the estimated 15,000 Republican and 12,000 Loyalists who were imprisoned throughout the Troubles (Conflict

Transformation Papers, 2003). To help alleviate fears in the general public about the mass release of former combatants, the prisoners were released under licence, which meant they could be returned to prison if they (a) supported an organisation not on ceasefire, (b) became involved in the commission, preparation or instigation of acts of terrorism or (c) became a danger to the public (Shirlow & McEvoy, 2008). Since the early release of prisoners only 23 have had their licence suspended and been returned to prison, and of these 23, only 10 had been returned for involvement in terrorist offences (Northern Ireland Prison Service, 2010). This recidivism rate of 5% is surprisingly low, considering that the normal recidivism rate for Northern Irish prisoners is 48% (Shirlow & McEvoy, 2008).

The reintegration of ex-prisoners back into Northern Irish society was also formally written into the Belfast Agreement (Agreement, 1998: 25) which stated that

> The Governments continue to recognise the importance of measures to facilitate the reintegration of prisoners into the community by providing support both prior to and after release, including assistance directed towards availing of employment opportunities, re-training and/or re-skilling, and further education.

However, the reintegration of prisoners has been highly divisive in Northern Ireland. For former prisoners who are returning to their communities and joining the thousands of other former prisoners in their communities, the idea that they need to be reintegrated to communities which they went to prison to defend is absurd, while for their many victims the idea that they would be rewarded for their violence was abhorrent (Shirlow & McEvoy, 2008). In reality, the depth of governmental assistance in the reintegration of former combatants has been very shallow: there was no strategic or comprehensive programme of reintegration. Instead, the funding of prisoner reintegration came from the European Union and the Community Foundation for Northern Ireland (CFNI, previously titled Northern Ireland Voluntary Trust), a local NGO. Between 1995 and 2003 the CFNI distributed £9.2 million in EU funding to ex-prisoner groups, which was about 0.9% of the total Peace I and II monies (Rolston, 2007; Shirlow & McEvoy, 2008) while the current Peace III programme is supporting a number of ex-prisoner projects.

The individual reintegration projects were managed by groups which broadly represented the paramilitary groupings the former combatants belonged to. Coiste na n-Iarchimí was the umbrella group for former Provisional IRA prisoners, EPIC served former UVF and Red Hand Commando (RHC) prisoners, UDA and Ulster Freedom Fighters (UFF) used Prisoners Aid, An Eochair works with Official IRA prisoners, Expac works mainly with Republican prisoners based in the Republic of Ireland, and Teach na Failte services Irish National Liberation Army (INLA) former prisoners. The reintegration projects were diverse and included counselling and training for former prisoners, self-help initiatives, advocacy work, restorative justice projects, youth and community work, community capacity building, conflict transformation initiatives, dispute resolution at community interfaces, not-for-profit employment etc. (see McEvoy & Mika, 2002; Shirlow & McEvoy, 2008).

The impact of imprisonment on the prisoners

In contrast with these developments the groups which service these paramilitary prisoners feel that the civic and political elite are antagonistic to the former prisoner community, ex-prisoners are discriminated against in the labour market and face legislative barriers which curb their full rights as UK citizens (Conflict Transformation Papers, 2003). Ex-prisoners face barriers in terms of ineligibility for employment in many sectors of employment, restrictions on international travel, problems securing bank loans and access to Public Service Vehicle (PSV) licences; they are ineligible to adopt or foster children and have restricted pension entitlements.

Recent studies of Northern Irish ex-prisoners (Jamieson & Grounds, 2002; Shirlow & McEvoy, 2008; Spence, 2002; Jamieson et al., 2010; Hamber, 2006) and their families (Hall, 2010) are illustrative of the problems these ex-prisoners face and reflect the problems discussed by a number of ex-prisoners we interviewed. These experiences include estrangement from their families and friends, emotional stress for both the ex-prisoner and their family with the readjustment of the absent father returning to the family, and difficulties managing the practical day-to-day realities of living outside prison (e.g. household budgets, bank accounts, mortgages). A member of the UVF and former prisoner illustrates the problems faced with reintegration with the family and society on return from prison.

> A lot of people in these circumstances similar to myself, who went to jail as young men and came out in their 40s and didn't have too many dealings with the responsibilities of running a home, that was all they had left in them and when they come out, it's kind of hard to fit back in when a woman's well used to doing that and you're not really ready to take all that on again.

There is also a need for readjustment to the world they now find themselves in, which is culturally, technologically and physically different from the one they left behind.

> [Prison was] like a holiday camp, to them [current prisoners] it was like a holiday camp. It wasn't a holiday camp when I was there. You know what I mean, you still pissed in the corner. Now they've got their own toilets, their own cells, and TV's in their cells, DVD's. What the fucks a DVD? I couldn't even turn one on. There's things I have problems with, I can't use this, I can't do that. I can't use a computer. I can't use a video recorder. That's honest to God, I'm just getting used to using a mobile phone.

Release from prison can create myriad emotions; there is the sadness and guilt of leaving their friends and comrades behind on release, there is the elation and hero worship just after release, the need to try and 'get your life back', then feeling isolated and alien in the community they had fought to protect.

> Now I came out and I walked them streets, and it was like, I didn't feel a hero. I didn't want to be a hero, I didn't want no medals. But people used to look up to me, and go 'that's such and such'. And kids knew you who you where . . . You didn't want to disillusion them but you wanted to hit them a good boot, and say 'see what I done. Don't ever, don't think about it' . . . I mean it's took my life away. I mean I'll never get that back. Hopefully I'll go on and live a good life and be 80, I mean the other way round I could have been dead.

Prisoners also reported personal safety issues with working outside their local community area, difficulty establishing new relationships, lack of skills (or skills and qualifications no longer valid in the labour market) and psychological problems such as anxiety, PTSD, depression, alcohol misuse and high rates of suicide among former prisoners. Jamieson et al.'s (2010) survey of former Loyalist and Republican prisoners illustrates the profoundness of these problems among the Northern Irish ex-prisoner population. Their survey of 190 former politically motivated prisoners indicated that 40% of the sample produced GHQ-12 scores indicative of mental health problems. Thirty-three per cent had been prescribed antidepressants and 40% had been prescribed medication for anxiety or sleep problems in the 12 months beforehand. Over half of the former prisoners sampled (51%) were troubled by memories and intrusive dreams related to the Troubles and/or incarceration. In addition, 69% of former politically motivated prisoners engaged in hazardous drinking behaviour and 54% were alcohol dependent. For many, these psychological problems remain untreated in part due to the illegality of their actions as perpetrators of violence in creating their own Perpetration Induced Traumatic Stress (PITS; MacNair, 2002, 2005) and also by the macho culture involved in being a combatant which hinders many from seeking treatment, for fear of appearing weak (see Ferguson et al., 2010).

These problems contribute to high unemployment rates amongst ex-prisoners, and a reliance on employment in the informal low-paid cash-in-hand economy. For example, Shirlow & McEvoy (2008) surveyed both Republican and Loyalist ex-prisoners and found the rate of unemployment to be 40% for Republican and 29.3% for Loyalist ex-prisoners sampled from an area of Belfast with an average rate of unemployment running at 14%. Jamieson et al. (2010) explored the impact of their incarceration on being refused employment and found that 55% of ex-prisoners had been refused employment due to their imprisonment. These figures clearly indicate the overrepresentation of ex-political prisoners among the unemployed and the disadvantage their convictions and incarceration have on successful employment, even though there is a voluntary employers code (Recruiting People with Conflict-Related Convictions: Employers Guidance, 2007) which states that conflict-related convictions should not bar former politically motivated prisoners from employment, unless their conviction was 'manifestly incompatible' with the job (p.5). This problem is illustrated by a former Loyalist prisoner:

> I mean, I'm still running about chasing a wage and not having a full time job, so that's a problem. Any job I apply for, they want to know your record. Even though you're out 10 years, 12 years, they're not willing to give you a second chance. Some people will. Most people won't, you know.

These high rates of unemployment and difficulties faced gaining employment outside the informal economy leads to financial problems, with 78% of former politically motivated prisoners reporting money problems since their release (Jamieson et al., 2010). As the politically motivated former prison population is aging, with an average age of 52 years, and having spent long periods of time in prison or outside formal employment, fewer than 1 in 10 hold private pensions, while many will not be entitled to a basic state pension on reaching retirement age (see Jamieson et al., 2010). Therefore most will face future financial hardship in their retirement years.

The impact of former prisoners on the peace process

As mentioned previously only 10 prisoners on the early release scheme have been re-imprisoned for involvement in terrorist offences; however, that does not mean that the armed groups which these prisoners belonged to have followed a purely peaceful path from the ceasefires in the mid-1990s or the signing of the Belfast Agreement in 1998 until the paramilitary organisations finally disarmed. For example, mainstream Republicans attached to the Provisional IRA have been linked to nine murders since they resumed their ceasefire in 1997, Loyalist groups have killed 79 people since they went on ceasefire in 1994, mainly due to inter-faction feuding, and other Republican groups have been responsible for the murder of 59 people since the Belfast Agreement (this includes the 31 people killed in the Omagh bomb in 1998 (see Sutton, 2012)).

While these figures demonstrate that the conflict in Northern Ireland did not end when the ink dried on the Belfast Agreement, they do indicate a significant reduction in the level of political violence since the signing of the Agreement. So while some of the supposedly former combatants have been and are still engaged in political violence and the current threat from dissident Republican groups is at its highest level since the Omagh bombing in 1998 (BBC, 2010), the conflict is not as intense or widespread as it has been. This reduction in violence is reflected in how the general population of Northern Ireland feel much more positive about the future. For example, 65% of people surveyed in 2008 believed that relations between Catholics and Protestants were better than they had been five years before and 59% believed that relations between the two communities would improve further in the future (Northern Ireland Life and Times, 2010).

While the resurgent violence of dissident Republicans grabs the national and international headlines, many former combatants are involved in creating the conditions for peace on the ground in Northern Ireland. Indeed, as many as 62% of ex-prisoners are involved in some level of political activity since their release from imprisonment (Hamber, 2006), with many involved in positive conflict trans- formation initiatives which are actively improving the prospects of peace and increasing community cohesion and capacity across Northern Ireland (for an evalu- ation of projects, see Mika, 2006). These projects are diverse, from involvement in truth recovery and story-telling, co-ordinating restorative justice programmes, setting up mobile phone contacts to diffuse interfaith tension, developing sports and community activities, promoting racial tolerance, etc. These projects have helped transform grass-roots attitudes towards violence, build bridges between and within the communities, link with governmental structures and assist in community development (Rolston, 2007; Shirlow & McEvoy, 2008).

Counter-intuitively, the time spent behind bars in the Maze Prison or Long Kesh was the catalyst which led the way to taking up leadership roles in conflict transformation post-release. Particularly, for the prisoners who served in Long Kesh prior to the removal of SCS in 1976 and those who served in the Maze from the mid-1980s till release on licence, having political or *de facto* political status meant the prisoners ran their own affairs, were involved in their own education, had freedom of association and controlled their own prison blocks. This provided them with the space to develop their ideas and begin to explore non-violent alternatives to the political problems of Northern Ireland. The role of prison in providing this space to think is noted by a former Loyalist prisoner:

> I've been involved for something like thirty-five years and the next stage obviously when you get involved in the conflict, the more operations you carry out the more you get involved and the bigger chance you've got of getting caught or killed. So I was caught, and put in prison, so I had those prison years where, and it should be no surprise to anybody, because some of the best leaders in the world developed their political thinking in prisons, Nelson Mandela. Some of the world's best leaders are ex-prisoners of the British particularly . . . so it should come as no surprise that people in prison do develop because you've been removed from the conflict.

While having former combatants actively working in conflict transforma- tion seems counterintuitive, their 'macho' and violent past offers them a certain credibility when they are encouraging others to turn their back on violence that can be lacking in someone who has never experienced or engaged in violence first-hand, the quote below from a former UVF prisoner illustrates both this credibility and the desire among former prisoners to move away from the violence of the past:

> We were talking about the conflict days [with a group of young men in a community group] . . . and one of them or two or three of them eventually said 'I would love to live in those days', and I just lost it. I said 'do you have any idea, you know it seems glamorous now', I said 'but wait till you're

carrying a coffin of your mother and father dead in the street, or you're carrying a coffin of your wife or your brother, or your best mate down the street', and it's getting this message through that it wasn't glamorous, it wasn't nice, it was ugly, it was rotten, and it's people like myself and others, we have to get this message out to the younger generation, that it wasn't glamorous. You know it's easy sticking up murals glorifying [the violence of the past], but it wasn't [glorious], you know, which is why we are trying to get rid of them and replace them with other stuff. By constantly glamorising you are attracting, and filling the minds of the kids with crap, and it's only people who, like myself, who came through it and who were involved in the conflict and carried the coffins of their mates and seen the atrocities who can make them see the horror of the conflict.

It could also be argued that the former combatants are more active in peace-building than the middle-class moderate politicians who advocate peace at the elite level – a position well articulated by a former UVF prisoner:

Had we waited for politicians to create a peace process, we'd have waited for a very long time, in fact we did. The truth of the matter is the paramilitarists created the peace process – almost the reverse of the way politics is supposed to work. We bring our soldiers home, politicians bring the soldiers home. While here the soldiers got out of the trenches, some people don't recognise them as soldiers but they still got out of the trenches and the politicians said 'why are you getting out of the trenches, get back in the trench', we said 'fuck off'.

However, even when the ex-prisoners are actively engaged in conflict trans-formation they are still the subject of stigmatisation and distrust from other mainstream groups who are active in local politics, peace-building and community development. This makes their task more difficult, particularly when they are in competition with these groups for funding for conflict transformation activities (Ferguson, Burgess, & Hollywood, in press). While these former prisoner groups have been stigmatised by the mainstream, they have also identified with each other and much of their conflict transformational work is conducted in association with former prisoners from groupings which would have been designated as the enemy across the interfaces between the two conflicting communities. A former Loyalist prisoner reflects on this change of direction:

The real peace is happening at the very, very basic level of people on the ground who were the most affected by the violence and were a part of the violence, entering into dialogue on community development issues, and that is where the real peace can be seen, because I am now on a daily basis sitting in a room with people who 20 years ago I would probably have been conspiring to murder.

Former political prisoners have been able to work together across community boundaries in a way that is less apparent among mainstream political parties (Shirlow & McEvoy, 2008). Some researchers believe that the leadership shown by former prisoners is key in preventing the resumption of organised political and communal violence in Northern Ireland (Shirlow, Graham, McEvoy, O'hAdhmaill & Purvis, 2005) rather than successful policing or elite political accommodations, a point clearly articulated by another former Loyalist prisoner we interviewed:

> If anybody thinks that the PSNI [Police Service of Northern Ireland] are maintaining the peace in the interfaces they are living in cloud cuckoo land. The paramilitaries are maintaining the peace at the interfaces. But that's good news. Some people would say that's terrible, it shows the power they have, but given the year we had last year, and the year before that, and the year before that, and the year before that, it's not bad that we have this degree of calm at this point in time.

However, it must be remembered while shared working-class roots, mutual prison experiences and the desire to transform the Northern Irish conflict have allowed former political prisoners the opportunity to build relations in post-Agreement Northern Ireland, there are still substantial problems. Mutual negative stereotypes, a shared history of antagonism, radically different world views, mistrust caused by events such as IRA spying at Stormont in 2002, compounded by the continued threat from dissident Republicans (Shirlow et al., 2005; Ferguson et al., in press) transpire to make peace building and cross-community interaction difficult at times. A former UVF prisoner reflects on how a threat from Republican dissidents led to a breakdown in cross-community work:

> And then we got a threat. Girl lifted the phone, and said there's a threat. So we phoned the Shinners [Sinn Fein] and we said look what's the craic? . . . and basically their answer was well you know we can't speak for everyone . . . You know, some of them have moved, don't get me wrong, some of them moved but its just people fell back into their trenches and it was hard to get away from. It was hard to move on from there. And I know that some people within our own community are still not talking.

It must also be remembered that not all former prisoners are engaged in positive conflict transformation and community capacity building, many have employed the skill sets they learned as paramilitaries to carve out careers in organised crime. This point is acutely recognised by former prisoners trying to build a positive future for Northern Ireland:

> There are genuine people and they're trying to do that, but don't get me wrong there's also the scumbags out there who will do whatever they can, just as long as their back pockets are being bulged, you know.

This pull of criminality and the fear that fragmentation among paramilitary groups could lead to internecine feuds slows the pace of change within paramilitary groups and their ability to use wholly non-violent means to deal with the political problems in Northern Ireland. The balancing act involved in keeping the organisation together and resisting the pull of criminality and/or factionalism is discussed by a former prisoner and UVF commander:

> It would be a tragedy to see another LVF [Loyalist Volunteer Force] or another group in that guise, who is only interested in gangsterism and drugs, you know what I mean. So it's how do you keep them on board and how do you disarm them gracefully? That's what you're toying with the whole time.

Conclusions and lessons from Northern Ireland

Imprisonment and politically motivated prisoners have had a major impact on fuelling and transforming the conflict in Northern Ireland over the last 40 years. For Northern Ireland's former prisoners, their activities as paramilitaries, their subsequent incarceration and reintegration back into the communities they were born into have left them with numerous physical, financial and psychological problems. For many the depth of these problems will impact on their health and quality of life for the rest of their lives. While the Agreement promised to assist prisoners with their reintegration into post-Agreement society, these promises have remained unfulfilled. Instead the financial, physical and psychological problems they face are compounded by their residual criminalisation and legislative barriers which challenge their full rights as UK citizens and restrict their access to gainful employment.

While the media and security agencies are transfixed by the resurgence of Republican dissidents and how they are able to draw former Provisional IRA prisoners into their ranks, in the shadows of the Belfast peace walls many former prisoners are actively engaged in local day-to-day conflict transformation and community development. The activities of these former prisoners are fundamental to building positive relations between Northern Ireland's divided communities.

The challenges Northern Ireland faces as it re-positions itself as a post-conflict society (see Mac Ginty, Muldoon & Ferguson, 2007) are similar to those faced in other societies which share a history of intrastate conflict (Kabia, 2010). Therefore, the actions and experiences of Northern Irish former prisoners, both during incarceration and after their release, provide lessons which could benefit other post-conflict societies immersed in political violence or grappling with the transition from conflict to peace. The research literature and accounts of former prisoners presented here illustrate the barriers former political prisoners face when engaging in conflict transformation – barriers created through the stigma of being men of violence, competition with professional community groups, negative stereotypes, the pull of criminality and the legacy of decades of political violence.

The dominant theme which comes from the accounts provided here and from other studies with former prisoners (Ferguson, 2010; Ferguson et al., in press) is the importance of having the space to think and formulate political ideology and strategy which leads to a reformulation of the conflict inside the prison walls. This implies that it is important to create prison conditions which allow political prisoners the space and educational resources to constructively develop alternative strategies to achieve group goals without employing violence.

The research and accounts of former prisoners also illustrate how former enemies can find commonalities when given the space and conditions to do so. Indeed for the former Loyalist prisoners interviewed here, most report they have more in common with their Republican adversaries than their middle-class Unionist counterparts. These relationships demonstrate that barriers, both physical and psychological, can be broken down when individuals place the good of the society before community or individual gain.

Notes

1 Mark Burgess and Ian Hollywood also interviewed the former prisoners during this fieldwork in Northern Ireland.
2 The use of internment, was not new to Ireland or Northern Ireland and there had been earlier periods of internment without trial in Irish history.

References

Agreement, The: Agreement reached in multiparty negotiations. (1998). Belfast: HMSO.

BBC (2010). 'Dissident threat level increases'. Retrieved from http://news.bbc.co.uk/1/hi/northern_ireland/8638255.stm

CAIN (2012). 'Security related incidents in Northern Ireland, shootings, bombings, and incendiaries, 1969 to 2003'. Retrieved from http://cain.ulst.ac.uk/ni/security.htm#06

Conflict Transformation Papers (2003). *Ex. Prisoners and Conflict Transformation.* Belfast: Regency.

Darby, J. (1983). *Northern Ireland: The Background to the Conflict.* Belfast: Appletree Press.

Darby, J. (1997). *Scorpions in a Bottle: Conflicting Cultures in Northern Ireland.* London: Minority Rights Publications.

Fay, M. T., Morrissey, M., & Smyth, M. (1998). *Northern Ireland's Troubles: The Human Costs.* London: Pluto.

Ferguson, N. (2010). 'Disengaging from terrorism'. In A. Silke. *The Psychology of Counter-Terrorism* (pp. 111–122). London: Routledge.

Ferguson, N., Burgess, M., & Hollywood, I. (in press). 'Leaving violence behind: A study of disengagement from loyalist paramilitary groups in Northern Ireland'. *Political Psychology.*

Ferguson, N., Burgess, M., & Hollywood, I. (2010). 'Who are the Victims? Victimhood Experiences in Post Agreement Northern Ireland'. *Political Psychology*, 31, 6, 857–886.

Gardiner Report. (1975). *Report of a Committee to Consider, in the Context of Civil Liberties and Human rights, Measures to Deal with Terrorism in Northern Ireland.* London: HMSO.

Hamber, B. (2006). 'Flying flags of fear: The role of fear in the process of political transition.' *Journal of Human Rights*, 5, 127–142.

Hall, M. (2010). *'Time Stands Still': The Forgotten Story of Prisoners' Families.* Newtownabbey, Northern Ireland: Island Pamplets.

Jamieson, R., & Grounds, A. (2002). *No Sense of an Ending: The Effects of Long-term Imprisonment amongst Republican Prisoners and their Families.* Monaghan: Seesyu.

Jameison, R., Shirlow, P., & Grounds, A. (2010). *Ageing and Social Exclusion Among Former Politically Motivated Prisoners in Northern Ireland and the Border Region of Ireland*. Belfast: Changing Age Partnership.

Kabia, J. M. (2010). 'Peacebuilding in Liberia and Sierra Leone: A comparative perspective'. In N. Ferguson (Ed.), *Post Conflict Reconstruction* (pp. 133–150). Newcastle: CSP.

Mac Ginty, R., Muldoon, O. & Ferguson, N. (2007). 'No war, no peace: Northern Ireland after the Agreement'. *Political Psychology*, 28, 1, 1–12.

MacNair, R. M. (2002). *Perpetration-induced Traumatic Stress: The Psychological Consequences of Killing*. Westport, CT: Praeger.

MacNair, R. M. (2005). 'Violence begets violence: The consequences of violence become causation'. In M. Fitzduff & C. E. Stout (Eds.), *The Psychology of Resolving Global Conflicts: From War to Peace. Vol. 2. Group and Social Factors* (pp. 191–210). West Port, CT: Praeger.

McEvoy, K. (2001). *Paramilitary Imprisonment in Northern Ireland: Resistance, Management and Release*. Oxford: OUP.

McEvoy, K. & Mika, H. (2002). 'Restorative justice and the critique of informalism in Northern Ireland' *British Journal of Criminology*, 43, 3, 534–563.

Mika, H. (2006). *Community Based Restorative Justice in Northern Ireland: An Evaluation*. Belfast: Institute of Criminology and Criminal Justice, Queens University of Belfast.

Northern Ireland Life and Times (2010). *Northern Ireland Life and Times Survey 2008*. Retrieved from http://www.ark.ac.uk/nilt/2008/

Northern Ireland Prison Service (2010). *Early Releases: Accelerated Release Scheme*. Retrieved from http://www.niprisonservice.gov.uk/index.cfm/area/information/page/earlyrelease

Purdie, B. (1990). *Politics in the Streets*. Belfast: Blackstaff Press.

Recruiting People with Conflict-Related Convictions: Employers Guidance (2007) OFM/DFM: Belfast.

Rolston, B. (2007). 'Demobilization and reintegration of ex-combatants: The Irish case in international perspective'. *Social and Legal Studies*, 16, 2, 259–280.

Shirlow, P., Graham, B., McEvoy, K., O'hAdhmaill, F., & Purvis, D. (2005). *Politically Motivated Former Prisoner Groups: Community Activism and Conflict Transformation*. Belfast: NICRC.

Shirlow, P. & McEvoy, K. (2008). *Beyond the Wire. Former Prisoners and Conflict Transformation in Northern Ireland*. London: Pluto.

Smyth, M. & Hamilton, J. (2004). 'The human cost of the Troubles'. In O. Hargie and D. Dickson (Eds.), *Researching the Troubles: Social Science Perspectives on the Northern Ireland Conflict* (pp. 15–36). London: Mainstream Publishing.

Spence, L. (2002). *Unheard Voices: The Experience and Needs of the Children of Loyalist Political Ex-Prisoners*. Belfast: Epic.

Sutton, M. (2012). *An Index of the Deaths from the Conflict in Ireland*. Retrieved from http://cain.ulst.ac.uk/sutton/chron/index.html

INDEX